# The Academic Writer

## A BRIEF RHETORIC

**Fifth Edition**

### Lisa Ede
Oregon State University

Chapter 7, "Doing Research: Joining the Scholarly Conversation," with
### Anne-Marie Deitering
Oregon State University

"Strategies for Success" notes with
### Bernice Olivas
Salt Lake Community College

 bedford/st.martin's
Macmillan Learning
Boston | New York

*For students and teachers everywhere — and for Gregory*

Vice President: Leasa Burton
Program Director, English: Stacey Purviance
Senior Program Manager: Laura Arcari
Director of Content Development: Jane Knetzger
Executive Development Manager: Maura Shea
Development Editor: Cara Kaufman
Assistant Editor: Annie Campbell
Director of Media Editorial: Adam Whitehurst
Marketing Manager: Vivian Garcia
Senior Director, Content Management Enhancement: Tracey Kuehn
Senior Managing Editor: Michael Granger
Senior Manager of Publishing Services: Andrea Cava
Senior Content Project Manager: Lidia MacDonald-Carr
Lead Digital Asset Archivist and Senior Workflow Manager: Jennifer Wetzel
Production Coordinator: Brianna Lester
Director of Design, Content Management: Diana Blume
Interior Design: Maureen McCutcheon
Cover Design: William Boardman
Director of Rights and Permissions: Hilary Newman
Text Permissions Researcher: Elaine Kosta, Lumina Datamatics, Inc.
Photo Permissions Editor: Angela Boehler
Photo Researcher: Krystyna Borgen, Lumina Datamatics, Inc.
Director of Digital Production: Keri deManigold
Associate Media Project Manager: Emily Brower
Project Management: Lumina Datamatics, Inc.
Project Manager: Jogender Taneja, Lumina Datamatics, Inc.
Editorial Services: Lumina Datamatics, Inc.
Composition: Lumina Datamatics, Inc.
Printing and Binding: LSC Communications

Library of Congress Control Number: 2020936682
ISBN 978-1-319-24564-1

Printed in the United States of America.
1 2 3 4 5 6      25 24 23 22 21 20

### Acknowledgments

*Text acknowledgments and copyrights appear at the back of the book on page 389, which constitutes an extension of the copyright page. Art acknowledgments and copyrights appear on the same page as the art selections they cover.*

*For information, write: Bedford/St. Martin's, 75 Arlington Street, Boston, MA 02116*

students. It also creates bridges between the diverse ways that students now create and consume texts—in print or on their smartphone, tablet, or computer—and the reading and writing they do as students.

A substantially revised chapter on reading, listening, and viewing rhetorically emphasizes the extent to which reading, writing, speaking, and listening are all parallel processes and rhetorical acts. New to this chapter is a substantial discussion of "Reading, Listening, Viewing, and Believing (or Not) in an Age of Social Media." This new section supports and extends this text's goal of helping students to make bridges between their daily communicative activities—arguing with friends about politics, listening to a podcast on a controversial subject—and more formal academic writing. And as this section's title suggests, it addresses the challenges of reading, responding, and believing in an age of social media—providing helpful guidelines for students while also reminding them that the question of what (and whom) to believe is an age-old one. In so doing, this new section contributes to *The Academic Writer*'s aim of helping students become informed consumers, engaged citizens, and rhetorically sensitive communicators.

Part I concludes with a chapter on "Academic Writing: Committing to the Process." This chapter helps students gain insight into their own preferences as writers, enabling them to commit to a writing process that works for them and that results in successful academic writing.

**PART TWO, "WRITING IN COLLEGE,"** focuses, as its title suggests, on the demands that contemporary students face. Analysis, synthesis, argument, and research are central to academic writing, and this section provides coverage of each of these topics as well as a chapter on writing in the disciplines.

**PART THREE, "PRACTICAL STRATEGIES FOR COMPOSING TEXTS,"** provides concise, reference-friendly advice for students on the writing process: invention, planning, drafting, revising, editing, and proofreading. It also includes a revised chapter on multimodal composing, with strategies that are versatile and eminently practical for writers producing texts in our fluid, ever-changing technological present.

# Key Features

- **Every feature of the text, in every chapter, reinforces the book's primary aim: to help students learn to think rhetorically.** The text as a whole encourages transfer by emphasizing decision making over rules. In other words, as the old trope goes, it teaches students to fish rather than presenting them with a fish. **"Thinking Rhetorically"** icons flag passages where rhetorical concepts are explained and exemplified, and **"For Exploration,"** **"For Collaboration,"** and **"For Thought, Discussion, and Writing"** activities encourage students to apply and extend what they have learned.

- **A wide range of model student essays** includes a multipart case study and eleven other samples of student writing—including two new essays by Thai Luong—that serve both to instruct students and to inspire them.

- **Thoughtful discussions of visuals and of writing as design** in Chapters 1, 2, and 11 suggest strategies for reading, viewing, writing, and designing multimodal texts.

- **Strong coverage of reading, research, and writing in the disciplines** in Chapters 1, 2, and 5 through 10 emphasizes the importance of consuming and creating texts rhetorically and enables students to succeed as academic readers and writers.

- **Guidelines and Questions boxes** present key processes in flowchart format to reinforce the importance of decision making and active engagement in the processes of writing, thinking, and reading and to help students easily find what they need.

# New to This Edition

- **Now in full color!** For the Fifth Edition we have moved to a new four-color design as color is an essential part of visual rhetorical analysis. The images throughout the book now appear in color, prompting a deeper understanding of how to approach and interact with visuals as texts to be composed, read, and analyzed.

- **A new section** in Chapter 2 entitled **"Reading, Listening, Viewing, and Believing (or Not) in an Age of Social Media"** includes an extensive discussion that emphasizes that reading, writing, listening, and speaking are rhetorical acts. It addresses the challenge students face today of reading, responding, and believing in an age of social media and widespread misinformation. New **Guidelines for Reading, Listening, and Viewing Rhetorically** help students better determine what (and whom) to believe so that they can become informed consumers, engaged citizens, and rhetorically sensitive communicators.

- **New "Strategies for Success"** boxes in every chapter offer helpful tips and advice for *all* student writers regardless of their level or experience. These broadly relevant notes provide added support for beginning writers from a variety of academic and cultural backgrounds and offer a little extra help in navigating college writing and academic conventions.

- **Updated advice for conducting academic research** appears in Chapter 7, "Doing Research: Joining the Scholarly Conversation." This chapter was written in conjunction with Anne-Marie Deitering, an expert on research and learning technologies, who revised the chapter to highlight the importance of academic habits of mind to successful research and to provide up-to-date coverage of research tools, from understanding algorithmic searches to staying organized with citation managers.

# Instructors' Notes for
## *The Academic Writer*

We have designed *The Academic Writer* to be as accessible as possible to the wide variety of instructors teaching composition, including new graduate teaching assistants, busy part-time instructors, experienced instructors, and writing-program administrators. To that end, we provide detailed *Instructor's Notes*, written by Lisa Ede and Kristy Kelly (also of Oregon State University). This material (ISBN 978-1-319-30716-5) includes correlations to the Council of Writing Program Administrators' Outcomes Statement, multiple course plans, practical tips for meeting common classroom challenges and for teaching key concepts, detailed advice for working with each chapter in the text, and ten sample student writing projects. These new *Instructor's Notes* are available for download by authorized instructors from the instructor's tab on *The Academic Writer's* catalog page at **macmillanlearning.com**.

# Acknowledgments

Before I wrote *The Academic Writer*, acknowledgments sometimes struck me as formulaic or conventional. Now I recognize that they are neither; rather, acknowledgments are simply inadequate to the task at hand. Coming at the end of a preface—and hence twice marginalized—acknowledgments can never adequately convey the complex web of interrelationships and collaborations that make a book like this possible. I hope that the people whose support and assistance I acknowledge here not only note my debt of gratitude but also recognize the sustaining role that they have played, and continue to play, in my life and in my work.

I would like to begin by thanking my current and former colleagues in the School of Writing, Literature, and Film at Oregon State University who supported me while I wrote and revised this text. Though as an emeritus professor I no longer see these colleagues regularly in the hallway, I am mindful of their role in supporting my work on this project over the years. I am indebted to my colleagues Chris Anderson, Kristy Kelly, Vicki Tolar Burton, Anita Helle, Sara Jameson, Tim Jensen, Ehren Pflugfelder, and Ana Ribero for their friendship and their commitment to writing and to the teaching of writing. I am especially grateful for Kristy Kelly's commitment to and work on the *Instructor's Notes for The Academic Writer;* she is taking over for Sara Jameson, who worked on the Instructor's Manual for the first four editions of this text, and I wish Sara the happiest of retirements. I also owe a great debt of gratitude to another friend and colleague in OSU's library, Anne-Marie Deitering, who is at the cutting edge of all things involving digital literacies, research, and undergraduate learning. I am deeply grateful for her work on the chapter on research for *The Academic Writer*.

For this new edition of *The Academic Writer* Bernice Olivas of Salt Lake Community College revised what in earlier editions had been "Notes for

Multilingual Writers." The newly conceived boxed "Strategies for Success" are relevant for all student writers, whatever their level of experience, and thus are more helpful and inclusive. I want to thank Bernice for this significant contribution to *The Academic Writer*.

I would also like to thank the many dedicated teachers of composition I have worked and talked with over the years. By their example, comments, suggestions, and questions, they have taught me a great deal about the teaching of writing. A number of writing instructors took time from their teaching to look carefully at *The Academic Writer*. Their observations and suggestions enriched and improved this book. These reviewers include the following instructors: Felicita Carmichael, Oakland University; Danielle Hinrichs, Metropolitan State University; Jo Hsu, University of Arkansas; Shawna Lesseur, University of Connecticut; Meg Mikovits, Moravian College; Omar Montoya, University of Colorado at Colorado Springs; Alice Myatt, University of Mississippi; Craig Santer, Metropolitan State University; Kelli Sellers, The University of Southern Mississippi; Martha Smith, The University of Texas at San Antonio; Kelly Steidinger, Mid-State Technical College & Nicolet College; and Kate Watts, Washington State University.

Colleagues and students play an important role in nurturing any project, but so do those who form the intangible community of scholars that is one's most intimate disciplinary home. Here, it is harder to determine who to acknowledge; my debt to the composition theorists who have led the way or "grown up" with me is so great that I hesitate to list the names of specific individuals for fear of omitting someone deserving of credit. I must, however, acknowledge my friend and frequent coauthor Andrea Lunsford, who writes with me even when I write alone.

I wish to thank the dedicated staff of Bedford/St. Martin's. Any textbook is an intensely collaborative effort, and I count myself particularly fortunate in having had Cara Kaufman as the development editor on this project. From start to finish, I have valued Cara's expertise and insight. Working on a project like this is a bit like taking a roller coaster ride, with scary moments right next to fun ones. Cara helped me keep the book on track but was equally supportive when I needed to pull back from writing/revising to attend to other matters, and I appreciate that. I appreciate her editorial judgment and insight even more. I am sure that *The Academic Writer* is a better book as a result. In addition, I want to thank Senior Content Project Manager Lidia MacDonald-Carr, whose patient attention to detail proved especially valuable; Assistant Editor Annie Campbell, who kept us organized and on track; Senior Program Manager Laura Arcari, whose frequent reminders about the needs of instructors and students were always appreciated; and Marketing Manager Vivian Garcia, whose knowledge and enthusiasm for English composition informs this text.

Finally, I want to (but cannot adequately) acknowledge the support of my husband, Gregory Pfarr, whose passionate commitment to his own creative endeavors, and our life together, sustains me.

Lisa Ede

# Bedford/St. Martin's puts you first

From day one, our goal has been simple: to provide inspiring resources that are grounded in best practices for teaching reading and writing. For more than 35 years, Bedford/St. Martin's has partnered with the field, listening to teachers, scholars, and students about the support writers need. We are committed to helping every writing instructor make the most of our resources.

## HOW CAN WE HELP *YOU?*

- Our editors can align our resources to your outcomes through correlation and transition guides for your syllabus. Just ask us.
- Our sales representatives specialize in helping you find the right materials to support your course goals.
- Our learning solutions and product specialists help you make the most of the digital resources you choose for your course.
- Our Bits blog on the Bedford/St. Martin's English Community (**community .macmillan.com**) publishes fresh teaching ideas weekly. You'll also find easily downloadable professional resources and links to author webinars on our community site.

Contact your Bedford/St. Martin's sales representative or visit **macmillanlearning .com** to learn more.

## PRINT AND DIGITAL OPTIONS FOR *THE ACADEMIC WRITER*

Choose the format that works best for your course, and ask about our packaging options that offer savings for students.

Print
- *Paperback.* To order the paperback edition, use ISBN 978-1-319-24564-1.

Digital
- *Achieve for Readers and Writers.* Achieve puts student writing at the center of your course and keeps revision at the core, with a dedicated composition space that guides students through drafting, peer review, plagiarism prevention, reflection, and revision. Developed to support best practices in commenting on student drafts, Achieve is a flexible, integrated suite of tools for designing and facilitating writing assignments, paired with actionable insights that make students' progress toward outcomes clear and measurable. Achieve offers instructors a quick and flexible solution for targeting instruction based on students' unique needs. For details, visit **macmillanlearning.com/college/us/englishdigital**.
- *Popular e-book formats.* For details about our e-book partners, visit **macmillanlearning.com/ebooks**.
- *Inclusive Access.* Enable every student to receive their course materials through your LMS on the first day of class. Macmillan Learning's Inclusive Access program is the easiest, most affordable way to ensure all students have access to quality educational resources. Find out more at **macmillanlearning.com/inclusiveaccess**.

## YOUR COURSE, YOUR WAY

No two writing programs or classrooms are exactly alike. Our Curriculum Solutions team works with you to design custom options that provide the resources your students need. (Options below require enrollment minimums.)

- *ForeWords for English.* Customize any print resource to fit the focus of your course or program by choosing from a range of prepared topics, such as Sentence Guides for Academic Writers.

- *Macmillan Author Program (MAP).* Add excerpts or package acclaimed works from Macmillan's trade imprints to connect students with prominent authors and public conversations. A list of popular examples or academic themes is available upon request.

- *Mix and Match.* With our simplest solution, you can add up to 50 pages of curated content to your Bedford/St. Martin's text. Contact your sales representative for additional details.

- *Bedford Select.* Build your own print handbook or anthology from a database of more than 800 selections, and add your own materials to create your ideal text. Package with any Bedford/St. Martin's text for additional savings. Visit **macmillanlearning.com/bedfordselect**.

## INSTRUCTOR RESOURCES

You have a lot to do in your course. We want to make it easy for you to find the support you need—and to get it quickly.

The *Instructor's Notes for The Academic Writer*, Fifth Edition, is available as a PDF that can be downloaded from **macmillanlearning.com**. In addition to chapter overviews and teaching tips, the instructor's manual includes sample syllabi, correlations to the Council of Writing Program Administrators' Outcomes Statement, and classroom activities.

# How *The Academic Writer* Supports the WPA Outcomes

As the following table shows, *The Academic Writer* provides support that is well aligned for each of the outcome categories in first-year writing, giving programs confidence that using this text supports students fully through their first-year composition class and through the rest of their academic career.

# WPA OUTCOMES

## Rhetorical Knowledge:

By the end of first-year composition, students should

| *Rhetorical Knowledge Outcomes* | *The Academic Writer* |
| --- | --- |
| ● Learn and use key rhetorical concepts through analyzing and composing a variety of texts;<br><br>● Gain experience reading and composing in several genres to understand how genre conventions shape and are shaped by readers' and writers' practices and purposes;<br><br>● Develop facility in responding to a variety of situations and contexts calling for purposeful shifts in voice, tone, level of formality, design, medium, and/or structure;<br><br>● Understand and use a variety of technologies to address a range of audiences;<br><br>● Match the capacities of different environments (e.g., print and electronic) to varying rhetorical situations. | Part One emphasizes understanding rhetorical situations to achieve these outcomes, with attention to rhetorical reading and writing/composing as multimodal design and with focus on audience, purpose, text (genre and content), multimodal elements, and medium (print, online, etc.).<br><br>Part Two provides specific activities to practice responding to a variety of rhetorical situations, with special emphasis on academic writing.<br><br>Part Three, Chapter 11, "Strategies for Multimodal Composing," offers guidance for students to adapt their compositions to various technologies and platforms.<br><br>Section 4 of these *Instructor's Notes* along with the chapter-specific notes throughout Section 5 offer suggestions for using instructional technologies for teaching and learning as well as technologies for multimodal composing for students. |

**Faculty in all programs and departments can build on this preparation by helping students learn**

| | |
| --- | --- |
| ● The expectations of readers in their fields;<br><br>● The main features of genres in their fields;<br><br>● The main purposes of composing in their fields. | In addition to the overall information about understanding one's rhetorical situation, *The Academic Writer's* Chapter 8 relates directly to writing in different disciplines.<br><br>Faculty can also aid students by their willingness to meet with students to discuss the reading, research, and composing in that discipline. |

## Critical Thinking, Reading, and Composing:

By the end of first-year composition, students should

| Critical Thinking, Reading, and Composing Outcomes | The Academic Writer |
|---|---|
| ● Use composing and reading for inquiry, learning, critical thinking, and communicating in various rhetorical contexts; <br><br> ● Read a diverse range of texts, attending especially to relationships between assertion and evidence, to patterns of organization, to the interplay between verbal and nonverbal elements, and to how these features function for different audiences and situations; <br><br> ● Locate and evaluate (for credibility, sufficiency, accuracy, timeliness, bias, and so on) primary and secondary research materials, including journal articles and essays, books, scholarly and professionally established and maintained databases or archives, and informal electronic networks and Internet sources; <br><br> ● Use strategies — such as interpretation, synthesis, response, critique, and design/redesign — to compose texts that integrate the writer's ideas with those from appropriate sources. | Part One especially attends to the questions of language, knowledge, and rhetorical thinking. <br><br> Chapter 2, "Reading, Listening, and Viewing Rhetorically," and Chapter 5, "Analyzing and Synthesizing Texts," provide extensive reading and analyzing strategies that directly address this outcome. <br><br> Part Two, Chapters 5–8 especially focus on the role of inquiry in academic writing. <br><br> Chapter 5 focuses on ways to find, interpret, evaluate, analyze, synthesize, integrate, and document the ideas of others. <br><br> Chapter 6 offers guidance for supporting claims. <br><br> Chapter 7 provides guidance for locating and evaluating (as well as creating) primary and secondary research, with tools for new and emerging databases and search tools. <br><br> Chapter 8 focuses on writing across the disciplines, so it covers questions of reading, writing, research and evidence as they apply in various disciplines, offering opportunities for critical thinking and analysis by comparing audience expectations. |

Faculty in all programs and departments can build on this preparation by helping students learn

| | |
|---|---|
| ● The kinds of critical thinking important in their disciplines; <br><br> ● The kinds of questions, problems, and evidence that define their disciplines; <br><br> ● Strategies for reading a range of texts in their fields. | Chapter 7 on inquiry and Chapter 8 on writing in the disciplines directly engage writing as a method of critical thinking via writing and how that leads to knowledge and power. <br><br> In addition, activities throughout *The Academic Writer* encourage students to interview faculty and upper division students in their major to better understand the reading, critical thinking, and composing as done in their field. |

## Processes:

### By the end of first-year composition, students should

#### Process Outcomes

- Develop a writing project through multiple drafts;
- Develop flexible strategies for reading, drafting, reviewing, collaborating, revising, rewriting, rereading, and editing;
- Use composing processes and tools as a means to discover and reconsider ideas;
- Experience the collaborative and social aspects of writing processes;
- Learn to give and to act on productive feedback to works in progress;
- Adapt composing processes for a variety of technologies and modalities;
- Reflect on the development of composing practices and how those practices influence their work.

#### The Academic Writer

Chapters 4, 9, and 10 provide explanations and activities to guide students through understanding writing processes and creating multiple drafts, from invention to planning, drafting, and revision in a recursive manner, including collaboration, group work, peer review, editing, and proofreading, followed by frequent opportunities to reflect on the process.

Chapter 6 provides an extended, in-depth sequential case study of a student's essay from brainstorming to discover ideas through multiple revisions and reflections.

Part One and Chapter 11 relate especially to composing for a broad range of audiences via a variety of multimodal technologies and genres.

### Faculty in all programs and departments can build on this preparation by helping students learn

- To employ the methods and technologies commonly used for research and communication within their fields;
- To develop projects using the characteristic processes of their fields;
- To review work-in-progress for the purpose of developing ideas before surface-level editing;
- To participate effectively in collaborative processes typical of their fields.

WAC/WID programs can use *The Academic Writer* to enhance student writing in various disciplines. Section 3 of these Instructor's Notes offers some thoughts on that approach.

*The Academic Writer* offers frequent suggestions for students to interview faculty about the reading, research, writing, and presenting that are integral in their discipline.

Chapter 7 reflects on various research approaches in disciplines.

Chapter 8 focuses directly on the differences in rhetorical situations in disciplines with sample papers.

Section 6 of these *Instructor's Notes* provides sample student papers that composition faculty can use.

## Knowledge of Conventions:

By the end of first-year composition, students should

### Conventions Outcomes

- Develop knowledge of linguistic structures, including grammar, punctuation, and spelling, through practice in composing and revising;
- Understand why genre conventions for structure, paragraphing, tone, and mechanics vary;
- Gain experience negotiating variations in genre conventions;
- Learn common formats and/or design features for different kinds of texts;
- Learn to give and to act on productive feedback to works in progress;
- Explore the concepts of intellectual property (such as fair use and copyright) that motivate documentation conventions;
- Practice applying citation conventions systematically in their own work.

### The Academic Writer

Throughout, *The Academic Writer* focuses on the rhetorical grounding of conventions and the creation of ethos on the part of students with their attention to reader expectations for clear, correct writing.

In particular, Chapters 8 and 11 and the student samples throughout the book show various college writing assignments in terms of content and formatting along with the expectations for composing in various disciplines.

Chapter 7 discusses documentation approaches in different disciplines, with attention to ethics in research and intellectual property in using borrowed materials.

Chapter 10 covers revising, editing, and proofreading, again with attention to the rhetorical importance of correctness.

---

Faculty in all programs and departments can build on this preparation by helping students learn

- The reasons behind conventions of usage, specialized vocabulary, format, and citation systems in their fields or disciplines;
- Strategies for controlling conventions in their fields or disciplines;
- Factors that influence the ways work is designed, documented, and disseminated in their fields;
- Ways to make informed decisions about intellectual property issues connected to common genres and modalities in their fields.

Faculty can count on *The Academic Writer* to introduce students to appropriate writing for their field.

The frequent Strategies for Success notes help students of varied academic and cultural backgrounds to compose work that meets expectations in various disciplines.

Section 4 of the *Instructor's Notes* provides additional guidance for helping students adapt to academic conventions.

# Contents

# 7   Doing Research: Joining the Scholarly Conversation   177

## 8    Writing in the Disciplines: Making Choices as You Write    225

part

**3** Practical Strategies for Composing Texts

# Writing Rhetorically

**W**hat does it mean to be a writer today? In a media-saturated world where visual images surround us, does writing still matter, and if so, how much? How has the increasing emphasis on the visual influenced how ordinary people communicate? One need only search Google to notice the power that images hold. While drafting this chapter, for instance, I searched for *dog and owner* photos and promptly got more than 371 million hits. Clearly, dog owners are using the web to communicate how much they love their pets.

As a medium, photographs are not new, and neither is sharing them. Now, though, just about anyone with a smartphone can establish a visually rich presence on the web. On social media sites such as Facebook, Pinterest, Instagram, Snapchat, and Twitter; on video sharing sites like YouTube; and on many blogs, images and video or audio clips can be as important as the written text.

Written language has hardly lost its power, however. If anything, the power of the written word has grown. Individuals with access to online technologies are writing more than ever before. On the same day that I searched Google for photos of owners with their dogs, I also searched Amazon for the

The power of images: The love people have for their pets — and the power images have to communicate — is reflected in the huge number of pet photos online.

Suzanne Collins's *Hunger Games* trilogy and found 73,948 customer reviews of this novel. Outside of school, many students read and write virtually all the time, via texting, tweeting, posting on social media, and so on.

Technology, of course, has engendered many changes in the kinds of texts produced, and the design of these texts has become increasingly important, with more and more texts integrating video, photographs, music, and the spoken word.

You may think that the writing you do for fun is irrelevant to the writing you do for your classes. It's not. All your experiences as a writer, reader, speaker, and listener will help you learn how to meet the demands of academic writing. But to communicate effectively, you will need to develop your rhetorical sensitivity: your ability to make effective choices about your writing based on your purpose, your audience, and the genre and medium in which you're composing and presenting. As you well know, a text to a friend is very different from an essay for a history class. Learning how to recognize your rhetorical situation and to adjust your writing appropriately will play a powerful role in helping you transfer what you already know about writing to an academic setting. This chapter (and this book) will help you gain that understanding.

# Understanding the Impact of Communication Technologies on Writing

One helpful way to understand the impact of technology on writing is to consider the history of the printed text. For centuries, the only means of producing texts was to copy them by hand, as European scribes did in the Middle Ages. The limited number of manuscripts created meant that few people owned manuscripts and fewer still could read them. In 1440, Johannes Gutenberg invented the printing press, which could produce multiple copies of texts and therefore dramatically increased the availability of the written word. The rise of printing tended to deemphasize the role of visual elements, however, because the technologies for printing words and images were largely incompatible. In the 1800s, it became possible to print high-quality illustrated texts. Since that time, readers have come to expect increasingly sophisticated combinations of words and images.

The history of texts produced by individual writers differs from that of printed texts. The invention of the typewriter in 1868 enabled writers to produce texts much more efficiently than they could writing by hand, and by using carbon paper, they could even make multiple copies. But typewriters were designed to produce only words. Writers could manipulate spacing and margins, and they could underline words and phrases, but that was about it.

The development of the personal computer and of sophisticated software for writing, design, and illustration changed all that. Today anyone with access to the Internet can compose texts that have most, if not all, of the features of professionally produced documents, including integrated visual and auditory elements. An art history student who's convinced that graffiti represents an important genre of contemporary art could write a traditional print essay to make this argument, but she could also create a video, develop a PowerPoint or Prezi presentation, or record a podcast to make her point. If this student has an ongoing interest in graffiti art, she might even host a blog on this subject.

## for **exploration**

List all the kinds of writing you do, from traditional print and handwritten texts such as essays, class notes, and to-do lists to texts, tweets, social media posts, and blog comments.

Now turn your attention to the media you use to write.

- In writing essays for your classes, do you first brainstorm and write rough drafts by hand and then revise at your computer; do you write entirely in a digital medium (on your computer, laptop, tablet, or smartphone); or do you switch back and forth, depending on the project and situation?
- How many programs do you typically have open on your computer, and how often do you move back and forth from your word processing program to Google, social media, or some other site as you compose?
- Does your smartphone play a role in your writing?
- Do you ever incorporate images or graphics (yours or other people's) into your informal or formal writing? Are design elements and visual images more important to some kinds of writing that you do than to other kinds?

Take a few more minutes to reflect about what — and how — you write. What insights have you gained from this reflection?

The ability to compose in diverse media (print, digital, and oral) and to integrate words, images, and sounds represents an exciting opportunity for writers—but opportunity can also bring difficulties and dilemmas. Consider the art history student writing an essay on graffiti as art. If she followed the conventions of traditional academic writing, she would double-space her essay and choose a readable font (like 12-point Times New Roman) that doesn't call attention to itself. If she's using headings, she might make them bold; she might also include some photographs. In general, though, her essay would look and read much like one written twenty, or even fifty, years ago.

Suppose, however, that in addition to assigning an essay, her instructor required students to prepare a presentation on their topic using software like PowerPoint or Prezi. The student would still need to communicate her ideas in a clear and understandable way, but she might manipulate fonts and spacing to give her presentation an edgy, urban feel. Although she would hardly want to use a font like the graffiti-style BROOKLYN KID throughout, she might employ it at strategic points for emphasis and to evoke the graffiti she's writing about (see p. 4). She might choose visual examples of graffiti and arrange her images in prominent or unusual ways to create the kind of in-your-face feel that characterizes much graffiti. In each case the student is sharing her understanding of and enthusiasm for graffiti, but she is doing so in ways appropriate to her particular rhetorical situation.

# Settings for GRAFFITI

→ Subways
eliminated in
the late 1980s
as most popular
venue

→ Moved above
ground to walls
and buildings

→ Freight trains
took art across
continent

DON EMMERT/AFP/Getty Images

# Tools for GRAFFITI

→ Paint cans
using custom
spray nozzles

→ Keith Haring's
work with
chalk

→ Markers and
stickers

→ Cutouts and
posters applied
with glue

Andrew Burton/Getty Images

**PowerPoint Slides from a Student Presentation**

# Writing and Rhetoric

One of the most powerful resources that students, and other writers, can draw upon is one of the oldest fields of study in Western culture: rhetoric. Rhetoric was formulated by such Greek and Roman rhetoricians as Isocrates (436–338 B.C.E.), Aristotle (384–322 B.C.E.), Cicero (106–43 B.C.E.), and Quintilian (35–96 C.E.). Originally developed to meet the needs of speakers, rhetoric came to be applied to written texts as well. Thanks to recent developments in communication technologies, students today are increasingly communicating via multiple media, not just print. In this world of expanded media and modes of communication, rhetoric continues to provide essential guidance.✱

When you think rhetorically, you consider the art of using words, images, space and design elements, sounds, and gestures to engage — and sometimes to persuade — others. Writers who think rhetorically apply their understanding of human communication in general, and of texts in particular, to the decisions that will enable effective communication within a specific situation.

A rhetorical approach to writing encourages you to consider four key elements of your situation:

1. Your role as a *writer* who has (or must discover) something to communicate
2. One or more *readers* with whom you would like to communicate
3. The *text* you create to convey your ideas and attitudes
4. The *medium* (print, digital, oral) you use to communicate that text

The relationship among these elements is dynamic. Writers compose texts to express their meaning, but readers are equally active. Readers don't simply decipher the words on the page; they draw on their own experiences and expectations as they read. As a student, for instance, you read your economics textbook differently than you read a comic book or a popular novel. The more experience you have reading certain kinds of writing — textbooks in your major or the sports or financial pages of the newspaper, for example — the more you will get out of them.✱ (The same is true for viewers and listeners, of course.) Rhetoric is a practical art that helps writers make effective choices by taking each of these four elements into consideration within specific rhetorical situations.

Let's return to the student who wants to write an essay on graffiti as art. To analyze her situation, she would first consider her own position as a writer. As a student in a class, how much freedom does she have? In academic writing, this question leads immediately to the second element of the rhetorical situation: the reader. In academic writing, the reader is primarily the teacher, even when the student is asked to imagine another audience (an audience of interested nonexperts, for example). In an academic context, the student would

✱ To learn more about multimodal composing, see Chapter 11.
  For more about reading, see Chapter 2.

also need to consider the nature of her assignment, such as how open it is and what statement (if any) the teacher has provided about format and expectations. But the writer would also want to draw on her general understanding of writing in the humanities. Instructors in the humanities often favor a conservative approach to academic writing; they want to make sure students can develop and express clear, logical, and insightful prose. So while this student might use headings and images in her research project, her safest bet would be to focus primarily on the clear and logical development of the ideas.

This student would have more flexibility in approaching her PowerPoint or Prezi presentation. The conventions for presentations are more open than those of traditional academic writing. Moreover, instructors and students alike expect individuals who compose presentations to take full advantage of the medium. Since this presentation would be for a class, however, the student would still want to focus on the development of her ideas, and any visual and design elements would need to enhance and enrich the expression of those ideas.

In this example, the student's teacher has specified the media that should be used: a print essay and a presentation using PowerPoint or Prezi. For this reason, constructing a blog or creating a video would be an inappropriate response to the assignment, but the student could embed video clips of interviews with graffiti artists and images of their work in her presentation. As this example indicates, a rhetorical approach to writing encourages you to think in practical, concrete ways about your situation as a writer and to think and act like a problem solver.

## Composing and Designing Texts

thinking rhetorically

When you think and act like a problem solver, you use skills that have much in common with those used in the design profession. There are many kinds of design—from industrial design to fashion design—but writing is especially closely allied with graphic design, thanks in large part to the development of software programs like Adobe InDesign and Adobe Photoshop. In fact, given ongoing developments in communication technologies, conventional distinctions between these two creative activities seem less and less relevant. While it is true that in the humanities the most traditional forms of academic writing emphasize words over images and other design elements, student writers—like all writers—are integrating the visual and verbal in texts more than ever before.

In his influential book *How Designers Think*, Bryan Lawson lists the essential characteristics of design:

- Design problems are open-ended and cannot be fully specified.
- The design process is endless.
- There is no infallibly correct process of design; rather, design is a persuasive activity that involves subjective value judgments.
- The design process involves finding as well as solving problems.

These characteristics apply, Lawson argues, to all kinds of design, from product design to graphic design.

Like design, writing is a creative act that occurs within an open-ended system of opportunities and constraints, and the writing process, too, is potentially endless in the sense that there is no objective or absolute way to determine when a project is complete. Instead, writers and designers often call a halt to their process for subjective and pragmatic reasons: They judge the project to be ready when they believe that their audience or clients will be pleased or when they run out of time or money. Indeed, the open-ended nature of writing and design is typical of activities that require creativity.

Precisely because writing and design are creative processes, there is no infallibly correct process that writers and designers can follow. Experience enables writers and designers to determine the strategies appropriate to the task, but each project requires them to consider anew their situation, purpose, medium, and audience. As they do so, designers and writers do not just solve problems; they also find, or create, them. That may sound intimidating at first. "I don't want to find problems," you might think. "I want to solve them quickly and efficiently." Here's the rub: Often you can't do the latter until you do the former.

Let's say, for example, that two dormmates are frustrated because their room is always a mess. They talk it over and realize that the problem is that they don't have enough storage space, a common problem for students who live in dorms.

To address this problem, they have to go beyond the general recognition that they need more storage space to pinpoint the problem more specifically. After reading an online article on organizing and redecorating dorm spaces, they realize that the real problem is that they've neglected to systematically consider all their storage options. Once they've identified the crux of their problem, they can address it; in this case, they take measurements and head to the local discount store to look for inexpensive storage units that will fit the space. They've solved their storage problem in part by correctly identifying, or creating, it.

In writing and in design, as in everyday life, the better you are at identifying your problem, the better you will be at addressing it. In fact, the ability to identify complex and sophisticated problems is one feature that distinguishes experienced from inexperienced writers and designers. An interior designer might develop solutions to the roommates' dorm room problems more quickly, and possibly more innovatively, than the students do. Furthermore, as Lawson argues, design inevitably involves subjective value judgments and persuasion to convince clients to accept the designer's vision. One roommate, for instance, may argue for design purchases that reflect her commitment to sustainably produced products, while the other roommate may believe that the least expensive product that meets their needs is the best choice.

Both writing and design offer individuals the opportunity to make a difference in the world. Someone who redesigns wheelchairs to improve their comfort and mobility, for instance, will improve the quality of life for all who rely on them. It's easy to think of writers who have made a difference in the world. Most environmentalists agree, for example, that Rachel Carson's 1962 *Silent Spring* played a key role in catalyzing the environmental movement. But there are other, less visible but still important examples of the power that writing can have to effect economic, social, political, and cultural change. Writing is one of the most important ways that students can become members of a disciplinary or professional community. For example, in order to be recognized as professional civil engineers, engineering students not only need to learn how to plan, design, construct, and maintain structures; they also must learn to write like civil engineers. Besides playing a key role in most careers, writing also represents an important way that citizens express their views and advocate for causes (see the poster on p. 9). Think, for example, of the role that Twitter and Instagram now play in politics and public affairs. In these and other ways, writing provides an opportunity for ordinary people to shape the future of local, regional, and national communities.

## for **exploration**

Write for five to ten minutes in response to this question: What has this discussion of the connections between writing and design helped you better understand about written communication?

## for **collaboration**

Bring your response to the preceding Exploration to class and meet with a group of peers. Appoint someone to record your discussion and then take turns sharing your writing. Be prepared to share your discussion with the class.

# Developing Rhetorical Sensitivity

thinking
rhetorically

Both graphic designers and writers understand that to create a successful project they must do the following:

- Draw on all their resources, learning from their experiences, exploring their own ideas, and challenging themselves to express those ideas as clearly and powerfully as possible
- Consider their audience—who they are, what they know and like, and what they value and believe
- Assess the purpose and goals of the project—the meaning they wish to communicate and their reasons for composing
- Make use of all the tools available to them (such as word processing and image and sound creation and editing, as well as specialized programs), given the medium in which they are working

In all of these activities, experienced writers and designers practice *rhetorical sensitivity*.

tap
water
is, on
average,
500 times
cheaper than
bottled water.*
boycott the
bottle.

*The Chartered Institution of Water and Environmental Management (CIWEM) - Policy about Bottled Drinking Water - November 2005

© 2007 Stever Meyer-Rassow

Poster Advocating for a Cause

Designers and writers practice rhetorical sensitivity when they explore the four elements of rhetoric—writer/designer, audience, text/ project, and medium—in the context of specific situations. The student writing about graffiti art, for example, drew on her rhetorical sensitivity in determining how best to respond to her assignment. She realized that as a student writing for a class, she is constrained in significant ways and that her reader's (that is, her teacher's) expectations are crucial to her decision making. She also knew that the textual conventions governing essays are more conservative than those governing presentations and that differences in media—print versus PowerPoint or Prezi—reinforce this distinction. As a result of her analysis, this student realized that she had more freedom to experiment with visual elements of design in her presentation than in her essay.

To respond to her assignment, this student consciously explored her rhetorical situation. Writers and designers are particularly likely to do this when they undertake an important assignment or work for a new client. At other times, this kind of analysis takes the form of rhetorical common sense. In your daily life, you already practice considerable rhetorical sensitivity. As you make decisions about how to interact with others, you naturally draw on your commonsense understanding of effective communication. When you interview for a job, everything you do before and during the interview—what you wear, how you act, and what you say—is in an effort to make it a success. Much of your attention will focus on how best to present yourself, given the company you are applying to. You would dress differently if you were interviewing at your local fitness center rather than at a bank, for example. You would probably also recognize the importance of being well prepared and of interacting effectively with your interviewer. Savvy applicants know that everything they do is an effort to persuade the interviewers to hire them.

## strategies for success

It can be a challenge to "read" a rhetorical situation if you are new to the university or the local culture, or if the context the professor has provided for the assignment is unfamiliar. To better understand the rhetorical situation of an assignment, ask your professor or peers specific questions. Consult your peers or visit your teacher during office hours. This is time that professors have scheduled specifically to answer questions and help with assignments. Take advantage of that time and go visit!

You also employ rhetorical sensitivity when you "read" contemporary culture. As a consumer, for instance, you're bombarded with advertisements urging you to buy various products or services. Wise consumers know that ads are designed to persuade, and they learn ways to read them with a critical eye (even as they appreciate, say, a television commercial's humor or a magazine ad's design).

## Rhetorical Sensitivity and Kairos

Writers and designers who think rhetorically understand that writing and reading do not occur in a vacuum. The language you grow up speaking, the social and cultural worlds you inhabit, and the technologies available to you, among other factors, all influence how you communicate. For example, most students find that the writing they do in college differs considerably from the language they use in their everyday lives. The language that feels comfortable and natural to you when you speak with your family and friends may differ

from that required in academic reading and writing assignments. This is just one of many reasons why writing cannot be mastered via a handy list of rules. Instead, writers must consider their rhetorical situation; doing so is especially important when they are writing in a new or unfamiliar context.

Writers must also consider what the Greek rhetoricians called *kairos*. *Kairos* refers to the ability to respond to a rhetorical situation in a timely or appropriate manner. You can probably think of some obvious examples of kairos in action. Consider, for instance, President Lincoln's Gettysburg Address, which was delivered on November 19, 1863, four and a half months after the Battle of Gettysburg—which Union soldiers won at a terrible cost—and the day that the new Soldiers' National Cemetery in Gettysburg, Pennsylvania, was to be dedicated:

> Four score and seven years ago our fathers brought forth, on this continent, a new nation, conceived in Liberty, and dedicated to the proposition that all men are created equal.
>
> Now we are engaged in a great civil war, testing whether that nation, or any nation so conceived and so dedicated, can long endure. We are met on a great battle-field of that war. We have come to dedicate a portion of that field, as a final resting place for those who here gave their lives that that nation might live. It is altogether fitting and proper that we should do this.
>
> But, in a larger sense, we can not dedicate—we can not consecrate—we can not hallow—this ground. The brave men, living and dead, who struggled here, have consecrated it, far above our poor power to add or detract. The world will little note, nor long remember what we say here, but it can never forget what they did here. It is for us the living, rather, to be dedicated here to the unfinished work which they who fought here have thus far so nobly advanced. It is rather for us to be here dedicated to the great task remaining before us—that from these honored dead we take increased devotion to that cause for which they gave the last full measure of devotion—that we here highly resolve that these dead shall not have died in vain—that this nation, under God, shall have a new birth of freedom—and that government of the people, by the people, for the people, shall not perish from the earth.

President Lincoln was not the major speaker at the dedication, but his words have rung throughout subsequent history, while those of other speakers have not.

Historians generally argue that Lincoln's address, which lasted roughly two minutes, was so powerful because it took full advantage of its rhetorical situation and strongly appealed to kairos. In 1863, the Civil War had been going on for two bloody years, and it would continue another two years before it ended in 1865. In his address, Lincoln shifted the terms of the war, redefining what had largely been viewed as an effort to save the union between the North and the South to one dedicated to ensuring human equality.

The Gettysburg Address represents a pivotal moment in the Civil War and in U.S. history. World leaders often draw on kairos when they respond to a crisis or argue for an initiative. Many arguments about the necessity of addressing global warming rely on kairotic appeals. Kairos also plays a role in our daily lives. Advertisers recognize the power of kairos, even if they are not familiar with the term. For example, much of the advertising surrounding Black Friday, the day after Thanksgiving when brick-and-mortar retail stores advertise what are supposed to be their best sales of the year, draws on kairotic appeals as advertisers attempt to persuade people to embark on a day of frenzied bargain hunting.

As these examples suggest, those hoping to persuade an audience to value, believe, or do something must necessarily consider kairos. This is also true of academic writing, which often involves argumentation. For example, instructors in a writing course might ask students to identify and take a position on a campus issue that they believe needs to be addressed. A kairotic approach to argumentation would encourage students to explore the history of this issue so they could understand how best to resolve it and emphasize its urgency. It would also encourage them to pay careful attention to both explicit and implicit arguments made by others about this issue so they can better understand the most important areas of agreement and disagreement.

The first three chapters of this book will help you understand and apply a rhetorical approach to writing and reading. Chapter 4, "Academic Writing: Committing to the Process," will help you learn how to manage the writing process so you can be successful as a college writer. You may have a clear understanding of both the rhetorical situation and kairos as they apply to an essay you are writing, but if you procrastinate and begin working on your essay the night before it is due, the odds of writing a successful essay are against you.

As a college student, you may at times feel like the new writer on the block. Both this book and your composition course will help you build on the rhetorical sensitivity you already have, so you can use all the resources available to you to make timely and appropriate choices about your writing.

## strategies for success

Academic writing conventions can feel strange and uncomfortable, especially if they are different from the rhetoric or languages you grew up with, you learned in your early education, or you use in other writing spaces like at work or online. Many writers, from all backgrounds, struggle with negotiating between the ways they are expected to speak and write in the classroom and the ways they speak and write in other places. It's okay to be frustrated. Remember, your goal as a writer is to add new ways of speaking and writing to your skill set without giving up your own ways of writing and speaking.

## for **exploration**

Take a look at the advertisements for women's skin care products on p. 13. After carefully examining the two ads, respond in writing to these questions:

1. How do the designers of the ads use words, images, and graphics to persuade? Do some of these elements seem more important than others? Why?

**Advertisement from Dove's Campaign for Real Beauty**

**Advertisement for an Anti-Aging Face Cream by L'Oreal**

2. In what ways do the ads reinforce Lawson's observation that design involves "subjective value judgments"? Do they rely on culturally sanctioned stereotypes about women, beauty, and aging? If yes, how do these stereotypes reinforce the message?

3. In what ways do these ads demonstrate rhetorical sensitivity on the part of those who created them?

4. Advertisers often appeal to kairos in order to persuade consumers to buy something. In what ways do these two ads appeal to kairos?

*thinking rhetorically*

## for **thought, discussion, and writing**

1. Take a few moments to recall an incident when you were called on to demonstrate *rhetorical sensitivity* and write a paragraph describing it. Then write a paragraph or two stating your current understanding of the terms *rhetoric* and *rhetorical sensitivity*. Finally, write one or two questions that you still have about these terms.

2. Write an essay in which you describe and reflect on the many kinds of writing that you do and the role that visual and design elements play in your writing. After writing the essay, create a text that uses words, images, and (if you like) graphics to convey the ideas you discuss. You can use any mix of photographs, drawings, text, or other material that will help others understand your experience.

3. Interview two or three students in your current or prospective major to learn more about writing in this field. Ask these students the following questions:

   ● What kinds of writing are students required to do in classes for this field?
   ● How would they characterize the role of images and other graphic elements in this writing? What roles, if any, do multimedia play in their writing?
   ● How is their writing evaluated by their professors?
   ● What advice about writing would they give to other students taking classes in this discipline?

   Your instructor may ask you to report the results of these interviews to the class and to write an essay summarizing and reflecting on the results of your interview.

4. Choose a newspaper of interest to you. It could be a local, regional, or national newspaper or your school newspaper. Read the letters to the editor that are published each day in the newspaper and identify three letters that you believe depend strongly on appeals to kairos. In what ways do these letters attempt to persuade readers to value, believe, or do something through appeals to timeliness? Be prepared to share your examples and analysis with your classmates.

# 2

# Reading, Listening, and Viewing Rhetorically

**W**hy—and how—do people read? Not surprisingly, they read for as many different reasons and in as many different contexts as they write. They read to learn how to use their new smartphone, to decide which movie to see, or to explore ideas for writing. They read for pleasure, whether checking social media, browsing a magazine, or enjoying a novel. They read to engage in extended conversations about issues of importance to them, such as climate change, the economy, or contemporary music. In all these ways, people read to experience new ways of thinking, being, and acting.

Reading and writing are in some respects parallel processes. The process of reading a complex written work for the first time—of grappling with it to determine where the writer is going and why—is similar to the process of writing a rough draft. When you reread an essay to examine the strategies used or the arguments made, you're "revising" your original reading, much as you revise a written draft. Because writing requires the physical activity of drafting, you may be more aware of the active role you play as writer than as reader. Reading is, however, an equally active process. Like writing, it is an act of *composing*, of constructing meaning through language and images.

The same is also true, of course, of listening and viewing—activities that have unfortunately often been represented as more passive than writing and reading. And yet they too depend upon active engagement with aural and visual texts. Whether you are listening to a podcast on contemporary politics while taking the bus home or are reading an article on a controversial topic for your philosophy class, your *active* participation is essential. Equally essential is the recognition that, as humans, our emotions inevitably play a powerful role in our response to texts of all sorts. It is only human nature, in other words, to want to affirm positions that accord with our own experiences and inclinations. This chapter closes with Guidelines for Reading, Listening, and Viewing Rhetorically.

# Applying Rhetorical Sensitivity to Your Reading

thinking
rhetorically

Reading, like writing, is a *situated* activity. When you read, you draw not only on words and images (as well as video, animated graphics, and audio files for digital texts) but also on your own experiences to make cultural, social, and rhetorical judgments. The purposes you bring to your reading, the processes you use to scrutinize a text, your understanding of the significance of what you read, and other aspects of your reading grow out of the relationships among writer, reader, text, and medium.✱

## UNDERSTANDING YOUR PURPOSES AS A READER

Imagine two students reading in a café. One student is reading excerpts from Aristotle's *Nicomachean Ethics*, a foundational work in philosophy, for her Introduction to Philosophy class; the other is taking a break from studying and is browsing blogs and e-zines (online magazines) on his tablet. Both students are reading texts, but they are undoubtedly reading them in quite different ways.

The student reading excerpts from an ancient philosophical treatise knows that she will be expected to discuss the reading in class; she also knows that she can expect a question on this text to appear on her midterm exam. Consequently, she reads it slowly and with care. Because the writing is dense and many of the concepts and vocabulary are unfamiliar, she knows that she will need to look up terms she doesn't understand and do background research to grasp the important points. She also recognizes that she may need to read the text several times. Early readings focus on basic comprehension of the text; later readings allow her to interact with it via annotations that raise questions, note important passages, and articulate personal responses.

The student browsing blogs and e-zines, on the other hand, knows they can be put out by anyone with the time and inclination and can range from well-written and thought-provoking reflections on contemporary issues to poorly written diatribes. Before diving in, then, he skims the contents quickly to see if the topics are interesting and the writing worth reading. Because he has a personal interest in contemporary culture, he ends up spending a good deal of time on *Harlot: A Revealing Look at the Arts of Persuasion*, a well-written e-zine that explores the role of rhetoric in everyday life (p. 17).

## UNDERSTANDING HOW GENRE AFFECTS YOUR READING

The differences between how the two students in the café read reflect their purposes as well as their social and cultural understandings of the texts. These readers are also influenced by the texts' *genre*—that is, by the kind of text or the category to which each text belongs—be it textbook, blog, e-zine, scholarly article or book chapter, social media post, or newspaper article. When we recognize that a text belongs to a certain genre, we make assumptions about the form of the writing and about its purposes and subject matter.

✱ To learn more about the rhetorical situation, see Chapter 3.

Harlot: A Revealing Look at the Arts of Persuasion

*Harlot: A Revealing Look at the Arts of Persuasion*, an online journal (http://harlotofthearts.orq)

For example, a person reading their company's annual report understands that it is a document that follows specific conventions, including those of formal written English. When the same person goes online to read *Book Stalker* (p. 18), a blog by writer and editor Julia Bartz about "the NYC lit scene," he brings quite different expectations to his reading. Everything about the site—from its title to its colorful, playful design—suggests that the author will emphasize her personal opinions as she shares her "unabashedly subjective" views about literature and the literary life in New York City. So he is not surprised by the blog's conversational tone, occasional use of slang, and humorous touches.

You will be a stronger, more effective reader if you are attentive to genre. The following are some common genres organized by the context in which they might be produced or consumed:

**Personal writing:** letters, Instagram and Facebook posts, journal entries, personal essays, tweets, text messages

**Academic writing:** textbooks, scholarly articles and books, lab reports, essay exams, research projects

Screenshot from the blog *Book Stalker* (http://bookstalker.tumblr.com)

**Popular writing:** articles in mass-market magazines, reviews, fan publications

**Public writing:** editorials, letters to the editor, advocacy websites, public-service announcements

**Professional writing:** technical and scientific articles and books, job applications, workplace email

**Creative or literary writing:** poetry, stories, novels, graphic fiction, comics

When thinking about genre, it's important to remember two points. First, all genres have histories: They are not static forms, but rather are socially constructed responses to the specific needs of writers and readers.＊ Second, while some genres, such as lab reports, have changed little over time, others are more fluid. For instance, consider the variety of blogs that exist today, from personal blogs read only by a limited number of the author's friends and family members to blogs such as the *Huff Post* that circulate widely in ways similar to more traditional media.

When we move through our daily lives, we intuitively understand many genre differences and respond appropriately as readers. For example, we read instructions for our new television differently than we read the news feed on Facebook or a scholarly article for class discussion or a research project. As a college student, however, you need to develop a sophisticated response to an array of academic genres. A textbook written for students in an Introduction to Sociology course is very different from a scholarly article or book published in this same area, and thus requires reading strategies appropriate to the genre. As you take courses in various disciplines, you will find it helpful to ask yourself what the defining features are of the genre you are reading.

## UNDERSTANDING HOW MEDIUM AND DEVICE AFFECT YOUR READING

Today, most college students have a variety of options about how and where to read texts: on paper or on-screen, and if on-screen, on a computer, tablet, or smartphone. The question of how to best take advantage of these options can be complicated, however. For example, the student discussed earlier who is reading excerpts of Aristotle's *Nicomachean Ethics* could read this text on her smartphone, but should she? How people read, what they remember, how they see information, and even what reading is can be radically altered when the medium or device changes. Imagine a person reading a detailed graphic in a print magazine. In that medium, the graphic appears across two pages and can be taken in all at once. Now imagine reading that graphic on the significantly smaller screen of a smartphone. Now consider him reading it on a tablet or laptop, on which the once-static graphic of the print magazine may now include animations, audio files, and other digital enhancements.

Some educators and critics worry that individuals who read texts on-screen are less likely to engage with the material with the same critical depth as individuals who read print texts. In his best-selling book *The Shallows: What the Internet Is Doing to Our Brains*, Nicholas Carr makes just such an argument. In a study grounded partly in his personal experience and partly in brain research, Carr argues that reliance on the Internet is reducing users' capacity for concentration and for sustained deep thought. Others, such as Clay Shirky (author of *Cognitive Surplus: Creativity and Generosity in a Connected Age*), applaud the opportunities for collaboration and creativity afforded by the web and praise the opening up of reading to multiple media, devices, and apps. They point out, as just one of many examples, the

＊ For more about the history of academic genres, see Chapter 8, pp. 225–52.

enhancements available to texts — including college textbooks — designed to be read on digital platforms, such as zoomable art, embedded videos and lectures, and tools for sharing reading notes with classmates.

At this point, the jury is still out: The research available on this topic is limited, and more data is needed before we can determine whether those in Carr's camp or those in Shirky's will be proved correct. (It's possible, of course, that a less extreme position than either Carr's or Shirky's may be more helpful and accurate.) Still, most of us will be reading at least some texts online. Today, academic research, for example, often begins with an online search for scholarly articles accessed through academic databases, so it is important to develop the rhetorical sensitivity needed to make informed decisions about how best to access and interact with these sources.

As a student negotiating the multiple demands of school, work, family, and friends, you must make decisions about how and when to access texts. (By the way, texts can include visual and auditory elements: Political cartoons, advertisements, and podcasts are all examples of texts.)✱ The student reading Aristotle's *Nicomachean Ethics*, for example, may need to review this text for an exam while doing her laundry and waiting for her wash to dry: It may not be the best device for the job, but if it's the device she has with her, it's better to review the material on her phone than not to review it at all. In a situation like this, the most pressing issue she faces becomes how she can use her mobile device to read actively and critically, taking a rhetorical approach to reading that recognizes the limits and opportunities afforded by the medium (and by programs or apps developed for that medium).

The more aware you are of the impact of your own experiences and preferences, particularly in terms of reading in print and on-screen, the more you can build on strengths and address limitations. The quiz on the next page will help you reflect on these issues.

This quiz can help you determine your preferences and habits as a reader. As you answer the questions, consider all the reading you do. Include your reading for school and work as well as the newspapers, magazines, fiction, comics, blogs, wikis, websites, social media posts, and so forth that you read for your personal satisfaction.

As a student reading academic texts, you need to read strategically, keeping in mind the constraints and opportunities of your rhetorical situation, including those of your chosen medium and (in the case of digital texts) device. Do you need to absorb names and dates to prepare for an exam, or do you need to synthesize information from a number of sources to get a sense of an academic research topic? What practical constraints are you facing, such as competing deadlines or the need to do laundry while studying for a big test? Each of these purposes (and many others) will influence your approach to a text.

What should you take into consideration when you are deciding how to access and interact with an academic text? At the most general level, you would do well to remember that your instructors — whatever their discipline — share

✱ For more help with reading visuals, see pp. 39–45 later in this chapter.

## Quiz: Reading on Page or Screen

1. **As a reader, not just of academic writing but of all kinds of writing, how would you describe your preferences in terms of reading in print and on-screen?**
   a. I still prefer print when possible, especially for demanding academic or work-related texts.
   b. I prefer to read on-screen when possible.
   c. I move back and forth from reading print to reading online depending on my situation, purpose for reading, nature of the texts, and so on.

   *How do you think these preferences affect your ability to engage with academic texts critically and in depth?*

2. **If you selected option c, how do you decide which medium (print or digital) and device (computer, e-reader, tablet, or smartphone) to use for the different types of reading you do?**

   _____

   _____

   _____

3. **If you have a smartphone, how would you characterize your use of it? To what extent has it replaced your tablet, laptop, or desktop computer, and why?**
   a. It's important in my daily life, but I use it mainly for communicating with others (texting, chatting on the phone, sending Snapchats, posting social media updates, and so forth).
   b. I use my smartphone for communicating but also for navigating, shopping, and streaming music.
   c. I use my smartphone for all the above purposes, but I also use it as a watch, a calendar, and an e-reader if the text isn't too complex.
   d. I pretty much use my smartphone for everything: to read assigned texts, study and prepare for exams, do online research, take notes, and so forth.

   *How does your choice of medium and platform affect your reading experience?*

4. **What are the most important questions you have about your current practices as a reader?**

   _____

   _____

   _____

5. **What are the most important goals you would like to set for yourself as a reader and, especially, as a student reader of academic texts?**

   _____

   _____

   _____

a strong commitment to a deep engagement with texts (whether scientific or humanistic) and to critical reading and writing, so your ability to interact with a text—whether in print or on-screen—is key. The kind, or genre, of text you are reading (and the reason you are reading it) is also important when determining how best to access and interact with texts. For example, if you're reading an op-ed for a research paper you are writing, using a smartphone makes sense. After all, op-eds are relatively short and nontechnical. If you decide that you might quote from the op-ed and thus need to take notes, you might want to read it on a device with a keyboard that makes note-taking easier. Reading an op-ed is a very different experience from that of reading a scholarly book or article that puts forward a complex argument, a novel like *War and Peace* that depicts complicated relationships and events, or a graphic novel that depends on the relationship between image, frame, and text for its meaning. When reading an academic text for the first time, you may want to read in print or on a large screen so that you can focus on, annotate, and critically engage with the text. When reviewing that same reading for a test, you might want the convenience of studying on your laptop or smartphone, especially if you are in the midst of a long commute to campus.

Another factor to consider is the complexity and importance of the work you need to read. The more intensively you need to read—the more challenging and complex the reading and the more central the reading is to your coursework or writing project—the greater the effect the medium can have. Some readers find, for instance, that they can more easily grasp the "big picture" of an argument and engage it deeply and critically when they read and annotate a print text rather than a digital one, or they may find it easier to focus when not tempted to surf the web or respond to a friend's latest text message. Others prefer to read a text on a device that allows them to look up the meaning of a word by clicking on it, zoom in on detailed images, watch a video of a process, or access a dictionary or other texts that can aid understanding.

## strategies for success

If navigating the reading material is a challenge, you may appreciate e-book features like definitions, pronunciation guides, enhanced visuals, and audio options. Sometimes we learn better if we can listen to the text or if the information is more visual. Explore these features to enhance your experience as a reader and a learner.

When you are reading on-screen—whether on your phone, tablet, or laptop—be sure to take advantage of programs and apps such as Zotero and Mendeley that can make your life as an online reader, writer, and researcher easier.✱ If your instructor assigns an e-book as a textbook, take full advantage of its features, which may include embedded interactive video, self-quizzing, and linked glossary definitions.

✱ For more about annotation, see pp. 32–35 later in this chapter.

Remember that research suggests that people often read quite differently on-screen than when they read print texts. People who read on-screen often do so erratically and selectively, skimming and scanning rather than reading intensively and critically. If you are reading important academic texts online, you may need to consciously resist these behaviors. To help maintain your focus, close social media and other websites and programs that might distract you.

## UNDERSTANDING THE TEXT'S RHETORICAL SITUATION

Successful college readers recognize that they need to consider their own rhetorical situation when they make decisions about how to approach texts, but they also recognize that they must consider the rhetorical situation of the text they are reading. Obviously, they can't get inside the mind of the writer of the text, but they can learn a good deal about his or her purposes and intended audience by asking a series of rhetorically oriented questions about them.

*thinking rhetorically*

The questions on pp. 24–26 will help you understand how the rhetorical situation of the text affects you as a reader.

---

### strategies for success

If you are new to the college or university, it can be challenging to interpret texts that expect you understand unfamiliar cultural information. For example, if you are returning to the classroom, you may not know as much about online culture as some of your peers. You may also bring different rhetorical and cultural expectations to your reading from many of the other students in your classes. To better understand how you approach reading, reflect on how your background has influenced your expectations. It may be helpful to discuss these expectations with your teacher, your classmates, or a tutor in the writing center.

---

# Developing the Habits of Mind Needed for Academic Reading

Learning how to draw upon and develop your rhetorical sensitivity can play an important role in your success as an academic reader, but you must also develop habits of mind appropriate to college-level expectations. In grade school, your teachers emphasized first the ability to decode or read texts and later the ability to comprehend them. Your college teachers have something very different in mind, and their expectations are an important part of your rhetorical situation. Of course, college teachers still expect you to comprehend (and in some cases memorize) the texts you read. But they also expect you to go beyond comprehension to analyze, synthesize, and evaluate texts (including visual and aural texts).✶

*thinking rhetorically*

✶ Chapter 5 will help you learn to analyze and synthesize; Chapter 6, to make and support claims; Chapter 7, to evaluate the texts you read; and Chapter 11, to compose multimodal texts.

## Questions for Analyzing a Text's Rhetorical Situation

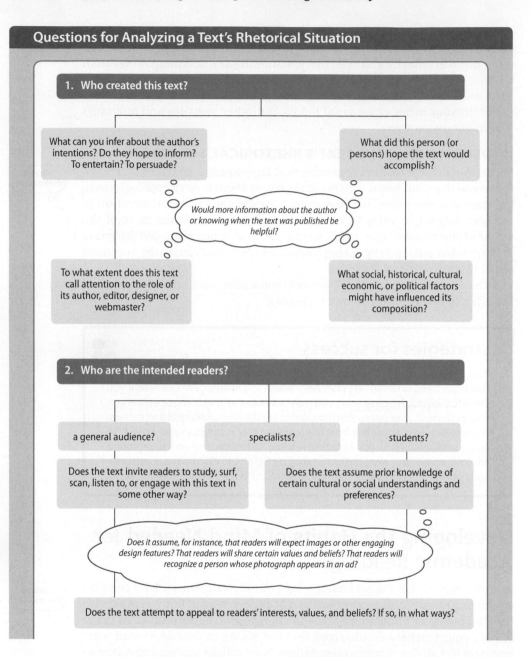

**1. Who created this text?**

What can you infer about the author's intentions? Do they hope to inform? To entertain? To persuade?

What did this person (or persons) hope the text would accomplish?

*Would more information about the author or knowing when the text was published be helpful?*

To what extent does this text call attention to the role of its author, editor, designer, or webmaster?

What social, historical, cultural, economic, or political factors might have influenced its composition?

**2. Who are the intended readers?**

a general audience?

specialists?

students?

Does the text invite readers to study, surf, scan, listen to, or engage with this text in some other way?

Does the text assume prior knowledge of certain cultural or social understandings and preferences?

*Does it assume, for instance, that readers will expect images or other engaging design features? That readers will share certain values and beliefs? That readers will recognize a person whose photograph appears in an ad?*

Does the text attempt to appeal to readers' interests, values, and beliefs? If so, in what ways?

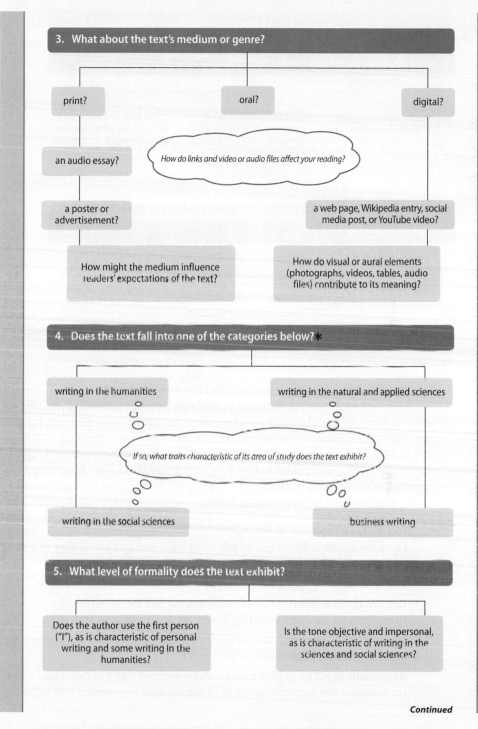

**3. What about the text's medium or genre?**

print?

oral?

digital?

an audio essay?

*How do links and video or audio files affect your reading?*

a poster or advertisement?

a web page, Wikipedia entry, social media post, or YouTube video?

How might the medium influence readers' expectations of the text?

How do visual or aural elements (photographs, videos, tables, audio files) contribute to its meaning?

**4. Does the text fall into one of the categories below? ✳**

writing in the humanities

writing in the natural and applied sciences

*If so, what traits characteristic of its area of study does the text exhibit?*

writing in the social sciences

business writing

**5. What level of formality does the text exhibit?**

Does the author use the first person ("I"), as is characteristic of personal writing and some writing in the humanities?

Is the tone objective and impersonal, as is characteristic of writing in the sciences and social sciences?

*Continued*

✳ For descriptions of these broad generic categories, see Chapter 8, pp. 225–52.

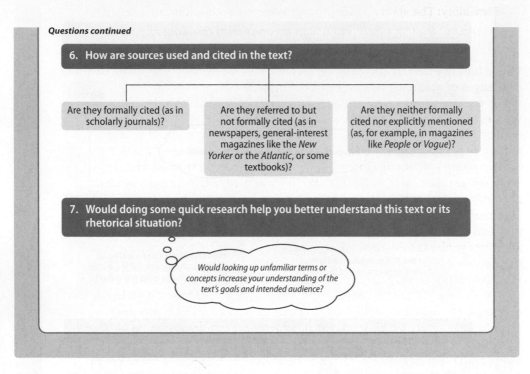

College teachers have understood for some time that certain habits of mind are essential to success in college. Several years ago, representatives from three national organizations involved with the teaching of writing—the National Council of Teachers of English, the Council of Writing Program Administrators, and the National Writing Project—came together to develop a formal list of habits of mind essential to academic success across the disciplines.[1] Called the "Framework for Success in Postsecondary Education," the list includes these habits:

**Curiosity:** The desire to know more about the world

**Openness:** The willingness to consider new ways of being and thinking in the world

**Engagement:** A sense of investment and involvement in learning

**Creativity:** The ability to use novel approaches for generating, investigating, and representing ideas

**Persistence:** The ability to sustain interest in and attention to short- and long-term projects

**Responsibility:** The ability to take ownership of one's actions and understand the consequences of those actions for oneself and others

---

[1]The habits of mind are discussed in *Framework for Success in Postsecondary Writing*, posted on the website of the Council of Writing Program Administrators, http://wpacouncil.org/aws /CWPA/pt/sd/news_article/242845/_self/layout_details/false.

**Flexibility:** The ability to adapt to situations, expectations, or demands

**Metacognition:** The ability to reflect on one's own thinking as well as on the individual and cultural processes used to structure knowledge

These habits of mind can play a powerful role in helping you meet the challenges of academic reading (and writing).

It goes without saying that academic reading is often demanding. Whatever the subject—whether it's the history of post-Stalinist Russia or the development of French Impressionist art—you are being exposed to subject matter that is new and complex. Rather than reading a summary of Karl Marx's *Capital: Critique of Political Economics* for your Introduction to Political Science class, for instance, your instructor may ask you to read one or more sections of Marx's original text, published in 1867. If you are taking this class to fulfill a requirement and have not previously been interested in political science, you may find the text daunting. Even when you are reading a textbook designed to introduce students to a subject, lack of background and unfamiliarity with the concepts and vocabulary may still make it a difficult read.

How you respond to such challenges will influence your success as a student. When you encounter reading that you find difficult and unfamiliar, one approach is to do the minimum and hope to get by, muttering to yourself that you wish you didn't have to take the class. Another approach is to recognize that difficult readings represent an opportunity. If you have developed the habits of mind of *curiosity* and *openness*, for instance, you are able to recognize that, although the reading is challenging, you will learn new things and new ways of thinking and being in the world. Recognition of these benefits allows you to maintain a sense of *engagement* in your own learning and increases your motivation. When you are fully committed to your reading and learning, you are much more likely to be able to draw on and express your *creativity*, to take *responsibility* for your learning, and to demonstrate *persistence*. As a learner, your *flexibility* is increased, particularly if you take time to reflect on and learn from your experiences via *metacognition*. In sum, these habits of mind encourage you to be a productive and successful learner, whether you are taking an introductory course in a discipline new to you or are transitioning from introductory to advanced courses in your major. These habits of mind are also as applicable in the professional world as on campus.

As you work to develop these habits of mind, be sure to take advantage of the following resources:

- **Talk with your instructor.** If you are finding the readings in a course difficult, make an appointment (the earlier the better) with your instructor. Describe the difficulties you are experiencing, such as understanding the vocabulary or underlying concepts or keeping up with reading assignments, and ask for help. Your instructor may work with you to understand the reading or point you to additional resources that can help you enter the scholarly conversation. Students are sometimes reluctant to ask their instructors for help, but most instructors enjoy talking with students. Instructors are deeply committed to their discipline—and to their students—so when a student indicates interest in a course, they are usually highly motivated to respond.

- **Take advantage of support services.** Many colleges provide services to help students transition from high school, or from years in the workforce, to college. These services may include peer mentoring, where you can meet with a more advanced student to talk about how you can respond to the challenges of college work, including college reading.
- **Visit your campus writing center.** Although writing centers generally focus on working with students on writing, many can also help you develop your skills as a reader, especially if the reading is connected with a writing assignment.
- **Use reference tools.** If you don't understand a word, look it up in a dictionary. An all-purpose dictionary like Merriam-Webster.com will be adequate in most situations, but for technical terms, you may need to consult a specialized dictionary for your discipline. (Most are now available through your library's online databases.) If you are reading a primary text by an author who is unfamiliar to you, be sure to look up the author for basic information.

Engaging in what the developers of the "Framework for Success in Postsecondary Education" refer to as *metacognition* is essential to your development as a reader. You might keep a reading journal, for instance, in which you reflect on the challenges—and successes—that you experience as a reader of academic texts. Or you might build in time for informal reflection and consider questions such as these: What are my strengths as a reader of academic texts? What are my limitations? How conscious am I of the various strategies I draw upon in reading different kinds of texts? How can I increase my repertoire of strategies?

When you encounter a particularly difficult reading, take the time to try to identify the sources of difficulty. Is it because of unfamiliar vocabulary and concepts, lack of clarity about the context in which the text was written (that is, its rhetorical situation), or inadequate background knowledge? Answering these questions can help you determine the most productive reading strategies to employ. After completing the reading, take a few minutes to ask yourself which strategies were particularly effective and which were less helpful.

## for **exploration**

Think of a recent time when you were required to read a text that you experienced as difficult. Take five minutes to freewrite✱ about the sources of the difficulty. Then freewrite for an equal amount of time about how you approached this challenge. Which of the strategies you used were productive? Which were not? Now take a few more minutes to write about what you have learned by reflecting on this experience. Conclude this exploration by identifying two positive ways that you could interact more productively with difficult texts.

## for **collaboration**

Meet with a group of classmates to discuss your response to the previous For Exploration activity. Begin by having each person state two important things he or she learned

✱ For more information about freewriting — what it is and how to do it — see Chapter 9, pp. 254–55.

as a result of the activity. (Appoint a recorder to write down each person's statements.) Once all members of the group have spoken, ask the recorder to read their statements aloud. Were any statements repeated by more than one member of the group? Working as a group, formulate two suggestions for how to engage productively with difficult texts. Be prepared to discuss your conclusions with your classmates.

# Developing Critical Reading Skills

Developing the necessary habits of mind can prepare you to engage college texts effectively. But you will also need to develop a repertoire of critical reading skills that you can employ depending on your rhetorical situation and the nature and complexity of the material you are reading. This section presents a number of useful strategies for engaging with texts. It also provides an opportunity for you to apply these strategies to a specific text, Frank Rose's "The Selfish Meme."

## PREVIEWING

When you preview a text, you survey it quickly to establish or clarify your purpose and context for reading, asking yourself questions such as those listed on p. 30. As you do so, recognize that print, online, and visual sources may call for different previewing strategies. With print sources, for instance, it's usually easy to determine the author and publisher. To learn the author of a website, however, you may need to drill through the site or decipher the web address. When skimming a printed text, it's easy to see all the text at once; skimming an article in an online magazine, however, might require navigating a variety of web pages. It can also be challenging to determine how accurate and trustworthy informally published texts are. Whereas such print texts as scholarly journals and books have generally undergone extensive review and editing to ensure their credibility, that may not be the case with online sources, which may appear or disappear with alarming frequency.✱

---

### strategies for success

All readers benefit from previewing texts because previewing gives you valuable information that can help you read the text efficiently and effectively. As you preview a text, be sure to formulate questions about specialized terms or about the text's general approach. Be sure to write down any questions that the preview brings up so that you can ask your professor or a tutor at the writing center to clarify it for you. Previewing, taking notes, writing down questions, and asking for clarification will help you to navigate even the most complex texts.

---

## for **exploration**

Using the Questions for Previewing a Text, preview "The Selfish Meme," an article by Frank Rose reprinted on pp. 31–32.

---

✱ For more on evaluating sources, see Chapter 7.

## Questions for Previewing a Text

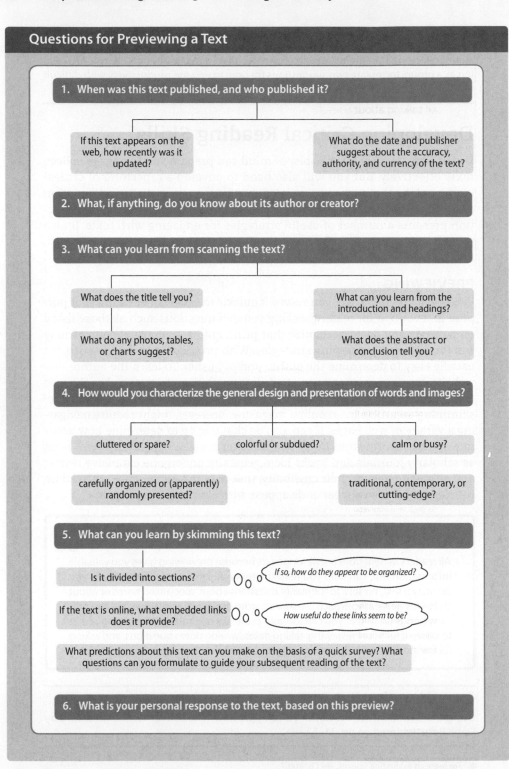

1. When was this text published, and who published it?

If this text appears on the web, how recently was it updated?

What do the date and publisher suggest about the accuracy, authority, and currency of the text?

2. What, if anything, do you know about its author or creator?

3. What can you learn from scanning the text?

What does the title tell you?

What can you learn from the introduction and headings?

What do any photos, tables, or charts suggest?

What does the abstract or conclusion tell you?

4. How would you characterize the general design and presentation of words and images?

cluttered or spare?

colorful or subdued?

calm or busy?

carefully organized or (apparently) randomly presented?

traditional, contemporary, or cutting-edge?

5. What can you learn by skimming this text?

Is it divided into sections?

If so, how do they appear to be organized?

If the text is online, what embedded links does it provide?

How useful do these links seem to be?

What predictions about this text can you make on the basis of a quick survey? What questions can you formulate to guide your subsequent reading of the text?

6. What is your personal response to the text, based on this preview?

## The Selfish Meme

Twitter, dopamine, and the evolutionary advantages of talking about oneself

Nicholas Blechman

Frank Rose

This spring, a couple of neuroscience researchers at Harvard published a study that finally explained why we like to talk about ourselves so much: sharing our thoughts, it turns out, activates the brain's reward system. As if to demonstrate the thesis, journalists and bloggers promptly seized the occasion to share their own thoughts about the study, often at a considerable cost to accuracy. "Oversharing on Facebook as Satisfying as Sex?" the Web site for the *Today* show asked.

Well, not really. The study, which combined a series of behavioral experiments and brain scans, didn't suggest that anyone, in the lab or elsewhere, had found sharing on Facebook to be an orgasmic experience. What it did suggest was that humans may get a neurochemical reward from sharing information, and a significantly bigger reward from disclosing their own thoughts and feelings than from reporting someone else's.

The Harvard researchers — Diana Tamir, a grad student in psychology, and Jason Mitchell, her adviser — performed functional MRI scans on 212 subjects while asking them about their own opinions and personality traits, and about other people's. Neuroimaging of this sort can reveal which parts of the brain are being activated; in this case, the researchers found that the mesolimbic dopamine system — the seat of the brain's reward mechanism — was more engaged by questions about the test subject's own opinions and attitudes than by questions about the opinions and attitudes of other people. The system has long been known to respond to both primary rewards (food and sex) and secondary rewards (money), but this was the first time it's been shown to light up in response to, as the researchers put it, "self-disclosure."

What the study really illustrated, then, was a paradox: when it comes to information, sharing is mostly about *me*. The researchers weren't trying to answer the thornier question of *why* — why, as they wrote, our species might have "an intrinsic drive to disclose thoughts to others." The paper nonetheless points to an intriguing possibility: that this drive might give us humans an adaptive advantage.

Researchers have previously shown that certain online activities — such as checking your e-mail or Twitter stream — stimulate the brain's reward system. Like playing a slot machine, engaging in these activities sends the animal brain into a frenzy as it anticipates a possible reward: often nothing, but sometimes a small prize, and occasionally an enormous jackpot. The response to this unpredictable pattern seems to be deeply ingrained, and for the most basic of reasons: precisely the same cycle of suspense and excitement motivates animals to keep hunting for food. E-mail inboxes and slot machines simply tap into an attention-focusing mechanism that's perfectly designed to make sure we don't lose interest in Job No. 1, which is to keep ourselves alive.

However unrelated food and Facebook may seem, this foraging impulse sheds light on why, by one count, 96 percent of the country's online population uses social-networking sites: we get high from being on the receiving end of social media. But that's only half the story. The Harvard study helps clarify why we are so eager to be on the sharing side as well. "This would certainly explain the barroom bore, wouldn't it?" said Brian Boyd, the author of the literary Darwinist treatise *On the Origin of Stories*, when I asked him about the brain's response to acts of self-disclosure. What about estimates that, while 30 to 40 percent of ordinary conversation consists of people talking about themselves, some 80 percent of social-media updates fall in the same category? "Ordinarily, in a social context, we get feedback from other people," Boyd told me. "They might roll their eyes to indicate they don't want to hear so much about us. But online, you don't have that."

At first blush, the notion that the self-disclosure impulse is somehow good for the species might seem counterintuitive. If all we did was prattle on about ourselves, we'd soon bore one another to extinction. Why would we have evolved to get a rush of pleasure from hearing ourselves talk?

A closer look at the advantages conferred by storytelling offers some clues: by telling stories effectively, we gain status, obtain social feedback, and strengthen our bonds with other people. And on the flip side, all of this nattering — or tweeting — by our fellow humans ensures that we don't have to discover everything on our own. We have no end of people competing to tell us what's what. Hence the *real* paradox of sharing: what feels good for *me* probably ends up benefiting us all.

## ANNOTATING

When you annotate a text, you highlight important words, passages, or images and write comments or questions that help you establish a dialogue with the text or remember important points. Some readers are heavy annotators, highlighting many passages and key words and filling the margins with comments and questions. Others annotate more selectively, preferring to write few comments and to highlight only the most important parts. In thinking about your own annotating strategies, remember that your purpose in reading should influence the way you annotate a text. You would annotate a text you're reading primarily for information differently than you would an essay that you expect will play a central role in an analytical essay you are writing for your history class.

One advantage of print texts is that there are an endless number of ways that readers can interact with them. If you look at three students' annotations of the same text, you might find that they look quite different but are equally effective in terms of engagement and critical thinking. Electronic or downloaded texts offer similar opportunities for interaction. Many devices make it possible for readers to highlight, bookmark, search, tag, add notes, and draw and embed images. Popular programs and apps—including iAnnotate, GoodReader, and Google Drive—are designed to increase the productivity of online reading and research, and new programs are being developed all the time.

Programs for note taking, sharing annotations, and making citations, as well as other tools for engaged reading, can help you read critically and deeply. The key is to choose a program that works for you, learn its strengths and limitations (depending on the complexity of the program, there can be a steep learning curve), and gain enough experience so that the benefits become real for you.

If you're working with print and have rented the text or prefer not to mark up your own copy, you can highlight and annotate a photocopy or scan or write questions and comments on a separate piece of paper or sticky notes. Some readers find it helpful to color code their annotations. For instance, you can underline main ideas in green and supporting evidence in orange. Color coding is easy to do in print, and many apps also allow for the use of color when annotating.

How can you know the most effective way to annotate a text? The Questions for Annotating a Text on p. 34 can help you make appropriate choices as you read and respond. In addition, see p. 35 for an excerpt from student Thai Luong's annotated copy of Charles Carr's essay "Reinstate the Fairness Doctrine!" which appears in Chapter 5 on pp. 115–17. Luong's essay responding to Carr's work can also be read in Chapter 5 on pp. 126–29.

## for **exploration**

Annotate "The Selfish Meme" by Frank Rose (pp. 31–32) as if you expected to write an essay responding to it for your composition class.

## for **collaboration**

Working in small groups, compare your annotations of the article. List all the various annotating strategies that group members used. To what extent did group members rely on similar strategies? What do these differences tell you about your own strengths and limitations as an annotator?

## Questions for Annotating a Text

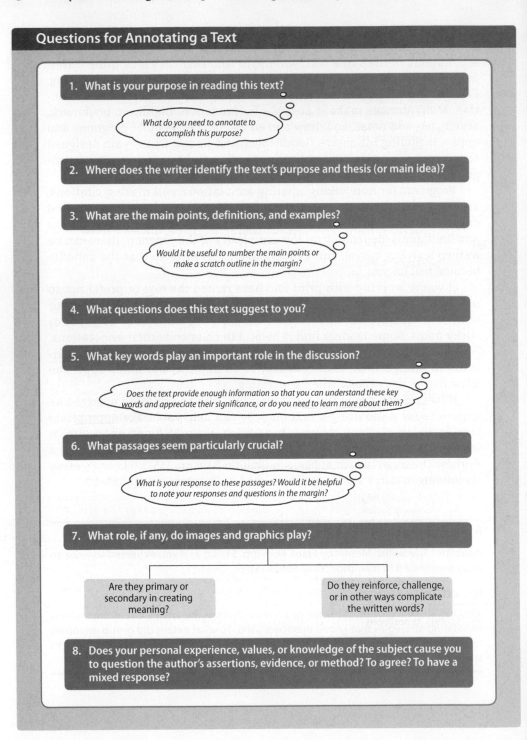

1. What is your purpose in reading this text?

   *What do you need to annotate to accomplish this purpose?*

2. Where does the writer identify the text's purpose and thesis (or main idea)?

3. What are the main points, definitions, and examples?

   *Would it be useful to number the main points or make a scratch outline in the margin?*

4. What questions does this text suggest to you?

5. What key words play an important role in the discussion?

   *Does the text provide enough information so that you can understand these key words and appreciate their significance, or do you need to learn more about them?*

6. What passages seem particularly crucial?

   *What is your response to these passages? Would it be helpful to note your responses and questions in the margin?*

7. What role, if any, do images and graphics play?

   Are they primary or secondary in creating meaning?

   Do they reinforce, challenge, or in other ways complicate the written words?

8. Does your personal experience, values, or knowledge of the subject cause you to question the author's assertions, evidence, or method? To agree? To have a mixed response?

*funny intro, hooks the reader in*

Like most people, there are certain things over which I have precisely zero will power. Junk food, for example. If it's anywhere in the house, I'll sniff it out like a Mangalitsa pig rooting truffles. Nearly three-quarters of a century ago some very wise lawmakers realized that America had something of a junk food problem of its own: the fact that people tend to believe that the opinions they already hold are correct and will not go far out of their way to subject them to scrutiny. It's only human nature. → *It's human nature to believe in what you believe in... it's hard to change mindsets*

To deal with it, just after WWII in 1949, our nation implemented a Federal Communications Commission (FCC) rule called the Fairness Doctrine. The Fairness Doctrine stated that all holders of broadcast licenses would be required to present controversial issues of public importance in a manner that was, in the FCC's language, "honest, equitable, and balanced." *BUT these are subjective terms.* Older readers may remember watching local news broadcasts in which editorial segments were immediately followed by a spokesperson presenting an "opposing viewpoint"—almost unthinkable in today's largely all-junk-news-all-the-time buffet. → *another food analogy*

*failed in 1987*

They did it, but they sure didn't like it and in 1987 pressured the FCC to eliminate it. It didn't take the ad boys and girls in TV and radio land to realize that its repeal could provide a massive revenue windfall. And those are pretty much the only two dots you need to connect to create the picture we've got today: 1) repeal the Fairness Doctrine 2) start capitalizing on people's basest instincts. Don't believe me? Here are just a few of the terms I pulled off of supposedly balanced political websites TODAY: smack-down, eviscerates, destroys, annihilates, slaughters, pulverizes, murders, and on and on . . . I only get a thousand words here. *→ But what about articles that have "fair" terms?*

*failed to save backup*

In the three decades since its repeal, there have been many attempts to reinstate the doctrine, so far without success. And, not coincidentally, over pretty much that exact period the severe ideological polarization in which America currently finds itself has increased dramatically. A recent Gallup poll revealed that, "Polarization in presidential approval ratings began to expand under Reagan and has accelerated with each president since Clinton." It has vaulted from a record 70 point gap under Barack Obama to 77 points under Donald Trump. News as sport. Opinion unfettered by correction. And dump trucks of bucks from a viewership kept too het up to risk turning away from the screen—a legislatively determinative number of people which has cocooned itself within a false reality so deep, so convincing, so perfectly — if cynically crafted that they are unable to see what they believe to be a perfect window into the world is, in fact, a mirror.

*while this may be true, there are a lot of factors that could contribute to it*

*→ important point here*

Reinstating the Fairness Doctrine or something much like it, would again require that opposing views be presented at the key moment viewers are being asked to make a decision. Keep your biases if you want, but only after someone with a different way of looking at the issue has had a shot at making their best pitch to you. Sort of like the nutrition label on that candy bar. You don't have to read it, but it's there. No wonder the food industry is always trying to get them removed. *→ BUT, people still eat it regardless of the label!*

? Reinstatement of the Fairness Doctrine would deliver a 9.9 shock directly to the tender bits of the news-as-sport industry and go a long ways to returning us to the days of Murrow, Cronkite, Sevareid, and the like—a world almost everyone purports to miss but hasn't the slightest idea

Thai Luong

**Thai Luong's Annotations of "Reinstate the Fairness Doctrine!"**

## SUMMARIZING

Never underestimate the usefulness of writing clear, concise summaries of texts. Writing a summary allows you to restate the major points of a book or an essay in your own words. Summarizing is a skill worth developing because it requires you to master the material you're reading and make it your own. Ideally, summaries should be as brief as possible, certainly no longer than a paragraph or two. The guidelines on p. 37 offer suggestions for writing your own summaries.

---

## for **exploration**

Following the guidelines on p. 37, write a one-paragraph summary of "The Selfish Meme" (pp. 31–32).

---

## ANALYZING A TEXT'S ARGUMENT

Previewing, analyzing visuals, annotating, and summarizing can all help you determine the central points in a text. Sometimes the central argument is explicitly stated. In the last paragraph of "The Selfish Meme," Frank Rose answers the question he raises in the first paragraph of why we like to talk about ourselves so much. We do so because "by telling stories effectively, we gain status, obtain social feedback, and strengthen our bonds with other people. . . . Hence the *real* paradox of sharing: what feels good for *me* probably ends up benefiting us all."

Not all authors are so direct. Someone writing about current issues in health-care ethics may raise questions rather than provide answers or make strong assertions. Whether an author articulates a clear position on a subject or poses a question for consideration, critical readers attempt to determine if the author's analysis is valid. In other words, does the author provide good reasons in support of a position or line of analysis? The questions on p. 38 provide an introduction to analyzing the argument of a text.✶

---

## for **exploration**

Using the Questions for Analyzing a Text's Argument, analyze "The Selfish Meme" (pp. 31–32). Be sure to answer all the questions.

---

✶ For a fuller discussion of this and related issues, see Chapter 3's discussion of ethos, logos, and pathos (pp. 64–69); Chapter 5's coverage of analyzing and synthesizing texts (pp. 103–38); and Chapter 7's coverage of evaluating a text (pp. 177–224).

## Guidelines for Summarizing a Text

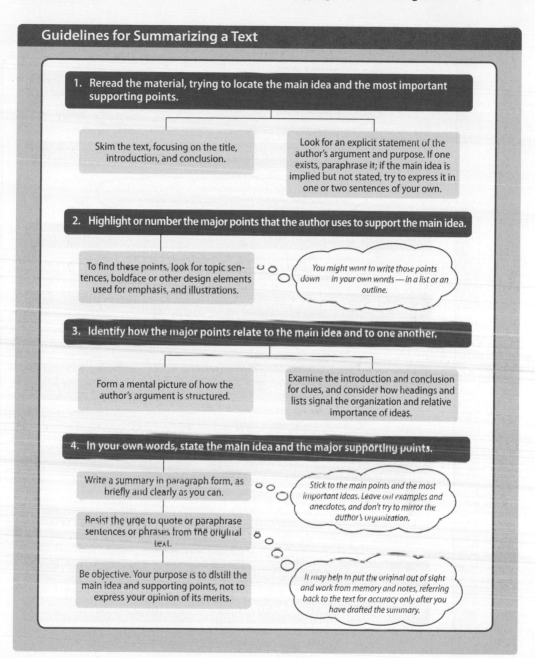

1. Reread the material, trying to locate the main idea and the most important supporting points.

Skim the text, focusing on the title, introduction, and conclusion.

Look for an explicit statement of the author's argument and purpose. If one exists, paraphrase it; if the main idea is implied but not stated, try to express it in one or two sentences of your own.

2. Highlight or number the major points that the author uses to support the main idea.

To find these points, look for topic sentences, boldface or other design elements used for emphasis, and illustrations.

*You might want to write those points down in your own words — in a list or an outline.*

3. Identify how the major points relate to the main idea and to one another.

Form a mental picture of how the author's argument is structured.

Examine the introduction and conclusion for clues, and consider how headings and lists signal the organization and relative importance of ideas.

4. In your own words, state the main idea and the major supporting points.

Write a summary in paragraph form, as briefly and clearly as you can.

*Stick to the main points and the most important ideas. Leave out examples and anecdotes, and don't try to mirror the author's organization.*

Resist the urge to quote or paraphrase sentences or phrases from the original text.

Be objective. Your purpose is to distill the main idea and supporting points, not to express your opinion of its merits.

*It may help to put the original out of sight and work from memory and notes, referring back to the text for accuracy only after you have drafted the summary.*

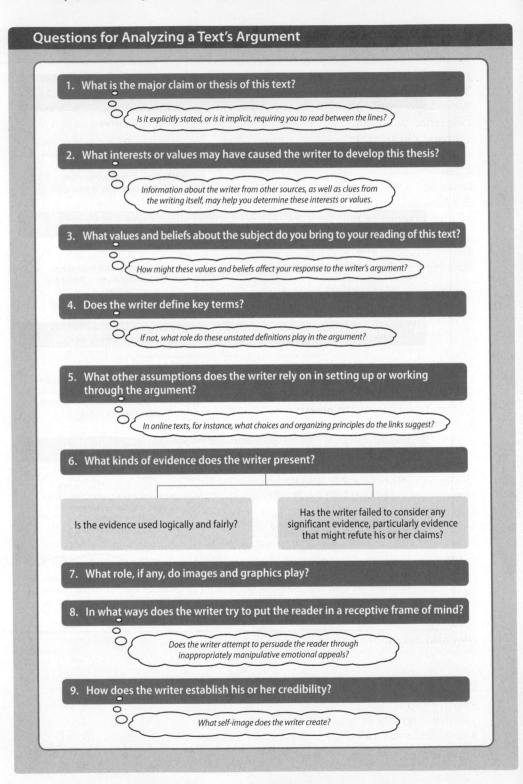

**Questions for Analyzing a Text's Argument**

1. What is the major claim or thesis of this text?

    *Is it explicitly stated, or is it implicit, requiring you to read between the lines?*

2. What interests or values may have caused the writer to develop this thesis?

    *Information about the writer from other sources, as well as clues from the writing itself, may help you determine these interests or values.*

3. What values and beliefs about the subject do you bring to your reading of this text?

    *How might these values and beliefs affect your response to the writer's argument?*

4. Does the writer define key terms?

    *If not, what role do these unstated definitions play in the argument?*

5. What other assumptions does the writer rely on in setting up or working through the argument?

    *In online texts, for instance, what choices and organizing principles do the links suggest?*

6. What kinds of evidence does the writer present?

    Is the evidence used logically and fairly?

    Has the writer failed to consider any significant evidence, particularly evidence that might refute his or her claims?

7. What role, if any, do images and graphics play?

8. In what ways does the writer try to put the reader in a receptive frame of mind?

    *Does the writer attempt to persuade the reader through inappropriately manipulative emotional appeals?*

9. How does the writer establish his or her credibility?

    *What self-image does the writer create?*

# Reading Visual Texts

As noted at the start of this chapter, when you read rhetorically, you draw not just on the text before you but also on all aspects of your rhetorical situation. You think about your purpose as a reader: What are your immediate goals? What do you need to "do" with your reading? Do you need to prepare for class discussion or an exam, or write an essay using the reading as one of several sources? You also think about issues of genre: What kind of text are you reading, and how might this constrain or facilitate your reading? Are you reading a genre with which you are already familiar, or are you reading a genre with unfamiliar and challenging content and conventions? And you also consider the medium. If you are reading a difficult text on your laptop, for instance, you may recognize that closing down multiple windows and programs will increase your ability to focus. Reading rhetorically means being an active, engaged reader, one who is not just reading passively to comprehend and absorb content but who is actively participating in the creation of meaning.

thinking
rhetorically

## strategies for success

The Questions for Analyzing a Text's Argument reflect one approach that you can use as you read. This approach uses North American English writing conventions. These conventions ask writers to announce their major claim or thesis in the introduction. Not all cultures or communities use the same conventions. As you read, consider the different argumentation conventions you have encountered. Bring up the differences in class so that everyone can benefit from your experience.

It may be easy for you to recognize the importance of reading rhetorically when you are reading traditional academic texts. Of course, the student reading excerpts from Aristotle's *Nicomachean Ethics* recognizes that this text requires her full attention, whether she is reading it in print or on her laptop. She also recognizes that to engage in the reading critically she must read proactively, looking up new terms and learning more about concepts she needs to understand. If she is unfamiliar with the branch of philosophy called ethics, for instance, she might do some quick online research to familiarize herself with its origin, history, and significance.

It can be harder for students to realize that just as they need to read verbal texts—texts that emphasize the use of words to create meaning—rhetorically, they also need to read visual texts rhetorically. This is not to suggest that you should read all texts, whether primarily verbal or visual, with the same level of attention and engagement. If you are reading your grocery list, all you need to know is that the abbreviation *mayo* means you should buy mayonnaise. Some visual texts function in similar ways—traffic signs, for instance, at least when you are traveling in your home country. Anyone who has traveled abroad knows that even traffic signs can require considerable cultural and rhetorical knowledge. To see why, search Google for "traffic signs around the world." You may be surprised by how much traffic signs in various countries can differ.

**Two Magazine Advertisements from 1955**

Reading and analyzing visual texts can be important in a variety of courses and disciplines. Students in art history are regularly asked to analyze reproductions of artwork; doing so is central to the discipline. Instructors in other disciplines may also create assignments that highlight the significance of visual texts. An instructor teaching an Introduction to Women's Studies class might ask students to analyze the pair of 1955 magazine advertisements on the previous page to gain insights about this era. A historian teaching a class on the lives of the urban poor in Victorian England might present students with a series of photographs from pioneering photographer John Thompson's 1877 *Street Life in London*. Their assignment? To choose several photographs that help illuminate one of the readings for the course and write an essay explaining what they have learned via this analysis.

Analyzing one or more visual texts is also a common assignment in many writing classes. You may be asked, for instance, to choose an advertisement and analyze it. If you haven't done so before, writing about visual texts can seem intimidating. How can you get enough out of a photograph or advertisement to write about it? How do you go about understanding the relationship between text and image? The Questions for Analyzing Visual Texts below will give you a place to start.

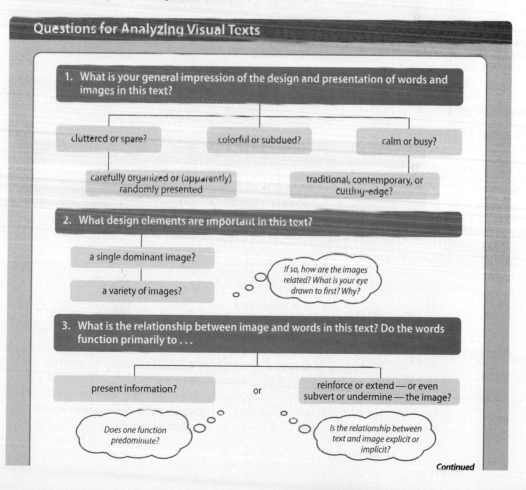

## Questions for Analyzing Visual Texts

1. **What is your general impression of the design and presentation of words and images in this text?**

   cluttered or spare?     colorful or subdued?     calm or busy?

   carefully organized or (apparently) randomly presented     traditional, contemporary, or cutting-edge?

2. **What design elements are important in this text?**

   a single dominant image?

   a variety of images?     *If so, how are the images related? What is your eye drawn to first? Why?*

3. **What is the relationship between image and words in this text? Do the words function primarily to . . .**

   present information?     or     reinforce or extend — or even subvert or undermine — the image?

   *Does one function predominate?*     *Is the relationship between text and image explicit or implicit?*

*Continued*

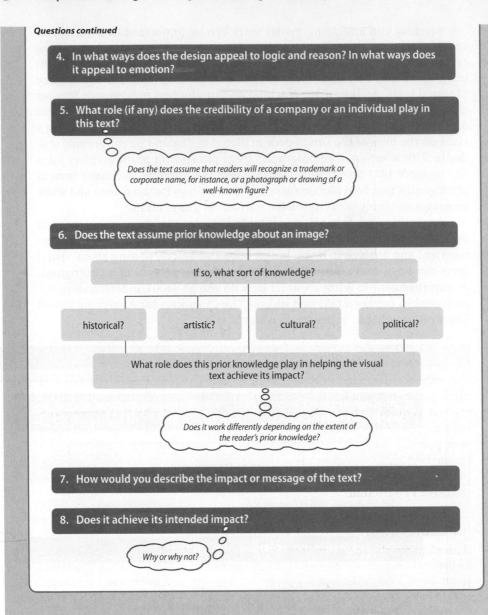

*Questions continued*

4. In what ways does the design appeal to logic and reason? In what ways does it appeal to emotion?

5. What role (if any) does the credibility of a company or an individual play in this text?

*Does the text assume that readers will recognize a trademark or corporate name, for instance, or a photograph or drawing of a well-known figure?*

6. Does the text assume prior knowledge about an image?

If so, what sort of knowledge?

historical?     artistic?     cultural?     political?

What role does this prior knowledge play in helping the visual text achieve its impact?

*Does it work differently depending on the extent of the reader's prior knowledge?*

7. How would you describe the impact or message of the text?

8. Does it achieve its intended impact?

*Why or why not?*

If you find it difficult to answer any of these questions, be sure to follow up by doing a little research. Let's say you are analyzing a political ad. The name of the group that created the ad is identified in the ad, but you are not familiar with this group. It doesn't take long to enter the group's name in your web browser and locate helpful information that will enable you to determine the group's credibility. Online research can also help you fill in gaps in your prior knowledge about an image. You may be familiar with the well-known photograph of a group of soldiers raising the U.S. flag during

Raising the Flag on Iwo Jima, February 23, 1945

the battle of Iwo Jima in World War II. You're aware that it is a famous photograph, but you know little about its historical, political, and cultural context. A quick web search can help you understand why this photograph became one of the most significant images of World War II. Depending on your purpose, this may be all the information you need. If you are writing a research paper on the role that news media played in World War II, however, you would need to learn more about the history of the photograph and the controversy surrounding it.

## for **exploration**

Illustrations can play an important role in texts that rely primarily on linguistic elements for their meaning. Such is the case with Frank Rose's "The Selfish Meme," which appears on pp. 31–32. At the top of the first page of Rose's text is a simple image. A man and a woman are facing each other holding what are clearly smartphones. Above each head is a bubble: The bubble above the man's head contains an "m," and the bubble above the woman's head contains an "e." Together they spell "me."

Using the Guidelines for Analyzing Visual Texts, analyze the illustration that accompanies "The Selfish Meme." After you have responded to the guideline's question, take a few minutes to explain the extent to which you feel the illustration reinforces the message of Rose's essay.

Even apparently simple visual texts can have rich cultural histories. On the next page, for instance, is a well-known photograph of the Marxist revolutionary Che Guevara. An Argentinian by birth, Ernesto "Che" Guevara

© 2019 Estate of Alberto Korda/Artists Rights Society (ARS), New York/ADAGP, Paris

**Ernesto "Che" Guevara, Photographed by Alberto Korda on March 5, 1960**

played a key role in the Cuban Revolution. This photo of Guevara was taken by photographer Alberto Korda on March 5, 1960, in Havana, Cuba. Korda recognized the power of the photo, but it was not distributed broadly until after Guevara's October 9, 1967 execution. After Guevara's death, this photograph quickly achieved near-mythic status.

Today, this image—and manipulations of it—persists in global culture as a powerful symbol of countercultural and political resistance. On p. 45, for instance, is a stylized version of the original photograph. In this rendering, the historical Guevara has become a widely recognized image, one that appears today in countless reproductions in every imaginable context, adorning posters, T-shirts, bumper stickers, Cuban currency, and even ice-cream wrappers, wine labels, and condoms.[2] Guevara's image has also become a popular tattoo, sported by Angelina Jolie and Mike Tyson, among many others.

The widespread use of Guevara's image has also given rise recently to "meta" references to its popularity—that is, to uses of the image that make tongue-in-cheek reference to how frequently the image is used. For instance, a T-shirt sold online by *the Onion* depicts Guevara wearing a T-shirt with his own image. In a similar vein, the cartoon from the *New Yorker* on the next page depends on readers recognizing not only Guevara's iconic image but also that of Bart Simpson (an image that vies with Guevara's in terms of its ubiquity).

As meta references, these uses of Guevara's image call into question the ways in which the image has been and continues to be used. Rather

---

[2]For additional examples accompanied by intelligent discussion, see Michael Casey's *Che's Afterlife: The Legacy of an Image*, Vintage Books, 2009.

"Che" Clip Art  Cartoon: Che and Bart

*www.openclipart.org*

*Matthew Diffee/Cartoon Collections*

than invoking Guevara as a symbol of countercultural and political resistance, they seem to suggest something about the image's commercialization and about its (mis)appropriation as a fashion statement and a means of perpetuating a consumer culture that the historical Guevara rejected.

## for **exploration**

Find a visual text that you believe has a rich cultural history. That history could be serious or humorous, high culture or pop culture. Take ten minutes to brainstorm everything you can think of about this visual text:

- What makes it interesting culturally?
- What are the specifics of its history?
- How has it been used in various contexts?
- What can it help writers better understand about how images and other visual elements create meaning?

Be prepared to share your visual text and brainstormed notes with others.

## for **collaboration**

Bring your visual text and brainstormed notes to class. Meet with a group of peers, dividing the time your instructor has allotted for this collaborative activity so that each student has roughly the same amount of time to present his or her visual text and brainstormed notes. Reserve at least five minutes for general group discussion about what you have learned as a result of this activity. Appoint a recorder/reporter who will share your group's results with the class. What has this activity helped you better understand about analyzing visual texts?

Chapter 6 presents an extended case study of one student's analysis of a visual text, a public-service ad (PSA) for the National Center for Family Literacy. This case study shows student Daniel Stiepleman moving from his early explorations of this PSA through planning, drafting, and revising. Notice how much attention he pays to visual elements in his preliminary annotation and analysis of the PSA (p. 161). Daniel struggled at times with his analysis, as is clear from the two rough drafts included in the chapter, but his effort paid off. His final essay represents a thought-provoking and engaging analysis of a visual text, one in which image, text, and design work together in powerful ways. Daniel's case study appears on pp. 173–76.

Daniel's analysis of the PSA for the National Center for Family Literacy emphasizes the importance of being able to analyze the visual texts we encounter in our daily lives. When driving down the street, watching television, skimming a magazine, or reading online—and in many other situations—we're continually presented with visual texts, most of which are designed to persuade us to purchase, believe, or do certain things. Often these texts can be a source of pleasure and entertainment, but informed consumers and engaged citizens recognize the value of being able to read them with a critical eye.

# Reading, Listening, Viewing, and Believing (or Not) in an Age of Social Media

Like many students today, you may feel that you face new and unusual challenges in your effort to be an informed consumer and engaged citizen, a rhetorically sensitive communicator who reads, writes, listens, and speaks respectfully and who values reasoned and evidence-based inquiry. After all, many people today argue that we live in a "Post-Truth" world, one that is threatened by a rapid increase in what is sometimes referred to as "fake news."

But is this really the case?

From one perspective, it is. You need only think about the rise of sophisticated photographic and video altering techniques that have resulted in difficult-to-identify fakes or the role that social media trolls played in the 2016 presidential election in the United States to worry about the future of both public and private discourse. In an article published in the *Washington Post* in June, 2019 titled "Seeing Isn't Believing: The Fact Checker's Guide to Manipulated Video," the authors discuss a variety of ways in which images and videos can be altered to deceive.

- Misrepresentation, such as identifying a photo by an incorrect date or location or sharing a brief clip from a longer video that distorts the message of that video.
- Omission, which occurs when someone similarly distorts or misrepresents an original context or narrative.
- Splicing, such as taking sound bites or video clips from multiple sources and editing them together, possibly adding new material.

- Doctoring, as happens when photos or videos are altered via cropping or other editing tools in programs such as Photoshop, alternating the speed, dubbing audio, and so on.

- Outright fabrication, of which what are called "deepfake videos" are an example.

In the case of deepfake videos, it is especially important to recognize that the old saying "Seeing is believing" no longer represents helpful guidance. Deepfake videos, which are so named because they use "deep learning" techniques developed in the field of AI (artificial intelligence), can in their simpler form be created by anyone with basic video-editing equipment: An example of a relatively straightforward deepfake video appears to show Facebook cofounder Mark Zuckerburg saying [falsely] that "whoever controls the data controls the future." (In the original video on which the "deepfake" version was based, Zuckerburg is discussing the Russians' efforts to interfere in the 2016 election via attacks on Facebook; to view the video, search Google for "Mark Zuckerburg deepfake video whoever controls the data.") Increasingly, however, the techniques are becoming more sophisticated. Some deepfakes use big data sets and algorithms to engage in sophisticated disinformation campaigns.

But from another perspective, this problem is as old as humanity itself. As Chris Mooney, author of "The Science of Why We Don't Believe in Science" observes, humans' neurological and biological makeup is such that our emotions often take priority over logic and reasoning, especially when we feel our pre-existing identities and commitments are under threat. Here is how Mooney explains this process:

> In other words, when we think we're reasoning, we may instead be rationalizing . . . We may think we're being scientists, but we're actually being lawyers. Our "reasoning" is a means to a predetermined end — winning our "case" — and is shot through with biases. These include "confirmation bias," in which we give greater heed to evidence and arguments that bolster our beliefs, and "disconfirmation bias," in which we expend disproportionate energy trying to debunk or refute views and arguments that we find uncongenial.[3]

In periods of extreme partisanship and strife, such as many countries throughout the world are currently experiencing, it can be particularly important to resist the urge to give into confirmation or disconfirmation bias. Especially in times like these, it is essential to attempt to genuinely *listen* to those with whom we disagree, not just to discover potential weaknesses in their argument but rather to understand and empathize with their experiences and commitments. As Krista Ratcliffe notes in *Rhetorical Listening: Identification, Gender, and Whiteness*, in Western culture listening has been valued less than

---

[3]Chris Mooney, "The Science of Why We Don't Believe Science," *Mother Jones*, May/June 2011, https://www.motherjones.com/politics/2011/04/denial-science-chris-mooney/.

writing, speaking, and reading. One reason for this may be that listening has mistakenly been viewed as passive, rather than active. (As noted earlier in this chapter, this has also at times been the case with reading.) But this is an incomplete understanding: Listening (like reading) is an active process that challenges communicators to invest time and energy in an effort to better understand others' assumptions, practices, and experiences.

As an example, think of arguments about climate change. Each side in this debate provides evidence and reasoning to support their views. Those on both sides of the debate are likely to cite scientific studies in support of their position, hoping perhaps that the scientific data and evidence presented would stand on their own. But of course they can't; they require interpretation and context. For this reason, both sides also draw on broader pre-existing assumptions and commitments. An advocate for measures to reduce the impact of climate change in the future might, for instance, point to the current generation's responsibilities to their children and grandchildren as an argument. Those who take a different position might emphasize instead the job losses that could occur for the *present* generation if such efforts were encouraged, and might instead emphasize the importance of rolling back regulations that they view as overly restrictive. Each side raises issues that the other side could fruitfully consider—but they most often don't.

If you think about it, this tension—between what we want to believe (based on who we are as people, what our experience as individuals and community members has been) and what others whose assumptions and experiences may differ considerably from our own believe just as firmly—has been present from the start of human civilization and surfaces any time we attempt to persuade someone to believe or do something. After all, we want to believe that our own assumptions, values, and practices must be correct, but we can learn a lot once we are able to identify and question them.

Doing so has always been difficult, but in an age when social media play a prominent role, this can particularly be the case. It is helpful to remember, however, that what we currently think of as social media are hardly new. In his book *Writing on the Wall: Social Media—The First Two Thousand Years,* for instance, Tom Standage takes a long view of the history of social media, noting that people have been sharing information with peers through informal, non-peer-reviewed networks for centuries. Standage cites as an example the graffiti on walls that played such an important role in the spreading of news (whether real or false) during the Roman Empire to the hand-printed tracts of the Reformation, including Luther's ninety-five theses which he posted on a door in Wittenburg, Germany, in 1517 and which led to the Protestant Reformation.

One way to think about our contemporary moment is to recognize that those who are negotiating media today—who are trying to determine what to read, listen to, or view and how best to do so—are dealing with an age-old problem: Who can you believe, and what reasoning and evidence should you expect to support these arguments?

## Guidelines for Reading, Listening, and Viewing Rhetorically

1. Remember the golden rule for reading, viewing, and listening rhetorically: Keep an open mind, just as you would wish others to keep an open mind when they read your writing or converse with you.

Empathy is essential in reading and listening rhetorically. Seeing another person's experiences, assumptions, and beliefs from their perspective is difficult, but it is also invaluable.

*This is much harder than you might imagine. It includes a willingness to consider new (and at times disagreeable) points of view. Ideally, doing so will allow you to gain perspective on the issue that concerns you; you might even try to argue the other side as an experiment. The reward? A richer, more thoughtful response that is likely to engage more readers, listeners, and viewers.*

Be willing to admit that your own experiences, assumptions, and beliefs might be not so much *right* or *wrong* as simply different from that of others.

Recognize that rhetorical reading, listening, and viewing are not passive: In engaging the views of others you are not passively accepting them. Rather, you are actively engaging them in open inquiry, whose goal is the greater good of the entire community.

2. Read, view, and listen proactively, checking for facts, misinformation, and lies. Having an open mind does not mean that you should automatically accept what you read, see, and hear, some of which could in fact be false or manipulated to deceive or confuse you. If you are concerned about the accuracy of a text, image, or video, follow these steps.

Check the source. Review the "about" page for helpful information. If you can't find the source, that's a sign that you should be concerned.

*Be alert to the possibility that photos or videos may have been manipulated. To determine the authenticity of an image, do a reverse image search using Google Image or TinEye. Additionally, pay attention to such details as shadows and light and distortions along the edges of people or objects for signs of digital manipulation.*

Look up other sources, including any research that the text quotes, and see if the original publication is reasonable.

Check facts using such independent, nonpartisan sites as Snopes or FactCheck.org.

Pay attention to the language used. Is it inflammatory or in other ways designed to encourage either a strongly negative or strongly positive response?

*Continued*

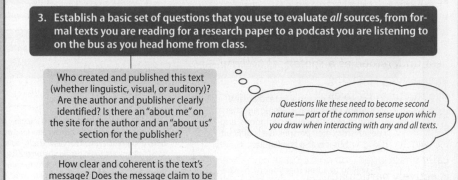

*Guidelines continued*

3. Establish a basic set of questions that you use to evaluate *all* sources, from formal texts you are reading for a research paper to a podcast you are listening to on the bus as you head home from class.

Who created and published this text (whether linguistic, visual, or auditory)? Are the author and publisher clearly identified? Is there an "about me" on the site for the author and an "about us" section for the publisher?

*Questions like these need to become second nature — part of the common sense upon which you draw when interacting with any and all texts.*

How clear and coherent is the text's message? Does the message claim to be fact or opinion? If it is a news story, what is its date — and has it been updated? Are sources cited, and are any statements attributed to them in quotation marks (to indicate they are exact quotes)?

What can you learn by looking at the text's context? Why was it created? How did you find the text?

Chapters 5 through 8 in Part II of this textbook, Writing in College, address these questions. These four chapters will help you to analyze and synthesize texts, make and support claims, conduct research—and do so in the context of the relevant academic discipline given your course and project. These chapters provide suggestions for meeting the demands of formal academic writing assignments: analyses, arguments, research papers, and assignments across the discipline.

As a student—and also as a citizen—you read (and increasingly view and listen to) a variety of texts. You will respond to some formally, but in many cases your response will be informal. Your instructor may ask you to read an essay and prepare to discuss it in class, for instance, or to listen to a podcast on a controversial subject. How can you best keep an open mind as you do so? The preceding guidelines can help you keep an open mind as you engage controversial or difficult texts, whatever their medium. You may also find it helpful to review the Guidelines for Analyzing Your Own Values and Beliefs on p. 144. Finally, remember that your rhetorical situation should play a key role in determining how you can most effectively read and listen to both texts and to people with whom you are conversing. If you are reading an essay to prepare for your writing or history class, you will certainly want to consider what biases you bring to the text, and you would do well to write responses and questions for class discussions in the margin (on screen or in print). If you are working on a more substantial project, such as a research paper, you might want to engage in a more systematic effort to analyze and evaluate your sources. In either situation, the Guidelines for Reading, Listening, and Viewing Rhetorically provide helpful suggestions.

This chapter encourages you to recognize that reading, like writing, is best understood as a rhetorical activity—and the same, of course, applies to listening, speaking, and viewing—all basic communication skills that we use in our daily lives. A rhetorical approach to these activities encourages you to consider your rhetorical situation as a student, community member, and citizen. It also encourages you to be aware of and take responsibility for your preferences and processes. Reading, viewing, and listening rhetorically challenges you to become an engaged and ethical communicator who is actively participating in the creation of meaning.

## for **thought, discussion, and writing**

1. For at least one full day, keep track of all the reading you do. Be sure to include both informal and formal material, from reading grocery lists and checking social media to reading class assignments, and doing so in print or on screen. Do you see any patterns in terms of preferences and habitual practices? Take a few minutes to write about what you have learned as a result of this reflection.

2. Write an essay in which you describe who you are as a reader today and how you got to be that way. Alternatively, create a poster-size collage that uses words, images, graphics, and even material objects to describe who you are as a reader today. For an example of such a collage, see Mirlandra Neuneker's collage on p. 89 portraying who she is as a writer.

   To prepare for this activity, spend at least an hour reflecting on your previous experiences as a reader and brainstorm responses to the following questions:

   - What are your earliest memories of learning to read?
   - Can you recall particular experiences in school or on the job that influenced your current attitude toward reading?
   - What images come to mind when you hear the word *reader*?
   - What kinds of reading do you enjoy or dislike?
   - What kinds of reading do you do outside of school?
   - How much of your outside-of-school reading is in print? How much is on screen?
   - What do you enjoy most—and least—about the reading process?
   - What goals would you like to set for yourself as a reader?

3. Interview either a professional or an advanced student in your intended major. Ask that person about the reading he or she does for professional or academic work and about the other kinds of reading he or she does for different purposes and for relaxation. What devices does your interviewee use? What patterns emerge in his or her reading practices? What does that person see as the greatest challenges and opportunities for readers today? What advice would the interviewee give to a student just entering this area of study?

4. Choose an advertisement or a public-service announcement that interests you. Using the Questions for Analyzing Visual Texts (pp. 41–42), write a response to each question. Finally, write one or two paragraphs about what you have learned as a result of this analysis.

5. Write an essay in which you respond to "The Selfish Meme" by Frank Rose (pp. 31–32).

6. Professors Carl Bergstrom and Jevin West of the University of Washington have created a popular course at their institution entitled Calling Bullshit. This course helps students learn how to negotiate fake or misleading information. As part of their course, these professors developed the website *Which Face Is Real*. Check it out by googling the title. You might also like to check out another site, *Spurious Correlations*, created by Tyler Vigan when he was a law student at Harvard that "pairs unrelated trends, based on actual data that have no meaningful relationship — other than they show a mathematical correlation." Is there a correlation between a decrease in Kentucky's marriage rate that happens to correspond with a drop in drowning on fishing trips, for example? The correlation is statistically valid, but there is no causal relationship. What do projects like this help you better understand about how what Bergstrom and West call "bullshit" spreads so rapidly?

# 3

# Analyzing Rhetorical Situations

As Chapters 1 and 2 emphasize, whenever you write — whether you're drafting an essay for class or designing a website for a student organization — you are writing in the context of a specific rhetorical situation involving you as the writer, who you're writing for, what you're writing, and the medium you're using to share what you have written. Each rhetorical situation comes with unique opportunities and demands: A management trainee writing a memo to her supervisor, for example, faces different challenges than an investigative journalist working on a story for the *New York Times* or a student preparing a slide presentation for a psychology class. Successful writers know that they need to exhibit rhetorical sensitivity — an understanding of the relationships among writer, reader, text, and medium — to help them make decisions as they write and revise.

In this chapter, you will learn how to ask questions about your rhetorical situation, questions that will enable you to determine the most fruitful way to approach your topic and respond to the needs and expectations of your readers. You will also learn how to recognize the textual conventions that characterize different communities of language users. This kind of rhetorically sensitive reading is particularly helpful when you encounter new genres of writing, as is the case, for example, when you enter college or begin a new job.

## Learning to Analyze Your Rhetorical Situation

Rhetoric involves four key elements: writer, reader, text, and medium. When you think about these elements and pose questions about the options available to you as a writer, you are analyzing your rhetorical situation.

The process of analyzing your rhetorical situation challenges you to look both within and without. Your intended meaning — what you want

thinking rhetorically

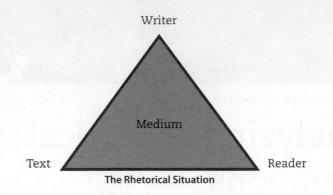

**The Rhetorical Situation**

to communicate — is certainly important, as is your purpose for writing. Unless you're writing solely for yourself in a journal or notebook, though, you can't ignore your readers or the kind of text you're writing. You also need to consider which medium (print, oral, digital) is most appropriate given your rhetorical situation. Both at school and on the job, sometimes your medium will be predetermined; at other times you will have options. Analyzing your rhetorical situation helps you respond creatively as a writer and yet keeps you aware of limits on your freedom.

## THE RHETORICAL SITUATION

In your daily life, you regularly analyze your rhetorical situation when you communicate with others, although you most often do so unconsciously and intuitively. Imagine, for instance, that you've been meaning to contact a close friend. Should you call, email, text, send a handwritten note, or contact him some other way? The answer depends on your situation.

## strategies for success

This chapter's approach to rhetoric and rhetorical sensitivity is grounded in the Western rhetorical tradition, which values individual self-expression. Other cultures, traditions, and communities hold different values and assumptions about communication. Western rhetoric as is written in school, business, and everyday contexts values a straightforward style that can feel abrupt or even rude to those from other traditions or communities. As a college writer, your goal is to understand when to use the Western rhetorical tradition and when to use the rhetorical traditions with which you are most familiar. Your writing (and your thinking) will be enriched when you learn how to draw on all the rhetorical sensitivity you have gained as a speaker, listener, writer, and reader. Be sure to discuss the differences between the styles you are learning and the styles you already know with your professor or a writing tutor. The strongest writers are the ones who have mastered the most tools.

If you just want to let your friend know that you're thinking of him, you might choose to text him because of this medium's ease and informality. If your friend maintains an Instagram account, you might visit his profile, view some posts to see what he's been up to, and then leave a friendly comment. But what if you're writing because you've just learned of a death in your friend's family? The seriousness of this situation and its personal nature might prompt you to send a handwritten note or call instead.

## USING YOUR RHETORICAL ANALYSIS TO GUIDE YOUR WRITING

Effective writers draw on their rhetorical sensitivity to determine the best ways to communicate with readers. Often, they do so without thinking. For example, the student deciding how best to get in touch with a friend didn't consciously run through a mental checklist; rather, she drew on her intuitive understanding of her situation. When you face the challenge of new and more difficult kinds of writing as you do in college, however, it helps to analyze your rhetorical situation consciously. The Questions for Analyzing Your Rhetorical Situation (pp. 56–57) can help you understand and respond to the constraints and opportunities.

---

### for exploration

Imagine that you need to compose the following texts:

- An application for an internship in your major
- A flyer for a march you are organizing to protest a tuition increase
- A response to a film you watched in class, posted to an online discussion board
- A substantial research-based essay for a class you are taking
- A status update for your social media page

Spend a few minutes thinking about how you would approach these different writing situations. Then write a brief analysis of each situation, using the following questions:

- What is your role as writer? Your purpose for writing?
- What image of yourself do you wish to present? How will you create this image?
- How will your readers influence your writing?
- How will the medium you use affect your communication?
- What role, if any, should images, design elements, and sound play?

---

## SETTING PRELIMINARY GOALS

Before beginning a major writing project, you may find it helpful to write a brief analysis of your rhetorical situation, or you may simply review these questions mentally. Doing so can help you determine your preliminary intentions or goals as a writer. Your intentions may shift as you write. It's natural to revise your understanding of your rhetorical situation as you

## Questions for Analyzing Your Rhetorical Situation

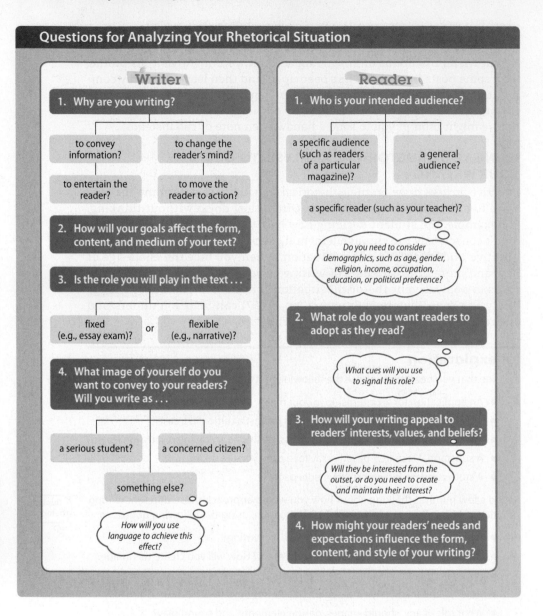

**Writer**

1. Why are you writing?
   - to convey information?
   - to change the reader's mind?
   - to entertain the reader?
   - to move the reader to action?

2. How will your goals affect the form, content, and medium of your text?

3. Is the role you will play in the text . . .
   - fixed (e.g., essay exam)? or flexible (e.g., narrative)?

4. What image of yourself do you want to convey to your readers? Will you write as . . .
   - a serious student?
   - a concerned citizen?
   - something else?

   *How will you use language to achieve this effect?*

**Reader**

1. Who is your intended audience?
   - a specific audience (such as readers of a particular magazine)?
   - a general audience?
   - a specific reader (such as your teacher)?

   *Do you need to consider demographics, such as age, gender, religion, income, occupation, education, or political preference?*

2. What role do you want readers to adopt as they read?

   *What cues will you use to signal this role?*

3. How will your writing appeal to readers' interests, values, and beliefs?

   *Will they be interested from the outset, or do you need to create and maintain their interest?*

4. How might your readers' needs and expectations influence the form, content, and style of your writing?

write. Despite its tentativeness, however, your analysis of your situation will give you a sense of direction and purpose.

Here's an analysis of a rhetorical situation by Alia Sands, whose essay appears on pp. 60–63. Alia analyzed her situation as a writer by using the Questions for Analyzing Your Rhetorical Situation above and on the facing page. She begins with some general reflections about her assignment.

## Questions for Analyzing Your Rhetorical Situation

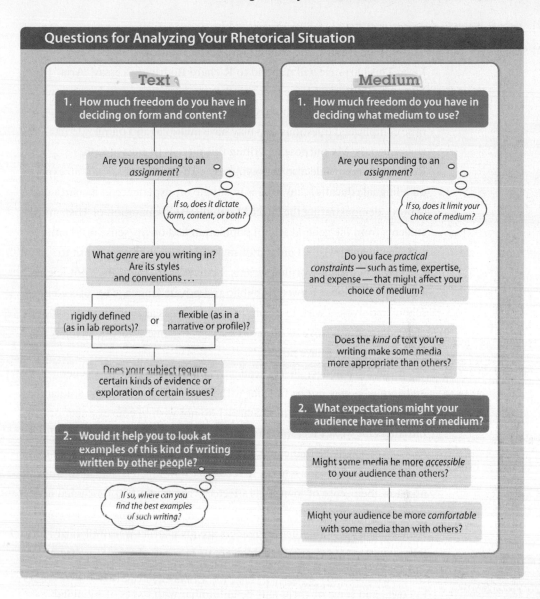

### Text

1. How much freedom do you have in deciding on form and content?

Are you responding to an *assignment*?

If so, does it dictate form, content, or both?

What *genre* are you writing in? Are its styles and conventions . . .

rigidly defined (as in lab reports)? **or** flexible (as in a narrative or profile)?

Does your subject require certain kinds of evidence or exploration of certain issues?

2. Would it help you to look at examples of this kind of writing written by other people?

If so, where can you find the best examples of such writing?

### Medium

1. How much freedom do you have in deciding what medium to use?

Are you responding to an *assignment*?

If so, does it limit your choice of medium?

Do you face *practical constraints* — such as time, expertise, and expense — that might affect your choice of medium?

Does the *kind* of text you're writing make some media more appropriate than others?

2. What expectations might your audience have in terms of medium?

Might some media be more *accessible* to your audience than others?

Might your audience be more *comfortable* with some media than with others?

### ALIA SANDS'S ANALYSIS

I am writing an essay for my first-year writing class. The assignment asked us to read an essay by Richard Rodriguez titled "Aria." This essay is included in Rodriguez's literacy narrative *Hunger of Memory*. The assignment asked us to respond personally to Rodriguez's text but also to engage with and synthesize his assertions about bilingual education.

**Writer:** I am writing a personal narrative regarding my experiences as a half-Hispanic, half-Caucasian middle-school student in Marshalltown, Iowa. This narrative will respond to Richard Rodriguez's essay "Aria" from *Hunger of Memory*. I hope that by using my own experience I can show how special programs for bilingual students, however well-intentioned, raise complicated questions and may have multiple (and unintended) consequences. My purpose in writing this piece is to engage with Rodriguez's text while also conveying my own story. As I am not an expert on bilingual education, my goal is to situate my experience in its particular context, demonstrating the effect Marshalltown's separation of Hispanic students from the general school population had on my sense of identity.

The image I wish to present of myself is of particular concern to me. I am not the child of immigrants. Unlike Rodriguez, I have not felt that I had to choose between a public and private language to succeed in school and work. I wish to portray my experiences as unique to myself and decidedly *not* indicative of all or even most Hispanic students, as many have struggled in ways I have not.

I will use language that is academic while appropriate to a general audience who may not be familiar with issues faced by Hispanic students in public schools in the United States. I do not wish to convey anger or bitterness for what I feel was an error on the part of the school, but I do wish to use language that emphasizes the gravity of the situation and how important I feel it is for schools to recognize how much is denied to students and how their sense of identity is affected when they are not included in mainstream instruction.

**Reader:** I am assuming that my readers are my instructor as well as my fellow students at Oregon State University. I assume that they are from diverse backgrounds; some of them may have had experiences similar to my own, and some of them may be unfamiliar with issues of bilingual education or the feeling of not having a public language or identity. As issues pertaining to race and education are often sensitive ones, I'm hoping to communicate in a way that acknowledges differences in opinion while still taking a clear stance based upon my own experience and my understanding of Rodriguez's text. I am trying not to be reductive when it comes to complicated situations. I don't want to imply that I know what kind of education will be beneficial to everyone. I do hope to show how my experiences overlap with the ideas discussed by Rodriguez and how those experiences have led me to conclusions about what can happen when students are excluded, rather than included, in the use of public language. **Text:** I only have a few pages to do the following: summarize Rodriguez's text, convey a meaningful story about my own experiences, and discuss the connections between the two. The length of the paper, then, will be a significant constraint. I will have to carefully edit my narrative, deciding on the most essential details to include, and also figure out what elements (examples, quotes, ideas) of Rodriguez's text I need to discuss. I will not be using multimedia or images, so I must engage my readers through my prose. I'll have to write clearly and succinctly because I have so little space, but I'll also need to use vivid language that will bring my experiences and other examples to life. (For example, I will be mentioning a movie, *Stand and Deliver*, that I was required to watch repeatedly in middle school. I will need to summarize its plot in order to convey its significance, but I'll also want to give readers a clear sense of what watching it felt like—the impression it made on me when I saw it for the first, second, third, etc., time.) **Medium:** I currently am not choosing to include any images, graphics, or multimedia in my essay. If I were writing a research paper on this topic, I would probably include graphics or images that would help readers better understand the information I am presenting. As most of my paper will respond to and synthesize Rodriguez's work, I do not feel that images or graphics are necessary to help readers better understand my own experiences or those of Rodriguez.

Here is Alia's essay. As you read it, keep her analysis of her rhetorical situation clearly in mind. In what ways did her analysis inform the essay she wrote?

Alia Sands
Professor Rhoads
Writing 121
May 2, 2019

A Separate Education

Bilingual education and support for nonnative English speakers in
classrooms are widely debated topics in academia today. While some
argue that students benefit from learning in their native languages,
others, like writer Richard Rodriguez, argue that bilingual education
deprives students of a shared public identity, which is critical to their
full participation in civic life. In middle school, as a half-Hispanic
student who only spoke English, I was surprised to find myself in a
special class for Hispanic students. My experience in the class brought
Rodriguez's misgivings about the effects of separate education vividly
to life: Being excluded from mainstream instruction even for a few
class periods a week caused me to reevaluate my identity and question
whether or not I was actually a member of the broader community.

In the essay "Aria" from *Hunger of Memory: The Education of
Richard Rodriguez*, Richard Rodriguez discusses his own experience
of second-language acquisition. Rodriguez, who describes himself as
"socially disadvantaged—the son of working-class parents, both Mexican
immigrants" (10), did not receive bilingual instruction and was actively
discouraged by the nuns running his school from speaking Spanish at
home. Though at first Rodriguez was reluctant to embrace English as his
primary language because he could not believe "that English was [his] to
use" (18), he grew increasingly comfortable with it. His experience learning English led him to believe that the common practice of separating
students from mainstream classroom instruction and from that public
language "dangerously . . . romanticize[s] public separateness and . . .
trivialize[s] the dilemma of the socially disadvantaged" (27).

My story is different from Rodriguez's. My sister Hannah and I
grew up in Marshalltown, Iowa, the children of a Hispanic mother

and an Anglo father, both college-educated. In school, I remember at some point checking off a box identifying myself as "Hispanic." In sixth grade, I received a small slip of paper instructing me to go to a basement classroom after lunch rather than to math class. When I arrived at the classroom, my older sister, Hannah, and about ten other students—all of whom were Hispanic—were already there.

There was a large Hispanic population in Marshalltown; many recent immigrants were employed in farming as well as in a local meat-packing plant. While there weren't many Hispanic students in my middle school, there were enough for the district to feel it necessary to send an instructor who said she would help us "integrate" more fully into the general school population. We were "at risk," she said. She promised to help us learn English and to value our home culture while also becoming meaningful parts of American culture.

Unfortunately, our instructor did not speak Spanish and assumed that none of us spoke English. In fact, more than three-fourths of the students in the class were bilingual, and those who weren't bilingual only spoke English. None of them spoke *only* Spanish. My older sister and I had never spoken Spanish; many of the other students were from Mexico and had only recently come to the United States, but they had improved their English throughout the school year attending regular classes and spoke enough English to understand what was said in classrooms. It was clear we were all being singled out based solely upon ethnicity. We had no idea that we were "at risk" until the instructor told us we were.

Statistics showed, she said, that most of us would not go to college. Many of us would drop out of school. She told us she sympathized with how uncomfortable we must be in class, not understanding English. Her first act as instructor was to go around the room pointing to objects and saying their names, drawing out the vowels slowly. Oooverhead projeeectoor. Blaaackboard. Liiight. She stopped in front of me and held up a pencil. My blank expression must have confirmed her suspicions about our substandard English skills, so she said "pencil" over and over again until I replied, "Uh, pencil?" hoping she

Sands 3

would go away. One of the boys across the room laughed loudly and said something in Spanish.

When our instructor moved to the next student to teach "notebook," I leaned over to a girl sitting at my table.

"What did he say?" I asked, pointing to the boy across the table.

"He said that stupid woman can't tell you don't speak Spanish."

He was right—but that was not the only thing she didn't seem to understand. We spent the next few weeks watching the movie *Stand and Deliver* over and over. *Stand and Deliver* is the story of how Jaime Escalante began teaching a remedial math class in East Los Angeles and developed a program that led his students to take and pass the AP calculus exam. Our teacher would beam happily after showing us the movie and would tell us that this movie was proof that we didn't need to cheat to excel. She told us we could stay in school, not join gangs, and not get pregnant. The implication, of course, was that because we were Hispanic, we were somehow more likely than others to cheat, to join gangs, and to have unprotected sex. The teacher, and the school, attempted to "empower" us by using stereotypical and racist assumptions about our knowledge of English and our abilities.

In "Aria," Rodriguez argues that his mastery of English represented a social change, not just a linguistic one: It made him a successful student and participant in the larger community (32). Rodriguez emphasizes the "public gain" that comes with language acquisition, advising that people be wary of those who "scorn assimilation" and discount the consequences of not having access to the public language of power and the public community (27). These consequences had most likely been considered at some point by the students in the Hispanic class I was a part of; the fact that the native Spanish speakers were all bilingual indicated their awareness of the importance of speaking English in order to function in and become part of the Marshalltown community. The instructor, however, continued to emphasize our difference from the larger community.

Sands 4

Unlike Rodriguez, before that class I had always had a sense of myself as part of the public community. I assumed I would go to college: If my family could not afford to send me, I would get scholarships and jobs to fund my education. I assumed that being a native speaker of English guaranteed me a place in the public community. Being put in the basement caused me to question these assumptions. I learned what I imagine other students in the classroom may have already known—that even if you were bilingual or spoke English perfectly, there was no guarantee that you would be considered part of the public community.

Richard Rodriguez describes how becoming part of public society is a process with both benefits and costs. He asserts that "while one suffers a diminished sense of *private* individuality by becoming assimilated into public society, such assimilation makes possible the achievement of *public* individuality" (26). This process of developing a public identity is not always a simple one, especially when it involves changes in language or in relationships. As my experience and Rodriguez's demonstrate, schools play an active role in shaping students' sense of themselves as individuals. With increasingly diverse student bodies like the one in my middle school, educators face the difficult question of how best to educate students from a variety of backgrounds, while at the same time helping all students become members of a broader public community.

I don't think my middle school had the answer, and I'm not sure there is a one-size-fits-all solution. What I am sure about is this: Educators in every community need to honestly evaluate what they're doing now, and then, working with students and their parents, find ways to help students realize their full potential, both as individuals *and* as members of the larger society.

Work Cited

Rodriguez, Richard. "Aria." *Hunger of Memory: The Education of Richard Rodriguez,* Dial Press, 1982, pp. 9–41.

*Note:* In an actual MLA-style paper, Works Cited entries start on a new page.

---

## for **exploration**

To what extent does Alia Sands's essay achieve the goals she established for herself in her analysis of her rhetorical situation? Reread Alia's analysis, and then reread her essay. Keeping her analysis in mind, list three or four reasons you believe Alia does or does not achieve her goals, and then find at least one passage in the essay that illustrates each of these statements. Finally, identify at least one way Alia might strengthen her essay were she to revise it.

---

# Using Aristotle's Appeals

*thinking rhetorically*

Analyzing your rhetorical situation can provide information that will enable you to make crucial strategic, structural, and stylistic decisions about your writing. In considering how to use this information, you may find it helpful to employ what Aristotle (384–322 B.C.E.) characterized as the three appeals. According to Aristotle, when speakers and writers communicate with others, they draw on these three general appeals:

- *Logos*, the appeal to reason
- *Pathos*, the appeal to emotion, values, and beliefs
- *Ethos*, the appeal to the credibility of the speaker or writer

As a writer, you appeal to logos when you focus on the logical presentation of your subject by providing evidence and examples in support of your ideas. You appeal to pathos when you use the resources of language to engage your readers emotionally with your subject or appeal to their values, beliefs, or needs. And you appeal to ethos when you create an image of yourself, a persona, that encourages readers to accept or act on your ideas.

These appeals correspond to three of the four basic elements of rhetoric: writer, reader, and text. In appealing to ethos, you focus on the writer's character as implied in the text; in appealing to pathos, on the interaction of writer and reader; and in appealing to logos, on the logical statements about the subject made in your particular text. In some instances, you may rely predominantly on one of these appeals. A student writing a technical report, for instance, will typically emphasize scientific or technical evidence (logos), not emotional or personal appeals. More often, however, you'll draw on all three appeals to create a fully persuasive document. A journalist writing a column on child abuse might open with several examples designed to gain her readers' attention and convince them of the importance of this issue (pathos). Although she may rely primarily on information about the negative consequences of child abuse (logos), she will undoubtedly also endeavor to create an image of herself as a caring, serious person (ethos), one whose analysis of a subject like child abuse should be trusted.

This journalist might also use images to help convey her point. One or more photographs of physically abused children would certainly appeal to pathos. To call attention to the large number of children who are physically abused (and thus bolster the logos of her argument), she might present important statistics in a chart or graph, which also contribute to her ethos. In so doing, the journalist is combining words, images, and graphics to maximum effect.

Kairos might also play a role in her column on child abuse. (Kairos, discussed in Chapter 1, pp. 10–12, refers to the ability to respond to a rhetorical situation in a timely or appropriate manner.) In presenting statistics about child abuse, for instance, the journalist might call attention to a recent substantial increase in the number of cases of child abuse reported to authorities. In so doing, she is appealing to kairos and encouraging readers to recognize that child abuse is an urgent problem that must be addressed. The journalist might also refer to several recent cases of child abuse that have been widely discussed in the media. Doing so also emphasizes the need to address a significant social and familial problem.

In the following example, Brandon Barrett, a chemistry major at Oregon State University, uses Aristotle's three appeals to determine how best to approach an essay assignment for a first-year writing class that asks him to explain what his major is and why he chose it. He also considers how his essay can take advantage of kairos.

In presenting the assignment, Barrett's teacher informed students that their two- to three-page essays should include "information about your major that is new to your readers; in other words, it should not simply repeat basic course information about your major. Rather, it should be your unique perspective, written in clear, descriptive language." The teacher concluded with this advice: "Have fun with this assignment. Consider your audience (it should be this class unless you specify a different audience). Remember Aristotle's three appeals: How will your essay employ the appeals of logos, pathos, and ethos? Remember the importance of kairos as a way of gaining the attention and interest of your readers. Finally, as you write, keep these questions in mind: What is your purpose? What do you hope to achieve with your audience?" Brandon's essay is preceded by his analysis of his rhetorical situation and of his essay's appeals to logos, pathos, ethos, and kairos.

thinking
rhetorically

### BRANDON BARRETT'S ANALYSIS

I'm writing this essay to explain how I made the most important decision in my life to date: what to major in while in college. I want to explain this not only to my audience but to myself as well, for bold decisions frequently need to be revisited in light of new evidence. There are those for whom the choice of major isn't much of a choice at all. For them, it's a *vocation*, in the strict *Webster's* definition of the word: a summons, a calling.

I'm not one of those people, and for me the decision was fraught with anxiety. Do I still believe that I made the right choice? Yes, I do, and I want my essay not only to reflect how serious I feel this issue to be but also to convey the confidence that I finally achieved.

**Writer:** I'm writing this as a student in a first-year writing class, so while the assignment gives me a lot of flexibility and room for creativity, I need to remember that finally this is an academic essay.

**Reader:** My primary reader is my teacher in the sense that she's the one who will grade my essay, but she has specified that I should consider the other students in the class as my audience. This tells me that I need to find ways to make the essay interesting to them and to find common ground with them.

**Text:** This assignment calls for me to write an academic essay. This assignment is different, though, from writing an essay in my history class or a lab report in my chemistry class. Since this is based on my personal experience, I have more freedom than I would in these other classes. One of the most challenging aspects of this essay is its limited page length. It would actually be easier to write a longer essay on why I chose chemistry as my major.

**Medium:** Our assignment is to write an academic essay. While I could potentially import graphics into my text, I should only do so if it will enrich the content of the essay.

After analyzing his rhetorical situation, Brandon decided to use Aristotle's three appeals to continue and extend his analysis. He also decided to consider kairos, making his essay timely.

**Logos:** This essay is about my own opinions and experiences and therefore contains no statistics and hard facts. What it should contain, though, are legitimate reasons for choosing the major I did. My choice should be shown as following a set of believable driving forces.

**Pathos:** Since my audience is composed of college students, I'll want to appeal to their own experiences regarding their choice of major and the sometimes conflicting emotions that accompany such a decision. Specifically, I want to focus on the confidence and relief that come when you've finally made up your mind. My audience will be able to relate to these feelings, and it will make the essay more relevant and real to them.

**Ethos:** The inherent danger in writing an essay about my desire to be a chemistry major is that I may be instantly labeled as boring or a grind. I want to dispel this image as quickly as possible, and humor is always a good way to counter such stereotypes. On the other hand, this is a serious subject, and the infusion of too much humor will portray me as somebody who hasn't given this enough thought. I want to strike a balance between being earnest and being human. I also need to write as clearly and confidently as I can manage. If I seem insincere or uncertain, then my audience may question the honesty of my essay.

**Kairos:** Thinking about kairos reminds me that even though I have analyzed logos, pathos, and ethos separately, they are really interconnected and work together to achieve the same effect: to turn an essay that could be boring into an essay that my classmates feel is timely and of interest. My use of humor is important in this regard, and so is my appeal to our shared experiences as college students. But the bottom line is that I have to persuade my readers that I have good reasons for my decision.

Brandon Barrett
Professor Auston
Writing 101
Jan. 20, 2019

## The All-Purpose Answer

When I was a small child, I would ask my parents, as children are apt
to do, questions concerning the important things in my life. "Why is
the sky blue?" "Why do my Cocoa Puffs turn the milk in my cereal
bowl brown?" If I asked my father questions such as these, he always
provided detailed technical answers that left me solemnly nodding
my head in complete confusion. But if I asked my mother, she would
simply shrug her shoulders and reply, "Something to do with chemistry,
I guess." Needless to say, I grew up with a healthy respect for the
apparently boundless powers of chemistry. Its responsibilities seemed
staggeringly wide-ranging, and I figured that if there was a God he was
probably not an omnipotent deity but actually the Original Chemist.

In my early years, I regarded chemistry as nothing less than magic
at work. So what is chemistry, if not magic—or a parent's response
to a curious child's persistent questions? Chemistry is the study of the
elements, how those elements combine, how they interact with one
another, and how all this affects Joe Average down the street. Chemists,
then, study not magic but microscopic bits of matter all busily doing
their thing.

When all those bits of matter can be coerced into doing something that humans find useful or interesting—like giving off massive
quantities of energy, providing lighting for our homes, or making
Uncle Henry smell a little better—then the chemists who produced the
desired effect can pat themselves on the back and maybe even feel just a
little bit like God.

Chemists solve problems, whether the problem is a need for a new
medicine or a stronger plastic bowl to pour our Wheaties into. They
develop new materials and study existing ones through a variety of

Barrett 2

techniques that have been refined over the decades. Chemists also struggle to keep the powers of chemistry in check by finding ways to reduce pollution that can be a by-product of chemical processes, to curb the dangers of nuclear waste, and to recycle used materials.

Chemistry is a dynamic field, constantly experiencing new discoveries and applications—heady stuff, to be sure, but heady stuff with a purpose.

Chemistry isn't a static, sleepy field of dusty textbooks, nor does it—forgive me, geologists—revolve around issues of questionable importance, such as deviations in the slope of rock strata. Those who know little about chemistry sometimes view it as dull, but I am proud to say that I plan to earn my B.S. in chemistry. And from there, who knows? That's part of the beauty of chemistry. After graduating from college, I could do any number of things, from research to medical school. The study of chemistry is useful in its own right, but it is also great preparation for advanced study in other fields since it encourages the development of logical thought and reasoning. In one sense, logical thought (not to mention research and medical school) may seem a giant step away from a child's idle questions. But as chemistry demonstrates, perhaps those questions weren't so childish after all.

## for **exploration**

Where can you see evidence of Brandon's attention to Aristotle's three appeals? Write one or two paragraphs responding to this question. Be sure to include examples in your analysis.

# Analyzing Textual Conventions

When you analyze your rhetorical situation, you ask commonsense questions about the elements of the rhetorical situation: writer, reader, text, medium. As you do so, you draw on your previous experiences as a writer, reader, speaker, and listener to make judgments about the text's purpose, subject matter, and form. For familiar kinds of texts, these judgments occur almost automatically. No one had to teach you, for instance, that a letter applying for a job should be written differently than a quick text

*thinking rhetorically*

asking a friend to meet up for pizza: Your social and cultural understanding of job hunting would cause you to write a formal letter. Similarly, if you are designing a flyer to announce an event—one that will be distributed both in print and online—you recognize that, although it is important to include basic information about the event, the visual design of the flyer and the images used in it will play a particularly important role in gaining the attention of your audience.

When faced with less familiar kinds of texts, you may have to work harder to make judgments about purpose, subject matter, and form. I recently received an email from a former student, Monica Molina, who now works at a community health center, where one of her responsibilities is to write grant proposals. In her email, she commented:

> It took quite a while before I could feel comfortable even thinking about trying to write my first grant proposal. Most of the ones at our center run 50 to 100 pages and seem so intimidating—full of strange subheadings, technical language, complicated explanations. I had to force myself to calm down and get into them. First I read some recent proposals, trying to figure out how they worked. Luckily, my boss is friendly and supportive, so she sat down with me and talked about her experiences writing proposals. We looked at some proposals together, and she told me about how proposals are reviewed by agencies. Now we're working together on my first proposal. I'm still nervous, but I'm beginning to feel more comfortable.

Like Monica, those entering new professions often must learn new forms of writing. Similarly, students entering a new discipline will often have to work hard to master unfamiliar language or genres.✱

Indeed, writers who wish to participate in any new community must strive to understand its reading and writing practices—to learn how to enter its conversation, as the rhetorician Kenneth Burke might say. The forms of writing practiced in different communities reflect important shared assumptions. These shared assumptions—sometimes referred to as *textual conventions*—represent agreements between writers and readers about how to construct and interpret texts. As such, they are an important component of any rhetorical situation.

The term *textual convention* may be new to you, but you can understand it easily if you think about other uses of the word *convention*. For example, social conventions are behaviors that reflect implicit agreement among the members of a community or culture about how to act in particular situations. At one time in the United States, for example, it was acceptable for

---

✱ Chapter 8, "Writing in the Disciplines: Making Choices as You Write," will help you make your way across the curriculum.

persons who chewed tobacco to spit tobacco juice into spittoons in restaurants and hotel lobbies. This particular social convention has changed over time and is no longer acceptable.

If social conventions represent agreements among individuals about how to act, textual conventions represent similar agreements about how to write and read texts. Just as we often take our own social conventions for granted, so too do we take for granted those textual conventions most familiar to us as readers and writers. Even though many of us write more texts and emails than letters, we still know that the most appropriate way to begin a letter is with the salutation "Dear . . ."

Textual conventions are dynamic, changing over time as the assumptions, values, and practices of writers and readers change. Consider some of the textual conventions of texting and other electronic writing. If you're texting your mom, you may not start with "Dear Mom." Instead, you might begin with something like "Hi there" or just jump into your message with no greeting. (Note: Although leaving out a salutation is considered acceptable in electronic contexts, rhetorically savvy writers know that when they're writing a work- or school-related text or email to a supervisor or teacher, they should include a clear statement of their subject and adopt a more formal tone.) If you're texting a friend, you might use abbreviations, such as R U for "are you" because it's easier to type on your phone.

When you think about the kind of writing you are being asked to do, or genre, you are thinking in part about the textual conventions that may limit your options as a writer in a specific situation. Textual conventions bring constraints, but they also increase the likelihood that readers will respond appropriately to your ideas.

The relationship between textual conventions and medium can be critical. Students organizing a protest against increased tuition, for example, would probably not try to get the word out by writing an essay on the subject. To get as many students as possible to participate in the protest, they would more likely put together an attention-getting flyer that they could post online and around campus while also sending tweets using a newly created hashtag. After the protest march, they might draft a letter to the editor to summarize the speakers' most important points, they might set up a Facebook group or blog to post announcements and to encourage student participation, and they might even post a manifesto online.

Some textual conventions are specific. Lab reports, for example, usually include the following elements: title page, abstract, introduction, experimental design and methods, results, discussion, and references. By deviating from this textual convention you run the risk of confusing or irritating readers.

Other textual conventions are more general. Consider, for instance, the conventions of an effective academic essay:

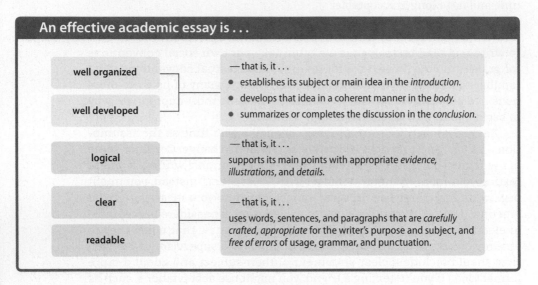

**An effective academic essay is . . .**

**well organized**

**well developed**

— that is, it . . .
- establishes its subject or main idea in the *introduction*.
- develops that idea in a coherent manner in the *body*.
- summarizes or completes the discussion in the *conclusion*.

**logical**

— that is, it . . .
supports its main points with appropriate *evidence*, *illustrations*, and *details*.

**clear**

**readable**

— that is, it . . .
uses words, sentences, and paragraphs that are *carefully crafted*, *appropriate* for the writer's purpose and subject, and *free of errors* of usage, grammar, and punctuation.

In writing an academic essay, you usually have more freedom in deciding how to apply the conventions than you do, say, when writing a lab report. For example, in an academic essay, an introduction is called for, but its specific form is not prescribed: How you begin depends largely on your audience, the reason you're writing, the disciplinary context in which you're writing, your chosen medium, and other factors.

# Observing a Professional Writer at Work: Comparing and Contrasting Textual Conventions

One way to strengthen your own writing skills is to observe successful writers in action. Let's look at three texts by psychologist Jean M. Twenge to see how one writer tackles the problem of creating an effective and appropriate essay. Each text is based on Twenge's research on differences between earlier and current generations in the United States, especially as these differences inform their use of technology, a subject she investigated in her 2017 book, *iGen: Why Today's Super-Connected Kids Are Growing Up Less Rebellious, More Tolerant, Less Happy—and Completely Unprepared for Adulthood.* Twenge's research draws on four large national surveys of 11 million Americans since the 1960s and focuses on what she terms the "iGen" generation, persons born in 1995 and later. Her book *iGen* is addressed to a general audience, but she has also published a good deal of academic research on this same topic. In addition to her book publications, she has published more than one hundred scholarly articles in such journals as *Clinical Psychological Science*, *American Psychologist*, *Journal of Personality*, and the *Journal of Personality and Social Psychology*. Twenge has also written for such publications as *Time*, *Newsweek*, the *New York Times*, *USA Today*, and the *Washington Post*.

The first selection (pp. 74–75) is an excerpt from the introduction to Twenge's *iGen*, a book written, as noted earlier, for a general audience. The second (pp. 76–77), an excerpt from "Has the Smartphone Destroyed a Generation?," was published in June 2017 in the *Atlantic*, a magazine that emphasizes in-depth analysis and reporting. The third (pp. 78–79), an excerpt from an article titled "Increases in Depressive Symptoms, Suicide-Related Outcomes, and Suicide Rates among U.S. Adolescents after 2010 and Links to Increased New Media Screen Time," was coauthored with Thomas E. Joiner, Megan L. Rogers, and Gabrielle N. Martin and published in the November 2017 issue of *Clinical Psychological Science*.

Few academics attempt to reach such diverse audiences, and Twenge has clearly been successful in doing so. Her research has been featured on *Today*, *NBC Nightly News*, *Fox and Friends*, *Dateline NBC*, and National Public Radio, for instance. (For more information on Twenge, including access to her blog, see www.jeantwenge.com.) You can learn a good deal about what it means to be a rhetorically sensitive and an intellectually agile writer by studying these three Twenge selections.

# Introduction

# Who Is iGen, and How Do We Know?

When I reach 13-year-old Athena around noon on a summer day, she sounds as if she just woke up. We chat a little about her favorite songs and TV shows, and I ask her what she likes to do with her friends. "We go to the mall," she says. "Do your parents drop you off?" I ask, remembering my own middle school days in the 1980s when I'd enjoy a few parent-free hours with my friends. "No—I go with my family," she says. "We'll go with my mom and brothers and walk a little behind them. I just have to tell my mom where we're going. I have to check in every hour or every thirty minutes."

Hanging out at the mall with your mom around isn't the only difference in teens' social lives these days. Athena and her friends at her middle school in Houston, Texas, communicate using their phones more than they see each other in person. Their favorite medium is Snapchat, a smartphone app that allows users to send pictures that quickly disappear. They particularly like Snapchat's "dog filter," which inserts a cartoonish dog nose and ears on people's heads as they snap photos. "It's awesome—it's the cutest filter ever," she says. They make sure they keep up their Snapstreaks, which show how many days in a row they have Snapchatted with each other. Sometimes they screenshot particularly ridiculous pictures of friends so they can keep them—"it's good blackmail."

Athena says she spent most of the summer hanging out by herself in her room with her phone. "I would rather be on my phone in my room watching Netflix than spending time with my family. That's what I've been doing most of the summer. I've been on my phone more than I've been with actual people." That's just the way her generation is, she says. "We didn't have a choice to know any life without iPads or iPhones. I think we like our phones more than we like actual people."

1

*iGen*

Introduction 2

iGen has arrived.

Born in 1995 and later, they grew up with cell phones, had an Instagram page before they started high school, and do not remember a time before the Internet.

The oldest members of iGen were early adolescents when the iPhone was introduced in 2007 and high school students when the iPad entered the scene in 2010. The *i* in the names of these devices stands for *Internet*, and the Internet was commercialized in 1995. If this generation is going to be named after anything, the iPhone just might be it: according to a fall 2015 marketing survey, two out of three US teens owned an iPhone, about as complete a market saturation as possible for a product. "You have to have an iPhone," said a 17-year-old interviewed in the social media exposé *American Girls.* "It's like Apple has a monopoly on adolescence."

The complete dominance of the smartphone among teens has had ripple effects across every area of iGen'ers' lives, from their social interactions to their mental health. They are the first generation for whom Internet access has been constantly available, right there in their hands. Even if their smart-phone is a Samsung and their tablet is a Kindle, these young people are all iGen'ers. (And yes, even if they are lower income: teens from disadvantaged backgrounds now spend just as much time online as those with more resources — another effect of smartphones.) The average teen checks her phone more than eighty times a day.

BY JEAN M. TWENGE

ILLUSTRATIONS BY JASU HU

# HAS THE SMARTPHONE DESTROYED A GENERATION?

**58** SEPTEMBER 2017 THE ATLANTIC

The post-Millenials were raised on the iPhone—and the effects have been seismic. More comfortable online than out partying, they are safer, physically, than adolescents have ever been. But they're on the brink of a mental-health crisis.

One day last summer, around noon, I called Athena, a 13-year-old who lives in Houston, Texas. She answered her phone — she's had an iPhone since she was 11 — sounding as if she'd just woken up. We chatted about her favorite songs and TV shows, and I asked her what she likes to do with her friends. "We go to the mall," she said. "Do your parents drop you off?," I asked, recalling my own middle-school days, in the 1980s, when I'd enjoy a few parent-free hours shopping with my friends. "No — I go with my family," she replied. "We'll go with my mom and brothers and walk a little behind them. I just have to tell my mom where we're going. I have to check in every hour or every 30 minutes."

Those mall trips are infrequent — about once a month. More often, Athena and her friends spend time together on their phones, unchaperoned. Unlike the teens of my generation, who might have spent an evening tying up the family landline with gossip, they talk on Snapchat, the smartphone app that allows users to send pictures and videos that quickly disappear. They make sure to keep up their Snapstreaks, which show how many days in a row they have Snapchatted with each other. Sometimes they save screenshots of particularly ridiculous pictures of friends. "It's good blackmail," Athena said. (Because she's a minor, I'm not using her real name.) She told me she'd spent most of the summer hanging out alone in her room with her phone. That's just the way her generation is, she said. "We didn't have a choice to know any life without iPads or iPhones. I think we like our phones more than we like actual people."

I've been researching generational differences for 25 years, starting when I was a 22-year old doctoral student in psychology. Typically, the characteristics that come to define a generation appear gradually, and along a continuum. Beliefs and behaviors that were already rising simply continue to do so. Millennials, for instance, are a highly individualistic generation, but individualism had been increasing since the Baby Boomers turned on, tuned in, and dropped out. I had grown accustomed to line graphs of trends that looked like modest hills and valleys. Then I began studying Athena's generation.

Around 2012, I noticed abrupt shifts in teen behaviors and emotional states. The gentle slopes of the line graphs became steep mountains and sheer cliffs, and many of the distinctive characteristics of the Millennial generation began to disappear. In all my analyses of generational data — some reaching back to the 1930s — I had never seen anything like it.

At first I presumed these might be blips, but the trends persisted, across several years and a series of national surveys. The changes weren't just in degree, but in kind. The biggest difference between the Millennials and their predecessors was in how they viewed the world; teens today differ from the Millennials not just in their views but in how they spend their time. The experiences they have every day are radically different from those of the generation that came of age just a few years before them.

What happened in 2012 to cause such dramatic shifts in behavior? It was after the Great Recession, which officially lasted from 2007 to 2009 and had a starker effect on Millennials trying to find a place in a sputtering economy. But it was exactly the moment when the proportion of Americans who owned a smartphone surpassed 50 percent.

The more I pored over yearly surveys of teen attitudes and behaviors, and the more I talked with young people like Athena, the clearer it became that theirs is a generation shaped by the smartphone and by the concomitant rise of social media. I call them iGen. Born between 1995 and 2012, members of this generation are growing up with smartphones, have an Instagram account before they start high school, and do not remember a time before the internet. The Millennials grew up with the web as well, but it wasn't ever-present in their lives, at hand at all times, day and night. iGen's oldest members were early adolescents when the iPhone was introduced in 2007, and high-school students when the iPad entered the scene, in 2010. A 2017 survey of more than 5,000 American teens found that three out of four owned an iPhone.

*Empirical Article*

# Increases in Depressive Symptoms, Suicide-Related Outcomes, and Suicide Rates Among U.S. Adolescents After 2010 and Links to Increased New Media Screen Time

Clinical Psychological Science
2018, Vol. 6(1) 3–17
© The Author(s) 2017
Reprints and permissions:
sagepub.com/journalsPermissions.nav
DOI: 10.1177/2167702617723376
www.psychologicalscience.org/CPS

Jean M. Twenge[1], Thomas E. Joiner[2], Megan L. Rogers[2], and Gabrielle N. Martin[1]
[1]San Diego State University and [2]Florida State University

## Abstract

In two nationally representative surveys of U.S. adolescents in grades 8 through 12 ($N = 506,820$) and national statistics on suicide deaths for those ages 13 to 18, adolescents' depressive symptoms, suicide-related outcomes, and suicide rates increased between 2010 and 2015, especially among females. Adolescents who spent more time on new media (including social media and electronic devices such as smartphones) were more likely to report mental health issues, and adolescents who spent more time on nonscreen activities (in-person social interaction, sports/exercise, homework, print media, and attending religious services) were less likely. Since 2010, iGen adolescents have spent more time on new media screen activities and less time on nonscreen activities, which may account for the increases in depression and suicide. In contrast, cyclical economic factors such as unemployment and the Dow Jones Index were not linked to depressive symptoms or suicide rates when matched by year.

## Keywords

depression, sociocultural factors, suicide prevention, interpersonal interaction, mass media

Received 4/25/17; Revision accepted 7/6/17

Depression and suicide are significant public health concerns, with over 40,000 Americans dying by suicide each year (Centers for Disease Control [CDC], 2017). Beyond the lives lost to suicide, death by suicide has significant emotional and economic costs, resulting in approximately $44.6 billion a year in combined medical and work loss costs in the United States alone (CDC, 2017). As such, suicide — and factors that may increase risk for suicide, including depression — is a serious public health concern that warrants extensive empirical investigation.

In recent years, clinicians heading university counseling centers have reported markedly increased caseloads, with many more students seeking help for mental health issues in the years after 2010 compared to a few years prior (Beiter et al., 2015; New, 2017; Novotney, 2014). One analysis found a 30% increase in caseloads between 2009–2010 and 2014–2015 at 93 university counseling centers, especially in mood and anxiety disorders and suicidal ideation

(Center for Collegiate Mental Health, 2015). Reports of increases in counseling use among high school students have also surfaced (Anderssen, 2013; Noguchi, 2014). If true, that would mean more young people than in previous years are suffering from mental health issues, putting them at risk for suicide and other negative outcomes (Berman, 2009).

However, these increases in counseling center caseloads could be due to other factors, such as more students with already-diagnosed mental health issues enrolling in college, improved outreach by counseling centers, and students being more willing to seek help. As Collishaw (2014) notes in his review of research on trends in the prevalence of psychiatric

**Corresponding Author:**
Jean M. Twenge, Department of Psychology, San Diego State University, 5500 Campanile Drive, San Diego, CA 92182-4611 E-mail: jtwenge@mail.sdsu.edu

disorders in child populations, "substantial increases in diagnosis and treatment of child psychiatric disorders in clinical practice do not necessarily reflect changes in population prevalence. Like-for-like comparisons using unselected cohorts are required to test mental health trends" (p. 19).

Thus, it would be useful to determine trends in mental health in general samples of adolescents, preferably with data collected concurrently over several years, rather than retrospectively, to minimize issues with recall (Klerman & Weissman, 1989). Previous studies examining such concurrent samples over time up to the 2000s found incongruent results, with some identifying significant increases in psychopathology (Collishaw, Maughan, Goodman, & Pickles, 2004; Collishaw, Maughan, Natarajan, & Pickles, 2010; Twenge et al., 2010) and others concluding that no changes occurred (Costello, Erkanli, & Angold, 2006; for reviews, see Collishaw, 2014; Twenge, 2011). In some cases, these disparate findings may have been caused by changes in the measurement of mental health issues, emphasizing the importance of using the same measures over time. In addition, research on trends in mental health after 2010, the time when mental health issues were rumored to have increased, is scant (Mojtabai, Olfson, & Han, 2016), though suicide rates appear to have increased (Curtin, Warner, & Hedegaard, 2016).

Furthermore, if mental health issues have increased among adolescents, the reasons are unclear (Collishaw, 2014; Glowinski & D'Amelio, 2016). Some have speculated that increased academic pressure and homework loads are the culprit (Galloway, Conner, & Pope, 2013; Neighmond, 2013), whereas others point to the severe recession of the late 2000s (Cummins, 2016). Continuing changes in family structure (e.g., Brown, Stykes, & Manning, 2016), in patterns of substance misuse (e.g., opioids; but see McCabe et al., 2017), and in obesity rates (e.g., Ogden et al., 2016) may also be implicated.

Another possible reason for the suspected increase in mental health issues is the growing popularity of electronic communication, especially social media. Some studies link frequency of social media use to poor psychological well-being (Augner & Hacker, 2012; Kross et al., 2013; Huang, 2017; Shakya & Christakis, 2017; Tromholt, 2016), although other studies instead find links with positive well-being (e.g., Dienlin, Masur, & Trepte, 2017; Oh, Ozkaya, & LaRose, 2014; Valkenburg, Peter, & Schouten, 2006), with outcomes depending on motivation for using social media (Valkenburg & Peter, 2007) and whether the frequency of use qualifies as addictive (Andreassen et al., 2016). However, most of these studies use convenience samples of adults,

with few using nationally representative samples and even fewer including the especially vulnerable population of adolescents.

Examining how adolescents spend their time — including both screen and nonscreen activities — may be especially important, as iGen[1] adolescents in the 2010s spent more time on electronic communication and less time on in-person interaction than their Millennial and Generation X (GenX) predecessors at the same age (Twenge, 2017; Twenge & Uhls, 2017). It is worth remembering that humans' neural architecture evolved under conditions of close, mostly continuous face-to-face contact with others (including nonvisual and nonauditory contact; i.e., touch, olfaction; Baumeister & Leary, 1995; Lieberman, 2013) and that a decrease in or removal of a system's key inputs may risk destabilization of the system (e.g., Badcock, Davey, Whittle, Allen, & Friston, 2017).

In-person social interaction (also known as face-to-face communication) provides more emotional closeness than electronic communication (Sherman, Minas, & Greenfield, 2013) and, at least in some studies, is more protective against loneliness (Kross et al., 2013, cf. Deters & Mehl, 2013). Some research suggests that electronic communication, particularly social media, may even increase feelings of loneliness (Song et al., 2014), and time spent on electronic communication has increased considerably since the smartphone (a mobile phone with Internet access) was introduced in 2007 and gained market saturation around 2012 (Smith, 2017).

These changes in social interaction are especially relevant for suicide and suicide-related outcomes, as posited by the interpersonal theory of suicide. Briefly, the interpersonal theory of suicide (Joiner, 2005; Van Orden et al., 2010) proposes that the desire for suicide results from the combination of two interpersonal risk factors: thwarted belongingness (i.e., social disconnection/alienation, loneliness) and perceived burdensomeness (i.e., feeling as though one is a burden on others). Empirical support for the theory's propositions is considerable. For example, Chu et al. (2017) meta-analyzed work on 122 published and unpublished samples and found support for theory predictions; both perceived burdensomeness and thwarted belongingness displayed robust connections to suicidal ideation (with some evidence for burdensomeness having a stronger connection). Given the recent shifts in adolescent social interaction, increases in both perceived burdensomeness and thwarted belongingness may be particularly salient risk factors for suicide in this population. As such, exploring trends in mental health and examining possible causes (e.g., changes in the mode and quantity . . . .

---

## for **exploration**

Read the Twenge selections (pp. 74–79) carefully, and write three paragraphs — one for each selection — characterizing their approaches. (Be sure to read the abstract and the footnote on the first page of the article from *Clinical Psychological Science*, which provide important cues about Twenge's rhetorical situation and the interests and expectations of her scholarly readers.) Here are some questions for you to keep in mind as you read.

- How would you describe Twenge's tone in each selection?
- What kinds of examples are used in each selection and what function do they serve?
- What relationship is established in each selection between writer and reader, and what cues signal this relationship?
- What assumptions does Twenge make in each selection about what readers already know?
- How would you describe the persona, or image of the writer, in each selection?

---

By glancing at the first pages of Twenge's three texts, you'll notice some important clues about the publications they appear in and about Twenge's expectations about their readers. For example, the first two pages of the introduction to Twenge's *iGen* begin with a story about Athena, a 13-year-old living with her family in Houston, Texas. Like many members of the iGen generation (born between 1995 and 2012), Athena spends a good deal of time on her phone: "I've been on my phone," Athena observes, "more than I've been with actual people" (2). Even though the title of Twenge's book makes it clear that she will be generalizing about an entire generation, Twenge begins with a specific story, as if to say to readers that although the author is a psychologist and is drawing on empirical research, this book will be relevant to them in their personal lives. Twenge is clearly aware that the market is flooded with books about a diverse range of topics, from how to survive a divorce to how to succeed in business. She knows that her introduction needs to invite readers into the story that she will tell in her book, and her introduction does just that. Twenge's introduction does not include any illustrations, but whether potential readers have looked at her book in a brick-and-mortar bookstore, on Amazon.com, or on some other online site, most of them will have already viewed its cover. If you would like to see a reproduction of the cover, just search Google for the author and title. If you do so, you will be struck immediately by the bright red color of the cover's background and how dramatically it contrasts with the title, which itself draws the reader's (or potential buyer's) interest and attention. Though the cover focuses primarily on identifying the author and title, and does so using attention-getting type and color, you will note that it also includes an image of a smartphone, with the first ten words of the much longer title shown as text on the phone. Even though the first two pages of the book are free of imagery or other forms of visual embellishment, the eye-catching cover of the book plays a similar role—and it does so whether you are reading a print text or an e-book.

In the remainder of the introduction to her book, Twenge describes how she became interested in the topic of generational differences and birth cohort studies. She informs readers about her own education as a psychologist and about the research that grounds her studies. The story of her own engagement with her topic, and the challenges she has faced as the mother of three daughters born in 2006, 2009, and 2012, complements and enriches the story of Athena that begins the introduction. She concludes the introduction by asking the question to which the rest of the book is the response: "So what's really different about iGen?" (16).

Now consider Twenge's second text, an article titled "Has the Smartphone Destroyed a Generation?" that was published in the September 2017 issue of the *Atlantic*. In her *Atlantic* essay, Twenge paints a concerning picture of a generation that is "safer, physically, than adolescents have ever been. But they're on the brink of a mental-health crisis" (58). She briefly mentions the methodology and data on which her research are based, but she focuses more strongly on the social and cultural implications of her findings. The full article does include several graphs designed to convey the changing beliefs and practices of the iGen generation.

Twenge's final text, "Increases in Depressive Symptoms, Suicide-Related Outcomes, and Suicide Rates among U.S. Adolescents after 2010 and Links to Increased New Media Screen Time," appears in *Clinical Psychological Science*, a specialized publication that has the most cramped and least inviting first page. Twenge's article is coauthored with three other scholars, a common practice in the social sciences, where the nature and scope of research projects often require collaboration. Twenge, however, is the first author and the corresponding author (see the note at the bottom of the page), which indicates to colleagues reading the article that her contributions to the research have been particularly important.

Rather than using an attention-getting title or an inviting design, Twenge and her coauthors straightforwardly describe the focus of their research project. The article begins with an abstract and keywords designed to help readers decide whether they want to read the entire article.

Twenge and her coauthors' essay in *Clinical Psychological Science* is seventeen densely argued pages long. In subsequent sections, the authors explain the importance of their research, describe their methodology (which relied upon data collected in two large, nationally representative surveys of U.S. adolescents that have been conducted annually in recent decades), and report their results. Their essay includes several tables that summarize and evaluate data, as well as graphs and other figures that help readers grasp the significance of their research. Clearly, the authors assume that scholars who choose to read their article will want the opportunity not only to understand and evaluate the authors'

> thinking
> rhetorically

conclusions but also to critique their methodology. Twenge and her coauthors conclude their article by considering the strengths and limitations of their own study.

Unlike her commentary in the *Atlantic*, where Twenge reports some of the most important results of her research on generational differences and considers some of the issues her research raises, in the article in *Clinical Psychological Science* Twenge and her coauthors take pains to make every step of their research process visible and available for other scholars to critique. Such critique might include efforts to replicate the studies described in the article. Clearly, Twenge expects much more of the readers of this scholarly article than she does of the readers of her commentary in the *Atlantic* or her popular book, *iGen*. She takes great care to document her sources and follow the correct citation format, knowing that her readers value and expect that.

Twenge also understands that readers of *Clinical Psychological Science* bring specific expectations to their reading of the journal. Like readers of the *Atlantic*, subscribers to *Clinical Psychological Science* don't have time to read every article, but they don't make their reading choices based on inviting titles, illustrations, or opening anecdotes. Instead, they skim the table of contents, noting articles that affect their own research or have broad significance for their field. The abstract in Twenge and her coauthors' article matters very much to these readers; they can review it to determine not only *if* but also *how* they will read the article. Some will read only the abstract, others will skim the major points, and others will read the entire article with great care, returning to it as they conduct their own research.

Although the excerpts of Twenge's three texts are grounded in the same research project, they differ dramatically in structure, tone, language, and approach to readers. Textual conventions play an important role in these differences. As shared agreements about the construction and interpretation of texts, textual conventions enable readers and writers to communicate successfully in different rhetorical situations.

---

## for **exploration**

Take five to ten minutes to freewrite about your experience of reading the introductions to Twenge's three texts, as well as the subsequent analysis of them. What has this experience helped you better understand about the role that textual conventions — and rhetorical sensitivity — play in writing? If this experience has raised questions for you as a writer, be sure to note them as well.

---

### strategies for success

The conventions of academic writing vary from culture to culture and community to community, and they change over time. You may have written successful texts that followed very different textual conventions than what you are learning now. Be open to trying new ways of writing successful texts and taking risks with your writing. Some of the conventions that might be different from what you are used to include the rhetorical strategies that introduce essay topics, the presence and placement of thesis statements, the kinds of information that qualify as objective evidence in argumentation, the use (or absence) of explicit transitions, and the use (or absence) of first-person pronouns. Given these and other potential differences, you may find it helpful to compare your previous writing experiences with the conventions of academic writing that are being introduced in your writing class. It might also help to discuss your writing experiences with your professor or a writing center tutor.

## Using Textual Conventions

You already know enough about rhetoric and the rhetorical situation to realize that there can be no one-size-fits-all approach to every academic writing situation.

What can you do when you are unfamiliar with the textual conventions of a particular discipline or of academic writing in general? A rhetorical approach suggests that one solution is to read examples of the kind of writing you wish to do. Jean M. Twenge, whose selections you read earlier in this chapter, undoubtedly drew on her experience as a reader of the publications in which her work would later appear as she wrote these texts. Discussing these models with an insider—your teacher, a tutor in the writing center, or an advanced student in the field—can help you understand why these conventions work for such readers and writers. Forming a study group or meeting with a tutor can also increase your rhetorical sensitivity to your teachers' expectations and the conventions of academic writing.

Finally, a rhetorical approach to communication encourages you to think strategically about writing—whether personal, professional, or academic—and to respond creatively to the challenges of each situation. As a writer, you have much to consider: your own goals as a writer, the nature of your subject and writing task, the expectations of your readers, the textual conventions your particular situation requires or allows, and the medium in which to express your ideas. The rhetorical sensitivity you have already developed can help you respond appropriately to these and other concerns. But you can also draw on other resources, such as textual examples and discussions with teachers, tutors, and other students. As a writer, you are not alone. By reaching out to other writers, in person or by reading their work, you can become a fully participating member of the academic community.

## for **thought, discussion, and writing**

1. From a newspaper or a magazine, choose an essay, an editorial, or a column that you think succeeds in its purpose. Now turn back to the Questions for Analyzing Your Rhetorical Situation on pp. 56–57, and answer the questions as if you were the writer of the text you have chosen. To answer the questions, look for evidence of the writer's intentions in the writing itself. (To determine what image or persona the writer wanted to portray, for instance, look at the kind of language the writer uses. Is it formal or conversational? Full of interesting images and vivid details or serious examples and statistics?) Answer each of the questions suggested by the guidelines. Then write a paragraph or more reflecting on what you have learned from this analysis.

2. Both Alia Sands and Brandon Barrett did a good job in anticipating their readers' expectations and interests. In writing their essays, they focused not just on content (what they wanted to say) but also on strategy (how they might convey their ideas to their readers). Not all interactions between writer and reader are as successful. You may have read textbooks that seemed more concerned with the subject matter than with readers' needs and expectations, or you may have received direct-mail advertising or other business communications that irritated or offended you. Find an example of writing that in your view fails to anticipate the expectations and needs of the reader, and write one or two paragraphs explaining your reasons.

3. Analyze the ways in which one or both of the following public service advertisements (pp. 85–86) draw on Aristotle's three appeals: logos, pathos, and ethos.

**Public Service Ad: "Dating Abuse Affects 1 in 3 Young People"**

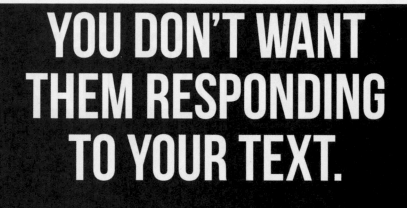

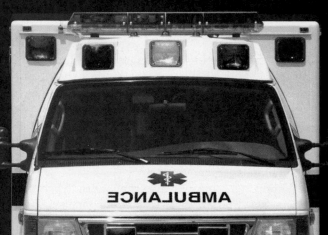

National Highway Traffic Safety Administration (NHSTA), Concept Farm, and the Ad Council

Public Service Ad: "You Don't Want Them Responding to Your Text"

# 4

# Academic Writing: Committing to the Process

**A** rhetorical approach to writing encourages you to build upon and apply your understanding of human communication in general, and of texts in particular, to make decisions that enable effective communication. That is true whether writing an essay for your composition course, a lab report for your biology class, a memo for your employer, or an audio essay to share with family and friends. Rather than emphasizing rigid rules, a rhetorical approach to writing asks you to consider all the elements of your rhetorical situation: writer, reader, text, and medium.

A rhetorical approach to writing also challenges the common assumption that those who write well possess a magical power. According to this view, people are either born with the ability to write well or not, and those who write well find writing easy: They just sit down, and the words and ideas begin to flow. Interestingly, people often feel the same way about those who work with images and graphics. They believe that designers and artists have a gift that enables them to create vivid and compelling designs, paintings, or other aesthetic objects.

In fact, most successful writers, designers, and artists study their craft for many years. What some would call "talent" or "a gift" might more aptly be characterized as interest, motivation, and commitment. Successful writers and designers know that their skills take time to mature. They also know that to develop their skills they must look for opportunities to practice them, reflecting on the strengths and limitations not only of the products they produce but also of the processes they use to create them. This reflection, in turn, allows them to develop strategies to cope with the complexities of writing and design and thus to experience the satisfaction of a job well done.

As a student, you probably know from experience that your writing is most successful when you give yourself ample time to develop your thoughts, draft, and revise. If you're like most students, though, you don't always act on this knowledge. This chapter will help you gain insight into your own preferences as a writer, enabling you to commit to a writing process that works for you and that results in successful academic writing.

## for **exploration**

Reflect on your own assumptions about writing and your experiences as a writer. Set aside half an hour, and respond in writing to the following questions. As you do so, be sure to reflect on both your academic and your personal writing and reading experiences.

1. What are your earliest memories of learning to read and write?
2. How were reading and writing viewed by your family and friends when you were growing up?
3. What role did reading play in your development as a writer? What kinds of texts were you drawn to: print texts; visually oriented texts, such as comics and graphic novels; a mix; or some other kind(s)?
4. Can you recall particular experiences in school or on the job that influenced your current attitude toward writing?
5. If you were to describe your history as a writer, what stages in your development would you identify? Write a sentence or two briefly characterizing each stage.
6. What images come to mind when you hear the word *writer*?
7. Draw up a list of metaphors describing who you are as a writer, such as "As a writer, I'm a turtle — slow and steady" or "As a writer, I'm a racehorse — fast out of the gate but never sure if I've got the stamina to finish." Write two or three sentences that use metaphors to characterize your sense of yourself as a writer.
8. What kinds of writing do you enjoy or dislike? What kinds of writing do you do outside of school? Do you regularly tweet or text, keep a personal journal, or blog? Do you write poetry, create podcasts, design flyers, or post to Instagram? Be sure to include any print or multimodal texts that you create simply because you enjoy doing so.
9. What do you enjoy most — and least — about the writing process?
10. What goals would you like to set for yourself as a writer?

## for **exploration**

Using the notes, responses, and reflections generated by the previous activity, write a letter to your classmates and teacher in which you describe who you are as a writer today and how you got to be that way. Alternatively, create a text that uses words and, if you like, images and graphics to describe who you are as a writer today. You can make it by hand or create it on the computer. (For her response to this assignment, student Mirlandra Neuneker created a collage, which is shown on p. 89.)

## for **collaboration**

Bring enough copies of the letter or visual text you created in response to the previous activity to share with your group. After you have all read one another's texts,

Mirlandra Neuneker's Collage, "Who I Am as a Writer"

work together to answer the following questions. Choose one person to record the group's answers so that you can share the results of your discussion with the rest of the class.

1. To what extent are your attitudes toward writing and experiences as writers similar? List three to five statements all group members can agree with.

2. What factors account for the differences in your attitudes toward writing and experiences as writers? List two or three factors that you agree account for these differences.

3. What common goals can you set for yourselves as writers? List at least three goals you can agree on.

---

# Managing the Writing Process

Successful writers know they must develop and commit to a writing process that enables them to succeed as students. But how do writers actually manage the writing process? Notice how differently the following students describe their process.

> My writing starts with contemplation. I let the topic I have chosen sink into my mind for a while. During this time my mind is a swirl of images, words, and ideas. Sometimes I draw clusters or diagrams that show how my ideas relate; sometimes I make lists. Whatever works works. But this period of letting my ideas develop is essential to my writing. Gradually my ideas take shape—and at a certain point I just know whether I have the right topic or approach or not. If I think I don't, I force myself to start over. If I do, then I make a plan for my essay. I can't really write without at least a skeleton plan that I can refer to: It stresses me out not to know where I'm headed. By the time I sketch out my plan, I usually have a pretty clear idea of where I'm going. Next I write a draft, possibly several drafts, before I do a final revision.—**Sara Steinman**

> Maybe it's just my personality, but when I get an assignment I have to leap right into it. It's hard to describe what I write at the beginning. It's part brainstorming, part planning, part drafting, part letting off steam. I just have to write to see what I think! I do most of this early writing by hand because I need to be able to use arrows to connect ideas, circle important points, draw pictures. At this point, no one but me could understand what I've written. I take a break if I can, and then I sit down and reread everything I've written (it can be a lot). That's when I move to the computer. Even at this point I still basically write without doing a lot of conscious planning—I'm going on

intuition. The time comes when I've got to change gears and become my own harshest critic. That's when I do a kind of planning in reverse. I might outline my draft, for instance, and see if the outline makes sense. It takes a lot of time and work for me to get to the point where my ideas have really jelled, and even then I've often got several drafts ahead of me. —**Eduardo Alvarez**

As a writer, I am first a thinker and then a doer. I've always had to think my ideas out in detail before I begin drafting. Even though for me this is essentially a mental process, it still involves words and images. I can't really describe it—I just keep thinking things through. It's always felt like a waste of time to me to sit down to write without having a clear idea of what I want to say. Since I have two children and work part-time, I also don't have a lot of time to focus solely on my writing, so I try out different ideas while folding laundry, driving the kids to day care, after they're in bed. I'm a new media major, so part of my mental planning always involves thinking about media. If the assignment specifies the medium, then I always think how to make the best possible use of it. If it doesn't, then I run through all my options. Eventually I have a pretty clear sense of what I want to say and what medium will best convey it. Sometimes I make a plan before I get to work, especially if it's a long or complicated project. But sometimes I just begin writing. With some projects, my first draft is strong enough that I just have to edit it. Of course, that's not always the case. —**Wei Liao**

On the surface, these students' writing processes seem to have little in common. Actually, however, all involve the same three activities: planning, drafting, and revising. These activities don't necessarily occur in any set order. Wei Liao plans in her head and postpones making a written plan until after she has generated a rough draft, whereas Sara Steinman plans extensively before she writes her first word. To be successful, however, all these writers must sooner or later think rhetorically and make choices about their own situation as writers, their readers, their text, and the medium. Then they must try out these choices in their heads or in writing; evaluate the effects of these choices; and make appropriate changes in their drafts. Rather than being a mysterious activity, writing is a process of planning, drafting, and revising.

thinking rhetorically

## IDENTIFYING COMPOSING STYLES

When designers and writers take their own composing processes seriously, they attempt to build on their strengths and recognize their limitations. They understand that they must vary their approach to a project depending on the task or situation. A student who prefers to spend a lot of time developing written or mental plans for writing projects simply doesn't have that luxury when writing an in-class essay exam. For this reason, it's more accurate to refer to *writing processes* rather than *the writing process*. As a writer and designer, you must be pragmatic: You decide how to approach a project based on such factors as the nature and importance of the task, the schedule, the nature and demands of the medium, and the experience you have with a particular kind of writing. Most experienced writers and designers do have a preferred way of managing the composing process, however.

**Heavy planners.** Like Wei Liao, heavy planners generally plan their writing so carefully in their heads that their first drafts are often more like other writers' third or fourth drafts. As a consequence, they revise less intensively and less frequently than other students. Many of these students have disciplined themselves so that they can think about their writing in all sorts of places—on the subway, at work, in the garden pulling weeds, or in the car driving to school.

Some heavy planners write in this way because they prefer to; others develop this strategy out of necessity. Wei Liao, for instance, has to do a great deal of her writing in her head because of the demands of her busy life. As a result, she's learned to use every opportunity to think about her writing while she drives, cooks, or relaxes with her family.

**Heavy revisers.** Like Eduardo Alvarez, heavy revisers use the act of writing itself to find out what they want to say. When faced with a writing task, they prefer to sit down and just begin writing.

Heavy revisers often state that writing their ideas out in a sustained spurt of activity reassures them that they have something to say and helps them avoid frustration. These students may not seem to plan because they begin drafting so early. Actually, however, their planning occurs as they draft and especially as they revise. Heavy revisers must often spend a great deal of time revising their initial drafts. To do so effectively, they must be able to read their work critically and, often, discard substantial portions of early drafts.

As you've probably realized, in both of these styles of composing, one of the components of the writing process is apparently abbreviated. Heavy planners don't seem to revise as extensively as other writers. Actually, however, they plan (and, in effect, revise) so thoroughly early in the process that they often don't need to revise as intensively later. Similarly, heavy revisers may not seem to plan; in fact, though, once they write their rough drafts, they plan and revise simultaneously and, often, extensively.

**Sequential composers.** A third general style of composing is exemplified by Sara Steinman. These writers might best be called sequential composers because they devote roughly equivalent amounts of time to planning, drafting, and revising. Rather than trying out their ideas and planning their writing mentally, as heavy planners do, sequential composers typically rely on

## Composing Styles: Advantages and Disadvantages

| Composing Style | Advantages | Disadvantages |
| --- | --- | --- |
| Heavy planners | • The writer spends less time drafting and revising. | • The writer may lose her or his train of thought if unexpected interruptions occur.<br><br>• The writer may miss out on fruitful explorations that result from reviewing notes, plans, or drafts.<br><br>• The writer may face substantial difficulties if sentences and paragraphs look less coherent and polished on paper than they did in the writer's head. |
| Heavy revisers | • The writer generates words and ideas quickly and voluminously.<br><br>• The writer remains open to new options because of the frequency with which he or she rereads notes and drafts. | • The writer may experience an emotional roller coaster as ideas develop (or fail to develop) through writing.<br><br>• The writer must have the ability to critique her or his own writing ruthlessly.<br><br>• The writer's work may suffer if he or she fails to allow adequate time for rewriting or, if necessary, for starting over. |
| Sequential composers | • The writer has more control over the writing process because roughly equivalent time is spent planning, drafting, and revising.<br><br>• Writers are unlikely to mistake a quickly generated collection of ideas or a brainstormed plan for adequate preparation. | • The writer may become too rigidly dependent on a highly structured writing process.<br><br>• The writer may waste valuable time developing detailed plans when he or she is actually ready to begin drafting. |

written notes and plans to give shape and force to their ideas. Unlike heavy revisers, however, sequential composers prefer to have greater control over form and subject matter as they draft.

Sequential composers' habit of allotting time for planning, drafting, and revising helps them deal with the inevitable anxieties of writing. Like heavy revisers, sequential composers need the reassurance of seeing their ideas written down: Generating notes and plans gives them the confidence to begin drafting. Sequential composers may not revise as extensively as heavy revisers because they generally draft more slowly, reviewing their writing as they proceed. Revision is nevertheless an important part of their composing process. Like most writers, sequential composers need a break from drafting to be able to critique their own words and ideas.

There is one other common way of managing the writing process, although it might best be described as management by avoidance, and that's procrastination. All writers occasionally procrastinate, but if you habitually put off writing a first draft until you have time only for a final draft (at 3 A.M. on the day your essay is due), your chances of success are minimal. Although you may tell yourself that you have good reasons for putting off writing ("I write better under pressure"; "I can't write until I have all my easier assignments done first"), procrastination makes it difficult for you to manage the writing process in an efficient and effective manner.

Is procrastination always harmful? Might it not sometimes reflect a period of necessary incubation, of unconscious but still productive planning? Here's what Holly Hardin—a thoughtful student writer—discovered when she reflected about her experiences as a writer.

> For me, sometimes procrastination isn't really procrastination (or so I tell myself). Sometimes what I label procrastination is really planning. The trouble is that I don't always know when it's one or the other.
>
> How do I procrastinate? Let me count the ways. I procrastinate by doing good works (helping overtime at my job, cleaning house, aiding and abetting a variety of causes). I procrastinate by absorbing myself in a purely selfish activity (reading paperbacks, watching TV, going to movies). I procrastinate by visiting with friends, talking on the telephone, prolonging chance encounters. I procrastinate by eating and drinking (ice cream, coffee, cookies—all detrimental). Finally, I procrastinate by convincing myself that this time of day is not when I write well. I'd be much better off, I sometimes conclude, taking a nap. So I do.
>
> Part of my difficulty is that I can see a certain validity in most of my reasons for procrastinating. There are some times of day when my thoughts flow better. I have forced myself to write papers in the past when I just didn't feel ready. Not only were the papers difficult to write, they were poorly written, inarticulate papers. Even after several rewrites, they were merely marginal. I would much rather write when I am at my mental best.
>
> I need to balance writing with other activities. The trouble is—just how to achieve the perfect balance!

Holly's realistic appraisal of the role that procrastination plays in her writing process should help her distinguish between useful incubation and unhelpful procrastination. Unlike students who tell themselves that they should never procrastinate—and then do so anyway, feeling guilty every moment—Holly knows she has to consider a variety of factors before she decides to invite a friend over, bake a batch of cookies, or take a much-needed nap.

## strategies for success

Many writers experience a disconnect between the language they use with family and friends and the more formal communication required in their courses. Other writers may experience some frustration with reflective writing that asks the writer to examine their own motives or thinking process. This can especially be the case if your first or home language is not Standard American English or if your culture leans away from writing about their own experiences. However, it can be helpful for *all* writers to reflect on how their previous experiences as a writer, reader, speaker, and listener enhance or interfere with their efforts to negotiate the demands of academic writing. Take some time to freewrite about this issue. You may want to discuss the results of your reflection with your teacher or a tutor in the writing center.

## ANALYZING YOUR COMPOSING PROCESS*

The poet William Stafford once commented that "a writer is not so much someone who has something to say as he is someone who has found a process that will bring about new things he would not have thought if he had not started to say them." Stafford's remarks emphasize the importance of developing a workable writing process—a repertoire of strategies you can draw on in a variety of situations. The quiz on pp. 96–97 can help you analyze your writing process

thinking
rhetorically

## strategies for success

If you are a writer whose first or home language is not Standard Academic English (SAE), consider how your language background affects your process when you compose texts in SAE. How do you typically think, freewrite, brainstorm, or make notes? Do you shift between languages in your process? How might this affect your writing process? Don't be afraid to write in the way that works best for you and translate later.

## for **collaboration**

Meet with classmates to discuss your responses to the quiz on pp. 96–97. Begin by having each person state two important things he or she learned as a result of completing the quiz. (Appoint a recorder to write down each person's statements.) Once all members have spoken, ask the recorder to read their statements aloud. Were any statements repeated by more than one member of the group? As a group, formulate two conclusions about the writing process that you would like to share with the class. (Avoid vague and general assertions, such as "Writing is difficult.")

* For a case study of student Daniel Stiepleman's process of interacting with a text, exploring ideas, and developing an essay for a first-year writing class, see Chapter 6, pp. 160–76.

## Quiz: Analyzing Your Composing Process

You can use the following questions to analyze your composing process. Your teacher may ask you to respond to some or all of these questions in writing.

1. **What is your general attitude toward writing?**
   a. love it
   b. hate it
   c. somewhere in between
   *How do you think this attitude affects your writing?*

2. **Which of the composing styles described in this chapter best describes the way you compose?**
   a. heavy planner
   b. heavy reviser
   c. sequential composer
   d. procrastinator
   *If none of these styles seems to fit you, how do you compose?*

3. **How long do you typically work on your writing at any one time?**
   a. less than an hour
   b. from one to two hours
   c. more than two hours
   *Do you think you spend about the right amount of time at a given stretch, or do you think you should generally do more (or less)? Why?*

4. **Are you more likely to write an essay**
   a. in a single sitting
   b. over a number of days (or weeks)
   *Have you had success doing it this way? How do you think adjusting your approach would affect the essays you end up writing?*

5. **Do you have any writing habits or rituals?**
   a. yes
   b. no
   *If you answered "yes," what are they? Which are productive, and which interfere with your writing process? If you answered "no," can you think of any habits you would like to develop?*

6. **How often do you import visuals, graphics, or sound files into texts you are composing?**
   a. sometimes
   b. never
   c. often

   *If you do use visuals, sound, or graphics, do you enjoy doing so? Find it a challenge? Take it for granted? How have your instructors received your efforts?*✳

7. **What planning and revising strategies do you use?**
   a. specific strategies (e.g., outlining, listing, etc.)
   b. general strategies (e.g., "I develop a plan, and I reread what I've written.")
   c. no strategies I'm aware of

   *How do you know when you have spent enough time planning and revising?*

8. **What role do collaborations or exchanges with others (conversations, responses to work in progress from peers or tutors) play in your writing?**
   a. an important role
   b. an occasional role
   c. little or no role

   *Would you like to make more use of collaborations like these? Why or why not?*

9. **How often do you procrastinate? (Be honest! All writers procrastinate occasionally.)**
   a. I procrastinate very little.
   b. I start later than I should, but I get the job done.
   c. I don't start until it's too late to do a good job.

   *Do you need to change your habits in this respect? If you do need to change them, how will you do so?*

10. **Thinking in general about the writing you do, what do you find most rewarding and satisfying? Most difficult and frustrating? Why?**

   _____

   _____

   _____

Writing is a *process*, and taking time to think about your own composing process can prove illuminating. One of my students, for example, formulated an analogy that helped us all think fruitfully about how the writing process works. "Writing," he said, "is actually a lot like sports." Writing—like sports? Let's see what this comparison reveals about the writing process.

✳ See Chapter 11 for more about multimodal composing.

**Writing and sports are both performance skills.** You may know who won every Wimbledon since 1980, but if you don't actually play tennis, you're not a tennis player; you're just somebody who knows a lot about tennis. Similarly, you can know a lot about writing, but to demonstrate (and improve) your skills, you must *write*.

**Writing and sports both require individuals to master complex skills and to perform these skills in an almost infinite number of situations.** Athletes must learn specific skills, plays, or maneuvers, but they can never execute them routinely or thoughtlessly. Writers must be similarly resourceful and flexible. You can learn the principles of effective essay organization, for instance, and you may write a number of essays that are well organized, but each time you sit down to write a new essay, you have to consider your options and make new choices. This is the reason smart writers don't rely on formulas or rules but instead use rhetorical sensitivity to analyze and respond to each situation.

thinking
rhetorically

**Experienced athletes and writers know that a positive attitude is essential.** Some athletes psych themselves up before a game or competition, often using music, meditation, or other personal routines. But any serious athlete knows that's only part of what having a positive attitude means. It also means running five miles when you're already tired at three or doing twelve repetitions during weight training when you're exhausted and no one else would know if you did only eight. A positive attitude is equally important in writing. If you approach a writing task with a negative attitude ("I never was good at writing"), you create obstacles for yourself. Having a positive, open attitude is essential in mastering tennis, skiing—and writing.

**To maintain a high level of skill, both athletes and writers need frequent practice and effective coaching.** "In sports," a coach once said, "you're either getting better or getting worse." Without practice—which for a writer means both reading and writing—your writing skills will slip (as will your confidence). Likewise, coaching is essential in writing because it's hard to distance yourself from your own work. Coaches—your writing instructor, a tutor at a writing center, or a fellow student—can help you gain a fresh perspective on your writing and make useful suggestions about revision as well.

**Experienced athletes and writers continuously set new goals for themselves.** Athletes continuously set new challenges for themselves and analyze their performance. They know that coaches can help but that *they* are ultimately the ones performing. Experienced writers know this too, so they look for opportunities to practice their writing. And they don't measure their success simply by a grade. They see their writing always as work in progress. Successful athletes, like successful writers, know that they must *commit* to a process that will enable them to perform at the highest possible level.

# Writing Communities

## FINDING A COMMUNITY

For many people, one big difference between writing and sports is that athletes often belong to teams. Writers, they think, work in lonely isolation. In fact, this romanticized image of the writer struggling alone until inspiration strikes is both inaccurate and unhelpful. If you take a careful look at the day-to-day writing that people do, you quickly recognize that many people in various professions work as part of one or more teams to produce written texts. In many cases, these individuals' ability to work effectively with others is key to a successful career. Those who write for school, community-based projects, or even for personal enrichment also often turn to others for ideas and advice.

Even when writers do a good deal of their composing alone, they often find it helpful to talk with others before and while writing. A group of neighbors writing a petition to their city council requesting that a speed bump be installed on their street might well ask one person to compose the petition. To generate the strongest ideas possible, the writer would have to talk extensively with her neighbors. She would probably also present drafts of the petition for her neighbors' review and approval.

Most writers alternate between periods of independent activity (composing alone at a desk or coffee shop table) and periods of social interaction (meeting with friends, colleagues, or team members for information, advice, or responses to drafts). They may also correspond with others in their field, or they may get in touch with people doing similar work through reading or research. These relationships help them learn new ideas, improve their skills, and share their interest and enthusiasm.

Sometimes these relationships are formal and relatively permanent. Many poets and fiction writers, for instance, meet regularly with colleagues to discuss their writing. Perhaps more commonly, writers' networks are informal and shifting, though no less vital. A new manager in a corporation, for instance, may find one or two people with sound judgment and good writing skills to review important letters and reports and to mentor her as she enters her profession. Similarly, students working on a major project for a class may meet informally but regularly to compare notes and provide mutual support.

Online technologies and the web have increased the opportunity for writers to work collaboratively. Using online spaces, from course websites to blogs and public writing communities such as Writing.com ("for writers and readers of all interests and skill levels"), writers everywhere are sharing their writing and getting responses to works in progress.

## WORKING COLLABORATIVELY

Because you're in the same class and share the same assignments and concerns, you and your classmates constitute a natural community of writers. Whether your instructor makes it a requirement or not, you should explore the possibility of forming a peer group or joining one that already exists. To work effectively, however, you and your peers need to develop or strengthen the skills that will contribute to effective group work.

As you prepare to work collaboratively, remember that people have different styles of learning and interacting. Some of these differences represent individual preferences: Some students work out their ideas as they talk, while others prefer to think through their ideas before speaking. Other differences are primarily cultural and thus reflect deeply embedded social practices and preferences. Effective groups are pragmatic and task oriented, but they balance a commitment to getting the job done with patience and flexibility. They value diversity and find ways to ensure that all members can comfortably participate in and benefit from group activities.

Effective groups also take care to articulate group goals and monitor group processes. Sometimes this monitoring is intuitive and informal, but sometimes a more formal process is helpful. If you're part of a group that meets regularly, you might begin meetings by having each person state one way in which the group is working well and one way in which it could be improved. If a problem such as a dominating or nonparticipating member is raised, deal with it immediately. The time spent responding to these comments will ensure that your group is working effectively.

Group activities such as peer response and collaborative troubleshooting can help improve your writing ability and prepare you for on-the-job teamwork. Remember, though, that groups are a bit like friendships. They develop and change, and they require care and attention. You have to be committed to keeping the group going, be alert to signs of potential trouble, and be willing to talk problems out.

Students juggling coursework, jobs, families, and other activities can sometimes find it difficult to get together or to take the time to read and respond to one another's writing. Getting together with classmates to share your writing is well worth the effort it takes. If it proves impossible, however, you may have one important alternative: a campus writing center. Many colleges and universities have established writing centers as places where you can go to talk with others about your writing, get help with specific writing problems, or find answers to questions you may have. If your campus does have a writing center, take advantage of the opportunity to get an informed response to your work.

## Guidelines for Group Work

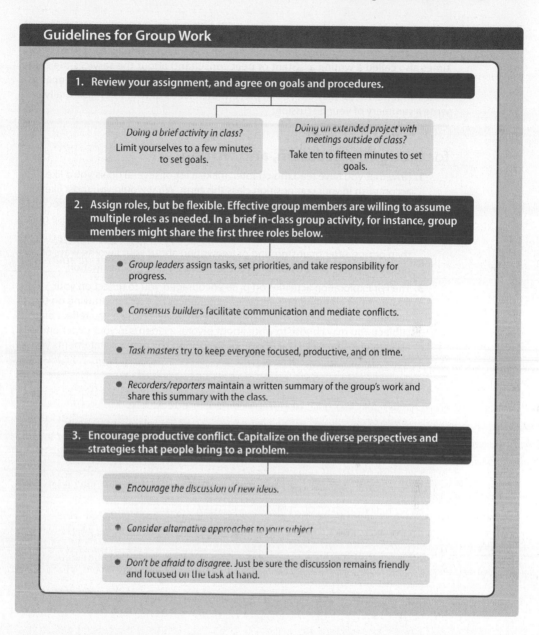

1. **Review your assignment, and agree on goals and procedures.**

   *Doing a brief activity in class?* Limit yourselves to a few minutes to set goals.

   *Doing an extended project with meetings outside of class?* Take ten to fifteen minutes to set goals.

2. **Assign roles, but be flexible. Effective group members are willing to assume multiple roles as needed. In a brief in-class group activity, for instance, group members might share the first three roles below.**

   ● *Group leaders* assign tasks, set priorities, and take responsibility for progress.

   ● *Consensus builders* facilitate communication and mediate conflicts.

   ● *Task masters* try to keep everyone focused, productive, and on time.

   ● *Recorders/reporters* maintain a written summary of the group's work and share this summary with the class.

3. **Encourage productive conflict. Capitalize on the diverse perspectives and strategies that people bring to a problem.**

   ● *Encourage the discussion of new ideas.*

   ● *Consider alternative approaches to your subject.*

   ● *Don't be afraid to disagree.* Just be sure the discussion remains friendly and focused on the task at hand.

## for **collaboration**

Meet with your group to discuss how you can most effectively work together. Begin by exchanging names, phone numbers, and email addresses, and take time to get to know each other. You might also see if your group can formulate some friendly rules to guide group activities. Be sure to write these rules down, and consult them as you work together. Try to anticipate problems, such as coordinating schedules, and discuss how to resolve them.

## for **exploration**

If your campus has a writing center, make an appointment to interview a tutor (sometimes also called a writing assistant or peer consultant) about the services the center provides. You may also want to ask the tutor about his or her own experiences as a writer. Your instructor may ask you to present the results of your interview orally or to write a summary of your discussion.

## for **thought, discussion, and writing**

1. Now that you have read this chapter, make a list of several goals you'd like to accomplish in your composition class this term. What would you most like to learn or improve? What would you like to change about your writing process? Then write a paragraph or two discussing how you plan to achieve these goals.

2. All writers procrastinate occasionally; some just procrastinate more effectively than others. After brainstorming or freewriting about your favorite ways of procrastinating, write a humorous or serious essay on procrastination.

3. The For Exploration activities on p. 88 encouraged you to reflect on your assumptions about writing and your experiences as a writer. Drawing on these activities and the rest of the chapter, write an essay in which you reflect on this subject. You may choose to write about pivotal incidents in your experiences as a writer, using particular occasions to support the general statements you make about your experiences.

# 5

# Analyzing and Synthesizing Texts

A rhetorical approach to writing looks at the various contexts in which you write. Even if you are writing alone, you are writing in the context of a specific rhetorical situation. By analyzing that situation, you can identify your purpose and goals as a writer, develop an appropriate persona or voice, and respond to the expectations of your readers. You also can understand and implement the appropriate textual conventions for courses across the curriculum.

thinking
rhetorically

## Understanding the Centrality of Reading to Academic Writing

One of the most important ways of recognizing and understanding the textual conventions appropriate to various disciplines is through reading. You already recognize that reading is central to academic writing. After all, as a student you are almost always writing in response to one or more texts. But you may not have realized that reading can help you understand how the methodologies that different disciplines are grounded in are reflected in their textual conventions.\* Whatever kind of text you are reading—from a chapter in your sociology textbook to a poem in your literature class to a research report for psychology—the ability to read critically and to engage your reading at multiple levels is essential.

In this chapter, you will learn how to master two skills essential to all reading: analysis and synthesis. When you *analyze*, you determine how a text, an object, or a body of data is structured or organized; you also often

---

\* Chapter 8 looks carefully at how the humanities, natural and applied sciences, social sciences, and business are reflected in each discipline's textual conventions.

assess its effectiveness or validity. Synthesis is a counterpart to analysis. When you *synthesize*, you explore connections and contradictions between two or more texts, objects, or bodies of data. Often you also bring your own experience to bear on the subject under consideration, indicating where you agree and where you disagree with those whose words and thoughts you are exploring.

# Considering Analysis and Synthesis in the Context of the Academic Community

Gaining an understanding of context is particularly important when you enter a new community of writers and readers. Accordingly, as you enter the academic community, you need to develop an insider's understanding of the conventions that characterize academic writing. Some of these conventions apply across the disciplines; for example, a successful academic argument must reflect an open, unbiased intellectual engagement with the subject, whether that subject is a Renaissance painting or the Federal Reserve System. Moreover, whatever your subject, the logic behind your conclusions and the evidence for them play key roles in any academic argument.

Most college instructors believe that *all* academic writing involves argument. But the model of argument they have in mind isn't about winning or losing a debate; rather, it involves using evidence and reasoning to discover a version of truth about a particular subject. I use the words *a version* here to emphasize that in academic writing what constitutes the "truth" is always open to further discussion. A political scientist who makes a convincing argument about federal policy on harvesting timber in national forests knows that others will add to, challenge, or refine that argument. In fact, having others respond to an argument is a sign that the writing has successfully raised questions that others consider important. In this sense, the scholarly work of the academy is a conversation rather than a debate.

# Understanding Your Audience

Because your instructors are the primary readers of your college writing, you need to understand their values and their goals for you and other students. They all share a commitment to the ideal of education as inquiry. Whether they teach in business, liberal arts, agriculture, engineering, or other fields, your instructors want to foster your ability to think, write, and speak well. When they read your papers and exams, they're looking for evidence of both your knowledge of a subject and your ability to think and write clearly and effectively.

But your instructors will not necessarily bring identical expectations to your writing. Methods of inquiry and research questions vary from discipline to discipline, and textual conventions reflect these differences. Despite such disciplinary differences, college instructors generally agree that educated, thoughtful, and knowledgeable college students share certain characteristics.* They believe, for instance, that perhaps the worst intellectual error is oversimplifying. They want their students to go beyond simplistic analysis and arguments to achieve deeper and more complex understandings. Thus a historian might urge students to recognize that more was at stake in the American Civil War than freeing the slaves, and an engineer might encourage students to realize that the most obvious way to resolve a design problem isn't necessarily the best way.

Most college instructors want students to be able to do more than memorize or summarize information. Indeed, they strive to develop students' abilities to analyze, apply, question, evaluate, and synthesize information. What do instructors look for in students' writing? Most broadly, they want evidence of learning and a real commitment to and engagement with the subject. They also want you to adhere to academic standards of clear thinking and effective communication. More specifically, most instructors hope to find the following characteristics in student writing:

- A limited but significant topic
- A meaningful context for discussion of the topic
- A sustained and full development of ideas, given the limitations of the topic, time allotted, and length assigned
- A clear pattern of organization
- Fair and effective use of sources
- Adequate detail and evidence as support for generalizations
- Appropriate, concise language
- Conventional grammar, punctuation, and usage

The essay on pages 107–08, written by Hope Leman for a class on politics and the media, meets these criteria. The essay was a response to the following assignment for a take-home midterm exam:

Journalists often suggest that they simply mirror reality. Some political scientists argue, however, that rather than mirroring reality journalists make judgments that subtly but significantly shape their resulting news reports. In

---

* See the discussion of academic habits of mind in Chapter 2, pp. 23–28.

so doing, scholars argue, journalists function more like flashlights than like mirrors. Write an essay in which you contrast the "mirror" and "flashlight" models of the role of journalists in American society.

Successful essays will not only compare these two models but will also provide examples supporting their claims.

**thinking rhetorically**

Because Hope was writing a take-home essay, she didn't have time to do a formal written analysis of her rhetorical situation. Still, her essay demonstrates considerable rhetorical sensitivity. Hope understands, for instance, that given her situation she should emphasize content rather than employ a dramatic or highly personal style. Hope's essay is, above all, clearly written. Even though it has moments of quiet humor (as when she comments on funhouses at the end of paragraph 2), the focus is on articulating the reasons the "flashlight" model of media theory is the most valid and helpful for political scientists. Hope knows that her teacher will be reading a stack of midterms under time pressure, so she makes sure that her own writing is carefully organized and to the point.

Leman 1

Hope Leman
Professor Roberts
Political Science 101
April 20, 2019

The Role of Journalists in American Society:
A Comparison of the "Mirror" and "Flashlight" Models

The "mirror" model of media theory holds that through their writing
and news broadcasts journalists are an objective source of information
for the public. This model assumes that journalists are free of bias and
can be relied on to provide accurate information about the true state
of affairs in the world. Advocates of the "flashlight" model disagree,
believing that a journalist is like a person in a dark room holding a
flashlight. The light from the flashlight falls briefly on various objects
in the room, revealing part—but not all—of the room at any one
time. This model assumes that journalists cannot possibly provide
an objective view of reality but, at best, can convey only a partial
understanding of a situation or an event.

In this essay, I will argue that the "flashlight" model provides a
more accurate and complex understanding of the role of journalists
in America than the "mirror" model does. The flashlight model
recognizes, for instance, that journalists are shaped by their personal
backgrounds and experiences and by the pressures, mores, and customs
of their profession. It also recognizes that journalists are under
commercial pressure to sell their stories. Newspapers and commercial
networks are run on a for-profit basis. Thus reporters have to "sell"
their stories to readers. The easiest way to do that is to fit a given news
event into a "story" framework. Human beings generally relate well to
easily digestible stories, as opposed to more complex analyses, which
require more thought and concentration. Reporters assigned to cover
a given situation are likely to ask "What is the story?" and then to
force events into that framework. Reality is seldom as neat as a story,

Leman 2

however, with neat compartments of "Once upon a time . . . ," "and then . . . ," and "The End." But the story framework dominates news coverage of events; thus the media cannot function as a mirror since mirrors reflect rather than distort reality (except in funhouses).

The "mirror" model also fails to acknowledge that journalists make choices, including decisions about what stories to cover. These choices can be based on personal preference, but usually they are determined by editors, who respond to publishers, who, in turn, are eager to sell their product to the widest possible audiences. Most people prefer not to read about seemingly insoluble social problems like poverty or homelessness. As a result, journalists often choose not to cover social issues unless they fit a particular "story" format.

In addition to deciding what to cover, journalists must determine the tone they will take in their reporting. If the "mirror" model of media theory were accurate, journalists wouldn't make implicit or explicit judgments in their reporting. But they do. They are only human, after all, and they will inevitably be influenced by their admiration or dislike for a person about whom they are writing or by their belief about the significance of an event.

From start to finish, journalists must make a series of choices. They first make choices about what to cover; then they make choices about whether their tone will be positive or negative, which facts to include or omit, what adjectives to use, and so on. Mirrors do not make choices—but a person holding a flashlight does. The latter can decide where to let the light drop, how long to leave it on that spot, and when to shift the light to something else. Journalists make these kinds of choices every day. Consequently, the "flashlight" model provides the more accurate understanding of the role that journalists play in American society, for the "mirror" model fails to take into account the many factors shaping even the simplest news story.

## for **collaboration**

Working in a group, respond to these questions about Hope Leman's essay. Appoint a recorder to write down the results of your discussion.

1. Hope begins her essay not by attempting to interest readers in her subject but by defining the "mirror" and "flashlight" models of media theory. Why might this be an effective way to begin her essay?

2. Writers need to have a working thesis, or controlling purpose, when they write.✳ Sometimes they signal this purpose by articulating an explicit thesis statement. Sometimes only subtle cues are necessary. (Students writing a personal essay might not want, for instance, to state their controlling purpose explicitly at the start of their essay but rather let readers discover it as they read.) In her essay, Hope includes an explicit thesis statement. Identify this statement, and then discuss the reasons that it is necessary in her particular situation.

3. Academic writing is sometimes viewed as dull and lifeless — as, well, *academic*. Yet even in this essay written under time pressure, Hope's writing is not stuffy, dull, or pompous. Examine her essay to identify passages where a personal voice contributes to the overall effectiveness of her essay. How does Hope blend this personal voice with the objective and distanced approach of her essay?

# Understanding How Analysis Works

As a student, you must respond to a wide range of writing assignments. For an American literature class, you may have to analyze the significance of the whiteness of the whale in *Moby Dick*, whereas a business management class may require a collaboratively written case study; you may need to write a lab report for a chemistry class and critique a qualitative research report for sociology. Although these assignments vary considerably, they all require and depend on analysis.

As noted earlier, analysis involves separating something into parts and determining how these parts function to create the whole. When you analyze, you examine a text, an object, or a body of data to understand how it is structured or organized and to assess its effectiveness or validity. Most academic writing, thinking, and reading involve analysis. Literature students analyze how a poem achieves its effect; economics students analyze the major causes of inflation; biology students analyze the enzymatic reactions that comprise the Krebs cycle; and art history students analyze how line, color, and texture come together in a painting.

As these examples indicate, analysis is not a single skill but a group of related skills. An art history student might explore how a painting by

✳ See also Chapter 9, pp. 253–75.

Michelangelo achieves its effect, for instance, by comparing it with a similar work by Raphael. A biology student might discuss future acid-rain damage to forests in Canada and the United States by first defining *acid rain* and then using cause-and-effect reasoning to predict worsening conditions. A student in economics might estimate the likelihood of severe inflation in the coming year by categorizing or classifying the major causes of previous inflationary periods and then evaluating the likelihood that such factors will influence the current economic situation. Different disciplines emphasize different analytic skills.✱ But regardless of your major, you need to understand and practice analysis. You will do so most successfully if you establish a specific purpose and develop an appropriate framework or method.

## ESTABLISHING A PURPOSE FOR YOUR ANALYSIS

*thinking rhetorically*

Your instructors will often ask you to analyze a fairly limited subject, problem, or process: Lily Briscoe's role in Virginia Woolf's novel *To the Lighthouse*, feminists' criticisms of Freud's psychoanalytical theories, Mendel's third law of genetics. Such limited tasks are necessary because of the complexity of the material, but the larger purpose of your analysis is to better understand your topic's role within a larger context—for example, a literary work that you are analyzing or a political or philosophical theory. When you analyze a limited topic, you're like a person holding a flashlight in the dark: The beam of light that you project is narrow and focused, but it illuminates a much larger area.

Even though the purpose of your analysis is to understand the larger subject, you still need to establish a more specific purpose for your analysis. Imagine, for instance, that your Shakespeare instructor has asked you to write an essay about the fool in *King Lear*. You might establish one of several purposes for your analysis:

- To explain how the fool contributes to the development of a major theme in *King Lear*
- To discuss the effectiveness or plausibility of Shakespeare's characterization of the fool
- To define the role the fool plays in the plot
- To agree or disagree with a particular critical perspective on the fool's role and significance

Establishing a specific purpose helps you define how your analysis should proceed. It enables you to determine the important issues to address or the questions to answer.

There are no one-size-fits-all procedures for establishing a purpose for your analysis. Sometimes your purpose will develop naturally as a result of reading, reflection, and discussion with others. In other instances, it may help to draw on the invention strategies described in Chapter 9; these strategies help you explore your subject and discover questions to guide

✱ For more on what's required in different disciplines, see Chapter 8.

your analysis. Since writing and thinking are dynamically interwoven processes, you may at times need to *write* your way into an understanding of your purpose by composing a rough draft and seeing, in effect, what you think about your topic.

## DEVELOPING AN APPROPRIATE METHOD FOR YOUR ANALYSIS

*thinking rhetorically*

Once you have a purpose, how do you actually analyze something? The answer depends on the subject, process, or problem being analyzed. In general, however, you should consider the methods of inquiry characteristic of the discipline in which you're writing. While students studying *To the Lighthouse* or Mendel's third law may use the same fundamental analytic *processes* — for example, definition, causal analysis, classification, and comparison — the relative weight they give to these different processes and the way they shape and present their final analyses may well differ.

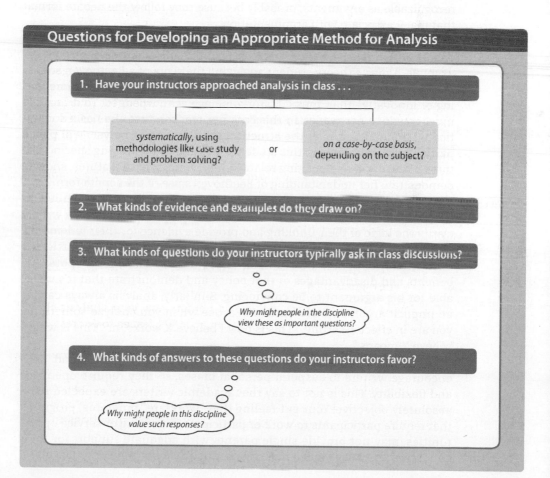

**Questions for Developing an Appropriate Method for Analysis**

1. Have your instructors approached analysis in class . . .

   *systematically*, using methodologies like case study and problem solving?

   or

   on a case-by-case basis, depending on the subject?

2. What kinds of evidence and examples do they draw on?

3. What kinds of questions do your instructors typically ask in class discussions?

   *Why might people in the discipline view these as important questions?*

4. What kinds of answers to these questions do your instructors favor?

   *Why might people in this discipline value such responses?*

The previous questions can help you develop an appropriate method for your analysis. If, after considering these questions and reflecting on your experiences in a class, you continue to have difficulty settling on an appropriate method, meet with your instructor to get help. You might ask him or her to recommend student essays or professional articles that clearly model the analytical methods used in the field.

# Understanding the Relationship between Analysis and Argument

All academic writing has an argumentative edge, and sometimes that edge is obvious. If a student writes a political science essay arguing that the government should follow a particular environmental policy, that student is explicitly arguing that the government should do something. Essays that discuss whether something should or should not be done are easily recognizable as arguments, probably because they follow the debate format that many associate with argumentation.

But writers can express judgments—can present good reasons for their beliefs and actions—without explicitly endorsing a course of action. For example, a music theory student analyzing the score of a Beethoven sonata may argue that the second movement of the particular sonata is more daring or innovative than music historians have acknowledged. To do so, she must convince her reader, in this case her teacher, that she has a sophisticated understanding of the structure of the sonata. Analysis will play a particularly central role in this student's writing: By identifying specific features of the score and positing relationships among these features, she will demonstrate her understanding of Beethoven's use of the sonata form.

*thinking rhetorically*

As this example demonstrates, analysis and argument are interdependent. Argumentation depends on analysis because through analysis writers clarify the logic of their thinking and provide evidence for their judgments. The student arguing that the government should follow a particular environmental policy, for example, would have to analyze the potential benefits and disadvantages of that policy and demonstrate that it's workable for his argument to be convincing. Similarly, analysis always carries an implicit argumentative burden because when you analyze something, you are in effect asserting, "This is how I believe X works" or "This is what I believe X means."

Academic analysis and argument call for similar habits of mind. Both encourage writers to suspend personal biases, so they require openness and flexibility. This is not to say that academic writers are expected to be absolutely objective. Your gut feeling that "workfare" programs, programs that require participants to work or participate in training or service opportunities, may not provide single parents with adequate support for their children may cause you to investigate this topic for an economics class.

This gut feeling is a strength, not a weakness, because it enables you to find a topic that interests you. Once you begin to explore your topic, however, you need to engage it dispassionately. You need, in other words, to be open to changing your mind.

If you do change your mind about the consequences of workfare programs, the reading and writing you have done probably have given you a more detailed understanding of the issues at stake. To write a successful essay about this topic, you will have to describe these issues and analyze their relationships and implications, developing logical connections that make your reasoning explicit. In these and other ways, you will demonstrate to readers that you have indeed understood your subject.

The essay by Hope Leman that begins on p. 107 is a good example of academic analysis. In this essay, Hope is not arguing that something should or should not be done. Rather, she is attempting to understand whether the "mirror" or "flashlight" model best describes the role of journalists in American society.

## ANALYZING ACADEMIC ARGUMENTS

Analysis plays a key role in all academic writing. It helps readers and writers understand the texts they encounter as they move across the disciplines and recognize, examine, and formulate arguments about them. In the world of academia, written, visual, and oral works—and even events, behaviors, and performances—can be considered "texts" susceptible to analysis. While written texts are still central to academic study, the ability to analyze texts that depend heavily on images, sounds, and graphics—whether they are television ads, multimedia presentations, or websites—has become increasingly important in our media-saturated culture.✱

The analysis of any complex text will feel less intimidating if you address three basic questions:

*thinking rhetorically*

- What question is at issue?
- What position does the author take?
- Do the author's reasons justify your acceptance of his or her argument?

## DETERMINING THE QUESTION AT ISSUE

When you determine the question at issue, you get to the heart of any argument and distinguish major claims from minor elements of support. You can then identify the author's position and evaluate whether he or she has provided good reasons for you to agree with this position.

Greek and Roman rhetoricians developed a method called *stasis theory* for determining the questions at issue in any argument. Stasis

---

✱ See Chapters 2 and 6 for advice on analyzing visuals (pp. 39–46) and a student's analysis of a public service ad (pp. 160–76).

theory encourages readers to identify the major point on which a particular controversy rests. This method presents six basic questions at issue in argumentative writing.[1]

As you determine the kinds of issues addressed in a particular argument, you will draw on your rhetorical sensitivity. You do this naturally in your everyday life. Imagine that a friend has urged you to drive with her to a concert in a city an hour away. You'd like to attend the concert, but it's on a midweek work night. Depending on your situation, the primary question at issue may be one of *value*. If you value the concert enough, you can justify the time, expense, and late-night bedtime involved in attending the concert. On the other hand, the primary question at issue for you may be one of *consequence*: This would be the case if you couldn't justify time away from study, work, and family, especially on a weeknight.

On the next page is an argument by journalist Charles Carr. In this opinion column, published in the Escondido, California *Times-Advocate*, Carr argues that reinstituting the Fairness Doctrine, which was in effect from 1949 to 1987, would diminish the "severe ideological polarization" in America today (p. 115). As you read his analysis, consider which of the six stasis questions—fact, definition, interpretation, value, consequence, and policy—are most clearly at stake in his argument.

---

## Stasis Questions

QUESTIONS OF FACT arise from the reader's need to know
   "Does _____ exist?"

QUESTIONS OF DEFINITION arise from the reader's need to know
   "What is _____?"

QUESTIONS OF INTERPRETATION arise from the reader's need to know
   "What does _____ mean?"

QUESTIONS OF VALUE arise from the reader's need to know
   "Is _____ good?"

QUESTIONS OF CONSEQUENCE arise from the reader's need to know
   "Will _____ cause _____ to happen?"

QUESTIONS OF POLICY arise from the reader's need to know
   "What should be done about _____?"

---

[1]In this discussion of stasis theory, I employ the categories presented in John Gage, *The Shape of Reason: Argumentative Writing in College*, 3rd ed., Allyn and Bacon, 1991, p. 40.

# Reinstate the Fairness Doctrine!

**CHARLES CARR**

Like most people, there are certain things over which I have precisely zero will power. Junk food, for example. If it's anywhere in the house, I'll sniff it out like a Mangalitsa pig rooting truffles. Nearly three-quarters of a century ago some very wise lawmakers realized that America had a something of a junk food problem of its own: the fact that people tend to believe that the opinions they already hold are correct and will not go far out of their way to subject them to scrutiny. It's only human nature.

To deal with it, just after WWII in 1949, our nation implemented a Federal Communications Commission (FCC) rule called the Fairness Doctrine. The Fairness Doctrine stated that all holders of broadcast licenses would be required to present controversial issues of public importance in a manner that was, in the FCC's language, "honest, equitable, and balanced." Older readers may remember watching local news broadcasts in which editorial segments were immediately followed by a spokesperson presenting an "opposing viewpoint"—almost unthinkable in today's largely all-junk-news-all-the-time buffet.

They did it, but they sure didn't like it and in 1987 pressured the FCC to eliminate it. It didn't take the ad boys and girls in TV and radio land to realize that its repeal could provide a massive revenue windfall. And those are pretty much the only two dots you need to connect to create the picture we've got today: 1) repeal the Fairness Doctrine 2) start capitalizing on people's basest instincts. Don't believe me? Here are just a few of the terms I pulled off of supposedly balanced political websites TODAY: smack-down, eviscerates, destroys, annihilates, slaughters, pulverizes, murders, and on and on. . . I only get a thousand words here.

In the three decades since its repeal, there have been many attempts to reinstate the doctrine, so far without success. And, not coincidentally, over pretty much that exact period the severe ideological polarization in which America currently finds itself has increased dramatically. A recent Gallup poll revealed that, "Polarization in presidential approval ratings began to expand under Reagan and has accelerated with each president since Clinton." It has vaulted from a record 70 point gap under Barack Obama to 77 points under Donald Trump. News as sport. Opinion

1

2                          Reinstate the Fairness Doctrine!

unfettered by correction. And dump trucks of bucks from a viewership kept too het up to risk turning away from the screen — a legislatively determinative number of people which has cocooned itself within a false reality so deep, so convincing, so perfectly — if cynically — crafted that they are unable to see what they believe to be a perfect window into the world is, in fact, a mirror.

Reinstating the Fairness Doctrine, or something much like it, would again require that opposing views be presented at the key moment viewers are being asked to make a decision. Keep your biases if you want, but only after someone with a different way of looking at the issue has had a shot at making their best pitch to you. Sort of like the nutrition label on that candy bar. You don't have to read it, but it's there. No wonder the food industry is always trying to get them removed.

Reinstatement of the Fairness Doctrine would deliver a 9.9 shock directly to the tender bits of the news-as-sport industry and go a long ways to returning us to the days of Murrow, Cronkite, Sevareid, and the like — a world almost everyone purports to miss but hasn't the slightest idea how to get back to. A world where the word "news" would no longer be what it has become in many quarters today — a four-letter-word.

It would be fair to ask, if the Fairness Doctrine couldn't survive way back in 1987 when the nation was far less polarized than it is now, what are the odds that it could ever be reimplemented in the hyper-partisan environment in which we currently find ourselves? Not great, I'll concede. But perhaps we can at least begin the conversation. Perhaps, as our nation continues toward 100% polarization, conversation will turn to action. Perhaps.

In the meantime, there's a lot we can do individually to create our own personal Fairness Doctrines of a sort. Modern online news aggregators have developed the uncanny ability to tailor web results to our exact tastes and opinions. We can show their smart-alecky AI we're not so easy to peg by going out of our way to visit a wider range of news and opinion sites than we have in the past. Before long, their algorithms will begin to a more diverse range of choices. And let's face(book) it, the way social networks have been shown time and time again to value profit over the welfare of their users, these sites are not our friends. Refusing to click on faux news stories, political ads, and divisive news stories will quickly make the pages unprofitable for the scammers who own them. Better yet, we can flag them as offensive, just as we would porn. In key ways, they are.

> Reinstate the Fairness Doctrine! 3
>
> When it comes to our junk news addiction, America needs an intervention. Let's return to the Fairness Doctrine and a true diversity of opinion. It will be like tasting something divinely fresh food after a long diet of nothing but junk food.
>
> That's all he wrote—for this year. See you in 2019. Got to go now; I think I figured out where my wife hid that Christmas box of Harry and David chocolate truffles!

## for **collaboration**

After you have read Carr's argument, list the two most significant stasis questions (see p. 114) at stake in his argument. Find at least one passage that you believe relates to each question. Then meet with a group of classmates and share your responses to this assignment. To what extent did you agree or disagree with other group members on the stasis questions at stake in Carr's analysis? As a group, choose the two stasis questions that you believe best apply to Carr's argument and agree on two or three reasons why each question is central to his argument.

## IDENTIFYING AN AUTHOR'S POSITION ON A QUESTION

You may find it helpful to identify an author's position in two stages: First, *read the text carefully to determine the main question that the author has presented.* If you review the first five paragraphs of Carr's column beginning on p. 115, for instance, you'll note that he introduces the column by comparing his personal obsession with junk food to the tendency that all humans have "to believe that the opinions they already hold are correct" (p. 115). Given the title of his column, "Reinstate the Fairness Doctrine!," Carr's position on this topic is already clear. But after providing several paragraphs of background information, Carr states his thesis explicitly at the beginning of the fifth paragraph: "Reinstating the Fairness Doctrine, or something much like it, would again require that opposing views be presented at the key moment viewers are being asked to make a decision" (p. 116). The remainder of Carr's column clarifies and supports his position on the issue, while also explaining the inclusion of "or something much like it" in his thesis statement, acknowledging that ". . . if the Fairness Doctrine couldn't survive way back in 1987 when the nation was far less polarized than it is now, what are the odds that it could ever be reimplemented in the hyper-partisan environment in which we currently find ourselves? Not great, I'll concede" (p. 116).

*After you have identified the author's position, you can read his or her argument critically.* Reading critically doesn't mean simply looking for logical flaws, poor evidence, and so on. Rather, critical readers shift stances as they read to develop a complex understanding of the issues at hand.

The following Questions for Critical Reading and Analysis can help you become a more active and critical reader who reads both with and against the grain of an author's argument.

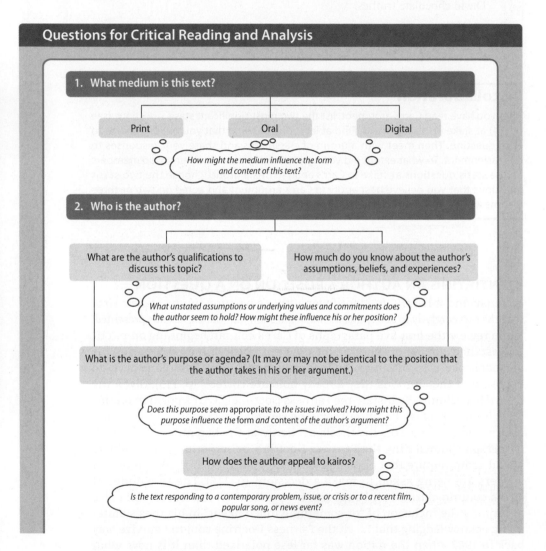

## Questions for Critical Reading and Analysis

1. What medium is this text?

Print     Oral     Digital

*How might the medium influence the form and content of this text?*

2. Who is the author?

What are the author's qualifications to discuss this topic?

How much do you know about the author's assumptions, beliefs, and experiences?

*What unstated assumptions or underlying values and commitments does the author seem to hold? How might these influence his or her position?*

What is the author's purpose or agenda? (It may or may not be identical to the position that the author takes in his or her argument.)

*Does this purpose seem appropriate to the issues involved? How might this purpose influence the form and content of the author's argument?*

How does the author appeal to kairos?

*Is the text responding to a contemporary problem, issue, or crisis or to a recent film, popular song, or news event?*

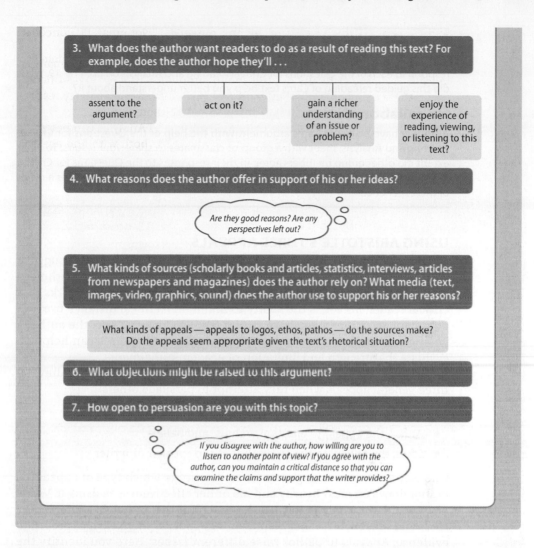

3. What does the author want readers to do as a result of reading this text? For example, does the author hope they'll . . .

- assent to the argument?
- act on it?
- gain a richer understanding of an issue or problem?
- enjoy the experience of reading, viewing, or listening to this text?

4. What reasons does the author offer in support of his or her ideas?

*Are they good reasons? Are any perspectives left out?*

5. What kinds of sources (scholarly books and articles, statistics, interviews, articles from newspapers and magazines) does the author rely on? What media (text, images, video, graphics, sound) does the author use to support his or her reasons?

What kinds of appeals — appeals to logos, ethos, pathos — do the sources make? Do the appeals seem appropriate given the text's rhetorical situation?

6. What objections might be raised to this argument?

7. How open to persuasion are you with this topic?

*If you disagree with the author, how willing are you to listen to another point of view? If you agree with the author, can you maintain a critical distance so that you can examine the claims and support that the writer provides?*

## strategies for success

The Questions for Critical Reading and Analysis may be particularly helpful for writers who are more familiar with acquiring and memorizing information than they are with analysis and critique.

## for **exploration**

Reread Charles Carr's "Reinstate the Fairness Doctrine!" (pp. 115–17). After doing so, respond to each of the Questions for Critical Reading and Analysis on pp. 118–19. What did this guided rereading of Carr's text help you better understand about it?

## for **collaboration**

After you have analyzed Carr's argument with the help of the Questions for Critical Reading and Analysis, meet with a group of classmates to share your results. To what extent did other group members agree in their responses to the Questions for Critical Reading and Analysis? To what extent did they disagree? What did you learn as a result of this experience?

## USING ARISTOTLE'S THREE APPEALS

As the Questions for Critical Reading and Analysis on pp. 118–19 suggest, you may agree with a writer's position on a subject but nevertheless question the support that he or she provides. One of the hallmarks of a critical reader, in fact, is the ability to maintain a critical distance from an argument, even when you have strong feelings for or against the author's position. Aristotle's three appeals, introduced in Chapter 3, can help you evaluate the strength and limitation of academic arguments.

In his *Rhetoric*, Aristotle determined that speakers and writers draw on three general appeals when they attempt to persuade others:

- *Logos*, the appeal to reason
- *Pathos*, the appeal to emotion, values, and beliefs
- *Ethos*, the appeal to the credibility of the speaker or writer

One way to analyze an argument is to determine which type of appeal the author draws on most heavily and his or her effectiveness in using it. When you consider appeals to logos, ask yourself if the author has articulated clear and reasonable major claims and supported them with appropriate evidence. Appeals to pathos raise different issues: Here you identify the strategies that the author has employed to appeal to readers' values and interests. Finally, appeals to ethos encourage you to consider the author's credibility and trustworthiness as demonstrated in his or her argument.

Appeals to logos are often considered especially trustworthy in academic contexts. Logical appeals include firsthand evidence—drawn from observations, interviews, surveys and questionnaires, experiments, and personal experience—and secondhand evidence—drawn from print and online sources. Critical readers do not automatically assume that support drawn from logical appeals is valid. After all, not all sources are equally valid, and facts can be outdated or taken out of context.✽

✽ For a discussion of how to evaluate print and online sources, see Chapter 7, pp. 197–98.

Critical readers look at all three of Aristotle's appeals in context. Appeals to pathos — to readers' emotions, values, and beliefs — can certainly be manipulative and inappropriate. We've all seen ads (like the one on the next page) that seem to promise one thing (youth, beauty, lust) to sell another. Nevertheless, emotional appeals play key roles in many kinds of arguments, including academic arguments. A student writing about humanitarian issues growing out of the conflict in Syria might begin her essay by describing the loss of life, order, and basic material necessities that have resulted from the conflict. In so doing, she would be appealing to readers' emotions and emphasizing the importance of her topic. The same is true for appeals to ethos. While we might be skeptical when we see an ad in which a movie star or sports hero praises a product, this doesn't mean that all appeals to ethos are suspect.

In this regard, let's return to Charles Carr's column "Reinstate the Fairness Doctrine!" (pp. 115–17). At the start of his op-ed, Carr presents a folksy, somewhat humorous image of himself as someone who has "precisely zero will power" when it comes to resisting junk food and goes on to compare his junk food obsession with the realization that America has "something of a junk food problem of its own: the fact that people tend to believe that the opinions they already hold are correct . . ." (p. 115). This is clearly designed to present a friendly, casual image of Carr, who knows that in today's heavily politicized world he is raising a contentious issue. Carr becomes much more serious in the body of his text, looking at the history of the Fairness Doctrine and to the possible benefits and difficulties of trying to reinstate it. Near the end of his piece, after acknowledging that the actual chances of reinstating the Fairness Doctrine are limited and arguing that "there's a lot we can do individually to create our own personal Fairness Doctrines of a sort," Carr returns to the junk food metaphor with which he began his column (p. 116). In his last paragraph, he makes gentle fun of himself: "Got to go now; I think I figured out where my wife hid that Christmas box of Harry and David chocolate truffles!" (p. 117). In these and other ways, Carr is paying careful attention to the role of pathos in his argument.

## for **exploration**

Drawing on your understanding of Aristotle's three appeals, analyze the op-ed column by Carr (pp. 115–17). What appeals does he draw on most heavily? How effective is he in using these appeals?

## for **collaboration**

Meet with a group of classmates to share your responses to the previous Exploration. Begin by addressing this question: To what extent did members of your group agree about Carr's effectiveness in his use of Aristotle's three appeals?

After responding, develop a group position on Carr's use of Aristotle's three appeals. To do so, first agree on a statement that conveys your group's sense of how Carr employed each appeal. Then find one or two examples from his text that support your analysis.

**The power of images: What is this ad promising viewers?**

## RECOGNIZING FALLACIES

When you analyze an argument, you should be aware of *fallacies* that may be at work. Fallacies are faults in an argument's structure that may call into question the argument's evidence or conclusions. Some fallacies are easy to recognize. If someone told you that Shailene Woodley's position on climate change and the environment is ridiculous because she's just a celebrity, you would probably recognize that this assertion is illogical and unfair. Such a statement is an example of an *ad hominem* fallacy, in which an attack on someone's character or actions masquerades as a critique of his or her position. This fallacy, like all fallacies, tends to shut down, rather than encourage, communication.

To determine whether an argument is grounded in a fallacy, you need to consider it in the context of its specific rhetorical situation, including the place and time in which the argument was or is being made. Sometimes judgments about a person's character or actions are relevant to an argument, for instance. In other words, just because a writer or speaker grounds part of an argument in such a judgment doesn't mean that he or she is committing an *ad hominem* fallacy.

Since the time of Aristotle, rhetoricians have developed diverse ways of naming, describing, and categorizing various fallacies. Often the fallacies are categorized according to Aristotle's three major appeals of argument: ethical appeals (appeals to ethos), emotional appeals (appeals to pathos), and logical appeals (appeals to logos).

The guidelines on pp. 124–25 list some of the most significant fallacies that appear in arguments. As you read the brief descriptions, remember that the point of studying fallacies is not to discredit the ideas of others, but rather to thoughtfully evaluate the arguments of others and to develop fair, well-reasoned arguments of your own.

---

## for **exploration**

Locate three of the fallacies described on the next page in such popular media as political websites, the editorial pages of your favorite newspaper, or advertisements in print or online. Identify the fallacy and explain how it functions in its particular context.

---

# Putting Theory into Practice I: Academic Analysis in Action

Readers engage in academic analysis not to criticize or dissect another's argument but rather to understand that argument as fully as possible. When you analyze an academic argument, you attempt to go beyond your

## Guidelines for Identifying Fallacies

### Ethical Fallacies

Writers who employ ethical fallacies attempt to discredit their opponents personally. Examples of ethical fallacies include the following:

**AN *AD HOMINEM*** attack is an unfair assault on a person's character or actions, one that diverts attention from the issue at hand.

> **"Any American who is in favor of gun control doesn't value our country's constitution."**
>
> *(A person's position on this topic does not indicate his or her commitment to the U.S. Constitution.)*

**GUILT BY ASSOCIATION** is an effort to damage a person's credibility by associating him or her with an unpopular or discredited activity or person.

> **"Hip-hop is bad because some hip-hop musicians have been involved in criminal activities."**
>
> *(The behavior of hip-hop musicians is separate from the music they create.)*

### Emotional Fallacies

Emotional appeals can play a valid and important role in argumentation, but when these appeals are overblown or unfair, they distract readers from attending to the point that is being argued. Examples of emotional fallacies include the following:

**A BANDWAGON APPEAL** argues that readers should support a person, an activity, a product, or a movement because it is popular. This appeal is particularly common in advertising:

> **"Frosty Puffs™ is the best-selling cereal in America!"**

**A SLIPPERY SLOPE** fallacy occurs when writers exaggerate the consequences of an event or action, usually with an intent to frighten readers into agreeing with their conclusion.

> **"If we ban *Beloved* from our school library, the next thing you know, we'll be burning books!"**

### Logical Fallacies

Logical fallacies are arguments in which the claims, warrants, or evidence are invalid, insufficient, or disconnected. Examples of logical fallacies include the following:

**BEGGING THE QUESTION** involves stating a claim that depends on circular reasoning for justification.

> **"Abortion is murder because it involves the intentional killing of an unborn human being."**

*(This statement is tantamount to saying, "Abortion is murder because it is murder." This fallacy often distracts attention from the real issues at hand because the question of whether a fetus should be considered a human being is complex.)*

**A HASTY GENERALIZATION** is drawn from insufficient evidence.

> **"Last week I attended a poetry reading supported by the National Endowment for the Arts, and several of the speakers used profanity. Maybe the people who want to stop government funding for the NEA are right."**

*(One performance doesn't constitute a large enough sample for such a generalization.)*

**A NON SEQUITUR** is an argument that attempts to connect two or more logically unrelated ideas.

> **"I hate it when people smoke in restaurants; there ought to be a law against cigarettes."**

*(Eliminating smoking in restaurants and the negative effects of secondhand smoke do not require the elimination of legal tobacco sales.)*

**A RED HERRING** is an argument that misleads or distracts opponents from the original issue.

> **"How can you expect me to worry about global warming when we're on the brink of war?"**

*(Whether or not we're on the brink of war is irrelevant to whether global warming is a problem.)*

**A STRAW MAN** fallacy occurs when a misrepresentation, an exaggeration, or a distortion of a position is attacked.

> **"My opponent argues that drugs should be legalized without taking into consideration the epidemic that selling heroin in every drugstore would cause."**

*(Arguing in favor of legalizing drugs does not mean that all drugs would be available over the counter.)*

immediate response—which often takes the form of binary-driven observations ("I agree/don't agree, like/don't like, am interested/not interested in X")—to achieve a fuller, more complex understanding of it.

On the next page is an example of a successful analysis of an academic argument. This essay by Thai Luong, a student at the University of Hawai'i, analyzes Carr's "Reinstate the Fairness Doctrine!" presented earlier in this chapter (pp. 115–17). As a student, Thai is particularly interested in issues of politics, culture, and entertainment. You can read his essay on Asian American representation in films on pp. 215–23 in Chapter 7, "Doing Research."

Luong 1

Thai Luong
Dr. Mallon
Composition 101
Oct. 10, 2019

Political Polarization in the News: Examining the Fairness Doctrine

**Summarizes Carr's basic argument**

In his essay "Reinstate the Fairness Doctrine!" award-winning journalist Charles Carr calls, as his title suggests, for the reinstatement of the 1949 Federal Communications Commission (FCC) rule called the Fairness Doctrine. The Fairness Doctrine required television stations to present issues to the public in a manner that was "honest, equitable, and balanced" (115). The rule was in effect until 1987, when it was eliminated. Carr argues that reinstating the Fairness Doctrine would reduce the polarization that has become such a significant and divisive feature of contemporary life, media, and politics.

**Indicates his initial agreement with Carr**

When I first read Carr's essay, which appeared as an opinion column in the Escondido California *Times-Advocate* on December 28, 2018, I found myself largely in agreement with him. Contemporary politics, media, and culture do seem, as Carr argues, to capitalize "on people's basest instincts" (115). Even those engaged in vitriolic debate bemoan this politicization—while they blame the alternate political party for it. So Carr is clearly raising an important issue.

**Describes questions that Carr's op-ed raises for him**

But is reinstating the Fairness Doctrine the best way to do so? If the Fairness Doctrine worked so well between 1949 and 1987, why was it repealed? What arguments successfully led to the repeal of the Fairness Doctrine? And how realistic is it to imagine that in 2019, thirty-two years after its repeal, the Fairness Doctrine can be successfully reinstated, especially in a world where social media (largely not under the control of the FCC) play a particularly powerful role in swaying public opinion.

**Shares background information on the FCC's Fairness Doctrine and a potential weakness in Carr's argument while acknowledging the limitations of a brief op-ed column**

In order to address these and related questions, I felt that I needed more information, so I did some quick background research on the FCC's Fairness Doctrine. I learned, first of all, that the Doctrine relied upon voluntary compliance, which raises questions in my mind as to its effectiveness. I also learned that concerns about threats to free

Luong 2

speech were among the factors that led to its demise. This exposes a weakness in Carr's analysis since he does not discuss the effectiveness of the doctrine during the time that it was in force or issues of free speech. This seems like a significant limitation, though it is only fair to recognize that as an opinion columnist Carr was limited in the issues he could discuss by space constraints.

There is much that I still agree with in terms of Carr's analysis. The humorous opening of Carr's essay which compares his urge to eat junk food with that of Americans "who have something of a junk food problem. . . [in that they] tend to believe that the opinions they already hold are correct. . ." is helpful (115). Such a belief, Carr observes, is "only human nature" (115). Carr clearly believes that the Fairness Doctrine addressed this problem in useful ways. His argument would have been stronger, however, if he had given more attention to the specifics: what the Fairness Doctrine did and did not do in practice given the voluntary nature of compliance. His analysis would also be stronger if Carr more fully addressed relevant counterarguments and issues.

**Gives credit to Carr for an attention-getting introduction but notes that Carr could have done more to address relevant counter-arguments**

In his commentary, Carr does a good job of showing that the dismantling of the Fairness Doctrine correlates well with the rise of contentious political ideologies: "not coincidentally," Carr argues, "over pretty much that exact period the severe ideological polarization in which America currently finds itself has increased dramatically" (115). Carr cites a recent Gallup poll to support his claim about the rise of political polarization since the removal of the Fairness Doctrine: "It [Gallup] has vaulted from a record 70 points gap under Barrack Obama to 77 under Donald Trump" (115). Ultimately, Carr argues that: "Reinstating the Fairness Doctrine, or something much like it, would again require that opposing views be presented at the key moments viewers are being asked to make a decision" (116). Carr goes on to suggest reinstating the Fairness Doctrine won't completely sway or convince viewers to change their preconceived opinions or biases: "Keep your biases if you want, but only after someone with a different way of looking at the issue has had a shot at making their best pitch to you" (116).

**Establishes his own ethos by providing a balanced assessment of Carr's analysis**

Luong 3

Raises additional questions about whether reintroducing the Fairness Doctrine would result in fair, equitable, and balanced presentation of the news

But how is "making their best pitch to you" the same as presenting the news in a way that is "fair, equitable, and balanced? And if the Fairness Doctrine were reintroduced, who would decide what constitutes a fair, equitable, and balanced presentation of the news? If the federal government had this power, couldn't it possibly be abused? How would it reduce the problem of political polarization if those who stridently oppose differing views simply ignore or, worse yet, belittle them? In my experience, the cable network CNN regularly tried to include panelists who champion opposing views as part of their on-air panels during the last election, but often the differing positions articulated on the panel are so extreme that it is impossible to come up with a "fair, balanced, and equitable" compromise.

Praises Carr's recognition of the difficulties inherent in any effort to reinstate the Fairness Doctrine and emphasizes the importance of these difficulties

It is important to point out that as much as Carr champions the Fairness Doctrine, he is realistic in pointing out its past failures and its uncertainty in being implemented today. Carr asks, "If the Fairness Doctrine couldn't survive way back in 1987 when the nation was far less polarized than it is now, what are the odds that it could ever be reimplemented in the hyper-partisan environment in which we currently find ourselves? Not great, I'll concede" (116). Carr's question highlights the pragmatism of his argument—that it is not just a right or wrong issue, but instead, it is layered with complexities and challenges. Carr is right to gesture to the fact that the Fairness Doctrine, although it could theoretically decrease partisan and polarizing reporting, has failed already failed once throughout its history. Its failure in the past rightfully makes it harder to be reinstated today.

Acknowledges the shift in Carr's argument from the value of reinstating the FCC's Fairness Doctrine to readers instituting their own personal fairness doctrines

Despite Carr's bleak concession, he swiftly shifts his conversation into a hopeful and productive tone. Carr writes that the even if we can't implement the Fairness Doctrine at the federal level, we can still execute it at an individual and personal level, "there's a lot we can do individually to create or own personal Fairness Doctrines of a sort" (116). Instead of relying on the federal government to dictate what is fair or biased reporting, Carr challenges us to reduce the spread of polarizing online news (by monitoring what we watch and click on).

Luong 4

To conclude, Carr's argument does an informative job in pointing
out the very real problem of ideological polarization in the news that
continues to divide our country. Although he falls short of making a
compelling case for the reinstatement of the Fairness Doctrine, he still
reminds readers of the important role we play in consuming (and in
some cases sharing) the news. In analyzing his argument, I have tried to
remember that given his chosen genre—an opinion column on the op-ed
page of the *Times-Advocate*—Carr couldn't have addressed all of his
counterarguments. His essay would have been stronger, however, if he had
made more of an effort to do so. For me, one of the major benefits of
Carr's essay was reminding me that while I tend to think of political and
cultural polarization and its impact on the news media as a contemporary
social problem, its history is much longer and more problematic.

> Concludes with a balanced assessment of Carr's column

Work Cited

Carr, Charles. "Reinstate the Fairness Doctrine!" *The Academic Writer:
A Brief Rhetoric*, 5th ed., by Lisa Ede, Macmillan Learning, 2021.
115–17.

Note: In an actual MLA-style paper, works cited entries start on a new page.

## for **exploration**

Now that you have read Carr's op-ed essay several times and have also read Thai Luong's analysis of it, reread Thai's essay to determine its strengths and limitations. Identify two or three passages from the essay that strike you as particularly significant and helpful, and write several sentences of explanation for each passage. Next, identify one or more ways this essay might be even more successful.

## for **collaboration**

Bring your response to the previous For Exploration to class to share with a group of peers. After all group members have shared their responses, answer these questions: (1) To what extent did other members of your group agree in their evaluation of Thai Luong's analysis? To what extent did they disagree? (2) Now that you have heard everyone's responses, what two or three passages does your group feel best demonstrate Thai's analytical skills? (3) How might Thai's essay be further strengthened?

# Understanding How Synthesis Works

Analysis often is connected with and leads to synthesis. When you analyze something, you examine it critically to understand how it is structured and how the parts work together to create the overall meaning. When you synthesize something, you draw on ideas or information from sources, as well as from your own experience, to create meaning of your own.

In much academic writing, synthesis is an important counterpart to analysis, for it enables you to make connections and identify contradictions within a text or group of texts that you have analyzed. Synthesis is an essential part of the research process. For a good example of synthesis, take a look at Thai Luong's essay in Chapter 7 (pp. 215–23). There Thai synthesizes a variety of sources as part of his exploration of the lack of diversity in Asian American films. As noted earlier, as a student Thai is particularly interested in issues of politics, culture, and entertainment, so he took advantage of an assignment in his Introduction to Film class to learn more about this topic.

In a research project you typically draw on multiple sources, as Thai does in his essay for his film class. Sometimes, however, an instructor will ask you to engage a limited number of texts. Your writing instructor might ask you, for instance, to read and respond to two or more articles on the same or a related topic, with the goal of analyzing and synthesizing these texts while also articulating your own views.

You might think of this kind of synthesis essay as a chronicle of your intellectual journey as you explore a topic and readings related to that topic. This is not to say that your essay should be a narrative; in most cases, it is more likely to be an academic argument. But readers of your essay should be able to see that you have interacted at a serious level with the texts to which you are responding and that you have done so to promote your own independent analysis. In other words, it should be clear that as a result of reading and reflecting on these texts you have gained new insights and perspectives.

Synthesis requires both the ability to analyze and to summarize, and this book contains a number of resources that you might want to review before undertaking a synthesis assignment.✱ But it is equally important that you develop your own views on your topic. This may feel difficult at first: How can you engage the arguments of published authors when you are just a college student? The best way to work your way through this

---

✱ Chapter 2 covers summary and reading critically (pp. 29–38); Chapter 7 covers summary and synthesis (pp. 202–03, 210). Elizabeth Hurley's essay in this chapter (pp. 133–37) is another good model of synthesis.

initial hesitation is to immerse yourself deeply in the texts to which you are responding.

As you begin your synthesis, focus on developing an understanding of the authors' positions, the reasons and evidence they use to support these positions, the contexts in which they are writing, and any motivating factors, such as their goals, interests, and priorities. Creating a chart in which you can record this information may help you keep track of what you are learning.

The Questions for Critical Reading and Analysis that appear on pp. 118–19 of this chapter will help you consider key aspects of the authors' rhetorical situation, such as each author's purpose or agenda and the values and beliefs that motivate him or her. The questions also encourage you to consider the reasons and evidence the authors provide, the objections that might be raised in response to the authors' positions, their use of evidence, and so forth. The Questions for Synthesizing Texts can help you synthesize the sources and develop your own approach to the issue.

## Putting Theory into Practice II: Academic Synthesis in Action

Synthesis assignments represent an exciting opportunity for students to enter into conversation with others, whether they are nonprofessionals expressing their ideas or professional journalists, politicians, or scholars. Throughout your college career, and later at work, you will regularly be asked to synthesize ideas and texts. Your psychology teacher may ask you to read two articles taking different positions on whether it is possible to become addicted to social media, such as Instagram and Twitter, and to articulate your own views on this topic. Your business teacher may ask you to study two bids for a hypothetical project and to write a response that includes an evaluation of each bid and a recommendation. Once you graduate and join a company, you may find yourself writing an evaluation of two bids that are anything but hypothetical. In each of these cases, you must carefully and respectfully analyze the texts before you, and you must articulate your own position.

Here is an example of a successful essay analyzing and synthesizing two texts. This essay by Elizabeth Hurley, a student at Oregon State University, was written in response to the following assignment:

> Choose two readings included in the Optional Readings section of our syllabus that address the same general topic, and write an essay that analyzes and synthesizes these two texts. Be sure to analyze these texts carefully, paying attention to their arguments, evidence, and rhetorical situations. Recognize that your goal in writing this essay is not just to respond to the two texts but also to advance your own views on this topic.

## Questions for Synthesizing Texts

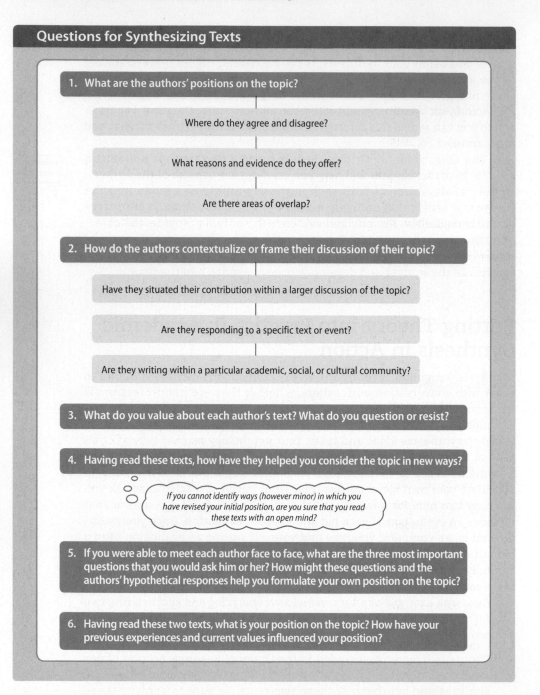

1. What are the authors' positions on the topic?

Where do they agree and disagree?

What reasons and evidence do they offer?

Are there areas of overlap?

2. How do the authors contextualize or frame their discussion of their topic?

Have they situated their contribution within a larger discussion of the topic?

Are they responding to a specific text or event?

Are they writing within a particular academic, social, or cultural community?

3. What do you value about each author's text? What do you question or resist?

4. Having read these texts, how have they helped you consider the topic in new ways?

*If you cannot identify ways (however minor) in which you have revised your initial position, are you sure that you read these texts with an open mind?*

5. If you were able to meet each author face to face, what are the three most important questions that you would ask him or her? How might these questions and the authors' hypothetical responses help you formulate your own position on the topic?

6. Having read these two texts, what is your position on the topic? How have your previous experiences and current values influenced your position?

Hurley 1

Elizabeth Hurley
Professor Braun
WR 121
October 26, 2019

The Role of Technology in the Classroom: Two Views

As a student and a future teacher, I have spent quite a bit of time
thinking about the role that technology has played in my education.
In many ways, I know that I am fortunate to be a college student
today. I have access to many resources — from word processing
software to an almost endless number of online databases that I
can consult when I'm researching a topic — that students as recently
as twenty years ago could not have imagined. Thanks to course
management systems like Blackboard and Canvas, I can easily submit
assignments electronically, and I can even take classes (and complete
entire degree programs) online. However, despite the many benefits
that modern technology offers, there are potential disadvantages.
One disadvantage that professors and students alike recognize is
the role that devices like laptops, tablets, and smartphones can play
in distracting students who should be engaged with lectures and
discussions, causing some teachers to consider banning the use of
such devices during class time.

    As a student, I have to admit that these concerns are valid.
Like many of my peers, I have been guilty of checking Facebook
or texting a friend during a lecture, hoping that my instructor
will assume that I am busily taking notes or looking through
my backpack for a pencil. I have often felt conflicted about this,
especially when I can sense how hard a professor is trying to make
the material matter to me, but in the past I quickly forgot my
momentary sense of guilt. Now that I have decided to major in
education, I have started to think about this issue from a different
perspective: that of the teacher. For these reasons, I was especially
interested to read two blog posts on this topic: Clay Shirky's

*Introduces the topic of her essay*

*Connects the topic of her essay with her personal experience and identifies the two essays she will analyze*

Hurley 2

"Why I Just Asked My Students to Put Their Laptops Away" and David Croteau's "Banning Technology in Classrooms: The False Dichotomy and a Boring Call for 'All Things in Moderation.' "

Though Shirky and Croteau come from different fields of study, they are both professors who have spent a lot of time thinking and writing about the role of technology in contemporary life. A noted writer, professor of social media at New York University, and advocate for the benefits of emerging technologies, Shirky focuses his research on the way that social networks and digital communication technologies benefit our culture. He has published two well-received books on the advantages of new digital and online technologies: *Here Comes Everybody: The Power of Organizing without Organizations* and *Cognitive Surplus: Creativity and Generosity in a Connected Age.* In his post, however, Shirky narrows his focus to reflect on issues regarding technology and education that he faces as a classroom teacher. He begins by recounting changes that he has observed in his classrooms, concluding that his students have grown more distracted over the years. The culprit, he believes, is technology, and in his article, he explains why he now requires students to put their laptops, tablets, and phones away during class.

**Provides background about Shirky and summarizes his position**

Aware how odd this decision might seem coming from a self-described "advocate and activist for the free culture movement," Shirky states that

> I came late and reluctantly to this decision — I have been teaching classes about the internet since 1998, and I've generally had a *laissez-faire* attitude towards technology use in the classroom. This was partly because the subject of my classes made technology use feel organic, and when device use went well, it was great. . . . it's my job to be more interesting than the possible distractions, so a ban felt like cheating. And finally, there's not wanting to infantilize my students, who are adults, even if young ones — time management is their job, not mine.

Shirky's essay describes the gradual changes in his thinking about the role of devices in his classroom. He is clearly a believer in placing

Hurley 3

considerable responsibility for learning on the student, but he is also keenly aware that devices can lead to mass distraction in what he calls the "Nearby Peer Effect." Shirky ultimately argues that devices used by students in the classroom have been engineered to distract and that multitasking during a lecture can be detrimental to the learning experience. Later in his essay he adds that:

> The fact that hardware and software is being professionally designed to distract was the first thing that made me willing to require rather than merely suggest that students not use devices in class. . . . The industry has committed itself to an arms race for my students' attention, and if it's me against Facebook and Apple, I lose.

Croteau responds to Shirky in his subsequent post. As a professor at Virginia Commonwealth University; a sociologist studying the effects of media, social movements, and class; and a specialist in the VCU Office of Online Learning, he has also had extensive experience with technology in classrooms. Though he admits that Shirky has some valid points, Croteau worries that Shirky's decision, which got a lot of attention in the media, will cause instructors with similar concerns to focus on the narrow issue of whether professors should ban devices in the classroom rather than on the larger question of student engagement and learning. Croteau does not take a strong position about devices in the classroom, though he does observe that "I've never banned tech in the classroom and don't think I would in the future." But he goes on to add that he can understand why in some circumstances instructors might want to do so. His view might best be characterized as "promote engagement rather than ban distraction." He ends his piece by reinforcing the concept of "all things in moderation."

*Provides background on Croteau and summarizes his position*

When I first read these two essays, I tried to fit them into a pro/con framework: Shirky was against allowing students to use

Hurley 4

personal devices in the classroom and Croteau was for it. But in rereading the articles, I realized that both authors' positions are more complicated—and closer—than I had originally thought. While Shirky spends a good deal of time explaining his decision to ban devices in the classroom, he concludes his article by noting that what is most important to him is not "a switch in rules, but a switch in how I see my role. . . . I'm coming to see student focus as a collaborative process." This comes very close to Croteau's emphasis on the importance of student learning and engagement. Croteau notes, for instance, that "stale PowerPoints and didactic lectures will likely be met with mental disengagement whether or not technology is present." In the end, both Shirky and Croteau argue that student engagement is central to effective learning.

**Discusses the evolution of her thinking and the relationship between Shirky's and Croteau's positions**

As a future teacher, I am glad that I took the time to analyze Shirky's and Croteau's essays carefully. Doing so has reminded me that in the midst of constant change (the implementation of the Common Core, debates about the role of testing in education, etc.), some essentials remain. Though Croteau focuses more on the role of the instructor and Shirky emphasizes the way that technology has impacted students' concentration in the classroom, together they raised an important point for me: that both the student *and* the instructor have important roles to play in the student's education. After much deliberation, I now believe that student–teacher relationships and engaged learning remain the most important aspect of education despite all of the technological changes. And as Croteau reminds readers in the closing sentence of his article, this is hardly a new issue: "The daydream," Croteau observes, "is a timeless distraction from a dull classroom."

**Concludes by articulating what she has learned as a result of her analysis**

Hurley 5

Works Cited

Croteau, David. "Banning Technology in the Classroom and a Boring
    Call for 'All Things in Moderation.'" *David Croteau*, 1 Oct. 2014,
    davidrcroteau.net/blog-post/banning-technology-in-classrooms-the
    -false-dichotomy-and-a-boring-call-for-all-things-in-moderation/.
Shirky, Clay. "Why I Just Asked My Students to Put Their Laptops
    Away." *Medium*, 8 Sept. 2014, medium.com/@cshirky/why-i-just
    -asked-my-students-to-put-their-laptops-away-7f5f7c50f368#
    .uip31nz3l.

## for **thought, discussion, and writing**

1. Interview an upper-level student majoring in your intended field of study or an
   area you are considering as a possible major. Ask the following questions and
   record his or her answers:

   - What caused you to choose this area as a major?
   - What kinds of texts do students in this major typically read?
   - What analytical skills are required to succeed in this major?
   - How are these analytical skills taught and reinforced in courses in this area?
   - How do these analytical skills reflect this area's dominant methodologies?
   - What advice would you give to someone who is preparing to major in this
     area?

   Be prepared to report the results of this interview to the class. Your instructor may also ask you to write an essay summarizing and commenting on the
   results of your interview.

2. Find an editorial or opinion column that interests you in a newspaper or
   general news magazine, such as *The Week* or *Time*.

   - Use the Questions for Critical Reading and Analysis on pp. 118–19 to analyze
     the text you have chosen. If your analysis has raised questions for you as a
     reader, articulate them as well.
   - Use stasis theory (p. 114) to determine the most important questions at issue
     in this editorial or column. Write a brief summary of what these activities
     have helped you understand about your reading.

- Use Aristotle's three appeals (pp. 120–22) to further analyze the text you have chosen. After doing so, reread the summary you wrote earlier. What has this additional analysis helped you better understand about your reading?

Your teacher may ask you to write an essay analyzing or responding to the editorial or opinion column you have chosen.

3. In this chapter, you read Elizabeth Hurley's essay on the role of technology as discussed in two blog posts:

- Clay Shirky's "Why I Just Asked My Students to Put Their Laptops Away"
- David Croteau's "Banning Technology in the Classroom and a Boring Call for 'All Things in Moderation'"

Locate and print these posts; then use the Questions for Critical Reading and Analysis on pp. 118–19 and the Questions for Synthesizing Texts on p. 132 to analyze these two selections. Based on the insights you have gained as a result of this analysis, write an essay responding to and synthesizing Shirky's and Croteau's posts.

# 6

# Making and Supporting Claims

As Chapter 5 emphasizes, analysis, synthesis, and argument are linked in powerful ways. To write an effective argument, you must analyze both your own ideas and those of others. But academic argument requires more than strong analytical skills. A successful academic argument also requires careful, well-supported reasoning that synthesizes or responds to ideas in sources and anticipates readers' interests and concerns.

## Understanding—and Designing—Academic Arguments

The first step in writing a successful academic argument is to understand the ways in which academic arguments are similar to and different from other kinds of arguments. Viewed from one perspective, all language use is argumentative. If you say to a friend, "You *have* to hear Billie Eilish's new album!" you're making an implicit argument that it's important (to be in the know, for sheer pleasure, or some other reason) to listen to that particular music. A sign that advertises the "Best Deep-Dish Pizza in Chicago" is also making an argumentative claim about the quality of the pizza relative to the competition. Even prayers can be viewed as arguments: Some prayers represent direct appeals to God; others function as meditations directed toward self-understanding. In either case, those who pray are engaged in an argument for change—either in themselves or in the world around them.

As these examples suggest, arguments serve many purposes beyond confrontation or debate. Sometimes the purpose is to change minds or to win a decision; this is particularly true in politics, business, and law. But winning isn't always the goal of argument—especially in the academy, where writers focus on contributing to the scholarly conversation in their fields. Given this focus, students who bring a debate model of argumentation to academic writing often encounter problems. Think about the terminology used in debate: Debaters *attack* their *adversaries*, hoping to *demolish* their *opponents'* arguments so that they can *win* the judge's approval and claim *victory* in the contest. In academic arguments, the goal is inquiry and not conquest. Your teachers aren't interested in whether you can attack or demolish your opponents. Rather, they value your ability to examine an issue or a problem from multiple perspectives. They want you to make a commitment not to "winning" but to using clear reasoning and presenting substantial evidence.

Not all scholarly arguments are identical, however. Because they reflect the aims and methods of specific disciplines, they can vary in significant ways. For example, interpretation—whether of literary texts, artwork, or historical data—is central to arguments in the humanities. Scholars in the social sciences often argue about issues of policy; they also undertake studies that attempt to help readers better understand—and respond to—current issues and events. For instance, a sociologist might review and evaluate recent research on the effects of children's gender on parents' child-rearing practices and then present conclusions based on her own quantitative or qualitative study. Argument is also central to research in the natural and applied sciences: Engineers who argue about how best to design and build trusses for a bridge or chemists who present new information about a particular chemical reaction are making claims that they must support with evidence and reasons.

Although scholarly arguments reflect disciplinary concerns, all scholars agree that the best arguments share the following traits:

1. They explore relevant ideas as fully as possible and from as many perspectives as possible.
2. They present their claims logically.
3. They include appropriate support for all significant claims.

These preferences distinguish academic arguments from other kinds of arguments. You and your friend might spend an hour on a Saturday night arguing about the merits of Billie Eilish's new album, but your discussion would undoubtedly be fluid and improvisational, with many digressions. In academic argument, great value is placed on the careful, consistent, and logical exploration of ideas.

In a way, what is true of design is also true of academic arguments. (See the discussion of writing as design in Chapter 1.) Most academic arguments are open-ended and cannot be solved once and for all. Philosophers have been arguing for centuries, for instance, about whether it is possible to justify warfare, just as historians continue to argue about the significance and consequences of specific wars. In this sense, those writing academic essays are participating in an ongoing scholarly conversation.

The process of identifying problems is central to writers of academic arguments, just as it is for designers. A literary scholar who believes that other critics of Toni Morrison's *Beloved* have failed to recognize the importance of religious imagery in that novel is describing a problem. Since literary texts—like other complex data sets—are open to multiple interpretations, this critic's argument (her response to the problem) will depend in part on subjective value judgments. The same occurs when a historian argues that previous accounts of the fall of Saigon near the end of the Vietnam War overemphasize the Western media's role in this event.

Perhaps most important is that those composing academic arguments are, like designers, concerned with what might, could, and should be. A biologist proposing a new method for protecting wetlands, a sociologist reporting the results of a new study on children in foster care, and a historian reconsidering previous studies of the spread of the Black Death in medieval Europe are all composing writing that *matters*: writing that addresses complex problems, expands the scholarly conversation, and makes a difference.

# Exploring Aristotle's Three Appeals

Academic writing places a high premium on logical appeals, or the quality of ideas, evidence, and organization — *logos*. This doesn't mean, however, that as a writer you should avoid emotional appeals (*pathos*) and ethical appeals (*ethos*).

*thinking rhetorically*

All writers — whether they're composing a message to a friend, an editorial for the student newspaper, or an essay for a history class — need to establish their ethos, or credibility. Academic writers generally do so by demonstrating knowledge of their subject and of the methodologies that others in their field use to explore it. They reinforce their credibility when they explore their subject evenhandedly and show respect for their readers. Writers demonstrate this respect, for instance, when they anticipate readers' concerns and address possible counterarguments. In these and other ways, academic writers demonstrate *rhetorical sensitivity*.✻

Just as all writers appeal to ethos, so too do they appeal to pathos — to emotions and shared values. Sometimes this type of appeal is obvious, as in requests for charitable contributions that feature heart-wrenching stories and images. Even texts that are relatively objective and that emphasize appeals to logos, as much academic writing does, nevertheless draw on and convey emotional appeals. An academic argument that uses formal diction and presents good reasons and evidence is sending readers a message based on pathos: "This subject is much too important for me to treat it frivolously. It requires the attention that only reasoned argument can give."

In academic writing, appeals to pathos can also emphasize just how much is at stake in understanding and addressing a problem or an event. Scholars writing about the Holocaust, for instance, often use vivid descriptions to encourage readers to connect personally with their texts. Moreover, to bring immediacy and impact to an argument, writers often employ figurative language, such as metaphors, similes, and analogies.

---

✻ For more on analyzing rhetorical situations and on Aristotle's three appeals, see Chapter 3.

(For example, some scholars who have written about the massacre that occurred when Nanking, China, fell to the Japanese on December 13, 1937, refer to this event as the Rape of Nanking.) They also may use images and graphics to lend visceral impact to their point.

# Understanding the Role of Values and Beliefs in Argument

When you write an academic argument, you give reasons and evidence for your assertions. A student arguing against a Forest Service plan for a national forest might warn that increased timber harvesting will reduce access to the forest for hikers or that building more roads will adversely affect wildlife. This writer might also show that the Forest Service has failed to anticipate some problems with the plan and that cost-benefit calculations unfairly benefit logging and economic-development interests. These are all potentially good reasons for questioning the plan. Notice that these reasons necessarily imply certain values or beliefs. The argument against increasing the timber harvest and building more roads, for instance, reflects the belief that preserving wildlife habitats and wilderness lands is more important than the economic development of the resources.

Is this argument flawed because it appeals to values and beliefs? Of course it isn't. When you argue, you can't suppress your own values and beliefs. After all, they provide links between yourself and the world you observe and experience.

Suppose that you and a friend are getting ready to go out for breakfast. You look out the window and notice some threatening clouds. You say, "It looks like rain. We'd better take umbrellas since we're walking. I hate getting soaked." "Oh, I don't know," your friend replies. "I don't think it looks so bad. I saw on my weather app that it wasn't going to start raining until the afternoon. I think we're OK." Brief and informal as this exchange is, it constitutes an argument. Both of you have observed something, analyzed it, and drawn conclusions — conclusions backed by reasons. Although you each cite different reasons, your conclusions reflect your different personal preferences. You're generally cautious, and you don't like getting caught unprepared in a downpour, so you opt for an umbrella. Your friend relies on expert opinion and might be more of a risk taker.

If your individual preferences, values, and beliefs shape a situation like this one, where only getting wet is at stake, imagine how crucial they are in more complicated situations, such as determining whether a controversial government proposal is right or wrong, just or unjust, effective or ineffective. Argument necessarily involves values and beliefs, held by both writer and reader, that cannot be denied or excluded — even in academic argument, with its emphasis on evidence and reasoned inquiry. The student arguing against the Forest Service plan can't avoid using values and beliefs as bridges between reasons and conclusions. And not all these bridges can be explicitly stated; that would lead to an endless chain of reasons. The standards of academic argument require, however, that writers explicitly state and defend the most important values and beliefs undergirding their argument. In this case, then, the student opposing the Forest Service plan should at some point state and support his belief that preserving wildlife habitats and wilderness lands should take priority over economic development.

It's not easy to identify and analyze your own values and beliefs, but doing so is essential in academic argument. Values and beliefs are often held unconsciously and function as part of a larger network of assumptions and practices. Your opinions about the best way for the government to respond to persons on welfare reflect your values and beliefs about family, the proper role of government, the nature of individual responsibility, and the importance of economic security. Thus if a political science instructor asks you to argue for or against programs requiring welfare recipients to work at state-mandated jobs in exchange for economic support, you need to analyze not just these workfare programs but also the role your values and beliefs play in your analysis. The guidelines on p. 144 will help you do so, thus enabling you to respond more effectively to the demands of academic argument.

At the same time, when you argue, you must consider not only your own values and beliefs but also those of your readers. The student writing about the Forest Service plan would present one argument to a local branch of the Sierra Club (an organization that advocates for protecting the environment) and a very different argument to representatives of the Forest Service. The student would expect members of the Sierra Club to agree with his major assumptions and therefore might focus on how the group could best oppose the plan and why members should devote time and energy to this project.

His argument to the Forest Service would be designed quite differently. Recognizing that members of the Forest Service would know the plan very well, would have spent a great deal of time working on it, and would likely be strongly committed to it, the student might focus on a limited number of points, especially those that the Forest Service might be willing to modify. The student would be wise to assume a tone that isn't aggressive or strident to avoid alienating his audience. He would articulate his most important assumptions and align them whenever possible with the beliefs and values of those who work for the Forest Service.

In the case of the arguments you'll write as an undergraduate, of course, your reader is generally your instructor. In this rhetorical situation, the most useful approach is to consider values and beliefs that your instructor holds as a member of the academic community. In writing for an economics or a political science instructor, the student arguing against the Forest Service plan should provide logical, accurate, and appropriate evidence. He should avoid strong emotional appeals and expressions of outrage or bitterness, focusing instead on developing a succinct, clearly organized, carefully reasoned essay.

thinking
rhetorically

## Guidelines for Analyzing Your Own Values and Beliefs

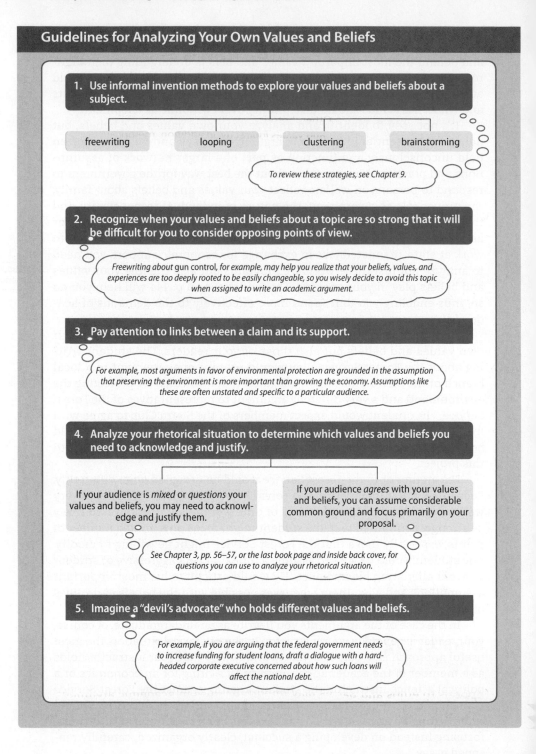

1. Use informal invention methods to explore your values and beliefs about a subject.

freewriting    looping    clustering    brainstorming

*To review these strategies, see Chapter 9.*

2. Recognize when your values and beliefs about a topic are so strong that it will be difficult for you to consider opposing points of view.

*Freewriting about gun control, for example, may help you realize that your beliefs, values, and experiences are too deeply rooted to be easily changeable, so you wisely decide to avoid this topic when assigned to write an academic argument.*

3. Pay attention to links between a claim and its support.

*For example, most arguments in favor of environmental protection are grounded in the assumption that preserving the environment is more important than growing the economy. Assumptions like these are often unstated and specific to a particular audience.*

4. Analyze your rhetorical situation to determine which values and beliefs you need to acknowledge and justify.

If your audience is *mixed* or *questions* your values and beliefs, you may need to acknowledge and justify them.

If your audience *agrees* with your values and beliefs, you can assume considerable common ground and focus primarily on your proposal.

*See Chapter 3, pp. 56–57, or the last book page and inside back cover, for questions you can use to analyze your rhetorical situation.*

5. Imagine a "devil's advocate" who holds different values and beliefs.

*For example, if you are arguing that the federal government needs to increase funding for student loans, draft a dialogue with a hard-headed corporate executive concerned about how such loans will affect the national debt.*

## strategies for success

The standards of academic argument that are discussed in this book reflect the Western rhetorical tradition as it is taught in the United States. This tradition encourages writers to clearly articulate and directly defend their values and beliefs. Other rhetorical traditions encourage writers to convey their assumptions and values indirectly. In addition, rhetorical traditions change over time.

Identifying differences between the ways in which writers are encouraged to address their values and beliefs in your educational experience and in the Western rhetorical tradition, and discussing them with your teacher and classmates, will enrich everyone's understanding of the way rhetorical practices differ in various contexts.

## for **exploration**

Think of an issue that concerns you, such as a campus controversy, a recent decision by your city council, or a broad national movement (e.g., to provide an on-campus food bank, house the homeless, or improve public transportation). After reflecting on this issue, use the guidelines presented on p. 144 to analyze your values and beliefs. Then respond to the following questions.

1. Given your values and beliefs, what challenges would writing an academic essay on this subject pose for you?

2. To what extent did your analysis help you understand that others might reasonably hold different views on this subject? Make a list of the possible opposing arguments. Then briefly describe the values and beliefs that underlie these counterarguments. How might you respond to these arguments?

3. Now write the major assertions or arguments that you would use to support your controlling idea, or thesis. Below each assertion, list the values or beliefs that your readers must share with you to accept that assertion.

4. How have the guidelines on p. 144 and this For Exploration helped you understand how to write an effective academic argument? If you were to write an academic argument on this issue, how would you now organize and develop your ideas? What strategies would you use to respond to your readers' values and beliefs?

# Mastering the Essential Moves in Academic Writing

Appeals to ethos and pathos play important roles in academic argument. For an academic argument to be effective, however, it must be firmly grounded in logos. The remainder of this chapter presents strategies that you can follow to meet the demands of academic writing. These strategies will help you to do the following:

1. Determine whether a claim can be argued
2. Develop a working thesis (an appropriately limited claim)
3. Provide good reasons and sound evidence for your argument
4. Acknowledge possible counterarguments
5. Frame your argument as part of the scholarly conversation
6. Consider whether visuals or other media would strengthen your argument

## DETERMINING WHETHER A CLAIM CAN BE ARGUED

You can't argue by yourself. If you disagree with a decision to increase school activity fees, you may mumble angrily to yourself, but you'd know that you're not arguing. To argue, you must argue *with* someone. Furthermore, the person must agree with you that an assertion raises an arguable issue. If you like hip-hop music, for example, and your friend, who prefers jazz, refuses to listen to (much less discuss) hip-hop, you can hardly argue about her preferences. You'll both probably just wonder at the peculiarities of taste.

Similarly, in academic argument you and your reader (most often your instructor) must agree that an issue is worth arguing about if you're to argue successfully. Often this agreement involves sharing a common understanding of a problem, a process, or an idea. A student who writes an argument on the symbolism of Hester Prynne's scarlet A in *The Scarlet Letter*, for example, begins from a premise that she believes the teacher will share: that Hester's A has meaning for the impact and significance of the novel.

The guidelines on p. 147 can help you compose an effective and arguable claim.

## DEVELOPING A WORKING THESIS

Arguable claims must meet an additional criterion: They must be sufficiently limited so that both writer and reader can determine the major issues at stake and the lines of argument that best address them. In a late-night discussion with friends, you may easily slip from a heated exchange over the causes of the current unrest in world affairs to a friendly debate about whether Steph Curry or LeBron James is the better basketball player.

In an academic argument, however, you must limit the discussion not just to a single issue but to a single thesis, a claim you will argue for. It's not enough, in other words, to decide that you want to write about nuclear energy or the need to protect the wilderness. Even limiting these subjects — writing about the Fukushima nuclear disaster in 2011 or the

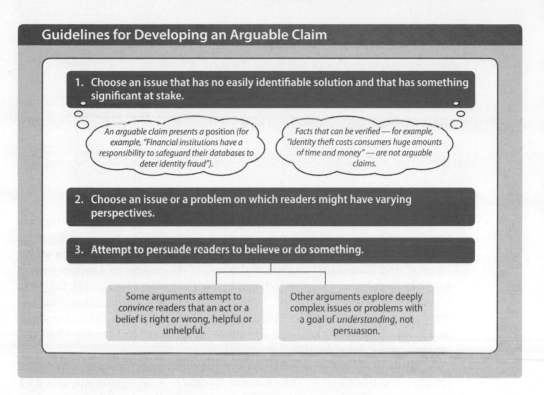

## Guidelines for Developing an Arguable Claim

1. Choose an issue that has no easily identifiable solution and that has something significant at stake.

   *An arguable claim presents a position (for example, "Financial institutions have a responsibility to safeguard their databases to deter identity fraud").*

   *Facts that can be verified — for example, "Identity theft costs consumers huge amounts of time and money" — are not arguable claims.*

2. Choose an issue or a problem on which readers might have varying perspectives.

3. Attempt to persuade readers to believe or do something.

   Some arguments attempt to *convince* readers that an act or a belief is right or wrong, helpful or unhelpful.

   Other arguments explore deeply complex issues or problems with a goal of *understanding*, not persuasion.

Forest Service's Land Management Plan for the White Mountain National Forest — wouldn't help much. That's because your thesis must be an *assertion*. In other words, it must be something to argue about.

An appropriately limited thesis makes it clear (for you and for your reader) what's at stake in your argument. For this reason, many instructors and writers suggest that academic arguments should contain an explicit thesis statement — a single declarative sentence that asserts or denies something about the topic. The assertion "The U.S. Forest Service's Land Management Plan for the White Mountain National Forest fails to protect New Hampshire's wilderness areas adequately" is an example of an arguable thesis statement.

Developing a clear, limited thesis statement can help you as a writer stay on track and include evidence or details relevant to the main point rather than extraneous or loosely related information. Readers — especially busy readers like your instructors — also find thesis statements helpful. A clearly worded thesis statement helps instructors read your writing more efficiently and critically.

Here is the first paragraph of an essay written for a class on Latin American history. The thesis statement is highlighted. Notice how it clearly articulates the student's position on the topic, the role of multinational and transnational corporations in Central America.

Over the past fifty years, Latin American countries have worked hard to gain economic strength and well-being. To survive, however, these countries have been forced to rely on multinational and transnational corporations for money, jobs, and technological expertise. In doing so, they have lost needed economic independence and have left themselves vulnerable to exploitation by foreign financiers.

A clear thesis statement can help both writer and reader stay on track as they "compose" or read an essay.

Often thesis statements appear early in an essay. In her analysis of the "mirror" and "flashlight" models of the role of journalists in American society that appears in Chapter 5, Hope Leman articulates an explicit thesis statement at the beginning of the second paragraph of her essay: "In this essay, I will argue that the 'flashlight' model provides a more accurate and complex understanding of the role of journalists in America than the 'mirror' model does" (p. 107).

Thai Luong takes a different tack in his analysis of Carr's op-ed calling for the reinstatement of the Fairness Doctrine. Thai begins his essay by summarizing Carr's s argument. Thai goes on in the second paragraph to note his initial acceptance of Carr's position but adds that he finds himself with some significant questions and reservations, which he details in his third paragraph. As will be discussed more fully later in this chapter, Thai spends the bulk of his essay carefully analyzing Carr's text, reserving final judgment until his concluding paragraph, where he summarizes his analysis by stating that "although [Carr] falls short of making a compelling case for the reinstatement of the Fairness Doctrine, he still reminds readers of the important role we play in consuming (and in some cases sharing) the news." (p. 129).

Both approaches represent thoughtful and effective responses to the writers' specific assignments. Hope Leman's assignment required her to take a position on her topic, so it made sense for her to present her thesis statement early on. (Hope was also writing under time pressure since she was completing a take-home midterm.) Thai Luong's assignment was more general: to respond to and evaluate Carr's column. It thus made equally good sense for him to defer his final judgment until he completed this analysis and demonstrated his ability to engage Carr's ideas via his own critique.

Sometimes you may develop a working thesis early in your writing process. This is especially likely if your assignment requires you to take a stand and specifies the options available to you, as Hope Leman's assignment did. At times, however, you may have to think—and write—your way to a thesis. In situations like this, you'll develop your thesis and gather evidence recursively as you deepen your understanding of your topic and your rhetorical situation. This chapter concludes with a case study of one student writer, Daniel Stiepleman, whose argument evolved in this way. Reading Daniel's prewriting and drafts will help you better understand how to work through the process of making and supporting claims in academic arguments. Often you will discover, as Daniel did, that you need to explore your ideas at considerable length before determining your thesis.

## PROVIDING GOOD REASONS AND SUPPORTING THEM WITH EVIDENCE

To support a claim in a way that readers will find truly persuasive, you'll need to provide good reasons. Chapter 5 discusses two tools for analyzing and evaluating arguments: stasis theory (p. 114) and Aristotle's three appeals (pp. 120–22). You can use the same analytical tools to construct and revise your own arguments.

Let's say that you've drafted an argument challenging increased standardized testing in public schools. You're majoring in education, and you have strong feelings about federally mandated assessments. Your draft explores your ideas as freely and fully as possible. Now it's two days later—time to step back and evaluate the draft's effectiveness. So you turn to Aristotle's three appeals.

As you reread your draft with the appeals of ethos, pathos, and logos in mind, you realize that you've gathered a lot of evidence about the limitations of standardized testing and thus made good use of appeals to logos. Your argument is much less successful in employing the appeals of ethos and pathos, however. Your rereading has helped you realize that the passion you bring to this subject caused you to write in a strident tone, which might make readers distrust your credibility and sense of fairness. You also haven't considered the advantages of standardized testing or the reasons that some people find such testing helpful and even necessary. Critical readers might well suspect that you've stacked the deck against standardized testing.

*thinking rhetorically*

Clearly, you need to strengthen your argument's appeal to ethos. You revise your tone so that it's more evenhanded; you also consider multiple points of view by presenting and evaluating possible counterarguments. Perhaps in the process you'll discover some shared values and beliefs that can strengthen your argument. (You could acknowledge your opponents, for instance, for recognizing the importance of education as a national, and not just a local, concern.) You'll want to find as many ways as possible to demonstrate that you realize your subject is complex and that reasonable people might have different ideas on the best way to address it.

What about pathos? In rereading your essay, you realize that in gathering strong evidence to support your claim, you've failed to give your subject a human face. You've got plenty of statistics and expert testimony but little that demonstrates how standardized testing affects real students and teachers. Based on your own experiences and those of peers, you have good examples of how standardized testing can have a negative impact, so you write yourself a reminder to include at least one such example in your revised draft. You also look for other ways to remind readers that national debates over standardized assessment aren't about impersonal test scores but about the real-life learning and teaching experiences of students and teachers across the United States.

As this example suggests, such analytical tools as Aristotle's three appeals can play a key role in the construction of arguments. You may not use these tools to write the first draft of your argument, but once you have a rough draft you can use them to test your ideas and identify problems that need to be addressed and areas that need to be strengthened. The student who's arguing that increases in standardized testing threaten the quality of students' education, for instance, might find it helpful to identify the most important questions at issue in her argument. Are they questions of fact? definition? interpretation? value? consequence? policy?

In addition to using analytical tools, you can ask commonsense questions about the evidence that you include to support your claims. (See Questions for Evaluating Evidence, p. 151.)

---

## for **exploration**

Think again about the issue you analyzed in response to the For Exploration on p. 145. Formulate a tentative, or working, thesis statement that reflects your current position on this issue. Articulate two or three reasons or claims that support your thesis, and then list the major evidence you would use to support these claims. Finally, write a brief statement explaining why this evidence is appropriate, given your thesis statement, the reasons or claims that you have written, and your intended audience.

---

## ACKNOWLEDGING POSSIBLE COUNTERARGUMENTS

Since academic argument is modeled on inquiry and dialogue rather than debate, as a writer you must consider multiple sides of an issue. Responding to counterarguments demonstrates that you've seriously analyzed an issue from a number of perspectives rather than simply marshalled evidence to support your predetermined position.

There are a number of ways to discover counterarguments. You could imagine dialogues with one or more "devil's advocates," or you could discuss your subject with a group of classmates. You might even interview someone who holds a different position. Being aware of your own values and beliefs can also help you identify counterarguments. The student arguing against the Forest Service plan might consider the views of someone with different values, perhaps a person who believes in the importance of economic development, such as the owner of a lumber company or individuals living in towns supported by the timber industry. Finally, reading and research can expose you to the ideas and arguments of others.

How you use counterarguments will depend on your subject and rhetorical situation. In some instances, counterarguments can play an important

## Questions for Evaluating Evidence

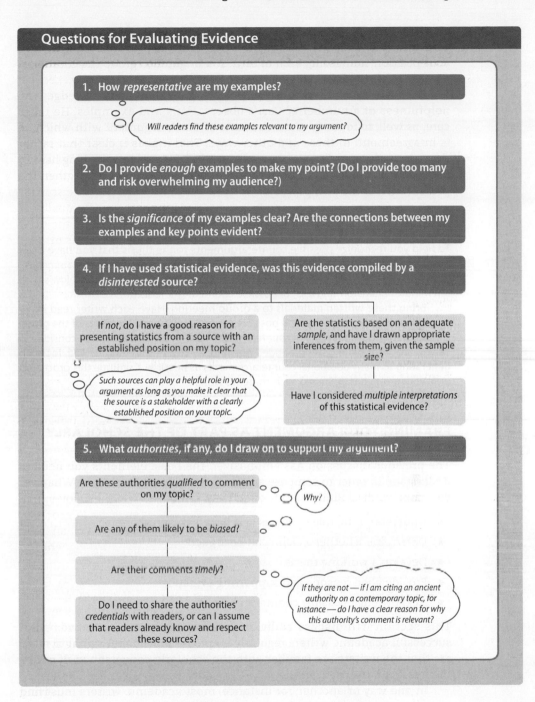

1. How *representative* are my examples?

> Will readers find these examples relevant to my argument?

2. Do I provide *enough* examples to make my point? (Do I provide too many and risk overwhelming my audience?)

3. Is the *significance* of my examples clear? Are the connections between my examples and key points evident?

4. If I have used statistical evidence, was this evidence compiled by a *disinterested* source?

If *not*, do I have a good reason for presenting statistics from a source with an established position on my topic?

> Such sources can play a helpful role in your argument as long as you make it clear that the source is a stakeholder with a clearly established position on your topic.

Are the statistics based on an adequate *sample*, and have I drawn appropriate inferences from them, given the sample size?

Have I considered *multiple interpretations* of this statistical evidence?

5. What *authorities*, if any, do I draw on to support my argument?

Are these authorities *qualified* to comment on my topic?

> Why?

Are any of them likely to be *biased*?

Are their comments *timely*?

> If they are not — if I am citing an ancient authority on a contemporary topic, for instance — do I have a clear reason for why this authority's comment is relevant?

Do I need to share the authorities' *credentials* with readers, or can I assume that readers already know and respect these sources?

structural role in your essay. After introducing your topic and indicating your thesis, for example, you might present the major counterarguments to your position, addressing each in turn. You might also group the counterarguments, responding to them all at once or throughout your essay.

In his essay in Chapter 5 (pp. 126–29), Thai Luong acknowledges the helpfulness of a number of Carr's observations and examples. He takes care, as well, to identify those elements of Carr's argument with which he is in agreement. In these and other ways, Thai makes it clear that rather than simply looking for reasons to disagree with Carr he is working hard to engage his ideas seriously and respectfully. The effect is to strengthen the presentation of his own position.

## for **collaboration**

To help you recognize possible counterarguments to the thesis that you have been developing in this chapter, first be sure that you have a clear, easy-to-read statement of your working thesis and of the major evidence you would use to support it. Now spend ten minutes brainstorming a list of possible counterarguments.

Bring these written materials to a group meeting. Have each writer read his or her working thesis, evidence, and possible counterarguments. Members of the group should then suggest additional counterarguments that the writer has not considered. As you proceed, avoid getting bogged down in specific arguments; instead, focus on generating as many additional counterarguments as possible. Continue this procedure until your group has discussed each student's work.

### FRAMING YOUR ARGUMENT AS PART OF THE SCHOLARLY CONVERSATION

The previous discussion has emphasized the basic elements you need to understand in order to compose an effective academic argument. Whatever your topic or discipline, to argue effectively you need to do the following:

- Understand the role of values and beliefs in argument
- Determine whether a claim can be argued
- Develop a working thesis
- Provide good reasons and supporting evidence
- Acknowledge possible counterarguments

This section will discuss additional essential rhetorical "moves" that successful academic writers regularly employ—moves that signal to readers that the writers are familiar with the scholarly conversation of which their essays are a part.

In one way or another, for instance, most academic writers must find a meaningful way to *enter the conversation* that grounds or motivates their topic. In her essay in Chapter 5, for instance, Hope Leman begins her discussion by contrasting the "mirror" and the "flashlight" models of media theory, making it clear that her essay will represent her own take on this ongoing controversy. In her essay synthesizing the views and positions of Clay Shirky and David Croteau on the role of technology in the classroom, also in Chapter 5, Elizabeth Hurley uses the opportunity to engage essays by these authors to remind herself "that student–teacher relationships and engaged learning remain the most important aspect of education despite all of the technological changes" (p. 136).

Fostering the ability of students to enter into and contribute to the academic conversation is a major goal of this book. Chapter 5 and this chapter provide essential information on such topics as analysis, synthesis, and making and supporting claims. Daniel Stiepleman's essay, at the end of this chapter, provides a detailed example of how one student moved from an initial mixed response to a public service announcement (PSA) on literacy to a final position on this topic, one that required him to do a careful, in-depth reading of both the text and the visual design of that PSA. The material in Chapter 7, "Doing Research: Joining the Scholarly Conversation," will also help you master such strategies as summarizing, quoting, and interpreting sources that are integral to the scholarly exchange on your topic.

Although you may not realize it, you already have considerable experience with the kind of rhetorical strategies, or "moves," that play a key role in academic arguments. Imagine that you and a group of friends are trying to decide where to go out to eat. One friend explains that since she had pizza for lunch she doesn't want that for dinner. Another suggests the new Ethiopian restaurant in town, which she tried a few weeks ago. The others aren't sure they're feeling that adventurous, so the friend who wants to go to the Ethiopian restaurant checks some online reviews of the restaurant and reads selected observations to the group, commenting as she reads. Other friends respond, raising issues about the cost, the atmosphere, and the spiciness of the food. In so doing, they add their own perspectives to the conversation. Finally, the group agrees to try the restaurant.

You've had countless conversations like this. What you may not have realized is that in these conversations you are enacting some of the fundamental rhetorical moves of academic writing:

- Explaining
- Synthesizing
- Responding

In the previous example, for instance, the first friend *explained* why she didn't want pizza for dinner. The friend arguing for the Ethiopian restaurant went online, found reviews of the restaurant, and *synthesized* those evaluations of it. The rest of the group *responded* by raising additional issues and, finally, agreeing to give the restaurant a try.

Of course, in academic argument these moves can be a bit more complicated. A student who is *explaining* the ins and outs of a topic or an argument may do so by summarizing her own ideas or those of others by paraphrasing or quoting. In academic writing, the process of *synthesizing* most often involves identifying connections and contradictions within a text or group of texts that you have analyzed. And *responding* can take a wide variety of forms—from agreeing or disagreeing to granting part of an argument or a position but resisting another part and so forth. In academic argument and analysis, writers rely on these moves to locate themselves in the scholarly conversation to which they wish to contribute.

Chapter 3 includes an essay by Alia Sands titled "A Separate Education" (pp. 60–63). In the excerpts below, notice how the highlighted words call attention to the moves Alia makes as she articulates her response to Richard Rodriguez's chapter "Aria," from *Hunger of Memory: The Education of Richard Rodriguez.*

*Explains* two major positions on bilingual education she will address

> While some argue that students benefit from learning in their native languages, others, like writer Richard Rodriguez, argue that bilingual education deprives students of a shared public identity, which is critical to their full participation in civic life. (par. 1)

*Responds* to incorrect assumption her teacher made about students in her class and provides correct information

> Unfortunately, our instructor did not speak Spanish and assumed that none of us spoke English. In fact, more than three-fourths of the students in the class were bilingual, and those who weren't bilingual only spoke English. (par. 5)

Distinguishes her experience from Rodriguez's and thus *responds* to his argument

> Unlike Rodriguez, before that class I had always had a sense of myself as part of the public community. (par. 12)

*Synthesizes* her experience and Rodriguez's

> As my experience and Rodriguez's demonstrate, schools play an active role in shaping students' sense of themselves as individuals. (par. 13)

Those engaged in scholarly conversation recognize that the ability to summarize the views of others accurately and fairly is an essential skill.

A final essential move in academic writing involves *showing what's at stake in your argument*—explaining why the issue you are discussing is important and why readers should care about it. In her essay on the "mirror" and the "flashlight" models of the role of journalists in Chapter 5, for instance, Hope Leman closes her essay by emphasizing that the power of the media makes it important for readers to have the richest possible understanding of the kinds of choices journalists make.

Whereas Hope makes this move at the end of her essay, Thai Luong begins his essay by summarizing Carr's work, emphasizing the importance of the issues Carr raises, and articulating some questions of his own. In so doing, he emphasizes what is at stake in his analysis and creates an opening for his own analysis of the issues raised by Carr's text.

This chapter began by discussing the model of argument that informs academic writing and emphasized that this model is based much more on inquiry than on debate: Rather than defeating opponents, the goal of academic argument is to enter the many rich scholarly conversations that occur in all the disciplines. The "moves" described thus far can help you enter these conversations in productive and rewarding ways.

## for **exploration**

Reread Thai Luong's essay in Chapter 5 (pp. 126–29) with an eye toward identifying rhetorical "moves" discussed in this chapter. Identify at least three moves that enable Thai to participate effectively in the scholarly conversation on his topic.

## USING MEDIA TO STRENGTHEN YOUR ARGUMENT

Images, sound, graphics, and video play an increasingly important role in communication today. Everywhere we turn—when we walk down the street, listen to a podcast, watch television, or surf the web—images, sound, and graphics compete for our attention (and, often, for our money: think of the power of such logos as Target's red-and-white bull's-eye or audio jingles such as State Farm Insurance Company's "Like a good neighbor, State Farm is there"). Most news media rely heavily on photographs, audio clips, video clips, interactive graphics, and so forth to heighten the impact of their stories.

The use of digital and oral media and visually rich print texts is not limited to professionals, though: Thanks to user-friendly software, we can all create texts that mix words, images, sound, and graphics. But what role should such texts play in the academic writing you do as a student? Because academic argument typically emphasizes logos over ethos and pathos, rhetorical common sense suggests that you should use digital and audio media and visually enriched alphabetic texts when they strengthen the substance of your argument. Tables, charts, graphs, maps, and photographs

thinking rhetorically

can usefully present factual information that appeals to logos and helps the writer build credibility as well.

In writing about the fragmentation of bobcat habitats in the Pocono Mountains of Pennsylvania, for example, biology student Suzanne Chouljian used a number of images and graphics to good effect. In her research proposal, Suzanne hypothesized that urbanization and barriers such as highways have cut off dispersal across urban areas, causing inbreeding among bobcat populations in her area. To help readers visualize her area of study, Suzanne included three maps: the first of the Pocono Mountains; the second of the area around the Tobyhanna and Gouldsboro State Parks, where the study was to take place; and the third of two state-designated Important Mammal Areas (or IMAs) in the study area.

Suzanne also included a table identifying the chromosomal characteristics of domestic cats, Canadian lynx, and local bobcat populations to show the ten characteristics she would be studying in the genomes of local bobcat populations. Through use of these visual elements, Suzanne strengthened her research proposal. The guidelines on p. 159 will help you make the most effective use of images and graphics in your academic writing.✱

✱  **For more about multimodal composing, see Chapter 11.**

Chouljian 8

## Research Design and Methods

### *Study Site*

Bobcats will be sampled from an area within Monroe County, located in the Pocono Mountains (Fig.1). The primary study area is approximately 832 km$^2$ and is surrounded by a 16.5 km buffer zone, producing a total area of roughly 3,900 km$^2$. The entire study site is bordered by heavily populated cities including Wilkes-Barre, Scranton, Pittston, Hazleton, Effort, Stroudsburg, and Tannersville, along with numerous smaller cities. Major roads and highways (I-380, I-80, I-84, routes 115 and 209) bisect the area.

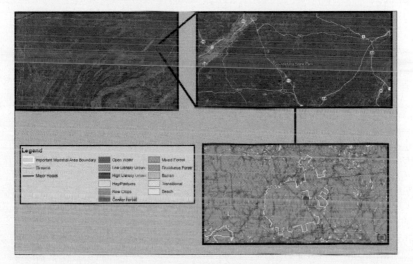

Figure 1. (a) The Pocono Mountains region of Pennsylvania. (b) Area near Tobyhanna and Gouldsboro State Parks, bisected by highways and major roads (I-380, I-80, I-84, routes 115 and 209, etc.) and surrounded by large cities (Wilkes-Barre, Scranton, and Stroudsburg). (c) Most of IMA 36 and a small part of IMA 35, and illustrating the types of land cover across the study site. Source: (a, b) Google Maps, (c) Pennsylvania Game Commission's website (http://www.portal.state.pa.us/portal/server.pt?open=514&objID=814362&mode=2).

Chouljian 15

*DNA Analyses*

Nuclear DNA will be extracted from hair and tissue samples using the DNeasy purification kit (Qiagen Inc.). Hair samples with at least five follicles are ideal for DNA extraction and will be utilized as often as possible, though Mills et al. (2000) describe successful extraction from samples with at least one hair follicle. Ten primers (Table 1) designed for microsatellite loci in the genomes of the domestic cat, the Canada lynx, and the bobcat will be used in polymerase chain reactions (PCR) to amplify microsatellite loci for each sample (Croteau et al. 2012; Reding et al. 2013).

[a]Table 1

Characteristics of domestic cat, Canada lynx, and bobcat microsatellites

| Locus | Species | Repeat Motif | [e]Chromosome | Size range (bp) |
|---|---|---|---|---|
| [b]FCA023 | Domestic cat | Di | B1 | 151–163 |
| [b]FCA045 | Domestic cat | Di | D4 | 166–178 |
| [b]FCA077 | Domestic cat | Di | C2 | 152–168 |
| [b]FCA090 | Domestic cat | Di | A1 | 117–129 |
| [b]FCA096 | Domestic cat | Di | E2 | 191–219 |
| [c]LC109 | Canada lynx | Di | Unknown | 182–202 |
| [c]LC110 | Canada lynx | Di | Unknown | 92–104 |
| [c]LC111 | Canada lynx | Di | Unknown | 157–217 |
| [d]BCE5T | Bobcat | Tetra | Unknown | 257–318 |

[a]As reported in Reding et al. (2013)
[b]Reding et al. (2013); taken from Menotti-Raymond et al. (1999)
[c]Reding et al. (2013); taken from Carmichael et al. (2000)
[d]Reding et al. (2013); taken from Faircloth et al. (2005)

**Student Essay Using a Table as Evidence**

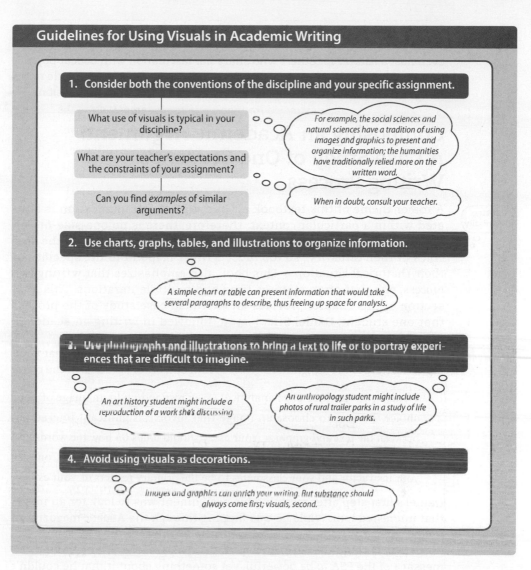

## Guidelines for Using Visuals in Academic Writing

**1. Consider both the conventions of the discipline and your specific assignment.**

What use of visuals is typical in your discipline?

*For example, the social sciences and natural sciences have a tradition of using images and graphics to present and organize information; the humanities have traditionally relied more on the written word.*

What are your teacher's expectations and the constraints of your assignment?

Can you find *examples* of similar arguments?

*When in doubt, consult your teacher.*

**2. Use charts, graphs, tables, and illustrations to organize information.**

*A simple chart or table can present information that would take several paragraphs to describe, thus freeing up space for analysis.*

**3. Use photographs and illustrations to bring a text to life or to portray experiences that are difficult to imagine.**

*An art history student might include a reproduction of a work she's discussing*

*An anthropology student might include photos of rural trailer parks in a study of life in such parks.*

**4. Avoid using visuals as decorations.**

*Images and graphics can enrich your writing. But substance should always come first; visuals, second.*

Suzanne Chouljian was writing a research proposal for a class using the medium of print. But what if she were creating a website to support her undergraduate thesis on this same topic? Her goal? To create a rich repository of information about local bobcat populations that would continue beyond her graduation. In this case, Suzanne might include real-time video of bobcats traversing known travel paths and the results of her DNA analysis of bobcat fur she collected at her study site. She might include links to research reports by other scientists studying bobcat populations or the effects of habitat fragmentation on other animals. She might also incorporate a podcast or video where she explains what attracted her to this project. The possibilities for communicating with others about her interest in this topic are almost unlimited. Suzanne might decide to create a blog on this topic. She could even host a listserv for others who share her fascination with bobcat populations and habitat fragmentation. In so doing, she would be, as Aristotle notes in *The Rhetoric*, taking advantage of all the available means of persuasion.

# Composing an Academic Argument: A Case Study of One Student's Writing Process

*thinking rhetorically*

A major theme of this textbook is that written communication is situated within a particular context; therefore, there is no one-size-fits-all approach to writing. Instead, just as designers must respond to the specifics of their situation, so too must writers respond to the specifics of their rhetorical situation.✱ This book also emphasizes that writing is a *process*, one that often requires time and multiple iterations. This final section of this chapter provides an extended case study of the process that one student, Daniel Stiepleman, followed in writing an academic argument.

When Daniel composed this essay, he was a student in a first-year writing class. Here is the assignment given to him and other students in the class:

> Write a two- to three-page analytical essay responding to an image of your choice. Be sure to choose an image that involves significant interaction between the text and graphics. Your essay should focus on how the words and graphics work together to generate the image's meaning and impact. Consider your instructor and your classmates to be the primary readers of your essay.

Daniel's first step after receiving his assignment was to look for an image that interested him. While he was flipping through the *Atlantic* magazine, a public service announcement (PSA) for the National Center for Family Literacy (NCFL) caught his eye. An aspiring English teacher, Daniel found the message of the PSA to be powerful, yet something about it that he couldn't quite put his finger on troubled him. In order to explore his initial response to the PSA, Daniel decided to annotate the text and image, using the Questions for Analyzing Visual Texts in Chapter 2 (pp. 41–42) as a guide. You can see the PSA with Daniel's annotations on p. 161. Daniel was working on a writing project that he would deliver in print, so his focus was on static visuals. If you were composing a writing project that would be delivered electronically, such as a presentation using PowerPoint or Prezi slides or a video presented online, you would want to consider a broader range of media. But the basic precepts in the Guidelines chart on p. 159 would remain true.

---

✱ To review the concept of the rhetorical situation, see Chapter 3.

When he first encountered the PSA, Daniel thought that the text's argument was easy to summarize: Literacy improves lives. While annotating, Daniel noticed some details that he didn't catch at first, such as the way the layout and type style underscore the simplicity of the PSA's message. The more he looked at his notes and re-examined the image and words, the more he wondered *why* simplicity was such a central part of the message. He also started to think about what the NCFL was trying to accomplish with the PSA and how other readers of the *Atlantic* might respond to it. And he still wasn't sure what it was about the message as a whole that troubled him.

## DANIEL STIEPLEMAN'S ANNOTATION OF THE PUBLIC SERVICE ANNOUNCEMENT

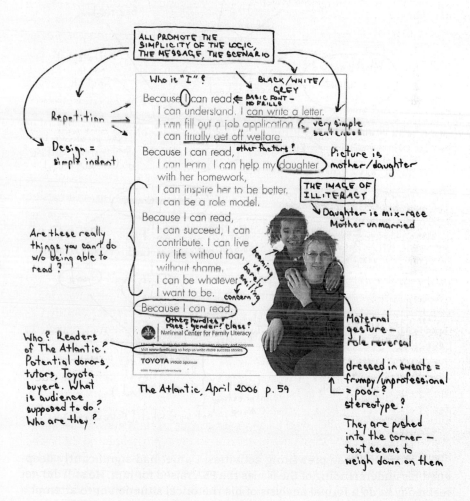

At this point in his writing process, Daniel's primary purpose was to engage as fully and critically as he could with the PSA that he had chosen to analyze. In order to explore his ideas more fully, Daniel decided to create a cluster on the word *illiteracy* to explore his response.✱ After evaluating his cluster, Daniel realized that the causes and effects of illiteracy are more complicated than the PSA acknowledges—and that he had a promising topic for an essay.

## DANIEL'S CLUSTER

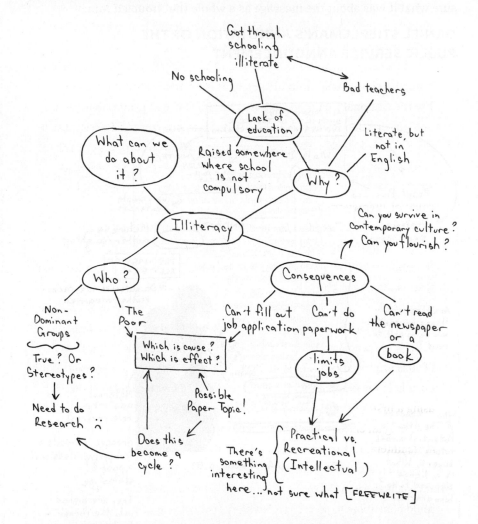

Thanks to these prewriting activities, Daniel had significantly deepened his understanding of the issues the PSA raised for him. He still did not feel ready to do a formal analysis of his rhetorical situation or to attempt a carefully structured first draft, so he decided to write a discovery draft.

✱ For more on invention strategies, see Chapter 9.

## DANIEL'S DISCOVERY DRAFT

Literacy, often taken for granted, is a gift. The ability to read text not only offers opportunities for escape and entertainment but gives access to ideas that challenge our own limited worldviews, thus allowing each of us to expand our understandings of our lives on our own terms, at our own pace. The generation of text allows for the further development and sharing of our own ideas with others, at a time when much of the world has lost reverence for oral traditions. Literacy is a gift.

Several organizations exist to help share this gift, but they are underfunded and need help from the public. It is for this reason that groups like the National Center for Family Literacy (NCFL) print public service announcements (PSAs). Obviously these announcements, which appear in magazines and newspapers, are directed toward an educated and literate audience. The task of the men and women who design these advertisements is to convince readers to donate time and/or money toward the cause of literacy training.

In my essay, I want to analyze a PSA that appeared in a recent issue of the *Atlantic* magazine. This PSA uses both text and an image to affect the emotions of the reader. The PSA consists of a series of "Because I can read" statements. The "I" is presumably the woman pictured with a young girl who seems to be the daughter mentioned in the advertisement, though they don't look that much alike. The woman pictured in the PSA stares directly at readers and explains some of the many real-world ways her life has improved because of literacy: "I can fill out a job application … I can help my daughter with her homework … I can be a role model." By using a first-person narrator, the advertisement is, I think, very successful at adding an emotional element that can inspire people to want to help more illiterate Americans improve their lives. Even though some of the things that are stated in the PSA may not be necessarily linked with literacy, such as when she says, "I can contribute" (certainly there are ways she could contribute to society even without being literate), I think this flaw in the logic of the PSA is subtle enough that an American who is flipping through his or her magazine would probably not notice it.

After reviewing his discovery draft, Daniel realized that while it represented a good start on his essay, he still had considerable work ahead of him. Here's what Daniel wrote about this draft in his journal.

**DANIEL'S JOURNAL ENTRY**

> Now that I've got some distance from this draft, I can see that it really is just a starting point. Right at the end something clicked with me: a flaw in the logic of the PSA. I tried to dismiss it; I even thought about deleting it because it would be easier for me to write about the value of literacy. But the fact of the matter is that the logic behind this ad really is problematic. This is going to be harder to write about, but it's also a more interesting and provocative idea. I think that I need to rewrite with this idea (or something like it) as my thesis. I'm a little frustrated at having to start over, but the truth is that I probably wouldn't have noticed this problem with the PSA if I hadn't written this draft.

Thanks to the preceding activities, which encouraged him to explore his response to the PSA, Daniel now felt ready to undertake a more formal exploration of his situation and goals as a writer. This was the moment, he decided, when it made sense for him to consider his controlling purpose and rhetorical situation and to do so in writing. Here is Daniel's analysis.

**DANIEL'S RHETORICAL ANALYSIS**

thinking
rhetorically

> I am writing an analytical essay for my composition class. I want to persuade my readers—my instructor and my classmates—that there are some disturbing assumptions behind the National Center for Family Literacy's public service announcement. If my readers are anything like I am, their first impressions will be that the ad must be good because it promotes literacy. I'm worried this will lead them to resist my argument that literacy isn't, as the ad implies, an easy solution to the problem of inequity. I've got to be convincing by using evidence, both from the text and from other sources.
>
> How will I persuade them to accept my argument? After all, I had to write my way to seeing it. What tone should I adopt—an objective tone or a passionate one? I'm inclined to try the latter, but I know our instructor said that being objective is usually a more effective strategy. Plus that may help it sound less like I'm arguing that the PSA's negative consequences are on purpose. I'll need to be careful in my analysis of the PSA.

Daniel also decided to develop a plan for his essay. As Daniel noted in his journal, he is a visual thinker, and so traditional outlines don't work well for him. So he came up with the visual map below, which helped him imagine how his essay might be organized. It includes several questions he thought he should address, reminders to himself, definitions of terms, and general comments. He used his plan to further explore his ideas and to determine the best organization for his essay. Although probably no one but Daniel could develop an essay from the diagrams and notes he created, the plan fulfilled his needs—and that's what counts.

## DANIEL'S PLAN FOR HIS ESSAY

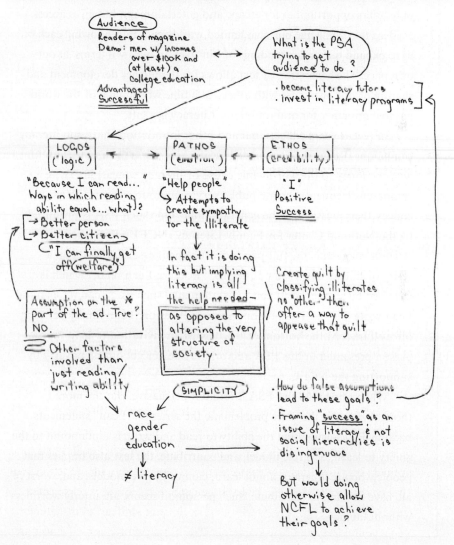

Daniel was now ready to write a formal draft. He had a clear controlling purpose: He wanted to critically examine the logic and design of the NCFL PSA and to convince his readers that although the ability to read and write is valuable, literacy cannot by itself solve the problem of poverty. Here is Daniel's first formal draft of his essay. (Notice that for Daniel's first draft, he has not yet created the necessary works cited page, and his in-text citations are incomplete.)

## DANIEL'S FIRST DRAFT

Literacy, often taken for granted, is a gift. The ability to read text not only offers opportunities for escape and entertainment, but gives access to ideas that challenge our own limited worldviews, thus allowing each of us to expand our understandings of our lives on our own terms, at our own pace. The generation of text allows for the further development and sharing of our own ideas with others, at a time when much of the world has lost reverence for oral traditions. Literacy is a gift.

In recent years educational and other foundations have run literacy campaigns designed to persuade literate Americans to donate their time and/or money to the worthwhile cause of literacy education. These campaigns frequently create public service announcements (PSAs) to convey their message to the general public. One such PSA is produced by the National Center for Family Literacy (NCFL). Published in *Atlantic* magazine, the full-page advertisement essentially sets up a series of linked statements. It begins, "Because I can read," which is followed by a series of "I can ..." statements, such as, "I can understand. I can write a letter. I can fill out a job application. I can finally get off welfare." At the bottom of the page is an invitation to help the person presented in this PSA and others like her get out of poverty by supporting the NCFL.

When I first read this PSA, I found it persuasive. But the more I thought about it, the more problematic the series of "I can" statements became. By asserting that the ability to read and write is tantamount to the ability to learn, be a role model, and contribute, the text also implies that people who are illiterate cannot learn, cannot be role models, and, worst of all, have nothing to contribute. Such persons, it seems, are utterly worthless without literacy.

The people reading *The Atlantic* are not illiterate. In fact, according to the magazine's website, the average reader of *The Atlantic* is a man in his early fifties with a college degree and a median household income of over $150,000. The image incorporated into the NCFL's "Because I can read" PSA is certainly not that of the typical reader of *The Atlantic*. The image is of a woman with an approximately ten-year-old girl, presumably her daughter, who is significantly darker skinned. The girl's father does not appear in the photograph. The image of illiteracy, then, is a single mother with a mixed-race child.

Can literacy solve this woman's problems? American society is immensely stratified; 58 percent of black and 62 percent of Hispanic children live in low-income households, as opposed to only 25 percent of white children (NCCP). According to the 1999 U.S. Census data, black and Hispanic Americans ("Hispanic" was still classified as a race in the 1999 census data) are twice as likely as European Americans to be unemployed. Those who work have a weekly income far less than whites—over $100 a week less for blacks, and almost $200 a week less for Hispanics (United States Census Bureau).

The NCFL PSA suggests that being able to read will magically get the woman portrayed in the ad off welfare. In reality, more highly educated black and Hispanic people are only slightly more likely to find work (as compared with equally educated whites) than their less-educated counterparts (United States Dept. of Education). Literacy does not equal social equality. Yet that is precisely what this PSA implies.

This PSA presents illiteracy as a problem of others who have not had the same advantages (role models, educational opportunities, membership in a dominant class or sex) as the readers. In so doing, it displays the inherent inequalities of our culture, but also offers an unrealistically simple solution to the problem—literacy. Given its purpose, the PSA is effective—but it is also a lie because it ignores the root causes of illiteracy. Granted, helping more Americans to become literate could be one step toward greater equality. So the question remains: Is the cumulative effect of this PSA harmful or good?

After writing this draft, Daniel knew that he would benefit from setting it aside for a while. After a day had passed, he decided to use the Questions for Evaluating Focus, Content, and Organization to analyze what he had written.✱ Here is his analysis.

✱ See Chapter 10, p. 280.

**Focus:** I think I do a good job of raising questions about the PSA. I wonder if I come on too strong, however. I also wonder if my focus is narrow and clear enough. I see that I don't write much about how the graphics and text interact. Our instructor specifically mentioned this in the assignment, so I need to pay more attention to that.

**Content:** I talk about how literacy affects income, and I think that's important. But looking back at the draft, I see that I don't really explain what other factors might cause a person to be poor. I definitely need to do some more research. I wonder, too, if I should include the PSA or describe it more thoroughly so that I can focus readers' attention on the parts of the PSA that are most important. I'd better go back to the PSA to decide which are the most important parts.

**Organization:** I'm not happy with my intro and conclusion. I kept the same introduction from my discovery draft mainly because I didn't want to worry about it. I'll need to change that. I like how I conclude with a question, but I wonder if it isn't more important to answer that question instead. There's still lots to do, but at least I can see that my ideas are taking shape.

When Daniel analyzed the first draft of his essay, he realized that although he had done a good job of exploring and raising questions about the PSA, his essay wasn't as effective as it could be.

Fortunately for Daniel, his teacher included in-class peer response sessions for all major writing assignments in their class, so Daniel was able to revise his essay and share it with members of his writing group for feedback. His second draft is presented here, with some of the group members' comments. (Notice that his essay now has a title and that he has revised it in significant ways. This early draft includes some source citations, not yet in final MLA form.)

## DANIEL'S SECOND DRAFT WITH PEER COMMENTS

Daniel's second draft had many strengths, which members of his writing group acknowledge. But they had suggestions for improvement as well. A number of them commented on the evidence in paragraph 3, asking for more background on what Daniel meant by "the systematic stratification of American society." Several readers wanted to know more about the PSA's goals and suggested that Daniel's negative tone made his overall argument less convincing than it could be.

Literacy in America: Reading between the Lines

Daniel Stiepleman

A woman and girl look straight at us. Their relationship to one another is unclear, but the girl, maybe ten, stands over the woman with a hand on her shoulder—she seems, unexpectedly perhaps, almost maternal. Huddled together in the lower right-hand corner, they are cradled between a thin border and text. A series of connecting statements takes up the bulk of the page. "Because I can read," it begins in the opposite corner in simple, black font, which is followed, in slightly indented gray, by a series of "I can" statements: "I can understand. I can write a letter. I can fill out a job application. I can finally get off welfare." The call and response repeats: "Because I can read . . . Because I can read . . . Because I can read." This page, a public service announcement (PSA) by the National Center for Family Literacy (NCFL), appears in the *Atlantic* magazine. From its short diction to its basic design to its three-color scheme, everything about this ad reinforces the simplicity of its logic: "Because I can read, I can succeed." This simplicity is reassuring and hopeful, but it's more than that; it's deceptive.

In order for the woman portrayed in this PSA to gain her worth through literacy, we are urged to accept that without reading and writing she is worthless. Asserting that once she learns to read, she can "learn . . . be a role model . . . [and] contribute," the PSA implies that people who cannot read or write cannot learn, cannot be a role model, and, worst of all, have nothing to contribute. It is here where both the simplicity and the logic of the NCFL's message begin to fall apart. The message becomes that people who are illiterate are worthless, and that must be why she is still on welfare. But perhaps even more astonishingly, literacy is supposed to magically solve her problems.

This assertion ignores the systematic stratification of American society. Is illiteracy alone the reason why 58 percent of all black children and 62 percent of all Hispanic children in America currently live in poverty, while only 25 percent of white children do (National Center for Children in Poverty)? Will literacy training change the fact

Great opening!
—Parvin

Really compelling description. I like the idea that the simplicity of the design reflects the simplicity of the logic. But I'm having trouble imagining the design: Can you show a picture of it?
—Eric

It sounds like you're saying the NCFL is deliberately insulting the people they help, but I don't think that's what you mean. Maybe you could start by explaining what they're trying to do with the ad?
—Kyong

Good evidence. Are there similar statistics for women?
—Parvin

**Where does this information come from?**
**–Kyong**

that, according to the 1999 U.S. Census data, black and Hispanic Americans are twice as likely as white Americans to be unemployed? Or that those who do work make an average of over $100 a week less than whites if they're black and almost $200 a week less if they're Hispanic? It seems unlikely that simply "Because I [or any illiterate

**I'm not sure I follow you. What are the other reasons? Why wouldn't being able to read help a person succeed? Maybe you could answer the questions that start the paragraph.**
**–Eric**

person] can read . . . I can succeed." The NCFL's suggestion otherwise is an unfortunate confirmation of the great American myth that anyone can pull him- or herself up by the bootstraps through simple, concerted effort, with only his or her ability and desire standing as obstacles in the way.

This PSA's potential for success relates directly to the degree to which it does not depict reality. The ad suggests that all the illiterate people in America need to achieve worth—based on its assumption that they are, without literacy, worthless—is to gain the ability to read and write; and it counts upon the readers' inexperience with both poverty and illiteracy to maintain its fiction. This is a safe bet as,

**This sounds a little harsh.**
**–Eric**

according to the *Atlantic*'s website, the magazine's average reader is a man in his early fifties with a college degree and a median household income of over $150,000.

**This is a strong conclusion. But your overall argument might be more effective if you acknowledged the positive aspects of the ad — maybe in the introduction?**
**–Parvin**

But the Census statistics portray a different image of America; it is a country in which the woman portrayed in the PSA will not so easily change her stake in the American dream. The injustice done by maintaining the myth of equal opportunity outweighs any good the NCFL can hope to accomplish with its ad. Looking at the woman more closely now, she seems somehow to know this. The girl is beaming, but there is a hesitance I see in the woman's smile. Am I projecting upon the image, or is there, in her face, concern? Her concern would be apt; she is shoved into the corner, held there, like so many Americans, beneath the

**I love how you circle back to the image in your conclusion.**
**–Kyong**

weight of a text that would take the rich and daunting complexity of our multicultural society and give it short diction, basic design, and a three-color scheme. The illusion of simplicity.

After Daniel contemplated his readers' responses, he recorded his reactions and ideas in his journal. Daniel's comments indicate that the peer response process helped him gain much-needed distance from his writing.

## DANIEL'S RESPONSE TO PEER COMMENTS

At first, I had some resistance to my writing group's comments. I've worked hard on this essay and taken it quite far, given my first draft. But after reading their comments and taking some time to think, I can see that they pointed out problems that I was just too close to my essay to see. Most important, I think I need to work some more on my tone so readers understand that I'm questioning the PSA's assumptions, not the value of literacy itself or the work of the NCFL.

Several readers suggested that I include a new introductory paragraph that sets up the situation and explains what the PSA is trying to do. I thought quite a bit about this and tried out a few new paragraphs, but I kept coming back to the paragraph as it was. I really like this paragraph, so I decided to try to address their concerns by writing a new second paragraph.

Parvin commented that while I have evidence to support my claims, none of it cites the situation of women. Now that I think about it, this is very odd, given the nature of the PSA. I'll check additional sources of information so I can include that.

The rest of the comments seem relatively minor — less revision than editing. I need to fix citations in the text and prepare the works-cited page. Then I'll be really close to a final draft!

In reflecting on his group's responses, Daniel does a good job of taking their comments seriously while also holding to his own vision of his essay. It's not possible to show all the stages that Daniel's draft went through, but the final draft demonstrates that his analysis of his readers' responses enabled him to revise his essay fully, to "see again" how he could most effectively make his point. Daniel's final draft begins on p. 173.

## DANIEL'S FINAL DRAFT

In the process of writing his essay, Daniel was able to articulate what was at first only a vague sense of unease about the National Center for Family Literacy PSA. As he moved from his first draft to the second, Daniel was able to identify why the ad concerned him. He clarified the problems with the PSA's logic in his third draft while also attending more carefully to the interplay of words and graphics in the PSA.

Daniel's final draft, you will probably agree, develops an argument that is not only persuasive but also stylish. His tone is more evenhanded, his paragraphs are more coherent, and his language is more polished than in his second draft. The effort that Daniel put into his essay more than paid off. This effort required planning: Daniel knew that he would have to work his way to a clear sense of purpose, audience, and organization, so he built in the necessary time for prewriting, drafting, and revising. The result is an engaged, persuasive analysis and a good demonstration of the inseparable nature of academic analysis and argument.

Stiepleman 1

Daniel Stiepleman
Professor Chang
English 100
21 March 2019

Literacy in America: Reading between the Lines

A woman and girl look straight at us. Though they look nothing alike, they are apparently mother and daughter. The girl, maybe ten, stands over the woman with a hand on her shoulder; it is she who seems maternal. Huddled together in the lower, right-hand corner of the page, they are cradled between a thin border and text. This text, presumably the words of the woman pictured, takes up the bulk of the page. "Because I can read" begins in the upper left-hand corner in simple, black font. This is followed, in slightly indented gray, by a series of "I can" statements: "I can understand. I can write a letter. I can fill out a job application. I can finally get off welfare." The call and response repeats: "Because I can read . . . Because I can read . . . Because I can read."

When I came across this page in *The Atlantic* magazine (see Fig. 1), the image of the girl and the woman was what first caught my eye, but it was the repeated statement "Because I can read" that captured my imagination. Its plainness was alluring. But as I read and reread the page, a public service announcement (PSA) designed to solicit donations of time and money for the National Center for Family Literacy (NCFL), I grew uncomfortable. The PSA, with its short diction, basic design, and black-and-white color scheme, reinforces the simplicity of its logic: "Because I can read, I can succeed." This simple message, though it promotes a mission I believe in, I fear does more harm than good.

The problem is with the underlying logic of this PSA. If we as readers believe the "Because I can read" statements, we must also believe that without literacy the woman in the PSA is worthless. Asserting that because a person can read, she "can learn . . . be a role model . . . [and] contribute," the PSA implies that people who cannot read or write cannot learn, cannot be role models, and, worst of all, have nothing to contribute to society. This is

*Margin notes:*

Stronger introduction focuses readers on image being analyzed

New paragraph extends context

Copy of PSA included so that readers can judge for themselves

Revised thesis statement is more balanced

Stiepleman 2

Fig. 1. NCFL Public Service Announcement. *Atlantic*, April 2006.

the real reason, the PSA suggests, why the woman portrayed in the photograph is still on welfare. But perhaps even more astonishing, literacy is supposed to be a quick fix to her problems.

This assertion ignores the systematic stratification of American society. Is illiteracy alone the reason why 60 percent of all black children and 61 percent of all Hispanic children in America currently live in poverty, while only 26 percent of white children do (National Center for Children in Poverty)? Will literacy training change the fact that, according to 1999 U.S. Census data, black and Hispanic Americans are twice as likely as white Americans to be unemployed? Or that those who do work make, on average, between $100 and 200 a week less than whites (406)? In the case of the woman pictured in the PSA, should literacy indeed lead her to a job, she is likely to make half as much money as a man with the same demographics

---

**New evidence added to strengthen argument**

**Sources are cited**

Stiepleman 3

who works in the same position (United States, Dept. of Education). It is not my intent to undermine the value of being able to read and write, but given the other obstacles facing the disadvantaged in America, it seems unlikely that simply because someone learns to read, he or she "can succeed."

**Less accusing tone wins readers over**

The benefits and opportunities for success extend well beyond a person's ability to fill out a job application. Race, class, and gender are powerful forces in our society, and the obstacles they present are self-perpetuating (Rothenberg 11–12). Even a well-educated person, if she is from a minority or low-income group, can find it overwhelmingly difficult to land a well-paying job with possibilities for advancement. The lack of simple things that middle-class readers of *The Atlantic* take for granted — the social connections of a network, the money for a professional wardrobe, a shared background with an interviewer — can cripple a job search. The NCFL's suggestion otherwise is an unfortunate reinforcement of the great American myth that anyone can pull him- or herself up by the bootstraps, with only his or her ability and desire standing as obstacles in the way.

**New paragraph provides examples of obstacles that could prevent a literate person from succeeding**

The PSA suggests that all the illiterate people in America need to achieve worth is the ability to read and write. But Americans disadvantaged by race, class, or gender will not so easily alter their position in our stratified culture. As long as we continue to pretend otherwise, we have no hope of changing the inequities that continue to be an inherent part of our society. For this reason, as much as I value this PSA's emphasis on the importance of literacy, I question its underlying logic.

**Language is more balanced**

Looking at the woman portrayed in the PSA more closely now, she seems somehow to know that her and her daughter's lives cannot improve so easily. Though the girl is beaming, there is a hesitance I see in the woman's smile and concern in her face. And it is apt; she is shoved into the corner, held there, like so many Americans, beneath the weight of a text that would take the rich and daunting complexity of our multicultural society and give it the illusion of simplicity.

Stiepleman 4

Works Cited

Koball, Heather. "Low-Income Children in the United States (2005)," National Center for Children in Poverty, Columbia University, Mailman School of Public Health, Sept. 2006, www.nccp.org /publications/pub_577.html.

National Center for Family Literacy. Advertisement. *The Atlantic*, Apr. 2006, p. 59.

Rothenberg, Paula S. *Race, Class, and Gender in the United States: An Integrated Study*. 9th ed., St. Martin's P, 2013.

United States, Census Bureau. "Labor Force, Employment, and Earnings." *Statistical Abstract of the United States: 1999*, Printing.

—, Department of Education, Institute of Education Sciences. National Center for Education Statistics, 1992 National Adult Literacy Survey, 1992, nces.ed.gov/pubsearch/pubsinfo .asp?pubid=199909.

## for **thought, discussion, and writing**

**1.** This chapter has presented activities designed to improve your understanding of academic argument. The For Exploration on p. 145, for instance, asks you to identify the values and beliefs that have led you to hold strong views on an issue. The one on p. 150 asks you to formulate a working thesis and to list the major evidence you would use to support it. Finally, the group activity on p. 152 encourages you to acknowledge possible counterarguments to your thesis. Drawing on these activities, write an essay directed to an academic reader on the topic you have explored, revising your working thesis if necessary.

**2.** This chapter focuses on argumentative strategies that apply across the curriculum. Now that you have read it once, take a few moments to review the chapter to remind yourself of the topics and strategies covered. Then take five minutes to list the most important understandings that you have gained as a result of reading this chapter.

**3.** Newspaper editorials and opinion columns represent one common form of argument. If your college or university publishes a newspaper, read several issues in sequence, paying particular attention to the editorials and opinion columns. (If your school doesn't publish a newspaper, choose a local newspaper instead.) Choose one editorial or opinion column that you believe represents a successful argument; choose another that strikes you as suspect. Bring these texts to class and be prepared to share your evaluations of them with your classmates.

# 7

# Doing Research: Joining the Scholarly Conversation

In some ways, learning to write for academic audiences is like traveling to a new country and learning a new culture: You may have to learn new approaches to familiar tasks, find ways to apply what you already know to a new environment, and master entirely new skills. And these are not things you will do just once. Since scholars in different disciplines examine similar topics in different ways, what works in one course may not work in another. What's important is developing the strategies and habits of mind that will help you determine how your academic audience approaches issues, frames questions, defines evidence, and uses research tools. These strategies and habits will guide you as you gather, analyze, and interpret the sources that are the backbone of a good academic argument. And they will also continue to serve you well long after you leave college: Strong researchers know how to adapt to new audiences, workplaces, and cultures, so they can communicate effectively in any situation.

In Chapter 1, rhetoric was defined as "a practical art that helps writers make effective choices . . . within specific rhetorical situations." Research is also a rhetorical process. Understanding your rhetorical situation will help you make good choices in every step of the way, from selecting topics, defining research questions, and developing strategies for exploration to filtering search results, supporting your claims with evidence, and documenting your sources appropriately and ethically. Asking yourself the Questions for Analyzing Your Rhetorical Situation as a Researcher (on the next page) can help you respond appropriately to your situation and assignment.

thinking rhetorically

## Habits of Mind for Academic Research

In Chapter 2, you learned about the habits of mind that are essential to success in college. (See pp. 23–28.) These same habits also drive successful researchers. Academic research is a learning process that can be

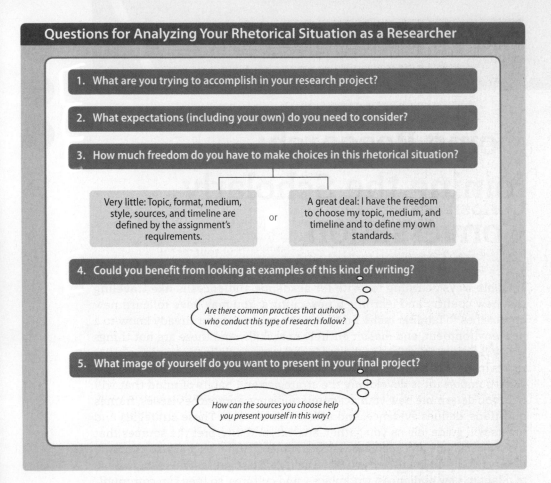

**Questions for Analyzing Your Rhetorical Situation as a Researcher**

1. What are you trying to accomplish in your research project?

2. What expectations (including your own) do you need to consider?

3. How much freedom do you have to make choices in this rhetorical situation?

Very little: Topic, format, medium, style, sources, and timeline are defined by the assignment's requirements.

or

A great deal: I have the freedom to choose my topic, medium, and timeline and to define my own standards.

4. Could you benefit from looking at examples of this kind of writing?

Are there common practices that authors who conduct this type of research follow?

5. What image of yourself do you want to present in your final project?

How can the sources you choose help you present yourself in this way?

simultaneously frustrating and rewarding. It requires you to take risks, to reconsider things you thought you knew, and to start before you know for sure where your process will lead. It is driven by curiosity, open-minded exploration, and engagement with new ideas. You will need flexibility, persistence, and creative thinking to get through it. And, in the end, you will synthesize your ideas with the ideas, facts, images, and concepts you find to create an argument or interpretation that is uniquely yours.

## ● CHOOSING A TOPIC AND FINDING YOUR FOCUS

Would it surprise you to hear that most undergraduates say that getting started is the most difficult part of the academic research process? It is natural to feel anxious and uncertain at this stage. Research requires a lot of time and effort, and early in the process there is a lot that you cannot know. Will you find enough sources on your topic? Will you figure out what you want to say? Many students feel pressure to choose a topic quickly so that they can start finding sources and making tangible progress. Writers who resist these feelings of urgency give themselves the gift of time — time that can be used to:

- Analyze the assignment and ask questions to ensure they clearly understand what they are being asked to do.
- Choose topics that spark their curiosity and interest.
- Choose topics that will support the type of research, learning, and thinking their instructors want to see.

# Curiosity

It takes courage to commit to a topic before you know whether it will work: Will it satisfy your instructor? Will you be able to find sources? Will you find a unique and compelling thesis? Some students try to manage this risk by sticking with topics they've used before (or that they know other students have used before). Fight this impulse! When you use a tired topic, it is unlikely that you will write a paper that really stands out. If you take a risk and go with a topic that you are genuinely curious about, you are more likely to create a project that is interesting to you and to your reader.

You may think that the things you are curious about are not scholarly enough to be the focus of an academic paper. Scholars study the world around them in all its complexity; do not immediately reject a topic because it seems lowbrow, niche, frivolous, or fun. The key is to figure out the types of questions scholars ask about a topic. Think about what makes you curious, and then read some articles to see how scholars approach those topics:

- Are you fascinated by puzzles or problems and interested in how things work? Engineers, scientists, and philosophers are some of the scholars asking these types of questions.
- Do you like to explore the world with your senses, discovering new tastes, smells, colors, textures, and sounds? So do psychologists, artists, anthropologists, and nutritionists — to name a few.
- Are you motivated to understand other people and their thoughts and feelings? So are scholars in fields like literature, history, marketing, psychology, and sociology.

All of these sparks can lead you to interesting, researchable topics. Curiosity is at the heart of a good research process. It is what drives scholars to discover new things. The amount of freedom you have to choose a topic can vary greatly. When you are allowed to choose your own topic, take the time to analyze your assignment carefully to make sure that your choice is appropriate. Consider the amount of time you have, what you are being asked to do with the topic (to report, to analyze, to argue), and the types of sources you are being asked to use.

# Source Requirements

When you are doing research on your own, you have control over all of your choices as a researcher. This is not the case when you are doing research to complete an assignment, and you can expect that any research assignment will place some constraints on you as a researcher. Sometimes, you are required to engage with specific types of sources. As soon as you get your assignment, review the requirements and make sure you understand them. If you don't know what "government documents" or "peer-reviewed articles" are, ask! You may have to read between the lines and confirm that you understand the types of sources that will let you do what the assignment is asking you to do. (Common source types are listed in the following chart.) For example, if you have an assignment that requires you to summarize the "current research" on a topic, your instructor probably expects you to find and read research articles in scholarly (or peer-reviewed) journals. If you need to discuss a current political debate, you will need to refer to articles in newspapers or magazines.

## Guidelines for Identifying Source Types

| Source Types | Purpose | Audience |
|---|---|---|
| Reference sources | Well-organized sources of factual information. | Varies. Some are broadly general (*Wikipedia, Webster's Dictionary*). Others are used by specific communities (*Sax's Dangerous Properties of Industrial Materials*). |
| Books | Longer, in-depth examinations that frequently place people, places, and events in a broader context. | Varies. Some books are written by experts for scholarly audiences. Others are written for general audiences by professional writers or journalists. |
| Magazines | A combination of news items and longer features and think pieces on a variety of topics. Usually published weekly or monthly. | Most are written for nonexpert audiences. Some focus on topics of general interest like politics (*Time, Economist*) or science (*National Geographic, Scientific American*). Many focus on narrower interests (*MacWorld, Cooking Light, Field & Stream*). |
| Scholarly journals | Used by scholars to share new research and discoveries. Usually published monthly or quarterly.* | Written by experts (scholars and scientists) for other experts in the same field. Most scholarly journals focus on work in a specific academic discipline or subfield. |

* For more about the peer review process, see p. 201.

| Source Types | Purpose | Audience |
|---|---|---|
| Newspapers and other published news sources | Factual coverage of breaking news in print or broadcast form. Most news outlets also publish reviews and opinion pieces (editorials, op-eds) on a variety of topics. Updated frequently, at least daily and sometimes more often. | Created for general audiences. Some have a national or international audience (*New York Times*, CNN, Al Jazeera). Others are local or regional (*Corvallis Gazette-Times*, *Syracuse Post-Standard*). |
| Blogs | Frequently updated websites on a variety of topics.<br><br>Most blogs also support reader's participation on social media and in comments. | Varies. Some are self-published with no defined audience. Some share expert or scholarly information with a broader public (*SciCurious*, *Archaeological Eye*). Others aggregate information on a topic (*TechCrunch*). Many traditional publications now include blogs on their websites (*Atlantic*, *New York Times*). |
| Government documents | Varies. Common purposes include:<br><br>● Information and education<br>● Establishing a historical record of actions taken by the government (*Congressional Record*)<br>● Reporting the results of expert research and scientific study | Varies. Most US government publications are openly accessible to all citizens (although there are exceptions), but some are primarily used by specialized audiences or communities.<br><br>● Educational publications are written for general audiences (*California Driver's Manual*).<br>● Research reports (*Morbidity and Mortality Weekly Report*) inform the public and support professionals working in relevant fields. |

Every one of these requirements tells you something important about the skills and learning that your instructor wants you to demonstrate in your final product. Even something as mundane as a page limit will tell you about the scope and depth of your analysis. You should think about these constraints when you consider different topic areas and choose a topic that will allow you to engage with the types of sources your instructor wants to see. If these sources are new to you, you probably won't be able to do this without some additional information. One of the best ways to understand the types of topics that are being discussed in your required sources is to browse through some examples. If you are required to use peer-reviewed journal articles, ask your instructor (or a librarian) to recommend some useful journals to browse. If you are required to use books, ask a librarian to point you to some potentially useful titles in the stacks, or use Google Books (books.google.com) to browse digital versions of relevant texts. Keep your mind open, and look for topics that spark your curiosity.

## Considering Multiple Perspectives

Here's another reason to let curiosity drive your research process: Keeping your mind open to different points of view is easier to do when you are learning about a topic than when you already have a specific argument or thesis in mind. Researchers in psychology and communications have demonstrated that when people feel strongly about an issue, they are less likely to notice sources that contradict their beliefs. As an academic writer, your ethos✱ is closely connected with openness, the habit of mind that welcomes new ways of thinking. When you show that you have critically examined all aspects of a topic, considered different points of view, and taken your readers' perspectives into account, your conclusions are likely to be more persuasive to academic readers.

*sense of right or wrong*

*thinking rhetorically*

Think about the types of topics that academic writers address. They are often big questions like "Should the government regulate hate speech?" or "Should there be cooperative international action against global warming?" On the surface, these are yes-or-no questions, but if you dig deeper, you will find that people who answer "yes" (or "no") to questions like these often have very different reasons for their position. You will want to explore all these reasons as you construct your own unique argument. Doing so will help you present yourself as the kind of thinker who carefully considers multiple perspectives, critically evaluates new ideas, and refines his or her ideas in light of new information—in short, as the ideal academic writer.

Remember what you learned in Chapter 2 about interacting with your texts and posing questions as you read and listen. Academic research is iterative; that is, it requires you to repeat steps in the process. As you learn more about your topic, you think of new questions to ask. It is the questions you ask, even more than the answers you find, that move your process forward. Think creatively as you explore.

## Hands-On Research

Direct, hands-on research activities can be a great way to generate new questions about your topic. Try some of these strategies, particularly if you are feeling blocked or stuck:

● Find an expert on your campus or in your community to interview.

✱ For more on Aristotle's appeals of logos, ethos, and pathos, see Chapter 5, pp. 120–21.

- Survey people who have had firsthand experience with the issue you are exploring.
- Go to public events or spaces on your campus, and spend some time intentionally observing what goes on.

Keep track of the ideas, thoughts, and questions that occur to you, and follow up on them when you search the published literature. Contextualize your observations by comparing them to research studies and other accounts. Use the literature on your topic to see if the themes that emerge in your interviews or observations are common or unusual. On the flip side, you can also use these hands-on methods to help you understand and analyze what you find in books and articles. Ask an expert to explain her perspective on a research study in her field; ask students to comment on claims made in the popular press about paying for college. The guidelines below can help make your hands-on research productive.

Do not expect to use the data you collect using hands-on methods as evidence to support broad claims. Researchers who use these methods to draw generalizable conclusions carefully design their surveys and studies according to established protocols. For example, the survey you do in your residence hall cannot be used to show what "most undergraduates in the

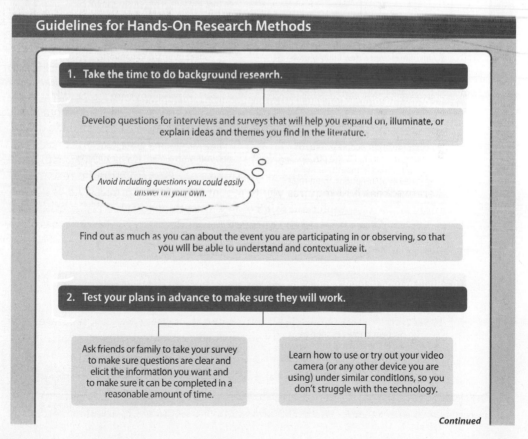

**Guidelines for Hands-On Research Methods**

1. **Take the time to do background research.**

Develop questions for interviews and surveys that will help you expand on, illuminate, or explain ideas and themes you find in the literature.

*Avoid including questions you could easily answer on your own.*

Find out as much as you can about the event you are participating in or observing, so that you will be able to understand and contextualize it.

2. **Test your plans in advance to make sure they will work.**

Ask friends or family to take your survey to make sure questions are clear and elicit the information you want and to make sure it can be completed in a reasonable amount of time.

Learn how to use or try out your video camera (or any other device you are using) under similar conditions, so you don't struggle with the technology.

*Continued*

*Guidelines continued*

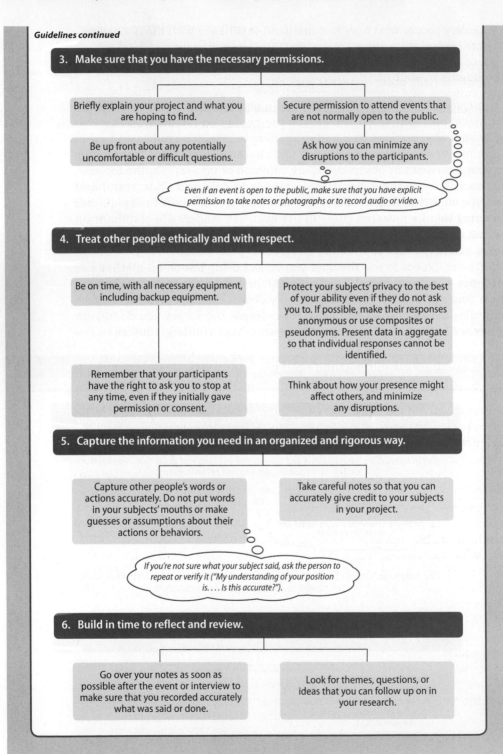

**3. Make sure that you have the necessary permissions.**

Briefly explain your project and what you are hoping to find.

Secure permission to attend events that are not normally open to the public.

Be up front about any potentially uncomfortable or difficult questions.

Ask how you can minimize any disruptions to the participants.

*Even if an event is open to the public, make sure that you have explicit permission to take notes or photographs or to record audio or video.*

**4. Treat other people ethically and with respect.**

Be on time, with all necessary equipment, including backup equipment.

Protect your subjects' privacy to the best of your ability even if they do not ask you to. If possible, make their responses anonymous or use composites or pseudonyms. Present data in aggregate so that individual responses cannot be identified.

Remember that your participants have the right to ask you to stop at any time, even if they initially gave permission or consent.

Think about how your presence might affect others, and minimize any disruptions.

**5. Capture the information you need in an organized and rigorous way.**

Capture other people's words or actions accurately. Do not put words in your subjects' mouths or make guesses or assumptions about their actions or behaviors.

Take careful notes so that you can accurately give credit to your subjects in your project.

*If you're not sure what your subject said, ask the person to repeat or verify it ("My understanding of your position is. . . . Is this accurate?").*

**6. Build in time to reflect and review.**

Go over your notes as soon as possible after the event or interview to make sure that you recorded accurately what was said or done.

Look for themes, questions, or ideas that you can follow up on in your research.

U.S. believe" because the sample of students isn't representative of all the different types of students across the country. But this does not mean that you cannot use what you learn firsthand in your project or paper. A survey of students in your dorm could be mined for data about the students on your campus, and quotations from students in your dorm could be used to personalize national research conducted by another researcher. Just be careful and precise about how you use your hands-on research, and be sure to connect it to the broader conversation.

**A note about ethics.** When you use any of the hands-on methods described previously, you have an important responsibility to treat anyone who agrees to help you with your project with respect. In a research context, this means ensuring that they consent to participate and doing everything you can to protect their privacy. When professional researchers study human subjects, they must prove that the research will be beneficial and adhere to a detailed set of ethical standards to minimize risk to the participants. Before they can even begin research, their projects must be reviewed and approved by their IRB (Institutional Review Board). For most classroom projects, you will not be required to undergo formal review even if you are gathering data from human subjects, but you should still take your ethical responsibilities seriously.

# ● LEARNING ABOUT YOUR TOPIC

Your main goal in exploring a topic is to figure out what you think and what you want to argue—to find a focus for your research. The goal of academic research isn't to find a point of view you agree with and repeat it. You are not looking for a single source that gives you the "truth." Instead, you're constructing your argument, building it out of the facts, figures, theories, concepts, ideas, and arguments that have been developed by a community of thinkers over the years. Your argument will still be original and creative, but it won't come out of nowhere. It will be a part of an ongoing conversation in which you have an opportunity to create connections between new ideas and what you already know. When you do not find a personal focus, academic writing can feel more like editing, paraphrasing someone else's ideas to fit a formula. It is in the connections among ideas that you show your own unique perspective and creative thinking.

In the early stages of a typical academic research process, you will read and consider many ideas that you do not end up using in your final project. Your goal is to explore ideas, and at first you will not know exactly what will be relevant in the end. As your focused argument emerges from your reading and thinking, deciding which sources to consider more carefully will become easier. Expand your perspective by reading widely in many genres. Read actively and critically, asking questions as you go.✱

✱ See Chapter 2 for more on genres (pp. 16–19) and reading critically (pp. 29–38).

---

## for **exploration**

As you explore, develop a system to capture the ideas that occur to you as you read. Post-it Notes can be very useful for capturing ideas because they are portable and easy to move around, but any method that will allow you to examine and re-examine your thoughts will work: note cards, a spreadsheet, or even a simple text document. Periodically, pull out your collection of ideas, lay it out, and look for connections. If you are a linear thinker, consider using timelines or outlines to organize your thoughts. If you are more visual, use sketches, a mind map, or a cluster diagram. (See Chapter 6, p. 162, and Chapter 9, p. 259.) As you recognize recurring themes or ideas, expand your system so that you can connect sources to themes. For example, you might use a different color or symbol for each theme and then mark your sources with that visual reminder.

---

# Search Terms and Keywords

The most important thing to understand about keyword searching in academic research is this: There is no such thing as a perfect search. In an academic research process, you will do dozens of different searches. You will try and retry different combinations of keywords, refining your initial broad search in many directions. You will try the same keyword combinations in different search tools, knowing that each tool might yield something new. Some of these attempts will succeed, and some will fail. Persistence is essential. Flexible thinking—a willingness to try new things and consider new sources—can help you along the way.

When you do a keyword search in a database or search engine, the computer looks for exact (or close to exact) matches for your terms in the information it has stored. Although some systems may be programmed to make common substitutions for you, for the most part computers do exactly what you tell them to do. This means that you will need to make some guesses about the specific words and phrases that are likely to be used in the articles, books, and other sources stored in your database. The better educated these guesses are, the more effective the search is likely to be. Thinking in terms of the rhetorical situation(s) that *produced* your potential sources will help. Once you realize that magazines, newspapers, journals, and websites are published with specific audiences or communities in mind, you can tailor your key terms to the communities for whom the texts were written in the first place.✱ The chart "Questions to Ask as You Devise and Revise Your List of Keywords" on p. 187 provides some useful strategies. For example, medical professionals use the term *hypertension* to describe the condition commonly called *high blood pressure*. Thinking rhetorically, you would use the specialized term to search for articles written by and for doctors and the more common term to search for news articles written for the general public.

*thinking rhetorically*

---

✱ For more about genres and source types, see Chapter 2, pp. 16–19.

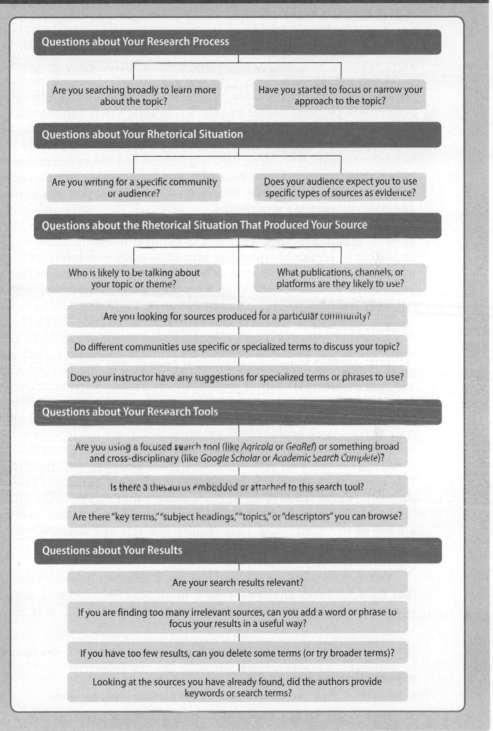

# Questions to Ask as You Devise and Revise Your List of Keywords

**Questions about Your Research Process**

Are you searching broadly to learn more about the topic?

Have you started to focus or narrow your approach to the topic?

**Questions about Your Rhetorical Situation**

Are you writing for a specific community or audience?

Does your audience expect you to use specific types of sources as evidence?

**Questions about the Rhetorical Situation That Produced Your Source**

Who is likely to be talking about your topic or theme?

What publications, channels, or platforms are they likely to use?

Are you looking for sources produced for a particular community?

Do different communities use specific or specialized terms to discuss your topic?

Does your instructor have any suggestions for specialized terms or phrases to use?

**Questions about Your Research Tools**

Are you using a focused search tool (like *Agricola* or *GeoRef*) or something broad and cross-disciplinary (like *Google Scholar* or *Academic Search Complete*)?

Is there a thesaurus embedded or attached to this search tool?

Are there "key terms," "subject headings," "topics," or "descriptors" you can browse?

**Questions about Your Results**

Are your search results relevant?

If you are finding too many irrelevant sources, can you add a word or phrase to focus your results in a useful way?

If you have too few results, can you delete some terms (or try broader terms)?

Looking at the sources you have already found, did the authors provide keywords or search terms?

# Evaluating Search Results

For the research you do to learn about your topic, you will probably use broad, general purpose search tools like search engines, discovery layers, or multidisciplinary databases.✲ Using these powerful tools, your exploratory searches will likely return thousands (even millions) of results. To make this manageable, these tools use algorithms—the mathematically based instructions that enable automated decisions—to predict which results will be most useful to you. To do this, the programmers who develop the tools will make some guesses, or assumptions, about what their typical user values. While most research tools will provide some helpful information to users, their algorithms and the assumptions that inform them are kept secret. As a user, you cannot make decisions based on how the algorithm works. Therefore, it is essential that you routinely and critically examine your results.

Commercial search engines like *Google* want their users to have a positive experience; they want you to get useful results. However, it is important to remember that they also have their own interests to promote, and that those interests inform the choices they make for you. Sometimes, your needs will align with their goals. Sometimes, they will not. Let's consider an example to better understand this. Search engines analyze user data so that they can deliver personalized—and hopefully more relevant—results. These companies are constantly gathering data about you as you do things online. This practice also makes it easier for these companies to personalize the advertisements that you see online, which is an essential part of their business model. A clear answer that is customized to your location or habits can be useful for some research questions. If you are looking to get your car tuned up, you might appreciate that a search engine filters out options that are not in your town or not suitable for the type of car you drive. A search engine that does this is making decisions for you—decisions about what you *don't* need to see. This can be useful when you need a simple, clear answer that is based on parameters (like "closest" or "highest rated") that can be easily quantified. However, as we discussed before, most academic research questions are not so straightforward. They require analysis and interpretation. To answer them, you must construct an argument from a variety of sources representing many perspectives.

You may be wondering, "Can I just use a different research tool? One that does not make choices for me?" In an academic research process, you can (and should) use a variety of research tools.✲ But it is crucial

---

✲ For more search tools, see pp. 191–92.

✲ See pp. 191–92 (Using Common Research Tools) for more information about your options.

that you understand that in the world of online search, every product you use will use algorithms to make some choices for you. Even library databases make assumptions—like prioritizing full-text resources, or the most recent articles—that shape your search experience. And because these algorithms are secret and proprietary, you can only make educated guesses about how they work. Your best strategy is to do multiple searches, using different tools and platforms. As you learn more about your topic, use what you know to critically evaluate what you're seeing. Talk to your instructor, to classmates, and to other experts about what you might be missing.

**A final thought about bias and objectivity.**  Most people have a high degree of confidence in the objectivity and accuracy of the results they get from search engines. This is partly based on experience—the information they have retrieved in the past has been useful—and partly based on the idea that because the results are computer-generated they are inherently objective and trustworthy. The first of these assumptions has merit, but the second does not. Search engines and databases are not created in isolation; they are created by people, using existing systems of organization and knowledge. Algorithmic predictions are based on historical patterns and assume that what happened in the past will happen again in the future. It would be extremely naïve to imagine that these people (and these systems) are free of the biases and inequalities that exist in the broader culture. There is a growing body of research documenting and analyzing what information scientist Safiya Umoja Noble calls "algorithmically driven data failures"[1]: situations where these factors combine to produce search results that are unequivocally racist or sexist. When researchers do not critically question these results, they run the risk of reproducing those oppressive assumptions in their own work.

# Refining Search Results

As noted earlier, many of the research tools you will use in an academic research process are designed to predict your needs and make choices for you, and for many of your searches these default options will work just fine. However, most research tools also give you advanced options that will let you define your own parameters and priorities. You can do this in two ways. **Advanced search** features let you limit your search to resources that meet certain conditions that you define. **Facets and filters** allow you to focus, sort, or manipulate your search results.

---

[1]Safiya Umoja Noble (2018). *Algorithms of Oppression: How Search Engines Reinforce Racism*. NYU Press. P. 4.

Computers break down large or complex pieces of information and store the pieces in categories called *fields*. If you do not specify which fields you want to search, the computer will usually look for your keywords in the fields that are most commonly useful, like *title* or *abstract*. Most search tools will also allow you to override or add to these default choices and specify field(s) you want to search. For example, you can use the *author* field to retrieve all the articles written by a specific person or the *journal title* field to retrieve articles published in a particular journal. Field searching is especially powerful in specialized databases that include unique fields that are useful to the communities or disciplines they serve.

Most databases will also provide a variety of *filters*, or *facets*, that you can use to focus your results. Filters allow you to set some parameters before you search. Look for drop-down menus or checkboxes on your search screen. However, it can be easier to figure out how you want to focus or streamline your search after you review some results. With most research tools you can do a broad keyword search, and then use facets to dig into your results in a more focused way. Look for a column of options next to your results, or a row of options underneath the search box. In academic databases, these options usually include publication type; publication date; language; subject or index terms; and availability. Sometimes, you will see a number in parentheses next to a particular option. That number indicates how many sources in your results list match that particular criteria. In specialized databases, you will find unique filters and facets that can be especially powerful. For example, a musician might want to search a music database for audio clips with a certain number of beats per minute, so she would add that filter to her search. Similarly, a psychologist who is considering treatment for a teenage patient might want to search for research studies focused on adolescents, and so he would use the *study population* facet to choose *adolescents*.

Facets for refining results

Facets Screen from a Discovery Tool

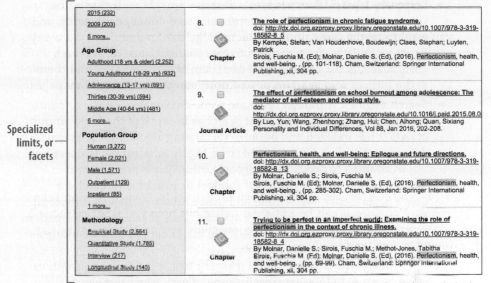

Specialized limits, or facets

Specialized Limits or Facets Available in PsycINFO (American Psychological Association)

# Using Common Research Tools

In a typical academic research process, you will use many different types of research tools. Some are broad, and some are specialized. Some are openly available on the web for anyone with an Internet connection, and others are proprietary, requiring a license or access code to use. Here is a brief overview of the tools you are likely to use during an academic research process:

- **Article (or periodical) databases:** These databases store information about articles, sometimes (but not always) including the full text of the articles. Most article databases are accessible only to subscribers or members of an institution that subscribes to them, so you will need to access these databases through your library's subscriptions. They range from broad collections of published sources (for example, EBSCO's *Academic Search Complete* or ProQuest's *Research Library*) to subject-specific tools (such as *Historical Abstracts* or *PubMed*). In between, you will find databases like *JSTOR* and *Web of Science*, multidisciplinary databases of scholarly research articles, and news databases like LexisNexis or *Ethnic NewsWatch*.

- **Library catalogs:** These databases store information about everything in a library's collection(s). This usually includes books and periodicals (but not the specific articles within those periodicals) and other useful materials specific to the library's user community. A school with a strong music program may collect sheet music, for example, or a chiropractic college may provide bones and skeletons for checkout.

- **Discovery layers:** Many academic libraries provide tools that allow you to search for content in several databases, library collections, and catalogs at the same time. The technology that makes these discovery layers work varies from campus to campus, and most of them are customized by the libraries that use them. You will usually find them in the form of search boxes posted prominently on library homepages.

- **Search engines:** Although there are some challengers, *Google* remains dominant in the area of Internet searches because of the huge amount of data it has indexed and because its ranking algorithm continues to deliver results that are perceived to be highly relevant by its users.

  In addition to *Google Search* (google.com), *Google* provides two focused search tools of particular interest to academic researchers: *Google Books* (books.google.com) and *Google Scholar* (scholar.google.com). Both tools allow you to search for specific types of scholarly information and to set your preferences to see if the materials you find are available at your library.

  While *Google* is a very useful research tool, it is not the only option when it comes to Internet search. Some privacy advocates worry about the amount of personal data it collects from its users. *Duck Duck Go* (duckduckgo.com) is a search engine that prioritizes user privacy.

# Retrieving Full Text

As you move through your research process it is almost certain that you will find yourself in this frustrating situation: You have enough information about an article to know that you want to see it, but you are not sure how to go about finding the full text. As a member of a college or university community, it is very likely that your library can help you get the books and articles you need. There is no room in this section to describe what to do in every possible scenario, but here are some useful guidelines to keep in mind:

- **Ask a librarian:** Most academic libraries are committed to getting their students access to all the resources they need to be successful in their research projects. If plan A does not work, your librarian will help you figure out plans B and C.

- **Cast a wide net:** Just because an article is not available in one database does not mean that it is not available in all databases. To find a specific article in your library collections, use the broadest, deepest research tool you can find. If your library has a discovery tool, start there. If you are not sure where to start, ask a librarian. Many libraries will provide tools, called *link resolvers*, which allow you to search quickly for your article in several databases. These tools are usually customized by the libraries that use them. If you are not sure if your library has a link resolver, ask a librarian.

Example of a Link-Resolver Button in an Article Database

- **Try your luck on the web:** You might get lucky and find a copy of your article on the author's personal website or available for free at the journal's website. You may want to check with a librarian or your instructor to make sure that the version you find this way is a good substitute for the published copy. (Authors may post prepublication [or *preprint*] versions of their articles that may be different from the version that has been peer reviewed and edited.)

- **Use interlibrary loans:** Most academic libraries will help you request articles that they do not have in their collections. These services are usually called *ILL (Interlibrary Loan)*. Today, articles are usually delivered digitally and arrive very quickly. You can also use ILL services to request books, videos, and items in less common formats. (Leave time in your schedule for the items you request to be delivered to you.)

As a rule, some types of information are more readily available on the web than others. Current newspaper articles are usually easy to find (though as a story slips off the front page it may be harder to locate). Scholarly books and articles are also easy to find on the web, but accessing the full text often costs money. You can get the same content from your library without these charges, but you may need to factor in delivery time if you request sources from other campuses or from other libraries. As you think through your research process, consider how your assignment's requirements might affect your time management.

To learn more about accessing articles that are not immediately available, use the Guidelines for Getting the Full Text of Articles on the next page.

## Guidelines for Getting the Full Text of Articles

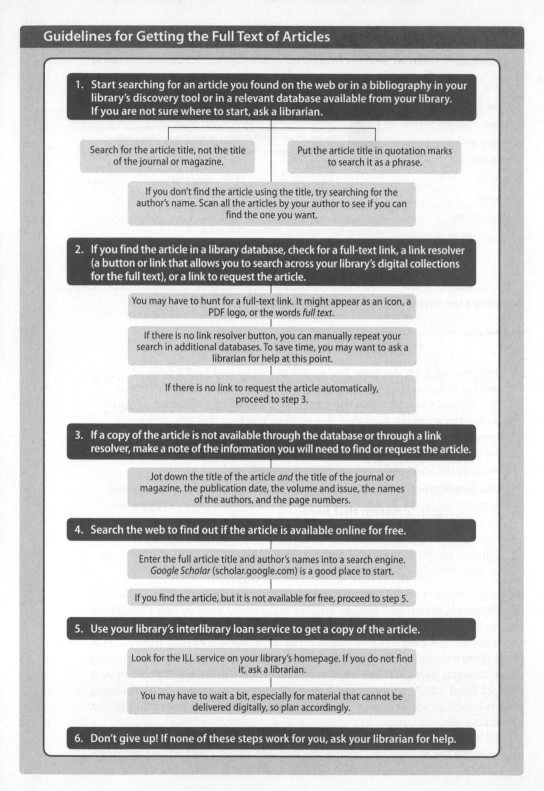

1. Start searching for an article you found on the web or in a bibliography in your library's discovery tool or in a relevant database available from your library. If you are not sure where to start, ask a librarian.

Search for the article title, not the title of the journal or magazine.

Put the article title in quotation marks to search it as a phrase.

If you don't find the article using the title, try searching for the author's name. Scan all the articles by your author to see if you can find the one you want.

2. If you find the article in a library database, check for a full-text link, a link resolver (a button or link that allows you to search across your library's digital collections for the full text), or a link to request the article.

You may have to hunt for a full-text link. It might appear as an icon, a PDF logo, or the words *full text*.

If there is no link resolver button, you can manually repeat your search in additional databases. To save time, you may want to ask a librarian for help at this point.

If there is no link to request the article automatically, proceed to step 3.

3. If a copy of the article is not available through the database or through a link resolver, make a note of the information you will need to find or request the article.

Jot down the title of the article *and* the title of the journal or magazine, the publication date, the volume and issue, the names of the authors, and the page numbers.

4. Search the web to find out if the article is available online for free.

Enter the full article title and author's names into a search engine. *Google Scholar* (scholar.google.com) is a good place to start.

If you find the article, but it is not available for free, proceed to step 5.

5. Use your library's interlibrary loan service to get a copy of the article.

Look for the ILL service on your library's homepage. If you do not find it, ask a librarian.

You may have to wait a bit, especially for material that cannot be delivered digitally, so plan accordingly.

6. Don't give up! If none of these steps work for you, ask your librarian for help.

# Staying Organized

As we've discussed at several points in this chapter, academic research is not a straightforward, linear process. It is messy and iterative. As you learn more about your topic, your argument will become clearer and more focused, but your search process may not. You might need to go back and do a whole set of new searches in a database you've searched before, or you might want to reread a chapter or article that previously seemed tangential. It is important to understand that this will not stop once you start to create your paper or presentation. Many academic writers use the process of drafting and revising as a way to develop their final argument. As you write, you may realize that you need to do some additional research, or revisit some of the sources you initially found. If you keep yourself organized as you go, your entire research process will be easier.

So why do we struggle so much with organization? Staying organized takes intent, effort, and discipline. In other words, you have to decide to stay organized, and then commit to doing a little extra work with every source you find. When you are on a roll, or coming up on a deadline, it can be easy to rationalize skipping some of these steps. Stick to your plan! Future you will be grateful.

## DEVELOP A SYSTEM

In this context, *staying organized* means keeping track of what you find, so that you can find it again when you need it. That seems simple, but it can get complicated. As you think about your system, keep these two scenarios in mind:

- You have an article in hand, or a quotation in your notes, but you are missing the identifying information you need to cite it.
- You know you read an article or excerpt that made a point you want to use, but you don't know where you read it and you can't find it again.

If you can develop a system that helps you avoid these two scenarios, you will be able to devote most of your time to the thinking, writing, and revising you need to do to create a paper that really stands out. Think about how you will record all of the necessary information about the sources you find, and how you will store your articles and notes so that they are useful to you when you begin to write.

Many students use analog methods like Post-it Notes, binders, note cards, and file folders to keep organized. These methods work just fine, especially if you tend to do most of your work in one place, like your room. There are also a host of digital tools available to help you stay organized, several of which are discussed below. Think about your workflow as a whole: How do you prefer to read? to write? to research? If you prefer to do all these things in the same digital space — on your computer or tablet — then it might make sense to find one tool that will support all of those processes. If you prefer to do one or more of these things offline — maybe you sketch out concept maps by hand or take notes in the margins of your books—you'll want to choose your tools accordingly. Each tool has different features; expect some trial and error as you figure out what works with your style.

## DIGITAL TOOLS AND CITATION MANAGERS

Most of the research tools designed for academic use—like the databases on your library's website—allow you to save useful sources temporarily, print or email them to yourself, and format the citation information. This is a useful way to stay organized during a single research session. Some database providers (like *EBSCO* or *JSTOR*) will allow you to create a personal account (separate from your library account) where you can save sources more permanently.

However, if you use several different databases and websites in a typical research project, you may want to consider a more robust option. With citation managers like *Zotero* (www.zotero.org) and *EndNote* (endnote.com), you can save, annotate, and organize sources wherever you find them. Citation managers also work with popular word processors to streamline your use of sources while you write.

Increasingly, people need to manage information across multiple computers and devices. To do this, many people are turning to tools like *Google Drive* (drive.google.com), *Dropbox* (www.dropbox.com), and *Evernote* (evernote.com). These services allow you to save your documents "in the cloud" so that you have immediate access to the most recent version from all your devices. Tools like these, and like the citation managers mentioned previously, also facilitate collaboration. When you save things online, it is much easier to share them with other people.

# Asking for Help

Many students avoid asking for help when they run into research problems because they think they should already know how to use the library or other research tools. Nothing could be further from the truth. Today's information landscape is so complex that everyone needs help navigating it sometimes.

Look for helpful resources on your library's website. Most academic libraries will provide research or subject guides to point you to useful resources for research on a topic or in a discipline. There may also be guides tailored to your specific course or assignment. You probably know that most libraries have a walk-up reference desk where you can ask questions about sources, databases, or the research process. Many libraries also provide these services online, by email, or even via a live chat. Finally, don't forget your instructor, frequently your first resource when you have questions about your research assignments.

# RESEARCH WRITING: JOINING THE SCHOLARLY CONVERSATION

Research and writing are sometimes presented as separate and sequential stages in a linear process. In reality, most academic writers move back and forth between these stages throughout their process. As you write, new questions or issues will emerge. While you are developing a supporting paragraph, you might notice that your evidence is a little weak. As you connect one idea to the next, you might realize that there is a gap in your thinking that makes the transition rough. These new questions will send you back to the sources. Academic research is iterative, nonlinear, and messy. Still, there is a point in your process when you will shift from broad exploration and learning to the more focused work of developing and supporting an academic argument.

## Synthesizing, Writing, and Citing

If research is the process of learning about a topic, how do we know when it is time to stop researching and start writing? Can't we keep learning forever? The answer to that is both simple and complex. The simple answer is: It depends when your paper is due! Academic writers are usually working against deadlines, usually deadlines set by someone else. Sometimes it is time to stop researching because the due date is approaching

On a deeper level, academic writers know that the learning process does not end when the assignment is due or the paper submitted. They think of their work as a contribution to an ongoing conversation, a conversation they may rejoin later. As an academic writer, your work should reflect your best understanding of your topic, based on your open-minded exploration of a wide variety of perspectives and ideas. But your mind should not close when your paper is done, and you may discover something in the future that inspires you to start reimmersing yourself in your topic.

People who do a lot of research often say that they know it is time to stop gathering information when they see the same themes over and over again in their sources. When that happens, you can be fairly certain that you have been thorough in your exploration and can start to focus on synthesizing the ideas, concepts, facts, and themes that have emerged along the way.

## Evaluating Sources

You start evaluating as soon as you start finding sources; sometimes you're not even aware that you're doing it. Every time you say to yourself, "That looks good" or "I think that's a tangent," you're evaluating. Once you decide to click on a source and scan it or download it to read carefully, you start evaluating at a different level. Critical reading is an essential part of this process.

In Chapter 2 you learned to question and interact with your sources constantly as you read them.✱ The questions you learned about in that chapter's discussion of analyzing a text's rhetorical situation are at the heart of critical evaluation: Who is the author? Why did he or she write this? What is her or his authority or expertise? What is the central argument? How does this source connect to the broader conversation(s) on this topic? These questions will frequently require you to do further research, and the answers you find may lead you to new questions, but they will also help you identify those sources that will push you to learn more about your topic in a complex and meaningful way. When you are choosing sources to support your own learning on a topic, your needs are your most important consideration. When you start developing an argument, however, you need to include your audience and their expectations in your evaluation process. As you figure out the claims you will be making, start thinking about supporting those claims with evidence. When you choose sources to support your claims, ask yourself, "Which of these sources will be the most convincing to my audience?" A source that is perfect in one rhetorical situation might not work in the next, even if you are writing about the same topic in both cases.✱

## Choosing Evidence

Students frequently complain that they feel disconnected from academic writing because they have to find experts who agree with their ideas; they are frustrated that teachers won't accept students' reasons and logic alone. But consider what you learned in Chapters 3 and 5 about Aristotle's appeal to ethos, or credibility.✱ The sources you choose to include in your writing say as much about you as a writer as they do about your argument. In other words, you're not just relying on your authors' ethos when you use outside sources; you're also building your own. When you use a variety of source types reflecting multiple perspectives and rigorously gathered information, you are presenting yourself as someone who is careful, thoughtful, thorough, open-minded, and able to deal with complexity. The "Questions to Consider as You Choose Sources" (pp. 199–200) can help you make sure that you are choosing the most appropriate evidence given your rhetorical situation.

---

✱ Take note of the different ways psychologist Jean Twenge uses evidence to convince her three audiences (Chapter 3, pp. 72–82).

## Questions to Consider as You Choose Sources

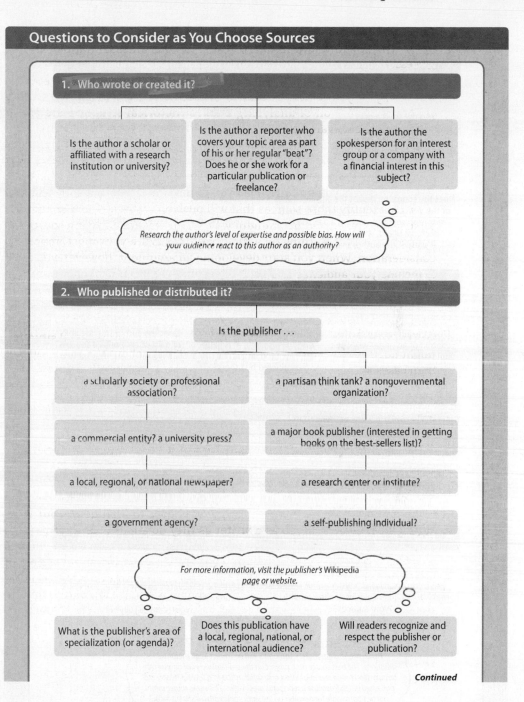

**1. Who wrote or created it?**

Is the author a scholar or affiliated with a research institution or university?

Is the author a reporter who covers your topic area as part of his or her regular "beat"? Does he or she work for a particular publication or freelance?

Is the author the spokesperson for an interest group or a company with a financial interest in this subject?

*Research the author's level of expertise and possible bias. How will your audience react to this author as an authority?*

**2. Who published or distributed it?**

Is the publisher . . .

a scholarly society or professional association?

a partisan think tank? a nongovernmental organization?

a commercial entity? a university press?

a major book publisher (interested in getting books on the best-sellers list)?

a local, regional, or national newspaper?

a research center or institute?

a government agency?

a self-publishing individual?

*For more information, visit the publisher's Wikipedia page or website.*

What is the publisher's area of specialization (or agenda)?

Does this publication have a local, regional, national, or international audience?

Will readers recognize and respect the publisher or publication?

*Continued*

Questions continued

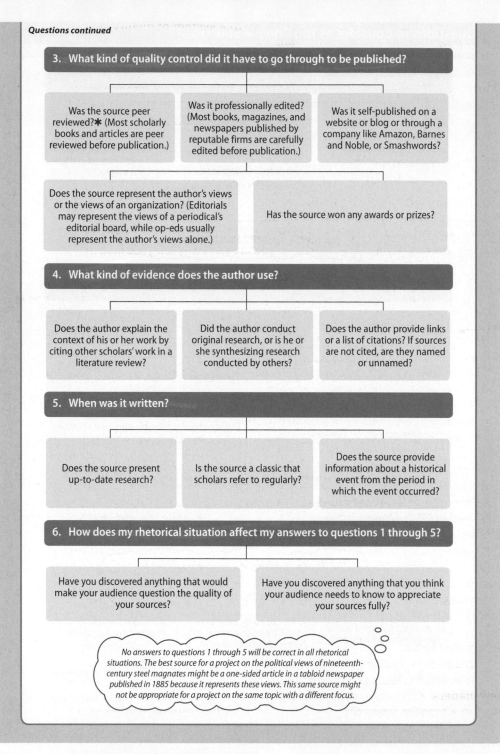

**3. What kind of quality control did it have to go through to be published?**

Was the source peer reviewed?✱ (Most scholarly books and articles are peer reviewed before publication.)

Was it professionally edited? (Most books, magazines, and newspapers published by reputable firms are carefully edited before publication.)

Was it self-published on a website or blog or through a company like Amazon, Barnes and Noble, or Smashwords?

Does the source represent the author's views or the views of an organization? (Editorials may represent the views of a periodical's editorial board, while op-eds usually represent the author's views alone.)

Has the source won any awards or prizes?

**4. What kind of evidence does the author use?**

Does the author explain the context of his or her work by citing other scholars' work in a literature review?

Did the author conduct original research, or is he or she synthesizing research conducted by others?

Does the author provide links or a list of citations? If sources are not cited, are they named or unnamed?

**5. When was it written?**

Does the source present up-to-date research?

Is the source a classic that scholars refer to regularly?

Does the source provide information about a historical event from the period in which the event occurred?

**6. How does my rhetorical situation affect my answers to questions 1 through 5?**

Have you discovered anything that would make your audience question the quality of your sources?

Have you discovered anything that you think your audience needs to know to appreciate your sources fully?

*No answers to questions 1 through 5 will be correct in all rhetorical situations. The best source for a project on the political views of nineteenth-century steel magnates might be a one-sided article in a tabloid newspaper published in 1885 because it represents these views. This same source might not be appropriate for a project on the same topic with a different focus.*

✱ For a discussion of peer review, see p. 201.

**A note about peer review.** *Peer review* refers to a system of quality control commonly used by academic journals. Peer-reviewed articles are usually written by scholars, people who are experts in a specific area of study and who develop that expertise by conducting original research. Before an article or book is published, it is reviewed by the author's peers (other experts in the same research area). These reviewers look at the research and decide if it makes a contribution to the broader conversation in the field. They may comment on the research question or method, or they may consider whether the data gathered supports the researcher's conclusions. They do not repeat the study to check its accuracy. The peer-reviewed (also called *refereed* or *scholarly*) article is one of the most common (and challenging) types of required sources. This is the type of writing that many of your professors do themselves. When you are required to use a peer-reviewed source, ask yourself, "Is this a research article published in a journal that uses peer review for quality control?" If you are not sure, ask your instructor or a librarian.

## UNDERSTANDING ACADEMIC AUDIENCES

Occasionally, you may be given an audience to consider in your academic writing. For example, in a course about grant writing, you could be told to write a proposal to a specific funding agency. Most of the time, however, you are writing for your professor (an audience of one) or more generally for an academic audience. In either case, you should find out what you can about your audience—what they do or do not value—and select your evidence wisely.

*thinking rhetorically*

There are cultures and subcultures within higher education, and what works well in one course or discipline may not be effective in another. Still, some broad generalizations apply. Most of your instructors are themselves researchers (or training to be). They write about their research, they do presentations about it, and they hope to publish their work in books and journals for other researchers to read. They build on the scholarly work that has been published before. They analyze, criticize, expand upon, and refine the work that has influenced theirs. They also do research to inspire further inquiry; they want others to build on their work. And many researchers want their work to have a positive impact on the world: to inform policy, professional practice, or cultural expression. What does this mean for you as an academic writer? It means you can assume that research and inquiry, and the kind of expertise that comes from those activities, will be valued by your academic audience. Sources that are based on research and data reflect that value.

In addition, academic audiences tend to value sources that are published in established and recognized outlets like journals, magazines, and newspapers. There are many reasons for this. Researchers ground their work in a broader scholarly conversation; they value sources that are organized and findable, now and in the future. They review one another's work, and they value sources that have also gone through some level of quality control or review. They have published (or hope to publish) their own work and understand the quality control methods embedded in the publication process.

This does not mean that all published sources are equal. As a new academic writer, you will not always know everything you need to know about the publications you want to cite. You should expect to do a little research to ensure that a publication will be credible to your readers. Here are some things to look for. Some newspapers have a national (or international) reputation and are recognized as authoritative sources, while others are written for local or regional audiences. Similarly, some magazines are widely read and will be familiar to most of your readers, while others are published for niche audiences, and you may need to explain their value. Some magazines are respected as sources of quality information, while others (like the tabloids you may have seen at the supermarket) should be read for entertainment only. Some scholarly journals have a better reputation than others. To find out about the scope, audience, and reputation of the publications you plan to use, you can go the "About" pages on their websites, use *Wikipedia*, or ask your instructor.

Finally, while these guidelines can help you make good choices when writing for academic audiences, they are not hard-and-fast rules. When you know the types of evidence your audience expects to see, you can choose sources that meet those expectations. Sometimes, however, your rhetorical situation will call for another type of source. For example, if a student writing a paper about etiquette in digital environments wanted to make a claim about the differences between Twitter and Tumblr, the best evidence they could use might be tweets and Tumblr posts, even though tweets and blog posts are not the type of sources most academic audiences would expect to see. Just be aware that if you are going to go against your audience's expectations, you should have reasons for doing so, and you should communicate those reasons to your reader. If you think you are really pushing the boundaries, talk to your instructor in advance. Academic audiences respect creative and original thinking. If you give your academic readers a good reason to consider an unfamiliar source—a reason that shows you understand and respect their expectations—they likely will agree that the source is appropriate.

# Synthesizing Information and Ideas

In Chapter 5, you learned that synthesis and analysis are closely related. In an academic research project, you will do both. As you learned in Chapter 2, effective readers interact with their sources as they read: breaking them down, asking questions, taking notes, and following up on unfamiliar ideas. This is analysis. Synthesis is the process of putting these ideas, facts, concepts, and theories together and creating something new.

Some writers find it much easier to do this as they write; the process of writing helps them make the necessary connections. These writers may write throughout their research process. Others prefer to explore their ideas in a separate planning process, outlining or mapping their ideas and then fleshing them out in a draft.

As you synthesize, you must focus on the connections among the ideas, concepts, and sources you've collected. Earlier you learned that you should develop a system for keeping organized that works with your habits and preferences as a writer. You can use this system as a starting point for your synthesis. Periodically go through your note cards, spreadsheets, documents, or pages looking for connections. Regroup or rearrange your sources to see if new themes emerge. An outline or chart (like the one below for a research paper on human trafficking in the US garment-manufacturing industry) is one way to do this. A visual map, like the one on p. 165, is another option. Post-it Notes and note cards can be grouped and regrouped into categories easily. Whatever method you use, be sure to record the source and page number along with the concept or idea to make attribution and citation easier later.

| Claims | Thought/Idea/Fact | Source | Page |
|---|---|---|---|
| Existing laws don't protect these workers | 3/4 textile manufacturing in NYC – "substandard wages and working conditions" | ITS video | n/a |
| | 61% garment manufacturers in LA violate wage/hour regs | Bonacich & Appelbaum | 3 |
| Traffickers prey on vulnerable members of society | 2/3 US cases involve foreign-born workers | USDOJ | 75–91 |
| | traffickers pretend to help those in need w/ jobs, housing, etc. | Van Impe | 114 |

# Structuring a Supporting Paragraph in a Research Project

In most research assignments, your goal is to synthesize information from a variety of reliable sources into a clear and coherent argument that is all your own. Many instructors express frustration with students who borrow their entire argument from a single source or expert or who stitch together quotes from other people without integrating their own ideas. To avoid these problems, consider using this three-part guideline for structuring supporting paragraphs in a research paper.

1. **Introduce the main point of the paragraph in a clear topic sentence.** This sentence should tell your reader what the paragraph is going to be about and how it supports your thesis. It may also make a connection to the paragraph that precedes it.

2. **Integrate your evidence.** This will usually (but not always) be material that you quote, paraphrase, or summarize from your sources. You may synthesize information from several sources to make an original point.

3. **Explain the evidence.** Do not assume that your evidence will "speak for itself." Use your own words to make the significance of your evidence clear to your reader. Use transitional words, phrases, and sentences to link the paragraph back to the thesis and to the paragraphs that precede and follow it. Leaving quotations or facts "dangling" at the end of a paragraph is a good indication that you are asking your reader to build your argument for you.

**thinking rhetorically**

You will find that this three-part structure will not work in every situation. As always, the choices you make as you write will be shaped by your rhetorical situation. It may be useful, however, to keep this structure in mind as you write and revise your papers. It will prompt you to carefully consider how well you have integrated and explained your evidence and may point out areas where you can improve your argument. Take a look this supporting paragraph from Thai Luong's essay, which appears at the end of this chapter. Notice how the paragraph connects to his central argument:＊

### Argument

With that fact in mind, it is crucial for the film industry to continue its efforts to diversify the representation of Asian Americans in American films . . . . The task ahead is two-fold: to ensure that Asian Americans are better represented in a diverse variety of roles in film and that their roles accurately reflect the complexities of the Asian American experience.

### Supporting Paragraph

While *CRA* [*Crazy Rich Asians*] has been both a success and a boost for Asian American diversity in films, it is important to acknowledge that despite its success *CRA* did not fully represent the complexities of Asian American experiences and ethnicities. Although *CRA* had a strong Asian American representation, most of the cast members were East Asians: missing were the voices and experiences of South and South East Asians, who are still largely underrepresented in American films. Clearly, in terms of representing a full range of Asian and Asian American experiences, much remains to be done. One of the main criticisms of the film was that "it entirely erases the 15% of those in Singapore who are Malay and the

---

＊ His central argument appears on p. 7 of his essay (p. 221).

6.6% who are Indian" (Ellis-Petersen and Kuo). So while it is important to appreciate the significance and the magnitude of *CRA*'s success, the film industry must continue to work toward a more inclusive display of Asian American and Asian experiences on the big screen.

The topic sentence makes it clear that in this paragraph Thai will address the part of his argument that focuses on the "complexities of the Asian American experience." He does this by integrating some relevant criticisms of the film *Crazy Rich Asians*. Because he has used the popularity of this film as a positive example of representation in the first part of his paper, this rhetorical choice adds important nuance and complexity to his argument. He uses concrete examples from the film to illustrate his argument and uses relevant quotations from his sources to build additional credibility. He does an excellent job of explaining how these examples fit into his argument with sentences like, "Clearly, in terms of representing a full range of Asian and Asian American experiences, much remains to be done."

# Quoting, Paraphrasing, and Summarizing

Academic writers integrate ideas and evidence from sources into their writing in three main ways:

- By *quoting*, or borrowing language exactly as it appears in the original source.
- By *paraphrasing*, or explaining an idea or concept from a source using their own words and sentences.
- By *summarizing*, or restating a source's central argument and main ideas concisely in their own words.

Novice academic writers frequently rely too heavily on the first practice: direct quotations. Sometimes this overquoting reflects a lack of confidence or the belief that it's always better to rely on the words of experts. As long as you cite your sources—whether you are quoting, paraphrasing, or summarizing—you can trust that your citation will tell your reader that your ideas are supported, even if you do not use direct quotations.

Sometimes overquoting occurs because transcribing a quotation requires less mental work than identifying or distilling another author's meaning. As you revise, look critically at your quotations. Relying on the words of others instead of integrating their ideas into your own prose can be a sign that you are still not entirely sure what you want to say, how your ideas fit together, or how to move from one part of your argument to another. The following guidelines can help you decide when to use quote, paraphrase, or summarize.

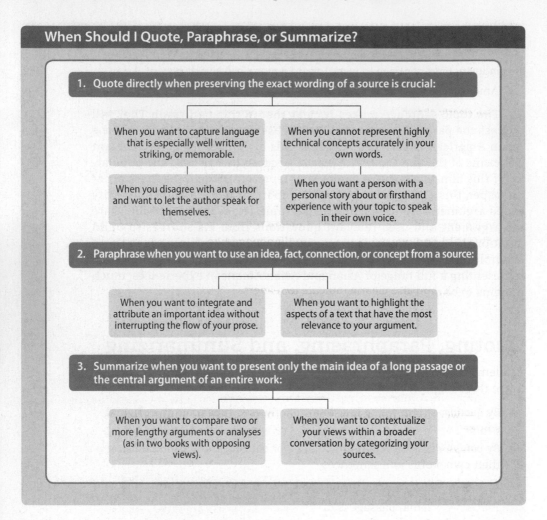

When Should I Quote, Paraphrase, or Summarize?

1. Quote directly when preserving the exact wording of a source is crucial:

When you want to capture language that is especially well written, striking, or memorable.

When you cannot represent highly technical concepts accurately in your own words.

When you disagree with an author and want to let the author speak for themselves.

When you want a person with a personal story about or firsthand experience with your topic to speak in their own voice.

2. Paraphrase when you want to use an idea, fact, connection, or concept from a source:

When you want to integrate and attribute an important idea without interrupting the flow of your prose.

When you want to highlight the aspects of a text that have the most relevance to your argument.

3. Summarize when you want to present only the main idea of a long passage or the central argument of an entire work:

When you want to compare two or more lengthy arguments or analyses (as in two books with opposing views).

When you want to contextualize your views within a broader conversation by categorizing your sources.

## USING SIGNAL PHRASES

Whether you quote, paraphrase, or summarize, it is essential to acknowledge sources accurately, both in the text of your paper and in the works cited list at the end. (Depending on your citation style, you may use *bibliography* or *references* to describe this list.) Within the text itself, you'll often want to use a signal phrase to introduce a source. A signal phrase includes the name(s) of the author(s) whose ideas you are discussing and a verb that communicates your attitude toward those ideas. For example, let's say that you are integrating a paraphrase of one of economist Amartya Sen's central claims into your paper. Consider how the following three signal phrases might help your reader understand how your ideas connect to Sen's:

| | |
|---|---|
| *Although Sen claims . . .* | This phrase suggests that you are going to question Sen's idea. |
| *Sen clearly shows . . .* | This phrase suggests that you agree with the idea you are about to discuss. |
| *Sen believes . . .* | This phrase is more neutral than the other two and could go either way. |

Signal phrases can also add clarity to your work. A good signal phrase can also help contextualize your source by sharing the analysis you did to evaluate it. For example, you could communicate the fact that an author's ideas are influential and well-known by using language like "In his best-selling book . . ." or "In her well-reviewed book . . ." in your signal phrase. Finally, by "bookending" borrowed ideas or information with a signal phrase and a page reference, you also clearly indicate to readers where your ideas stop and another author's begin.

**A note about citations.** As an academic writer, you know that you must cite the sources you quote directly, but you may be less clear about whether you must cite reworded information or ideas taken from sources. You must, and here's why: Your ideas are grounded in the conversation represented by your sources, and your citations show how all the ideas—yours and your sources'—work together. Even when you paraphrase or summarize, you want to point to the authors who have informed your thinking, both in the text and in your works cited list.

## QUOTING, PARAPHRASING, AND SUMMARIZING APPROPRIATELY AND ETHICALLY

The following original passage is drawn from the opening chapter of a book by psychologist Jennifer Eberhardt, who is an expert in the neuroscience behind racial bias. Read it closely. We will use this passage throughout the next section to show you how to quote, paraphrase, and summarize appropriately in MLA style.

### Original Passage

The brain is not a hardwired machine. It's a malleable organ that responds to the environments we are placed in and the challenges we face. This view of the brain runs counter to what most of us learned in science class. In fact, the whole idea of neuroplasticity runs counter to what scientists believed to be true about the brain for centuries. Only fairly recent advances in neuroscience have allowed us to peek inside the brain and track its adaptation over time. Slowly, we're beginning to understand the many ways the brain can be altered by experience.

—Jennifer Eberhardt, *Biased: Uncovering the Hidden Prejudice That Shapes What We See, Think, and Do*, pp. 15–16

**Quoting.** When you incorporate a quotation into your writing—for any reason—you must include the exact words from the source. Depending on your needs, you will do this in different ways.

**USING SHORT QUOTATIONS** In the following example, a student only quotes a brief snippet from the original text:

Eberhardt challenges the widely held view that the human brain is a "hardwired machine" (15).

This student did three important things when she integrated this quotation:

1. She introduced the source with a signal phrase: "Eberhardt challenges . . . ."

2. She used Eberhardt's words exactly and indicated the borrowed language with quotation marks.

3. She provided a page reference at the end of the sentence. (She needs to include the full citation for Eberhardt's book in the list of works cited at the end of her paper as well.)

**USING LONG QUOTATIONS** In this example, a student integrates a long quotation into his paper:

As scientists find new and innovative ways to see what is actually happening inside the human brain, it is becoming increasingly clear that the brain is deeply affected by the events and environments around it. Stanford psychologist Jennifer Eberhardt puts it this way:

In fact, the whole idea of neuroplasticity runs counter to what scientists believed to be true about the brain for centuries. Only fairly recent advances in neuroscience have allowed us to peek inside the brain and track its adaptation over time. Slowly, we're beginning to understand the many ways the brain can be altered by experience (15–16).

This student did three important things when integrating this quotation:

1. He introduced the quotation with a signal phrase: "Jennifer Eberhardt puts it this way."

2. He indented the quoted text as a block, without quotation marks.✱

---

✱ See the Writers' References appendix, pp. 328 and 364, for rules about indenting quotations as a block.

3. He included a page reference at the end of the quotation. (He will also need to include a complete citation in the list of works cited at the end of his paper.)

**EDITING A QUOTATION** Occasionally you will need to make some slight adjustments to a quotation to fit it into your text grammatically, to add a word, to change a lowercase letter to a capital letter, and so on. Follow these rules to do so:

- Use square brackets ([ ]) when you need to change a quotation to make it fit into your text. For example: "[T]he whole idea of neuroplasticity runs counter to what scientists believed to be true about the brain for centuries" (15).
- Use ellipses (. . .) to eliminate words from the original quotation. For example, "It's a malleable organ that responds to . . . the challenges we face" (15).

You should use these techniques sparingly, and always be sure that you do not change the author's original meaning in your edited quotation.

**Paraphrasing.** A paraphrase should be about the same length as the original text. It must accurately reflect the meaning of that text, without copying or borrowing key words, key phrases, or sentence structure. In this example, a student appropriately paraphrased Eberhardt's passage above:

> At Stanford, psychologist Jennifer Eberhardt has conducted extensive research on how the human brain works in an effort to understand how race affects our perceptions about the world, and about each other. She explains that the brain's functions are not rigid and unchanging. Instead, they are affected, and can be altered, by interactions with the world around them. This idea, called neuroplasticity, is relatively new, and is supported by recent discoveries by neuroscientists (15–16).

This student did three important things in this paraphrase:

1. They clearly distinguished their original ideas from the ideas they paraphrased by using a signal phrase and an in-text citation.
2. They used their paraphrase to communicate Eberhardt's ideas without editorializing.
3. They did not replicate Eberhardt's language or distinctive sentence structure. Note that this does not mean that the paraphrase doesn't share any words with the original, but instead that the student only used common words (*the, and*) and words for which there is no ready substitute (for example, variations on the word *neuroplasticity*).

Paraphrasing well is harder than it looks. It requires you to really understand the meaning of a text and to separate yourself enough from the original source so that you are not unduly influenced by it. It is not enough to
swap out individual words; you need to make the expression of the idea or
concept your own.

If you notice yourself "translating" a passage as you write—swapping
in synonyms or turning words around—take a step back. It is likely that you
haven't thought enough about the passage to figure out what meaning you
really want to capture from it. (Note: Some instructors consider this kind of
sloppy paraphrase a form of plagiarism. For more information, see the section on plagiarism on pp. 211–12.)

**Summarizing.**  When you summarize, you condense a long passage by conveying the main idea and key supporting points in your own words and
sentence structures. The long passage can be an excerpt, but it is more frequently a full article or even a full book. In this example, a student summarized Eberhardt's excerpt:

> Recent developments in neuroscience show that the human brain is deeply
> affected by experience and environment (Eberhardt 15–16).

This student did four things to effectively summarize the passage:

1. She significantly condensed the initial passage, distilling it into a
   single, clear message.
2. She used her own language and sentence structure to express
   Eberhardt's meaning.
3. She used her summary to communicate Eberhardt's message, not
   her own.
4. She clearly attributed the source of the idea in an in-text citation.

You have probably already realized that it is very difficult to do a surface-
level summary. To effectively summarize without distorting the original
meaning of your source, you must understand the author's message very
well. It requires careful, analytic reading. Take the time to summarize
your sources as you read them. It is much easier to figure out the main
point or points while the source is fresh in your mind; if you wait until
you are writing, you may have to reread before you can articulate the
main point.

If you get too bogged down in detail or worry that you are borrowing
too much from the original text, try drafting your summary without looking
back at the original source or take a short break to let the details fade. You
will still want to double-check your work against the original to make sure
that you have accurately captured the meaning in your own words.

# Avoiding Plagiarism

In academic culture, giving credit to others when you use their work—their ideas, examples, images, facts, theories, and more—is considered the right thing to do. On most campuses, there are also concrete consequences for students who plagiarize. Plagiarism is the intentional or unintentional use of others' words, ideas, or visuals as if they were your own. At some colleges, students who plagiarize fail not only the assignment but also the entire course; at colleges that have honor codes, students may even be expelled. This practice is not limited to academic settings. In recent years, professional authors, journalists, politicians, and news reporters have been caught in plagiarism scandals, leading to public apologies, embarrassment, and sometimes even job loss. On college campuses, a great deal of time and energy is spent adjudicating cases of plagiarism, intentional and unintentional. Some colleges and universities devote resources to plagiarism-detection software like SafeAssign or TurnItIn.

Could it be that plagiarism is more common now than it used to be? It is possible: Taking sloppy notes, forgetting where an idea was first seen, writing a faulty paraphrase, failing to mark a quotation in an early draft—all are easier in the era of copying and pasting from digital texts, and any one of these mistakes can lead to inadvertent plagiarism. Most people who plagiarize do so accidentally. But it is also easier to get caught today than it was in the past. The same tools that make it easy for you to copy and paste text into your paper make it easy for your instructors to copy and paste that same text into databases and search engines to track down the original source. If a text seems familiar or the language in a student's paper doesn't sound authentic, following up on that hunch is quick and easy. In a digital world, keeping track of where sources come from and when and how material from sources gets used is crucial. See the guidelines on p. 212 for strategies for avoiding plagiarism.

---

## strategies for success

The concept of plagiarism is central to Western academic writing. It rests on the notion of intellectual property: the belief that language can be "owned" by writers who create original ideas. This is not a universal belief. College students in the U.S are expected to follow Western documentation and citation practices. Citation is a critically important part of persuading your audience that you are aware of the conventions of Western research. However, citation practices are not always easy or straightforward, so if you find citation practices challenging, err on the side of caution. Ask your instructor, a librarian, or a writing-center tutor for help using citations.

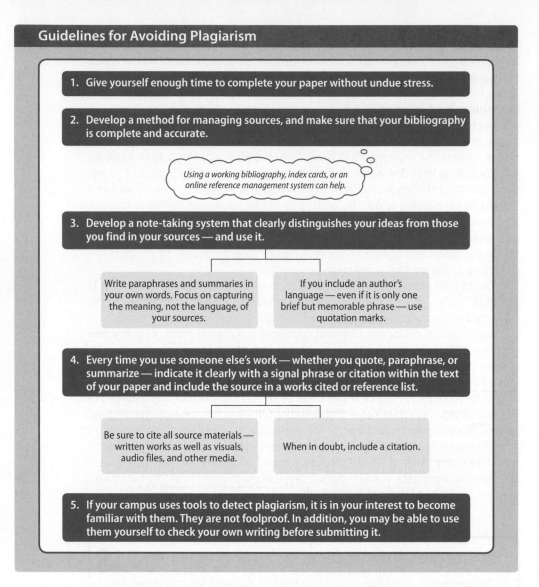

## Guidelines for Avoiding Plagiarism

1. Give yourself enough time to complete your paper without undue stress.

2. Develop a method for managing sources, and make sure that your bibliography is complete and accurate.

> *Using a working bibliography, index cards, or an online reference management system can help.*

3. Develop a note-taking system that clearly distinguishes your ideas from those you find in your sources — and use it.

Write paraphrases and summaries in your own words. Focus on capturing the meaning, not the language, of your sources.

If you include an author's language — even if it is only one brief but memorable phrase — use quotation marks.

4. Every time you use someone else's work — whether you quote, paraphrase, or summarize — indicate it clearly with a signal phrase or citation within the text of your paper and include the source in a works cited or reference list.

Be sure to cite all source materials — written works as well as visuals, audio files, and other media.

When in doubt, include a citation.

5. If your campus uses tools to detect plagiarism, it is in your interest to become familiar with them. They are not foolproof. In addition, you may be able to use them yourself to check your own writing before submitting it.

# Using Appropriate Citation Styles and Formatting

Academic communities, or disciplines, have different expectations when it comes to research writing. Some of these expectations are unwritten or tacit, but others have been defined in style guides. MLA (Modern Language Association) style and APA (American Psychological

Association) style are two of the most frequently required styles for undergraduates. (*Chicago* and Council of Science Editors are two other popular styles.) MLA style is typically used in English and other areas of the humanities; APA is common in the social sciences. It is important that you format your papers and your citations in a way that will meet your audience's expectations.

At the end of this chapter, you'll find a sample student essay using MLA documentation and formatting style (pp. 215–23). The documentation guidelines at the back of this book provide examples and explanations for MLA rules (pp. 327–63) and APA rules (pp. 364–88).

# Understanding Your Rights as a Content Creator

There is a very good chance that you are already creating content for others to view and publishing it on the web: Every time you post to Instagram, tweet, or make a TikTok video, you're creating content. Most social media platforms allow you to decide how public you want your contributions to be. Still, when you sign up for a service, you agree to share the rights to the intellectual property you create and publish on the site, even if you are allowed to adjust your privacy settings. You may not think of your social media content as intellectual property, but it is, and just by living in today's world you have experience making choices about sharing your intellectual property.

As you develop your skills as a researcher, you may have the opportunity to publish your own research, even as an undergraduate. When that happens, you will usually be asked to sign an agreement turning over some, or all, of your copyright to a publisher. You can negotiate with the publishers, keeping some rights to your work. Your professors and mentors can help guide you through this process.

There is no correct answer to the question, "How public should my intellectual property be?" There are arguments for keeping control of your intellectual property and arguments for sharing it. Your individual situation will determine what is right for you. One way that you can assert some control over content you do make public is by attaching a Creative Commons license to it (creativecommons.org). These licenses allow you to define, in advance, whether or not other people have permission to use your work, and they allow you to set conditions on that permission. There are a variety of licenses to choose from. These licenses do not eliminate your copyright, nor do they legally transfer ownership of your intellectual property to anyone else. They simply grant permission, in advance, to others who may want to use your work.

## Isn't There More to Say Here on Writing?

This final section might strike you as brief, when there's clearly so much to think about when writing with, and from, sources. Yet the brevity of this section illustrates something important about the recursive nature of the writing process and, indeed, of all rhetorical activities. While there's much to learn about how to do research, and while integrating sources into your writing takes practice, you will not (and should not) throw away everything you know about your writing process when you write with, and from, sources. The strategies you've explored throughout this book apply to research-based writing: Part One leads you to think broadly about reading, writing, and rhetoric; Part Two helps you accomplish specific kinds of reading and writing tasks; and Part Three gives you practical strategies for reading and writing effectively. So the short answer to the question posed in the heading above is that there is more to say — and you'll find it in the rest of the book.

## Sample Research Essay Using MLA Documentation Style

Here is a research essay by Thai Luong, a student at the University of Hawai'i. Read it carefully to see how he synthesizes information from sources and skillfully integrates that information to support his own ideas.

Luong 1

Thai Luong
Professor Clark
Introduction to Film 100
9 May 2019

Name, instructor, course, and date double-spaced and aligned at left margin

Representation Matters:

Asian American Representation in Films

Title centered

My earliest memory of watching a movie in a theater, rather than at home, was when I was six years old. I had just moved with my family from Vietnam to Hawai'i. In Vietnam, I loved watching movies; it was easy for me to identify with the actors, people who I wouldn't mind walking a day in their shoes just to see how it feels. In Vietnam, the biggest TV screen I had ever seen was around five inches tall and eight inches wide. In Hawai'i, staring at the massive screen ahead of me, I felt small and intimidated. After settling down, I was ready to enjoy *The Fast and the Furious,* my first big-screen movie. But my anticipation quickly turned to dismay: the loud noises, fast cars, violent action scenes, and (especially) the foreign actors all felt strange and distant to me. This was the first time I saw a movie where none of the actors looked like me. I was certain that no matter how hard I tried, my feet would never fit their shoes. As I left the movie theater with my family, I was confused. Why weren't there actors who looked like me? Once I got older and began to explore my interest in films, I realized that at six years of age I had understood something important: Asian Americans like myself have a lot of empty shoes to fill if we hoped to be represented in films in America.

Opens with a narrative to:
1) engage readers' interest and
2) establish the author's connection to the topic

Introduces the central argument, or thesis, of the paper

As a college student who studies as well as watches American films, I now know that research confirms my early insight. In a study done by Smith et al., on race and ethnicity in popular films, in 2014, only 4.4% of Asian Americans had a speaking line in their respective roles compared to 74.1% of their White counterparts (15). Asian Americans are not only underrepresented on screen, but they are also virtually invisible directing and producing them as well. In a more recent

Descriptive facts and statistics provide background information and establish the significance of the topic

Luong 2

2018 study analyzing over 1,100 popular Hollywood films and 1,223 directors spanning across 10 years (2007–2017), Smith et al. found that only 3.1% or 38 out of 1,223 directors were Asian or Asian Americans (see fig. 1).

What is even more startling is the gender disparity that is found within those already depleted numbers—out of 38 Asian or Asian American directors—three were female (Smith et al. 2018, 3). As these statistics show, Asian Americans are sorely underrepresented in films from acting to directing and producing. Independent Asian American film director Erik Lu describes the challenges that Asian Americans face in the film industry: "I just don't think there's enough exposure for us. In order for us to pop up on the Hollywood scene, we need to make sure that people who are writing Asian-American parts are coming through" (Chan). While Lu acknowledges the lack of exposure for Asian Americans in films, his statement offers a positive way forward, one that recognizes that Asian Americans are more than their stereotypes.

Currently, Asian American stereotypes too often portray characters who play either the quiet, smart, geeky, exotic, foreign, or submissive roles (Levin). This presents a dilemma for actors, who need

**Effective use of a source to support a transition from background information (there is a problem) to thesis (the author's suggested solution)**

**First subtopic: The prevalence of stereotypes in mainstream productions**

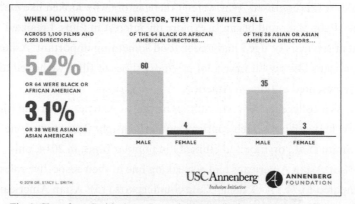

Fig. 1. Chart from Smith, Stacy L., et al. "Inequality in 1,100 popular films: Examining portrayals of gender, race/ethnicity, LGBT & disability from 2007 to 2017."
USC Annenberg School for Communication and Journalism

Luong 3

to make sure that they don't limit themselves to a stereotype in order to chase their dreams of acting. Although it is difficult to find a role that is unexpected for Asian Americans, it is not impossible. The success of Ki Hong Lee, for instance, demonstrates that Asian Americans can successfully be cast in nonstereotypical roles. Ki Hong Lee, 31, is an up-and-coming Asian American star in Hollywood. Lee's acting career started small; early in his career he was known as an actor for Wong Fu Productions on YouTube. Later, he played a professor in *Everything Before Us*, Wong Fu's first feature film. But he really hit it big with his role in *The Maze Runner* and its sequel *Maze Runner: The Scorch Trials*, dystopian science fiction thrillers. In the film, Lee plays Minho, who is strong and quick with an athletic body (see fig. 2). Minho is depicted as one of the alpha male characters in the book and film. In an interview with the Coalition of Asian Pacifics in Entertainment, Lee talks about the importance of playing an assertive role.

Fig. 2. Ki Hong Lee as Minho in *The Maze Runner*

Luong 4

> I have to do this role; there is no other role out there for me.
> I try my best to bring the alpha male, dominant, strong kind of
> characteristic to that role. I am really lucky and just truly blessed
> to showcase that Asian actors can be masculine and can run really
> fast, and can be strong. (Randall)

Lee's appearance in the film as a masculine, athletic Asian American
male is a momentous occurrence for all Asian American actors and
actresses. Lee didn't settle for weak supporting character roles; instead,
he chased a lead role that refreshingly emphasizes assertiveness and
leadership. In an interview with *Mochi Magazine*, Lee offers advice for
Asian-American actors who want to avoid stereotypical roles: "It's a
matter of finding them, looking for them, and being aware when they
pop up on your screen. Now, time is changing and there are a lot more
opportunities, but you still have to pick and choose what roles you want
to go out for" (Hwang).

**Second subtopic: Market for diverse representation**

Wong Fu Productions has played an important role in increasing
the opportunities available to Asian-American actors, directors, and
producers. They first started making small film projects and videos
in 2003 at UC San Diego. Since then, Wong Fu Productions has
accumulated 550 million views and over 3.2 million subscribers on their
YouTube channel.

In 2015, Wong Fu Productions released their first full-length movie
called *Everything Before Us* starring a predominately Asian-American
cast. Wong Fu Productions asked their fans to help fund their first full-
length movie via Indiego, an online crowdfunding site. Their goal was
to fund over $200,000 for their film. Within 40 days of setting up their
Indiegogo campaign, Wong Fu Productions, with the large contribution
from their fans, raised over $358,308 for their movie. *Everything Before
Us* proved to be a huge success for Wong Fu as their film garnered
high ratings from IMDb at 7/10 and Rotten Tomatoes at 75%. The film
also accumulated four out of five stars on Netflix. In so doing, Wong
Fu refuted the assumption that Asian-American films couldn't be
successful in the broad public market.

Luong 5

In an interview at Northwestern University, the founders describe
their motivation: Wang recounted a story of when Wong Fu tried to
produce a movie through mainstream media and producers told them
a large cast of Asians was "bad business" for attracting audiences.
"This is why it's really important to share this movie," Wang said.
"To show those companies: No, there is an audience." (Choi)

Through their dedication and support from the Asian American
community, Wong Fu Productions demonstrates that a group of Asian
American producers can create a successful movie starring Asian
American actors and actresses. As such, they are helping to expand the
market for Asian American actors, producers, and directors.

Although Asian Americans are still fighting an uphill battle
in terms of being represented in films, the release of *Crazy Rich
Asians* in 2018 definitely represents an important breakthrough.
*Crazy Rich Asians* is a film adaptation of a novel of the same title by
Kevin Kwan (see fig. 3). From the directors to the writers and actors,
*Crazy Rich Asians* (*CRA*) was mostly comprised of Asian American
artists. Not only did *CRA* become the first major Hollywood movie
starring a predominantly Asian American cast since *The Joy Luck
Club* in 1993, but *CRA* also amassed over $237 million worldwide
and was the highest-grossing romantic comedy in the past decade
showing that consumers are hungry for diversity (Abad-Santos). The
accomplishments and visibility of *CRA* have already boosted the
careers of Asian American actors like Nora Lum, who is also known
as Awkwafina. Before appearing in *CRA*, Awkwafina started her acting
career on YouTube. Since appearing on the big screen, Awkwafina has
upcoming roles in major movies like *The Angry Birds Movie 2*, *Jumanji:
The Next Level*, and *Shang-Chi and the Legends of the Ten Rings*. In an
interview with *TIME*, Awkwafina spoke out about the positive impact
of *CRA*. "So much has changed. It impacts everything, every day.
Asian American actors come to me and say, 'I couldn't get one audition
before *Crazy Rich Asians*—now I'm auditioning every day'" (Chow).

Third subtopic:
Studio,
big-budget
example

Luong 6

Fig. 3. Promotional picture of *Crazy Rich Asians* taken from IMDb

**Fourth subtopic: Representation is more complicated than box-office numbers**

While *CRA* has been both a success and a boost for Asian American diversity in films, it is important to acknowledge that despite its success *CRA* did not fully represent the complexities of Asian American experiences and ethnicities. Although *CRA* had a strong Asian American representation, most of the cast members were East Asians: missing were the voices and experiences of South and South East Asians, who are still largely underrepresented in American films. Clearly, in terms of representing a full range of Asian and Asian American experiences, much remains to be done. One of the main criticisms of the film was that "it entirely erases the 15% of those in Singapore who are Malay and the 6.6% who are Indian" (Ellis-Petersen and Kuo). So while it is important to appreciate the significance and the magnitude of *CRA*'s success, the film industry must continue to work toward a more inclusive display of Asian American and Asian experiences on the big screen.

Asian Americans are an increasing community in the United States. According to a study done by Pew Research (see fig. 4), the US Asian American population grew 72% between 2000 and 2015, which accounted for the fastest rate of growth for all racial or ethnic groups, and that trend is not slowing down any time soon (Lopez et al.).

Luong 7

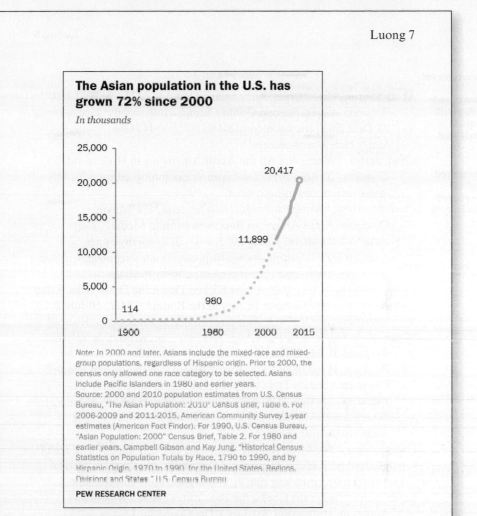

**The Asian population in the U.S. has grown 72% since 2000**

*In thousands*

Note: In 2000 and later, Asians include the mixed-race and mixed-group populations, regardless of Hispanic origin. Prior to 2000, the census only allowed one race category to be selected. Asians include Pacific Islanders in 1980 and earlier years.
Source: 2000 and 2010 population estimates from U.S. Census Bureau, "The Asian Population: 2010" Census Brief, Table 6. For 2006-2009 and 2011-2015, American Community Survey 1-year estimates (American Fact Finder). For 1990, U.S. Census Bureau, "Asian Population: 2000" Census Brief, Table 2. For 1980 and earlier years, Campbell Gibson and Kay Jung, "Historical Census Statistics on Population Totals by Race, 1790 to 1990, and by Hispanic Origin, 1970 to 1990, for the United States, Regions, Divisions, and States," U.S. Census Bureau

**PEW RESEARCH CENTER**

Fig. 4. Chart of Asian population in the United States from Pew Research Center
"Key facts about Asian Americans, a diverse and growing population" Pew Research Center, Washington, D.C. 2017, https://www.pewresearch.org/fact-tank/2017/09/08/key-facts-about-asian-americans/

With that fact in mind, it is crucial for the film industry to continue its efforts to diversify the representation of Asian Americans in American films. While much has been accomplished, as demonstrated by Wong Fu Productions, Ki Hong Lee, and *Crazy Rich Asians*, there is still more work to be done. The task ahead is two-fold: to ensure that Asian Americans are better represented in a diverse variety of roles in film and that their roles accurately reflect the complexities of the Asian American experience.

Conclusion provides a summary of the central argument

Luong 8

Works Cited

Abad-Santos, Alex. "Crazy Rich Asians Dared to Make Asian Lives
  Aspirational. Its Success Could Change Hollywood." *Vox*,
  21 Dec. 2018, www.vox.com/2018/12/21/18141213
  /crazy-rich-asians-success

Chan, Justin. "Where Are All the Asian Americans in Hollywood?"
  *Complex,* 20 Aug. 2014, www.complex.com/pop-culture/2014/08
  /asian-americans-in-hollywood

Choi, Matthew. "Wong Fu Productions Screens New Movie,
  Discusses Asian-American Representation in Media." *The
  Daily Northwestern,* 3 May 2015, www.dailynorthwestern.
  com/2015/05/03/campus/wong-fu-productions-screens-new-movie
  -discusses-asian-american-representation-in-media/

Chow, Andrew. "*Crazy Rich Asians* Kicked Down the Door. Now Asian
  Americans Are Fighting To Stay in the Room." *TIME,* 10 July 2019,
  www.time.com/5622913/asian-american-representation-hollywood/

"Crazy Rich Asians." *IMDb*, 15 Aug. 2018, www.imdb.com/title/tt3104988/.
  Accessed 31 July 2019.

Ellis-Petersen, Hannah and Lily Kuo. "Where Are the Brown People?
  *Crazy Rich Asians* Draws Tepid Response in Singapore" *The
  Guardian,* 21 Aug. 2018, www.theguardian.com/film/2018/aug/21
  /where-are-the-brown-people-crazy-rich-asians-draws-tepid
  -response-in-singapore

Hwang, Sora. "The Maze Runner's Ki Hong Lee Embraces the Maze of
  Hollywood." *Mochi Magazine,* 7 Oct. 2014, www.mochimag.com
  /mochi-magazine/maze-runner-ki-hong-lee-wong-fu-productions

Levin, Sam. "'We're the Geeks, the Prostitutes': Asian American
  Actors on Hollywood Barriers." *The Guardian*, 11 Apr. 2017,
  www.theguardian.com/world/2017/apr/11/asian-american
  -actors-whitewashing-hollywood

Lopez, Gustavo, et al. "Key Facts about Asian Americans, a Diverse
  and Growing Population." *Pew Research Center*, 8 Sep. 2017,
  www.pewresearch.org/fact-tank/2017/09/08/key-facts-about
  -asian-americans/

Randall. "AAPI Heritage Month: Daniel Dae Kim & Ki Hong Lee."
  *AsAmNews*, 28 May 2015, www.asamnews.com/2015/05/28/aapi
  -heritage-month-daniel-dae-kim-ki-hong-lee/

Luong 9

Smith, Stacy L., et al. "Inequality in 700 Popular Films: Examining
Portrayals of Character Gender, Race, & LGBT Status from
2007 to 2014." *Media, Diversity, & Social Change Initiative*, 2014,
pp. 1–29.

Smith, Stacy L., et al. "Inequality in 1,100 Popular Films: Examining
Portrayals of Gender, Race/Ethnicity, LGBT & Disability from
2007 to 2017." *Annenberg Inclusion Initiative*, 2018, pp. 1–37.

Wong, Tessa. "*Crazy Rich Asians*: The Film Burdened with 'Crazy'
Asian Expectations." *BBC News*, 18 Aug. 2018, www.bbc.com
/news/world-asia-45179503

## for **thought, discussion, and writing**

1. After reviewing this chapter's discussion of paraphrasing and summarizing, select one of the sample essays that appears in Chapter 8, "Writing in the Disciplines: Making Choices as You Write." Choose a paragraph from the essay that strikes you as particularly interesting or informative. After reading this paragraph carefully, first write a paraphrase of it, and then summarize the same passage. Finally, write a paragraph explaining why your paraphrase and summary of this passage are effective.

2. Identify an important journal for scholars in your major. You will probably have to ask someone (a major adviser, a professor, or a librarian) to recommend a journal that is important and useful in your field. If you do not have a major yet, ask the person who teaches your favorite class to recommend a journal of interest to scholars in that field.

   Now browse through a copy of that journal, taking note of the articles and the topics it covers. As you browse, ask yourself the following:

   ● How did you gain access to the journal? You might have found the journal online, if access is open. More likely, you needed to access the journal via your library. Think about access as an issue: How easy or difficult is it for people to use the content in this journal? What would the advantages and disadvantages be of changing its level of accessibility?

   ● What do the articles tell you about how scholars in your field write? Do the articles have common characteristics (abstracts, section headings, citation styles)? Do the authors write in first person or third person? Do they place their arguments into a context for you? What are some things they seem to assume that you, as the reader, already know?

   Write a paragraph reflecting on what you've learned.

**3.** Go to *ScienceBlogs* (scienceblogs.com) or *ResearchBlogging* (researchblogging.org). Find a post about an article written by a scholar in your major discipline or a post about an article on a topic discussed in one of your classes. Read the blog post and any responses to it. Take note of important issues or any points of controversy, and try to determine where this scholarly discussion fits within the larger field.

Now find and read the original article. (If the article is not available for free online, search for the article through your library instead.) Compare the discussion on the blog about the article to the article itself. What information is available in both places? What information is available only in the post or only in the article? How might each source be useful in an academic research process?

# 8

# Writing in the Disciplines: Making Choices as You Write

Part One of *The Academic Writer* began with this question: What does it mean to be a writer today? Despite the increasing prevalence and power of multimodal composition, writing does indeed still matter. In fact, those with access to computer and online technologies are writing more than ever before.

How can you negotiate the opportunities and challenges of communication in today's world? As Part One emphasizes, you can draw on your understanding of rhetoric, the rhetorical situation, and the writing process. Part Two of *The Academic Writer* builds on this rhetorical approach to writing. It applies this approach to the essential skills needed in college reading and writing. One of the challenges you face as an academic writer is learning how to apply these skills in a wide range of courses — from philosophy to chemistry to psychology. You can use your knowledge of rhetoric and of the writing process to negotiate the demands of academic writing in a broad variety of disciplines. This chapter will help you do so, and it will introduce you to the expectations and conventions of these disciplines.

thinking rhetorically

Meeting these expectations can be a significant challenge, especially when you take courses outside of your major. By thinking rhetorically about the nature and purpose of writing in the various academic disciplines, you can gain confidence, skill, and flexibility as a writer. By learning how writing works in different fields, you can become a successful academic writer in *all* the courses you take in college.

## strategies for success

An academic discipline is an area of study (e.g., philosophy, biology, mathematics) taught and researched in higher education. Each discipline accumulates a body of knowledge through specific research methods, produces theories and concepts to organize the knowledge, and uses specific terminologies or language to share that knowledge. Academic disciplines also have different writing conventions. For example, a writer who is a biology major must learn the conventions of writing in their discipline.

225

# Thinking Rhetorically about Writing in the Disciplines

thinking
rhetorically

The conventions of academic writing in different disciplines have histories worth noting. For example, scholars generally attribute the development of scientific writing to the rise of humanism and the scientific method during the Renaissance. When in 1660 a group of scientists in Great Britain founded the Royal Society (a body that still exists), they worked to standardize methods for reporting scientific results. Practitioners refined these textual conventions over time, but, as David Porush notes in A Short Guide to Writing about Science, "the basic outline of the scientific report has changed little in over a century."[1] There is no need for it to change because the scientific report still meets the day-to-day needs of working scientists: It encourages effective and efficient communication among scientists.

Textual conventions in the humanities, too, have a history. One particularly important impetus for those conventions was the desire to interpret religious texts, which has been a strong tradition in most of the world's major religions. Over time, interpretive practices for reading religious texts were applied to secular works as well. This tradition of textual interpretation is particularly important to such disciplines in the humanities as literature, philosophy, religious studies, and rhetoric, but it has influenced such other areas as history, music, and art.

Whereas scientists work to achieve objective and reliable results that others can replicate, those in the humanities often study questions for which there is no definitive answer. What constitutes a just war? How can we best interpret Shakespeare's The Tempest or best understand the concept of free will? Scholars in the humanities take it for granted that there are multiple ways to approach any topic. Although they hope that their writing will lead to a broader understanding of their subject, they don't expect that their research will result in the kind of knowledge generated by the scientific method. Indeed, in the humanities, originality is valued over replicability.

This brief discussion of the development of textual conventions in the humanities and sciences emphasizes that rather than being arbitrary forms to be filled in, the textual conventions that characterize different academic disciplines are deeply grounded in their history, nature, and goals. It is important to remember, however, that even though disciplines in these two broad areas share a number of general assumptions and practices, variations do exist. Moreover, disciplines in the social sciences, such as psychology, sociology, economics, anthropology, communication, and political science, include elements of both the sciences and the humanities, as does much writing in business.

As a college student, you can better understand your teachers' expectations as you move from, say, a chemistry class to a course in art appreciation by thinking rhetorically about the subject matter, methodology, and goals of the disciplines. The questions on the next page can guide this analysis.

---

[1]David Porush. A Short Guide to Writing about Science. Harper Collins, 1995, p. 8.

## for **exploration**

Take five minutes to write freely about your experience creating texts in various disciplines. Are you more confident writing for some disciplines than for others? Why? What questions seem most important to you as you anticipate writing in courses across the curriculum?

## for **collaboration**

Bring your response to the previous Exploration to share in class. After each person has summarized his or her ideas, spend a few minutes noting common experiences and questions.

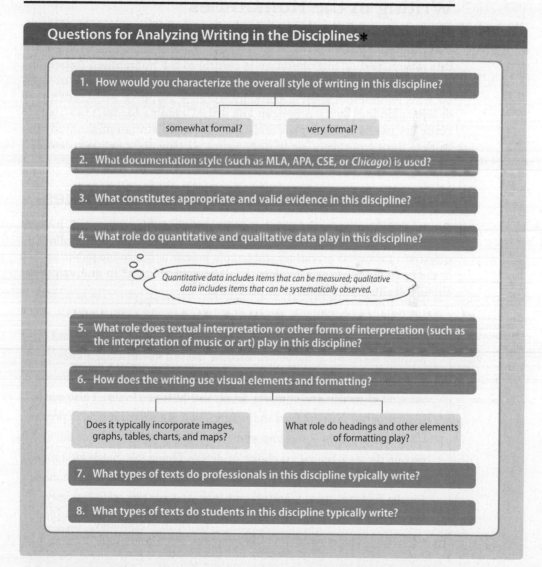

### Questions for Analyzing Writing in the Disciplines*

1. How would you characterize the overall style of writing in this discipline?

   somewhat formal?     very formal?

2. What documentation style (such as MLA, APA, CSE, or *Chicago*) is used?

3. What constitutes appropriate and valid evidence in this discipline?

4. What role do quantitative and qualitative data play in this discipline?

   *Quantitative data includes items that can be measured; qualitative data includes items that can be systematically observed.*

5. What role does textual interpretation or other forms of interpretation (such as the interpretation of music or art) play in this discipline?

6. How does the writing use visual elements and formatting?

   Does it typically incorporate images, graphs, tables, charts, and maps?     What role do headings and other elements of formatting play?

7. What types of texts do professionals in this discipline typically write?

8. What types of texts do students in this discipline typically write?

* To answer these questions, you'll need to read representative examples of writing from each field; your teacher or your own coursework can provide such examples.

---

**strategies for success**

The Questions for Analyzing Writing in the Disciplines may be especially helpful for writers who are new to university or college culture or writers who are returning to college or university culture. If your educational experiences didn't include navigating college or university culture, ask your instructor or a writing tutor any questions you may have about how the disciplines work.

---

# Writing in the Humanities

In a general sense, those studying the humanities are attempting to determine what something means or how it can best be understood or evaluated. For this reason, textual interpretation is central to the humanities. Depending on their discipline, scholars in the humanities may read the same or similar texts for different analytical and interpretive purposes. An art critic may analyze paintings by the American folk artist Grandma Moses (1860–1961) to study her use of brush strokes and color, while a historian might study her work to learn more about life in rural America in the mid-twentieth century.

## Sample Student Essay in the Humanities*

On pp. 229–31 is an essay written for an in-class exam in a U.S. history course. The author, Elizabeth Ridlington, was responding to the following question: *During his presidency, did Lincoln primarily respond to public opinion or did he shape public opinion more than he responded to it?* In analyzing her rhetorical situation, Elizabeth commented:

*thinking rhetorically*

My teacher phrased this as an either/or question, inviting a strong and clear position statement at the outset. Because this is a history class, I knew that I needed to provide evidence from primary documents we'd read, offering the kind of specific and concrete details that historians value. I also needed to incorporate material from the lectures. In thinking about how to present information, I knew it was important not just to provide evidence but also to explain the logic behind my choice of details. Doing this makes for a more coherent essay in which every paragraph supports my initial thesis statement. Finally, looking at events and actions from multiple perspectives is very important for historians, so I explained Lincoln's decisions in a variety of circumstances essentially as a series of mini case studies.

---

✱ For a research essay with citations and a list of works cited in MLA style, see Chapter 7, pp. 215–23.

Elizabeth Ridlington

Lincoln's Presidency and Public Opinion

This essay argues that Lincoln shaped public opinion more than he responded to it and examines the issues of military recruitment, Northern war goals, and emancipation as examples of Lincoln's interaction with public opinion.

Introduction frames response, lists supporting points

    At the start of the war, Lincoln needed men for the military. Because of this, he could hardly ignore public opinion. But even as he responded in various ways to public opinion, he did not significantly modify his policy goals. Lincoln's first call for seventy-five thousand soldiers was filled through militias that were under state rather than federal control. As the war progressed, the federal government took more control of military recruitment. The government set quotas for each state and permitted the enlistment of African American soldiers via the Militia Act. Kentucky, a slave state, protested, and Lincoln waived the requirement that blacks be enlisted so long as Kentucky still filled its quota. In so doing, Lincoln responded to public opinion without changing his policy goal. Another example of this strategy occurred when the first federal draft produced riots in New York City. When the riots occurred, Lincoln relented temporarily and waited for the unrest to quiet down. Then he reinstated the federal draft. Again, Lincoln responded to a volatile situation and even temporarily withdrew the federal draft. But he ultimately reinstated the draft.

Multiple examples for first supporting point

    Lincoln's efforts to shape public opinion in the North in favor of the war provide another example of his proactive stance. Whenever he discussed the war, Lincoln equated it with freedom and democracy. Northerners linked democracy with their personal freedom and daily well-being, and therefore Lincoln's linkage of the Union with democracy fostered Northern support for the war even when the conflict was bloody and Northern victory was anything but guaranteed. After the emancipation, Lincoln continued his effort to influence public opinion by connecting the abolition of slavery with democracy. The image of a "new birth of freedom" that Lincoln painted in his

Second supporting point

Gettysburg Address was part of this effort to overcome Northern racism and a reluctance to fight for the freedom of blacks.

The process that led to the emancipation provides perhaps the clearest example of Lincoln's determination to shape public opinion rather than simply respond to it. Lincoln's views on slavery were more progressive than those of many of his contemporaries. These views caused him personally to wish to abolish slavery. At the same time, Lincoln knew that winning the war was his highest priority. Consequently, retaining the border states early in the war was more important to Lincoln than emancipation, and for this reason he revoked Freemont's proclamation in the summer of 1861. In explaining this decision privately to Freemont, Lincoln admitted that he was concerned about public opinion in Kentucky since it would determine whether Kentucky stayed with the Union. However, in a letter that Lincoln knew might be made public, Lincoln denied that he had reacted to Kentucky's pressure and claimed that emancipation was not among his powers—a clear effort to gain public approval. Even when others such as Frederick Douglass (in a September 1861 speech) demanded emancipation, Lincoln did not change his policy. Not until July 1862 did Lincoln draft the preliminary Emancipation Proclamation. Rather than releasing it then, at the advice of his cabinet he waited for a time when it would have a more positive impact on public opinion.

Lincoln realized that the timing of the Emancipation Proclamation was crucial. While he was waiting for an opportune time to release the document, Horace Greeley published his "Prayer of Twenty Million," calling on Lincoln to abolish slavery. Lincoln's response, a letter for publication, emphasized the importance of the Union and the secondary importance of the status of slavery. By taking this position, Lincoln hoped to shape public opinion. He wanted Northerners to believe that he saw the Union cause as foremost, so that the release of the proclamation would create as few racial concerns as possible. The Emancipation Proclamation was released on January 1, 1863. Once it

**Several primary sources cited to support third point**

**Final section cites primary sources, gives dates**

was released, Lincoln stood by it despite strong public opposition. In 1864, when Democrats called for an armistice with the South, Lincoln stood by his decision to abolish slavery. He defended his position on military grounds, hoping voters would approve in the 1864 election.

As the examples I have just discussed indicate, Lincoln could not ignore public opinion, and at times he had to respond to it. But when Lincoln did so, this was always part of a larger effort to shape public opinion and to ensure Union victory.

Conclusion restates thesis

# Writing in the Natural and Applied Sciences

Whatever their skill level, students in the humanities expect that writing will play a key role in their education. Those majoring in other areas, particularly the natural and applied sciences, sometimes assume otherwise. They're wrong. Here's what David Porush tells students to expect if they enter the sciences:

> You will write to report your research. You will write to communicate with colleagues at other institutions. You will write to request financial support for your work. You will write to colleagues, managers, and subordinates in your own institutional setting. You will write instructions and memos, and keep lab notebooks.[2]

Porush's argument is supported by other scientists. Victoria McMillan, author of *Writing Papers in the Biological Sciences*, points out that "no experiment, however brilliant, can contribute to the existing fund of scientific knowledge unless it has been described to others working in the same field."[3]

Because established formats for scientific writing encourage efficient communication and facilitate replication of experiments, scientists use them whenever possible. At the same time, they pay particular attention to the effective presentation of data, often using figures, tables, images, and models. This attention to format and document design is equally important in student writing in the sciences.

---

[2]David Porush. *A Short Guide to Writing about Science.* Harper Collins, 1995, xxi–xxii.
[3]Victoria McMillan. *Writing Papers in the Biological Sciences.* 4th ed. Bedford/St. Martin's, 2006, 1.

Scientists write a variety of kinds of texts. Since maintaining and operating labs can be costly, scientists spend considerable time writing proposals to fund research projects. Most research proposals follow this format: title page, introduction, purpose, significance of the study, methods, time line, budget, and references. The format for research reports and journal articles is generally as follows: title, author(s), abstract, introduction, literature review, materials and methods, results, discussion, and references.

# Sample Student Essay in the Natural and Applied Sciences

Scientists value precision, clarity, and objectivity. The following essay, an undergraduate research proposal by Tara Gupta, demonstrates these traits. Note that Tara uses headings to mark the various sections of her proposal. She also uses the documentation style required by the Council of Science Editors (CSE). For details on this reference style, consult its handbook, *Scientific Style and Format: The CSE Manual for Authors, Editors, and Publishers,* 8th ed. (2014).

Field Measurements of
Photosynthesis and Transpiration
Rates in Dwarf Snapdragon
(*Chaenorrhinum minus* Lange):
An Investigation of Water Stress
Adaptations

Tara Gupta

Proposal for a
Summer Research
Fellowship
Colgate University
March 11, 2019

Complete title,
specific and
informative

Shortened title and page number

Headings throughout help organize proposal

Introduction states scientific issue, gives background information, cites relevant studies

Personal letter cited in parentheses, not included in references

Aims and scope of proposed study

Water Stress Adaptations 2

## Introduction

Dwarf snapdragon (*Chaenorrhinum minus*) is a weedy pioneer plant found growing in central New York during spring and summer. The distribution of this species has been limited almost exclusively to the cinder ballast of railroad tracks[1], a harsh environment characterized by intense sunlight and poor soil water retention. Given such environmental conditions, one would expect *C. minus* to exhibit anatomical features similar to those of xeromorphic plants (species adapted to arid habitats).

However, this is not the case. T. Gupta and R. Arnold (unpublished) have found that the leaves and stems of *C. minus* are not covered by a thick, waxy cuticle but rather with a thin cuticle that is less effective in inhibiting water loss through diffusion. The root system is not long and thick, capable of reaching deeper, moister soils; instead, it is thin and diffuse, permeating only the topmost (and driest) soil horizon. Moreover, in contrast to many xeromorphic plants, the stomata (pores regulating gas exchange) are not found in sunken crypts or cavities in the epidermis that retard water loss from transpiration.

Despite a lack of these morphological adaptations to water stress, *C. minus* continues to grow and reproduce when morning dew has been its only source of water for up to five weeks (R. Arnold, personal communication). Such growth involves fixation of carbon by photosynthesis and requires that the stomata be open to admit sufficient carbon dioxide. Given the dry, sunny environment, the time required for adequate carbon fixation must also mean a significant loss of water through transpiration as open stomata exchange carbon dioxide with water. How does *C. minus* balance the need for carbon with the need to conserve water?

## Aims of the Proposed Study

The above observations have led me to an exploration of the extent to which *C. minus* is able to photosynthesize under

Water Stress Adaptations 3

conditions of low water availability. It is my hypothesis that *C. minus* adapts to these conditions by photosynthesizing in the early morning and late afternoon, when leaf and air temperatures are lower and transpirational water loss is reduced. I predict that its photosynthetic rate may be very low, perhaps even zero, on hot, sunny afternoons. Similar diurnal changes in photosynthetic rate in response to midday water deficits have been described in crop plants[2 3]. There is only one comparable study[4] on noncrop species in their natural habitats.

*CSE documentation, citation-sequence format*

Thus, the research proposed here aims to help explain the apparent paradox of an organism that thrives in water-stressed conditions despite a lack of morphological adaptations. This summer's work will also serve as a basis for controlled experiments in a plant growth chamber on the individual effects of temperature, light intensity, soil water availability, and other environmental factors on photosynthesis and transpiration rates. These experiments are planned for the coming fall semester.

*States significance of study*

*Connects study to future research projects*

## Methods

*Methodology described briefly*

Simultaneous measurements of photosynthesis and transpiration rates will indicate the balance *C. minus* has achieved in acquiring the energy it needs while retaining the water available to it. These measurements will be taken daily at field sites in the Hamilton, NY, area, using an LI-6220 portable photosynthesis system (LICOR, Inc., Lincoln, NE). Basic methodology and use of correction factors will be similar to that described in related studies[5–7]. Data will be collected at regular intervals throughout the daylight hours and will be related to measurements of ambient air temperature, leaf temperature, relative humidity, light intensity, wind velocity, and cloud cover.

Water Stress Adaptations 4

## Budget

| | |
|---|---|
| 1 kg soda lime | $56.00 |
| (for absorption of $CO_2$ in photosynthesis analyzer) | |
| 1 kg anhydrous magnesium perchlorate | $280.75 |
| (used as desiccant for photosynthesis analyzer) | |
| Shipping of chemicals (estimate) | $15.00 |
| Estimated 500 miles travel to field sites in own car | $207.15 |
| @ $0.405/mile | |
| $CO_2$ cylinder, 80 days rental | $100.00 |
| (for calibration of photosynthesis analyzer) | |
| TOTAL REQUEST | $658.90 |

## References

1. Widrlechner MP. Historical and phenological observations of the spread of Chaenorrhinum minus across North America. Can J Bot. 1983;61(1):179–187.

2. Manhas JG, Sukumaran NP. Diurnal changes in net photosynthetic rate in potato in two environments. Potato Res. 1988;31:375–378.

3. Yordanov I, Tsonev T, Velikova V, Georgieva K, Ivanov P, Tsenov N, Petrova T. Changes in $CO_2$ assimilation, transpiration and stomatal resistance in different wheat cultivars experiencing drought under field conditions. Bulg J Plant Physiol. 2001;27(3–4):20–33.

4. Chaves MM, Pereira JS, Maroco J, Rodrigues ML, Ricardo CP, Osório ML, Carvalho I, Faria T, Pinheiro C. How plants cope with water stress in the field: photosynthesis and growth. Ann Bot. 2002;89(Jun): 907–916.

5. Jarvis A, Davies W. The coupled response of stomatal conductance to photosynthesis and transpiration. J Exp Bot. 1998;49(Mar):399–406.

6. Kallarackal J, Milburn JA, Baker DA. Water relations of the banana. III. Effects of controlled water stress on water potential, transpiration, photosynthesis and leaf growth. Aust J Plant Physiol. 1990;17(1):79–90.

7. Idso SB, Allen SG, Kimball BA, Choudhury BJ. Problems with porometry: measuring net photosynthesis by leaf chamber techniques. Agron J. 1989;81(4):475–479.

Before embarking on her grant proposal, Tara spent time analyzing her rhetorical situation. Here is her analysis:

thinking
rhetorically

I am writing to persuade a committee to grant me funds for working on my scientific project. Because I want the readers (scientists) to notice my ideas and not the medium, and because I want to convince them of my scientific merit and training, I will use the traditional medium and style for scientists—a written research proposal. A research proposal follows a standard format. Hence, I would say that my role as a writer, and my product, is relatively fixed. In the end, I want readers to hear the voice of a fellow scientist who is hardworking, trustworthy, and a creative observer.

To be persuasive, I need to understand the behaviors, motivations, and values of scientists. I expect the readers, as scientists, to immediately begin formulating questions and hypotheses as I present the background information. My job is to give them the best information to help them form the questions I would like them to be thinking about. In addition, it is important to include all logical steps in proceeding with my idea and background knowledge, especially since the scientists reading my proposal are not all in my research field and cannot fill in the information gaps. Nothing is more boring or painful for a scientist than reading something that has flawed logic which they have trouble following or understanding. I also need credibility, so I will have references for all background information.

Scientists value communication that is succinct, concrete, logical, accurate, and above all, *objective*. For example, if I want to discuss the environmental conditions these plants live in, I will not write a subjective account of how I've grown up in this area and know how hot and dry it can be in the summer. Instead, I will present an objective account of the environmental conditions using specific language (location, temperatures, moisture). In science, the hardest information to write about is ambiguous information, since it can be difficult to be succinct, concrete, logical, accurate, or objective; though in the end, this ambiguity is where the next experiment is and where the real work is to be done.

In reading Tara's analysis, you might be surprised by how extensive and complex her thinking is. After all, scientists just follow the conventions of scientific writing, don't they? Tara's analysis is a powerful demonstration of the kind of rhetorical sensitivity that scientists draw on when they write proposals, lab reports, and other scientific documents.

# Writing in the Social Sciences

The social sciences, disciplines such as sociology, psychology, anthropology, communications, political science, and economics, draw from both the sciences and the humanities. Many scholars in the social sciences address questions that interest humanities scholars, but their methods of investigating these questions differ. Consider the topic of aging. An English professor might study several novels with elderly characters to see how they are represented. A philosopher might consider the moral and political issues surrounding aging and longevity. A sociologist, on the other hand, might explore the ways in which the elderly are treated in a particular community and evaluate the impact such treatment has on elders' moods and activity levels.

In general, social scientists explore questions through controlled methods, including the following:

- Surveys and questionnaires
- Experiments
- Observation
- Interviews
- Case studies
- Ethnographic field work

Careful observation is central to all these methods because, like scientists, social scientists value the development of objective and reliable knowledge. As a result, they ground their arguments in quantitative data (data based on statistics) or qualitative data (data based on observations). An economist studying the effect of aging on earning power might gather statistics that enable him to generate a hypothesis about their relationship. A sociologist might use one or more surveys, interviews, and case studies to gain a nuanced understanding of the impact of aging on self-perception and self-esteem.

Writing is as important in the social sciences as it is in the natural and applied sciences and humanities. As Deidre McCloskey, internationally known economist and author of *Economical Writing*, points out, a person trained in economics "is likely to spend most of her working life writing papers, reports, memoranda, proposals, columns, and letters.

Economics depends much more on writing (and on speaking, another neglected art) than on the statistics and mathematics usually touted as the tools of the trade."[4]

# Sample Student Essay in the Social Sciences

Pages 240–48 present an example of effective writing in the social sciences. Tawnya Redding wrote this essay for a psychology class in clinical research methods. A major assignment was to write a review of the literature on a possible theoretical experiment. Tawnya chose to write her review on music preference and the risk for depression and suicide in adolescents. Note that this essay uses APA documentation style, required for this course.[5] For details on this reference style, see the APA Documentation Guidelines section at the back of this book.

---

[4]Deidre McCloskey. *Economical Writing*. 2nd ed. Waveland Press, 1999, 5.

[5]The formatting shown in the sample paper that follows is consistent with typical APA requirements for undergraduate writing. Formatting guidelines for papers prepared for publication differ in some respects; see pp. 364–88.

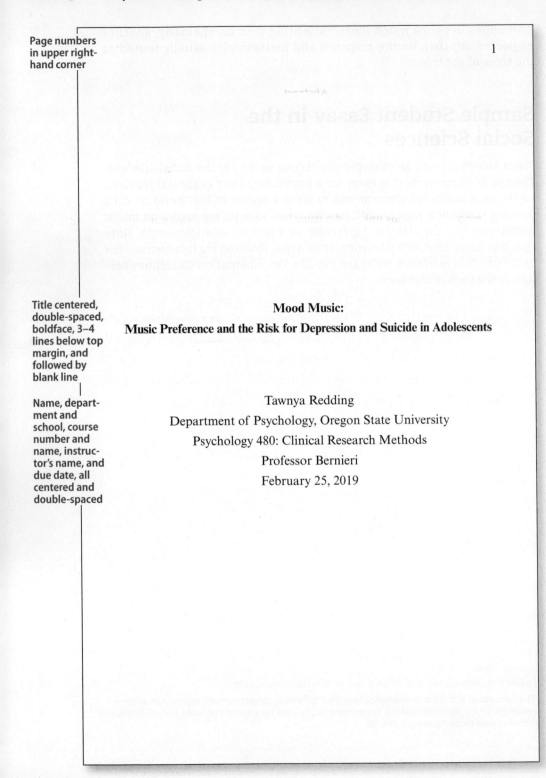

Page numbers in upper right-hand corner

1

Title centered, double-spaced, boldface, 3–4 lines below top margin, and followed by blank line

**Mood Music:**

**Music Preference and the Risk for Depression and Suicide in Adolescents**

Name, department and school, course number and name, instructor's name, and due date, all centered and double-spaced

Tawnya Redding

Department of Psychology, Oregon State University

Psychology 480: Clinical Research Methods

Professor Bernieri

February 25, 2019

2

## Abstract

The last 25 years have shown a growing concern for the effects that certain genres of music (such as heavy metal and country) have on youth. While a correlational link between these problematic genres and increased risk for depression and suicide in adolescents has been established, researchers have been unable to pinpoint what is responsible for this link, and a causal relationship has not been determined. This paper will begin by discussing correlational literature concerning music preference and increased risk for depression and suicide, as well as the possible reasons for this link. Finally, studies concerning the effects of music on mood will be discussed. This examination of the literature on music and increased risk for depression and suicide points out the limitations of previous research and suggests the need for new research establishing a causal relationship for this link as well as research into the specific factors that may contribute to an increased risk for depression and suicide in adolescents.

**Instructor-requested abstract; heading centered and boldface**

**Summary of literature review**

**Double-spaced**

3

**Mood Music: Music Preference and the Risk for Depression and Suicide in Adolescents**

Music is a significant part of American culture. Since the explosion of rock 'n' roll in the 1950s there has been a concern for the effects that music may have on those who choose to listen and especially for the youth of society. The genres most likely to come under suspicion in recent decades have included heavy metal, country, and even blues. These genres have been suspected of having adverse effects on the mood and behavior of young listeners. But can music really alter the disposition and create self-destructive behaviors in listeners? And if so, what genres and aspects of these genres are responsible?

The following review of the literature will establish the correlation between potentially problematic genres of music, such as heavy metal and country, and depression and suicide risk. First, correlational studies concerning music preference and suicide risk will be discussed, followed by a discussion of the literature concerning the possible reasons for this link. Finally, studies concerning the effects of music on mood will be discussed. Despite the link between genres such as heavy metal and country and suicide risk, previous research has been unable to establish the causal nature of this link.

**The Correlation between Music and Depression and Suicide Risk**

Studies over the past several decades have set out to establish the causal nature of the link between music and mood by examining the correlation between youth music preference and risk for depression and suicide. A large number of these studies have focused on heavy metal and country music as the main genre culprits in association with youth suicidality and depression (Lacourse et al., 2001; Scheel & Westefeld, 1999; Stack & Gundlach, 1992). Stack and Gundlach (1992) examined the radio airtime devoted to country music in 49 metropolitan areas and found that the higher the percentages of country music airtime, the higher the incidence of suicides

**Annotations (left margin):**

- Full title repeated, centered, and boldface
- Opening sentences set context for study, argue for significance
- Questions frame focus of report
- Second paragraph outlines paper's purpose, structure, and conclusion
- Heading, centered and boldface
- Opening sets chronological context
- APA-style parenthetical citation of three studies

4

among whites. Stack and Gundlach (1992) hypothesized that themes in country music (such as alcohol abuse) promote audience identification and reinforce preexisting suicidal mood and that the themes associated with country music were responsible for the elevated suicide rates. Similarly, Scheel and Westefeld (1999) found a correlation between heavy metal music listeners and an increased risk for suicide, as did Lacourse et al. (2001).

Source named in the body of the text

### Reasons for the Link: Characteristics of Those
### Who Listen to Problematic Music

Headings organize literature review; section discusses studies that fail to establish music as causal factor in suicide risk

Unfortunately, previous studies concerning music preference and suicide risk have been unable to determine a causal relationship and have focused mainly on establishing a correlation between suicide risk and music preference. This leaves the question open as to whether an individual at risk for depression and suicide is attracted to certain genres of music or whether the music helps induce the mood, or both.

Some studies have suggested that music preference may simply be a reflection of other underlying problems associated with increased risk for suicide (Lacourse et al., 2001; Scheel & Westefeld, 1999). For example, in research done by Scheel and Westefeld (1999), adolescents who listened to heavy metal were found to have lower scores on Linehan, Goodstein, Nielsen, and Chiles's Reasons for Living Inventory (1983) and several of its subscales, a self-report measure designed to assess potential reasons for not committing suicide. These adolescents were also found to have lower scores on several subscales of the Reason for Living Inventory, including responsibility to family along with survival and coping beliefs.

Identifies an important psychological measurement tool

Other risk factors associated with suicide and suicidal behaviors include poor family relationships, depression, alienation, anomie, and drug and alcohol abuse (Bobakova et al., 2012; Lacourse et al., 2001). Lacourse et al. (2001) examined 275 adolescents in the Montreal region with a preference for heavy metal and found that this

5

preference was not significantly related to suicide risk when other risk factors were controlled for. This was also the conclusion of Scheel and Westefeld (1999), in which music preference for heavy metal was thought to be a red flag for suicide vulnerability but which suggested that the source of the problem may lie more in personal and familial characteristics.

George et al. (2007) further explored the correlation between suicide risk and music preference by attempting to identify the personality characteristics of those with a preference for different genres of music. A community sample of 358 individuals was assessed for preference of 30 different styles of music, along with a number of personality characteristics including self-esteem, intelligence, spirituality, social skills, locus of control, openness, conscientiousness, extraversion, agreeableness, emotional stability, hostility, and depression (George et al., 2007). The 30 styles of music were then sorted into eight categories: rebellious (for example, punk and heavy metal), classical, rhythmic and intense (including hip-hop, rap, pop), easy listening, fringe (for example, techno), contemporary Christian, jazz and blues, and traditional Christian. The results revealed an almost comprehensively negative personality profile for those who preferred to listen to the rebellious and rhythmic and intense categories, while those who preferred classical music tended to have a comprehensively positive profile. Like Scheel and Westefeld (1999) and Lacourse et al. (2001), this study also supports the theory that youth are drawn to certain genres of music based on already existing factors, whether they be related to personality or situational variables.

### Reasons for the Link: Characteristics of Problematic Music

Another possible explanation for the correlation between suicide risk and music preference is that the lyrics and themes of the music have a negative effect on listeners. In this scenario, music is thought

Transitional sentence announces discussion of new group of studies

6

to exacerbate an already depressed mood and hence contribute to an increased risk for suicide. This was the proposed reasoning behind higher suicide rates in whites in Stack and Gundlach's (1992) study linking country music to suicide risk. In this case, the themes associated with country music were thought to promote audience identification and reinforce preexisting behaviors associated with suicidality (such as alcohol consumption).

Stack (2000) also studied individuals with a musical preference for blues to determine whether the themes in blues music could increase the level of suicide acceptability. The results demonstrated that blues fans were no more accepting of suicide than nonfans, but that blues listeners were found to have lowered religiosity levels, an important factor for suicide acceptability (Stack, 2000). Despite this link between possible suicidal behavior and a preference for blues music, the actual suicide behavior of blues fans has not been explored, and thus no concrete associations can be made.

**Year distinguishes this study from previously cited study conducted by same researcher**

### The Effect of Music on Mood

While studies examining the relationship between music genres such as heavy metal, country, and blues have been able to establish a correlation between music preference and suicide risk, it is still unclear from these studies what effect music has on the mood of the listener. Previous research has suggested that some forms of music can both improve and depress mood (Johnson, 2009; Lai, 1999; Siedliecki & Good, 2006; Smith & Noon, 1998).

**Heading and transitional sentence identify problem not yet answered by research**

Lai (1999) found that changes in mood were more likely to be found in an experimental group of depressed women versus a control group. The physiological variables of heart rate, respiratory rate, blood pressure, and immediate mood state were measured before and after the experimental group had listened to music of their choice for 30 minutes and the control group had listened to pink sound (similar to white noise) for 30 minutes. It was

7

found that music listening had a greater effect on participants' physiological conditions, as decreases in heart rate, blood pressure, and respiratory rate were greater in the experiment group than the control group (Lai, 1999). This study suggests that music can have a positive effect on depressed individuals when they are allowed to choose the music they are listening to.

In a similar study, Siedliecki and Good (2006) found that music can increase a listener's sense of power and decrease depression, pain, and disability. Researchers randomly assigned 60 African American and Caucasian participants with chronic nonmalignant pain to either a standard music group (offered a choice of instrumental music between piano, jazz, orchestra, harp, and synthesizer), a patterning music group (asked to choose between music to ease muscle tension, facilitate sleep, or decrease anxiety), or a control group. There were no statistically significant differences between the two music groups. However, the music groups had significantly less pain, depression, and disability than the control group.

**Mentions seemingly contradictory research findings**

On the other hand, Martin et al. (1993) identified a subgroup of heavy metal fans who reported feeling worse after listening to their music of choice. Although this subgroup did exist, there was also evidence that listening to heavy metal results in more positive affect for some, and it was hypothesized that those who experience negative affect after listening to their preferred genre of heavy metal may be most at risk for suicidal behaviors.

Smith and Noon (1998) also determined that music can have a negative effect on mood. Six songs were selected for the particular theme they embodied: (1) vigorous, (2) fatigued, (3) angry, (4) depressed, (5) tense, and (6) all moods. The results indicated that selections 3–6 had significant effects on the mood of participants, with selection 6 (all moods) resulting in the greatest positive change in mood while selection 5 (tense) resulted in the greatest negative

8

change in mood. Selection 4 (depressed) was found to sap the vigor and increase anger/hostility in participants, while selection 5 (tense) significantly depressed participants and made them more anxious. Although this study did not specifically comment on the effects of different genres on mood, the results do indicate that certain themes can indeed depress mood. The participants for this study were undergraduate students who were not depressed, and thus it seems that certain types of music can have a negative effect on the mood of healthy individuals.

### Is There Evidence for a Causal Relationship?

Despite the correlation between certain music genres (especially that of heavy metal) and an increased risk for depression and suicidal behaviors in adolescents, it remains unclear whether these types of music can alter the mood of at-risk youth in a negative way. This view of the correlation between music and suicide risk is supported by a meta-analysis done by Baker and Bor (2008), in which the authors assert that most studies reject the notion that music is a causal factor and suggest that music preference is more indicative of emotional vulnerability. However, it is still unknown whether these genres can negatively alter mood at all and, if they can, whether it is the themes and lyrics associated with the music that are responsible. Clearly, more research is needed to further examine this correlation, as a causal link between these genres of music and suicide risk has yet to be shown. However, even if the theory put forth by Baker and Bor (2008) and other researchers is true, it is still important to investigate the effects that music can have on those who may be at risk for suicide and depression. Even if music is not the ultimate cause of suicidal behavior, it may act as a catalyst that further pushes individuals into a state of depression and increased risk for suicidal behavior.

Heading and transitional sentence emphasize inconclusive nature of studies

Emphasizes need for further research and suggests direction research might take

9

**References**

Baker, F., & Bor, W. (2008). Can music preference indicate mental health status in young people? *Australasian Psychiatry, 16*(4), 284–288. https://doi.org/10.1080/10398560701879589

Bobakova, D., Madarasova Geckova, A., Reijneveld, S. A., & Van Dijik, J. P. (2012). Subculture affiliation is associated with substance use of adolescents. *Addiction Research, 18*(2), 91–96.

George, D., Stickle, K., Rachid, F., & Wopnford, A. (2007). The association between types of music enjoyed and cognitive, behavioral, and personality factors of those who listen. *Psychomusicology, 19*(2), 32–56.

Johnson, F. D. (2009). The effects of music on temporary disposition. http://clearinghouse.missouriwestern.edu/manuscripts/260.php

Lacourse, E., Claes, M., & Villeneuve, M. (2001). Heavy metal music and adolescent suicidal risk. *Journal of Youth and Adolescence, 30*(3), 321–332.

Lai, Y. (1999). Effects of music listening on depressed women in Taiwan. *Issues in Mental Health Nursing, 20*(3), 229–246. https://doi.org/10.1080/016128499248637

Linehan, M. M., Goodstein, J. L., Nielsen, S. L., & Chiles, J. A. (1983). Reasons for staying alive when you are thinking of killing yourself: The Reasons for Living Inventory. *Journal of Consulting and Clinical Psychology, 51*(2), 276–286. https://doi.org/10.1037/0022–006X.51.2.276

Martin, G., Clark, M., & Pearce, C. (1993). Adolescent suicide: Music preference as an indicator of vulnerability. *Journal of the American Academy of Child and Adolescent Psychiatry, 32*(3), 530–535.

Scheel, K., & Westefeld, J. (1999). Heavy metal music and adolescent suicidality: An empirical investigation. *Adolescence, 34*(134), 253–273.

Siedliecki, S., & Good, M. (2006). Effect of music on power, pain, depression and disability. *Journal of Advanced Nursing, 54*(5), 553–562. https://doi.org/10.1111/j.1365-2648.2006.03860.x

Smith, J. L., & Noon, J. (1998). Objective measurement of mood change induced by contemporary music. *Journal of Psychiatric & Mental Health Nursing, 5*(5), 403–408.

Snipes, J., & Maguire, E. (1995). Country music, suicide, and spuriousness. *Social Forces, 74*(1), 327–329.

Stack, S. (2000). Blues fans and suicide acceptability. *Death Studies, 24*(3), 223–231. https://doi.org/10.1080/074811800200559

Stack, S., & Gundlach, J. (1992). The effect of country music on suicide. *Social Forces, 71*(1), 211–218.

**Marginal annotations:**

References begin new page

First line of each entry begins at left margin; subsequent lines indent ½ inch

Online document identified with URL

Citation follows APA style for print journal article

Article from database identified with the article's DOI (digital object identifier)

References double-spaced (single-spaced here for length)

In reflecting on her experience writing this essay, Tawnya had this to say:

> My assignment was to write a literature review on a topic of my choice. Since the literature review is a fairly standard genre in psychology, my role as a writer was both fixed and flexible. It was fixed in that I had to follow the conventions for literature reviews; this includes conveying the tone of a serious scholar, in part by using the third person rather than the first person. But it was flexible in that I was able to determine what material to include in the review, the conclusions I drew from my analysis, and my suggestions for future research. My professor was the intended reader for this essay, but I also had a more general reader in mind as I wrote. I wanted to encourage readers to think critically about the studies being presented. What are the strengths and weaknesses of the studies? How might they be improved? What information is lacking in the current research? What problem has previous research not yet addressed, and how might future research do so?

# Writing in Business

Historians of business writing emphasize the roles that the spread of literacy in the Middle Ages and the invention of the printing press in the Renaissance played in this history. According to Malcolm Richardson, a contributor to *Studies in the History of Business Writing*, even before capitalism developed in Europe there were scribes and scriveners, who played a key role in both government and private communication.[6] In the fourteenth century, what some historians believe to be the first business writing school opened in England, and in the sixteenth century, Angell Day's *The English Secretary or Method of Writing Epistles and Letters*, one of the earliest texts on business communication (which at that time primarily took the form of letter writing), appeared.

The conventions that characterize modern business writing—particularly the preference for clear, concise, goal- and audience-oriented communication and an easy-to-read visual design—developed slowly but

---

[6]Douglas, George H., and Herbert William Hildebrandt, editors. *Studies in the History of Business Writing*, Association for Business Communication, 1985.

steadily. With the growth of the middle class and the increase of commerce, businesspersons needed to be able to communicate with both internal and external audiences. Basic forms of business writing, such as memos, letters, proposals, and reports, became more standard. As layers of management evolved and departments proliferated, written internal communication became increasingly important, as did changes in the technologies of communication. The typewriter and carbon paper (and, later, dictaphones and photocopiers) transformed the office through the mid-twentieth century.

Developments in online and digital communication are once again effecting powerful changes in business writing. Today's business writers communicate online as well as in traditional print environments. They must be able to work effectively in teams, and they need to be able to respond to the demands of working in a global environment. The essential characteristics of effective business writing, however, remain grounded in basic issues of rhetorical sensitivity. When writing for business, it's especially important to consider the differing needs—and situations—of your readers. You may need to consider readers spread geographically or across an organization chart, for instance.

# Sample Student Email for Business Writing

The email message memo shown on p. 251 was written by Michelle Rosowsky in a business class. The email presents an analysis and recommendation to help an employer make a decision. As you read, notice how the opening paragraph provides necessary background information and clearly states the email's purpose. Even if this email is forwarded to others, the subject line will make its purpose clear. Michelle also used bold type to emphasize the most important information.

This assignment took the form of a case study. The student's teacher provided a series of hypothetical facts about a potential business transaction. Michelle had to analyze this information, determine her recommendations, and communicate them in the most effective form possible.

In reflecting on the email, Michelle commented that the first and most important step in the writing process involved analyzing both the information that she was given and her rhetorical situation.

> I first had to analyze the facts of the case to come up with an appropriate recommendation and then present the recommendation within the format of a typical business email. Because it's written for a busy manager, I wrote the email as concisely as possible so that the

information would be available at a glance. I also put the most critical calculation, the manufacturing cost, at the beginning of the email and in bold so that the manager could find it easily and refer back to it later if necessary. The succinctness of the email reflects my confidence in the analysis, which gives me a strong and positive ethos and helps establish my reliability and competence.

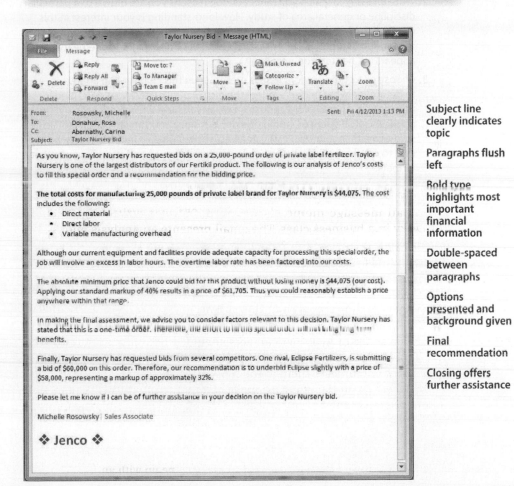

Subject line clearly indicates topic

Paragraphs flush left

Bold type highlights most important financial information

Double-spaced between paragraphs

Options presented and background given

Final recommendation

Closing offers further assistance

## for **thought, discussion, and writing**

1. Although you may not have determined your major area of study yet, you probably have some idea of whether you want to major in the humanities, social sciences, sciences, or business. Meet with a group of classmates who share your general interests. Working together, first make a list of the reasons you all find this area interesting. Next, make a list of the writing challenges that students in this area face. Finally, choose two of these challenges and brainstorm productive ways that students can respond to them.

2. Write an essay in which you reflect on the reasons you are drawn to a particular discipline or general area of study. How long-standing is your interest in this discipline? What do you see as its challenges and rewards? (Before writing, you might read Brandon Barrett's essay on his decision to major in chemistry, which appears in Chapter 3 on pp. 68–69.)

3. Choose one of the student essays presented in this chapter and analyze it to determine what features reflect the disciplinary preferences described in this chapter. Alternatively, choose an essay you have written for a class in the sciences, social sciences, humanities, or business, and similarly analyze it. In studying either your own essay or an essay that appears in this chapter, be sure to consider its vocabulary, style, method of proof, and use of conventional formats.

# 9

# Strategies for Invention, Planning, and Drafting

Part Three of *The Academic Writer* provides practical strategies that writers can use when they compose texts. The first two chapters provide pragmatic, action-oriented advice about how to meet the challenges of academic writing. They also model strategies that enable writers to move productively through the writing process. Many of these strategies apply to both print texts (or alphabetic texts that look like traditional print texts but are read on screens) and compositions that employ multiple modes. Whether you are writing a print essay for your geography class or creating a Prezi presentation or podcast for that same course, you need to come up with ideas, develop them, and embody them in a print, oral, or digital medium. As Chapter 11, "Strategies for Multimodal Composing," emphasizes, however, students are increasingly creating texts that take advantage of the multiple modes and media available to them. Students who want to share a personal story could write a personal essay, but they could also create a visually rich poster, podcast, collage, or video. Chapter 11 addresses some of the opportunities and challenges that writers face in our world of expanding opportunities for communication.

## Strategies for Invention

Like many writers, you may believe that finding ideas to write about is the most mysterious part of the writing process. Where do ideas come from? How can you draw a blank one minute and suddenly know the right way to support your argument or describe your experience the next? Is it possible to increase your ability to think and write creatively? Writers and speakers have been concerned with questions such as these for centuries. Ancient Greek and Roman rhetoricians, in fact, were among the first to investigate the process of discovering and exploring ideas. The classical Roman rhetoricians called this process *inventio*, for "invention" or "discovery." Contemporary writers, drawing on this Latin term, often refer to this process as *invention*.

In practice, invention usually involves both individual inquiry and dialogue with others. In working on a lab report, for example, you might spend most of your time writing alone, but the experiment you're writing about might have been undertaken by a group of students working together; you might look up some related research to be sure you understand the principles you're writing about; you might also ask other students or your instructor for advice in putting the report together. Every time you talk with others about ideas or consult materials for information, you're entering into a conversation with others about your topic, and, like all writers, you can benefit from their support and insights.

The strategies discussed in this section of the chapter aim to help you invent successfully, whether you're having a conversation with yourself as you think through and write about ideas or working with classmates. These methods can help you discover what you know—and don't know—about a subject. They can also guide you as you plan, draft, and revise your writing.

Read this section with a writer's eye. Which of these strategies do you already use? Which ones could you use more effectively? What other strategies might extend your range or strengthen your writing abilities? As you read about and experiment with these strategies, remember to assess their usefulness based on your own needs and preferences as a writer as well as on your particular writing situation. Most writers find that some of the following methods work better for them than others. That's fine. Just be sure to give each method a fair chance before deciding which ones to rely on.

---

## strategies for success

When you practice the methods of invention, you're focusing on generating ideas—not on being perfectly correct. There's no need to interrupt the flow of your ideas by stopping to edit your grammar, spelling, vocabulary, or punctuation. Feel free to invent in the languages that you are most comfortable using, especially if doing so increases your fluency and helps you generate ideas.

---

### FREEWRITING

Freewriting is the practice of writing as freely as possible without stopping. It's a simple but powerful strategy for exploring important issues and problems. Here is a description of freewriting by Peter Elbow, from his book *Writing with Power: Techniques for Mastering the Writing Process*:

> To do a freewriting exercise, simply force yourself to write without stopping for [a certain number] of minutes . . . . If you can't think of anything to write, write about how that feels or repeat over and over "I have nothing to write" or "Nonsense" or "No." If you get stuck in the middle of

a sentence or thought, just repeat the last word or phrase till something comes along. The only point is to keep writing.[1]

Freewriting may at first seem too simple to achieve very powerful results, but it can actually help you discover ideas that you couldn't reach through more conscious and logical means. Because it helps you generate a great deal of material, freewriting is also an excellent antidote for the anxiety many writers feel at the start of a project. It can also improve the speed and ease with which you write.

Freewriting is potentially powerful in a variety of writing situations. Writing quickly without censoring your thoughts can help you explore your personal experience, for example, by enabling you to gain access to images, events, and emotions that you've forgotten or suppressed. Freewriting can also help you experiment with more complex topics without having to assess the worthiness of individual ideas. The following shows how one student used five minutes of freewriting to explore and focus her ideas for a political science paper on low voter turnout.

This student's freewriting not only helped her explore her ideas but also identified a possible question to address and sources she could draw on as she worked on her project.

---

I just don't get it. As soon as I could register I did    it felt like a really import-ant day. I'd watched my mother vote and my sisters vote and now it was my turn. But why do I vote; guess I should ask myself that question—and why don't other people? Do I feel that my vote makes a difference? There have been some close elections but not all that many, so my vote doesn't literally count, doesn't decide if we pay a new tax or elect a new senator. Part of it's the feeling I get. When I go to vote I know the people at the polling booth; they're my neighbors. I often know the people who are running for office in local elections, and for state and national elections—well, I just feel that I should. But the statistics on voter turnout tell me I'm unusual. I want to go beyond statistics. I want to understand *why* people don't vote. Seems like I need to look not only at research in political science, but also maybe in sociology. (Check journals in economics too?) I wonder if it'd be okay for me to interview some students, maybe some staff and faculty, about voting—better check. But wait a minute; this is a small college in a small town, like the town I'm from. I wonder if people in cities would feel differently—they might. Maybe what I need to look at in my paper is rural/small town versus urban voting patterns.

---

[1]Elbow, Peter. *Writing with Power: Techniques for Mastering the Writing Process.* Oxford UP, 1981, p. 13.

## LOOPING

Looping, an extended or directed form of freewriting, alternates freewriting with analysis and reflection. Begin looping by first establishing a subject for your freewriting and then freewriting for five to ten minutes. This freewriting is your first loop. After completing this loop, read what you have written and look for the center of gravity or "heart" of your ideas—the image, detail, issue, or problem that seems richest or most intriguing, compelling, or productive. Select or write a sentence that summarizes this understanding; this sentence will become the starting point of your second loop. The student who wrote about low voter turnout, for example, might decide to use looping to reflect on this sentence: "I want to understand *why* people don't vote."

There is no predetermined number of loops that will work. Keep looping as many times as you like or until you feel you've exhausted a subject. When you loop, you don't know where your freewriting and reflection will take you; you don't worry about the final product. Your final essay might not even discuss the ideas generated by your efforts. That's fine; the goal in freewriting and looping is not to produce a draft of an essay but to discover and explore ideas, images, and sometimes even words, phrases, and sentences that you can use in your writing.

---

## for **exploration**

Choose a question, an idea, or subject that interests you, and freewrite for five to ten minutes. Then stop and read your freewriting. What comments most interest or surprise you? Write a statement that best expresses the center of gravity, or "heart," of your freewriting. Use this comment to begin a second loop by freewriting for five minutes more.

After completing the second freewriting, stop and reread both passages. What did you learn from your freewriting? Does your freewriting suggest possible ideas for an essay? Finally, reflect on the process itself. Did you find the experience of looping helpful? Would you use freewriting and looping in the future as a means of generating ideas and exploring your experiences?

---

## BRAINSTORMING

Like freewriting and looping, brainstorming is a simple but productive invention strategy. When you brainstorm, you list as quickly as possible all the thoughts about a subject that occur to you without censoring or stopping to reflect on them. Brainstorming can help you discover and explore a number of ideas in a short time. Not all of them will be worth using in a piece of writing, of course. The premise of brainstorming is that the more ideas you can generate, the better your chances will be of coming up with good ones.

Alex Osborn, the person generally credited with naming this technique, originally envisioned brainstorming as a group, not an individual, activity. Osborn believed that the enthusiasm generated by the group helped spark ideas. Group brainstorming can be used for a variety of purposes. If your class has just been assigned a broad topic, for instance, your group could brainstorm a list of ways to approach or limit this topic. Or the group could use email, an online discussion board, or a blog to generate possible arguments in support of or in opposition to a specific thesis. (See the guidelines for group brainstorming on the next page.)

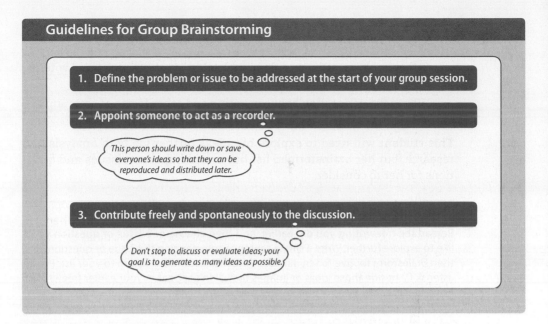

## Guidelines for Group Brainstorming

1. Define the problem or issue to be addressed at the start of your group session.

2. Appoint someone to act as a recorder.

   *This person should write down or save everyone's ideas so that they can be reproduced and distributed later.*

3. Contribute freely and spontaneously to the discussion.

   *Don't stop to discuss or evaluate ideas; your goal is to generate as many ideas as possible.*

There are also brainstorming resources available online that you may find useful. Some software, including Thinkature and Bubbl.us, allows you to brainstorm and diagram relationships between ideas.

Those who regularly write with teams or groups cite increased intellectual stimulation and improved quality of ideas as major benefits of brainstorming together, but solitary brainstorming can be just as productive. To brainstorm alone, take a few moments at the start to formulate your goal, purpose, or problem. Then list your ideas as quickly as you can. Include everything that comes to mind, from facts to images, memories, fragments of conversations, and other general impressions and responses. (You are the only one who needs to be able to decipher what you've written, so your brainstorming can be as messy or as organized as you like.) Then review your brainstorming to identify the most promising or helpful ideas.

After freewriting about low voter turnout, for example, the student whose writing you read on p. 255 decided to brainstorm a list of possible reasons people might not vote. Here is part of her list:

Some people (young people?) mistrust politicians

Alienated from the political process

Many political issues are highly polarized—abortion, research using stem cells, war, drugs, death penalty, health care, etc.

People in the middle may feel left out of the discussion

Don't know enough about the issues—or the candidates—to decide

"My vote won't make a difference"

Her brainstorming also raised several important questions:

What role does voter registration play?

Is the problem getting people to register—or getting registered voters to vote?

What's the connection between voting and other forms of community and civic engagement?

This student will need to explore her ideas further via both analysis and research, but her brainstormed list has raised important issues and questions for her to consider.

---

## for **exploration**

Reread the freewriting you did earlier, and then choose one issue or question you'd like to explore further. Write a single sentence summarizing this issue or question, and then brainstorm for five to ten minutes. After brainstorming, return to your list. Put an asterisk (*) beside those ideas or images that didn't appear in your earlier freewriting. How do these new ideas or images add to your understanding of your subject?

---

### CLUSTERING

Like freewriting, looping, and brainstorming, clustering emphasizes spontaneity. The goal of all four strategies is to generate as many ideas as possible, but clustering differs in that it uses visual means to generate ideas. Some writers find that it enables them to explore their ideas more deeply and creatively. (The cluster on the next page was done by the student whose writing appears on pp. 255 and 257.)

Start with a single word or phrase that best summarizes or evokes your topic. Write this word in the center of a page of blank paper and circle it. Now fill in the page by adding ideas connected with this word. Don't censor your ideas or force your cluster to assume a certain shape—your goal is to be as spontaneous as possible. Simply circle your key ideas and connect them either to the first word or to other related ideas. After clustering, put the material you've generated aside for a bit, and then return to it so that you can evaluate it more objectively. When you do return to it, try to find the cluster's center of gravity—the idea or image that seems richest and most compelling.✱

---

## for **exploration**

Reread the freewriting, looping, and brainstorming you have written thus far. Then choose one word that seems especially important for your subject, and use it as the center of a cluster. Without planning or worrying about what shape it's taking, fill in your cluster by branching out from this central word. Then take a moment to reflect on what you have learned.

---

✱ For another example of a cluster, see Chapter 6, p. 162.

**"Voter Apathy" Brainstorming Cluster**

## ASKING THE JOURNALIST'S QUESTIONS

If you have taken a journalism class or written for a newspaper, you know that journalists are taught to answer six questions in articles they write: *who, what, when, where, why,* and *how.* By answering these questions, journalists can be sure that they have provided the most important information about an event, an issue, or a problem for their readers. And because they probe several aspects of a topic, the journalist's questions can help you discover not just what you know about but also what you *don't* know — and thus alert you to the need for additional research.

You may find these questions particularly useful when describing an event or writing an informative essay. Suppose that your political science instructor has assigned an essay on the conflict in Syria. Using the journalist's questions as headings, you could begin working on this assignment by asking yourself the following:

- *Who* is involved in this conflict?
- *What* issues most clearly divide those engaged in this dispute?
- *When* did the conflict begin, and how has it developed over the last few years?
- *Where* does the conflict seem most heated or violent?
- *Why* have those living in this area found it so difficult to resolve the situation?
- *How* might this conflict be resolved?

Although you might discover much the same information by simply brainstorming, using the journalist's questions ensures that you have covered all the major points.

---

## for **exploration**

Using the journalist's questions, explore the subject that you have investigated in preceding For Explorations in this chapter. (If you believe that you have exhausted this subject, feel free to choose a different topic.)

Once you have employed this method, take a few moments to reflect on this experience. To what extent did the strategy help you organize and review what you already know, and to what extent did it define what you still need to find out?

---

# Exploring Ideas

The previous invention strategies have a number of advantages. They're easy to use, and they can help you generate a reassuringly large volume of material when you're just beginning to work on an essay. Sometimes, however, you may want to use more systematic methods to explore a topic. This is especially true when you've identified a potential topic but aren't sure that you have enough to say about it.

## ASKING THE TOPICAL QUESTIONS

One of the most helpful methods for developing ideas is based on the topics of classical rhetoric. In his *Rhetoric*, Aristotle describes the topics as potential lines of argument, or places (*topos* means "place" in Greek) where speakers and writers can find evidence or arguments. Aristotle defined twenty-eight topics, but the list is generally abbreviated to five: *definition*, *comparison*, *relationship*, *circumstance*, and *testimony*.

The classical topics represent natural ways of thinking about ideas. When confronted by an intellectual problem, we all instinctively ask such questions as these:

- What is it? (*definition*)
- What is it like or unlike? (*comparison*)
- What caused it? (*relationship*)
- What is possible or impossible? (*circumstance*)
- What have others said about it? (*testimony*)

Aristotle's topics build on these natural mental habits. The topical questions can help you pinpoint alternative approaches to a subject or probe one subject systematically, organizing what you know already and identifying gaps that require additional reading or research. Simply pose each question in turn about your subject, writing down as many responses as possible. You might also try answering the expanded list of questions for exploring a topic on p. 262.

---

## for **exploration**

Use the topical questions on p. 262 to continue your investigation of the subject that you explored with the journalist's questions in the For Exploration on p. 260. What new information or ideas do the topical questions generate? How would you compare these methods?

---

## RESEARCHING

You're probably already aware that many writing projects are based on research. The formal research paper, however, is not the only kind of writing that can benefit from looking at how others have approached a topic. Whatever kind of writing you're doing, a quick survey of published materials can give you a sense of the issues surrounding a topic, fill gaps in your knowledge, and spark new ideas and questions.

Chapter 7 covers the formal research process in detail. At the invention stage, however, loose, informal research is generally more effective. If you're interested in writing about skydiving, for example, you could pick up a copy of *Skydiving* magazine or spend a half hour browsing websites devoted to the sport to get a better feel for current trends and issues.

To cite another example, imagine that you're writing about the Americans with Disabilities Act (ADA) for a political science assignment. After freewriting and asking yourself the journalist's questions, you find

## Questions for Exploring a Topic

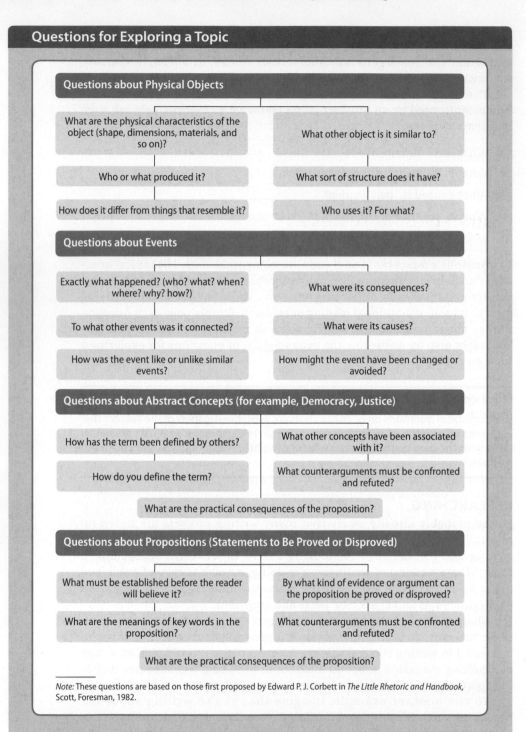

### Questions about Physical Objects

What are the physical characteristics of the object (shape, dimensions, materials, and so on)?

What other object is it similar to?

Who or what produced it?

What sort of structure does it have?

How does it differ from things that resemble it?

Who uses it? For what?

### Questions about Events

Exactly what happened? (who? what? when? where? why? how?)

What were its consequences?

To what other events was it connected?

What were its causes?

How was the event like or unlike similar events?

How might the event have been changed or avoided?

### Questions about Abstract Concepts (for example, Democracy, Justice)

How has the term been defined by others?

What other concepts have been associated with it?

How do you define the term?

What counterarguments must be confronted and refuted?

What are the practical consequences of the proposition?

### Questions about Propositions (Statements to Be Proved or Disproved)

What must be established before the reader will believe it?

By what kind of evidence or argument can the proposition be proved or disproved?

What are the meanings of key words in the proposition?

What counterarguments must be confronted and refuted?

What are the practical consequences of the proposition?

*Note:* These questions are based on those first proposed by Edward P. J. Corbett in *The Little Rhetoric and Handbook,* Scott, Foresman, 1982.

yourself wondering if the fact that President Franklin Delano Roosevelt was afflicted with polio had any influence on accessibility legislation. You type "FDR" and "disability" into a search engine, and, browsing the first few hits, you learn that while FDR is now considered an inspiration for Americans with disabilities, he spent years trying to keep his wheelchair hidden from public view. Realizing that you're very interested in this shift in attitude, you decide to focus on the question of how the ADA has influenced public perceptions of disability. A few keystrokes have given you a valuable idea.

## strategies for success

Your educational experiences may have taught you ways of discovering and exploring ideas that are different from those discussed in this chapter. How are they different? If you have been educated in another culture, do the invention methods used in that culture reflect different rhetorical and cultural values? What invention methods used in your community or in your experiences reflect different rhetorical values? If there are significant differences, how have you dealt with them?

## WRITING A DISCOVERY DRAFT

Sometimes the best way to develop and explore ideas is to write a very rough draft and see, in effect, what you think about your topic. This strategy, sometimes called *discovery drafting*, can work well as long as you recognize that your draft will need extensive analysis and revision.

Writing a discovery draft is a lot like freewriting, although the process tends to be more focused and usually takes more time. As you write, stick to your topic as best you can, but expect that your thoughts may veer off in unexpected directions. The goal is not to produce a polished — or even a coherent — essay, but to put your ideas into written form so that you can evaluate them. Once you have completed a discovery draft, you can use it to identify and fine-tune your most promising ideas, to clarify your goals, and to determine what remains to be done. In order to do so, you will need to put your draft aside for a bit so you can look at it objectively when you return to it.✱

✱ For an example of a discovery draft, see Daniel Stiepleman's draft on p. 163.

---

## for **collaboration**

Meet with a group of classmates to discuss the methods of discovering and developing ideas. Begin by having group members briefly describe the advantages and disadvantages they experienced with these methods. (Appoint a recorder to summarize each person's statements.) Then, as a group, discuss your responses to these questions: (1) How might different students' preferences for one or more of these strategies be connected to different learning, composing, and cultural preferences? (2) What influence might situational factors (such as the nature of the assignment or the amount of time available for working on an essay) have on the decision to use one or more of these strategies?

---

# Strategies for Planning

It may be helpful to think of planning as involving waves of play and work. When you're discovering and exploring ideas, for example, you're in a sense playing—pushing your ideas as far as you can without worrying about how useful they'll be later. Most people can't write an essay based on a brainstorming list or thirty minutes of freewriting, however. At some point, they need to settle down to work and formulate a plan for the project.

The planning activities described in this section of the chapter generally require more discipline than the play of invention does. Because much of the crafting of your essay occurs as a result of these activities, however, this work can be intensely rewarding.

### ESTABLISHING A WORKING THESIS

You can't establish a workable plan for your essay without having a tentative sense of the goals you hope to achieve by writing. These goals may change along the way, but they represent an important starting point for guiding your work in progress. Before you start to draft, then, try to establish a *working thesis* for your essay.

A working thesis reflects an essay's topic as well as the point you wish to make and the effect you wish to have on your readers. An effective working thesis narrows your topic, helps you organize your ideas, enables you to determine what you want to say and *can* say, helps you decide if you have enough information to support your assertions, and points to the most effective way to present your ideas.

thinking
rhetorically

A few examples may help clarify this concept. Suppose that you're writing an editorial for your campus newspaper. "What are you going to write about?" a friend asks. "The library," you reply. You've just stated your topic, but this statement doesn't satisfy your friend. "What about the library? What's your point?" "Oh," you say, "I'm going to argue that students should petition library services to extend the number of hours it is open each week. The current hours are too limited, which is inconvenient and unfair to students who work long hours to finance their education." This second statement, which specifies both the point you want to make and its desired effect on readers, is a clearly defined working thesis. Further, because the newspaper editorial is an established genre with specific writing conventions, you know before you start that your argument will need to be brief, explicit, and backed up with concrete details.

You can best understand and establish a working thesis by analyzing the elements of your rhetorical situation: writer, reader, text, and medium. This process (which is described in detail in Chapter 3) should give you a clearer understanding of both your reasons for writing and the most appropriate means to communicate your ideas. In some cases, you may be able to analyze your rhetorical situation and establish a working thesis early in the writing process by asking yourself the questions on p. 266. In many other instances, however, you'll have to think and write your way into understanding what you want to say.

A working thesis will help you structure your plan and guide your draft, but you should view it as preliminary and subject to revision. After you've worked on an essay for a while, your working thesis may evolve to reflect the understanding you gain through further planning and drafting. You may even discover that your working thesis isn't feasible. In either case, the time you spend thinking about your preliminary working thesis isn't wasted, for it has enabled you to begin the process of organizing and testing your ideas.

## FORMULATING A WORKABLE PLAN

Once you have established a working thesis, you should be able to develop a plan that can guide you as you work. As the discussion of differing composing styles in Chapter 4 indicates, people plan in different ways. Some develop detailed written plans; others rely on mental plans; others might freewrite and determine their goals by reflecting on their own written text. As a college student, you will often find written plans helpful. Some writers develop carefully structured, detailed outlines. Others find that quick notes and diagrams are equally effective.

Still others prefer plans that are more visual.✱ Whether a jotted list of notes, a diagram or chart, or a formal outline, developing a plan is an efficient way to try out ideas and engage your unconscious mind in the writing process. In fact, many students find that by articulating their goals on paper or on-screen, they can more effectively critique their own ideas—an important but often difficult part of the writing process.

There is no such thing as an ideal one-size-fits-all plan. An effective plan is one that works for you. Plans are utilitarian, meant to be used *and* revised. In working on an essay, you may draw up a general plan only to revise it as you write. Nevertheless, if it helps you begin drafting, your first plan will fulfill its function well.

---

✱ Daniel Stiepleman's visual plan appears in Chapter 6 (p. 165).

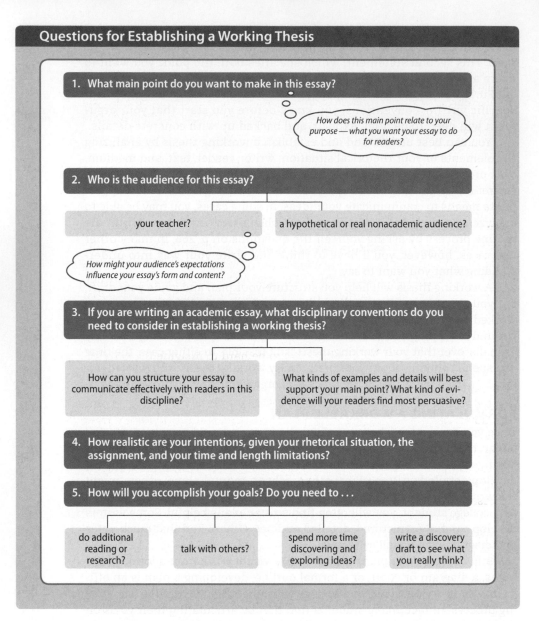

**Questions for Establishing a Working Thesis**

1. What main point do you want to make in this essay?

*How does this main point relate to your purpose — what you want your essay to do for readers?*

2. Who is the audience for this essay?

your teacher?

a hypothetical or real nonacademic audience?

*How might your audience's expectations influence your essay's form and content?*

3. If you are writing an academic essay, what disciplinary conventions do you need to consider in establishing a working thesis?

How can you structure your essay to communicate effectively with readers in this discipline?

What kinds of examples and details will best support your main point? What kind of evidence will your readers find most persuasive?

4. How realistic are your intentions, given your rhetorical situation, the assignment, and your time and length limitations?

5. How will you accomplish your goals? Do you need to . . .

do additional reading or research?

talk with others?

spend more time discovering and exploring ideas?

write a discovery draft to see what you really think?

## strategies for success

You may find it helpful to consider how your unique educational, cultural, or community knowledge of languages or dialects affects the way you formulate plans. Is it easier and more productive to formulate plans in one language and then translate these plans into another? Or is it more helpful to formulate plans in Standard Academic English because doing so encourages you to keep your audience's expectations in mind? You may want to experiment with both approaches so that you can determine the planning process that works best for you.

## for **exploration**

If you have ever created a plan for an essay or a project, what kinds of plans have you typically drawn up? Do you formulate detailed, carefully structured plans (such as detailed outlines or idea maps), do you prefer less structured ones (scratch outlines, lists), or do you just start writing? Use these questions to think about the plans you have (or have not) used in the past; then spend ten minutes writing about how you might develop more useful plans in the future.

# Strategies for Drafting

The British writer E. M. Forster once asked, "How can I know what I think until I see what I say?" You can see what he means if you take the writing process seriously: By working through drafts of your work, you gradually learn what you think about your subject. Although your process may begin with freewriting or brainstorming, drafting is the point in the process when you explore your ideas more fully and deeply, and it is through drafting that you create a text that embodies your preliminary goals.

## MANAGING THE DRAFTING PROCESS

When you sit down to begin writing, it can be hard to imagine the satisfaction of completing a rough draft. Just picking up pen or pencil or booting up your laptop can seem daunting. Once you pass the initial hurdle of getting started, you'll probably experience the drafting process as a series of ebbs and flows. You may write intensely for a short period, stop and review what you've written, make a few notes about how to proceed, and then draft again more slowly, pausing now and then to reread what you've written. It's important to keep your eye on the prize, though: Very few writers can produce anything worth reading without going through this messy, sometimes painful, process. (If, like most writers, you experience moments of writer's block, try the block-busting strategies suggested on p. 268 to get back on track.)

While no two people approach drafting the same way—indeed, even a single person will take different approaches at different times—the strategies discussed in this section can help make your process more efficient and productive.

**Overcoming resistance to getting started.** All writers experience some resistance to drafting, but there are ways to overcome this resistance. To get started, many writers rely on rituals such as clearing their writing space of clutter, gathering notes and other materials in a handy place, or queuing up a favorite playlist. Personal predispositions affect writing habits as well. Some people write best early in the morning; others, late at night. Some require a quiet atmosphere; others find the absence of noise distracting. Some find it easier to draft if they're doing something else at the same time; others shut off their devices so they can focus. The trick is to figure out what works best for you.

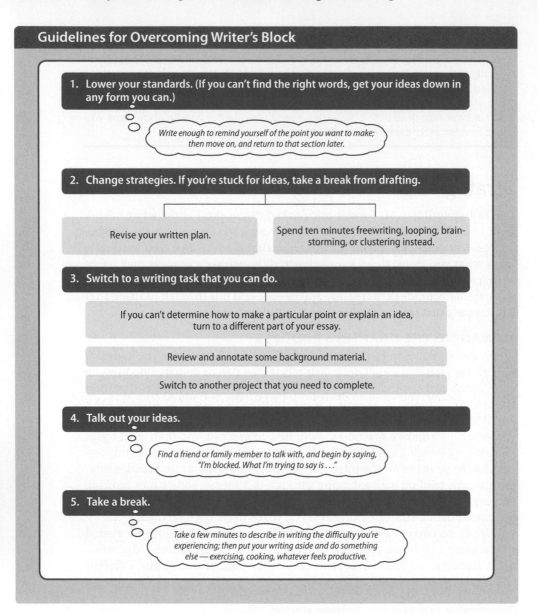

**Guidelines for Overcoming Writer's Block**

1. Lower your standards. (If you can't find the right words, get your ideas down in any form you can.)

   *Write enough to remind yourself of the point you want to make; then move on, and return to that section later.*

2. Change strategies. If you're stuck for ideas, take a break from drafting.

   Revise your written plan.

   Spend ten minutes freewriting, looping, brainstorming, or clustering instead.

3. Switch to a writing task that you can do.

   If you can't determine how to make a particular point or explain an idea, turn to a different part of your essay.

   Review and annotate some background material.

   Switch to another project that you need to complete.

4. Talk out your ideas.

   *Find a friend or family member to talk with, and begin by saying, "I'm blocked. What I'm trying to say is . . ."*

5. Take a break.

   *Take a few minutes to describe in writing the difficulty you're experiencing; then put your writing aside and do something else — exercising, cooking, whatever feels productive.*

Reading through early notes is an effective way to begin drafting. It can be reassuring to remind yourself that you're not starting from scratch, and you may find yourself turning fragmentary notes into full sentences or grouping them into paragraphs—that is, drafting—before you know it.

Perhaps the best motivation is to remind yourself that a draft doesn't have to be perfect. Your initial goal should simply be to *get something down.* If you can't think of a way to open your essay, for instance, don't force yourself; just begin writing whatever you're ready to write and return to the introduction later.

**Building momentum.** While it might seem easier said than done, it's important to keep at it—to keep producing something, *anything*—so that the momentum can help you move steadily toward your goal. Accept that your draft will be imperfect, even incomplete, and just focus on putting your thoughts into words. By giving yourself permission to create a messy draft, you free yourself to explore ideas and discover what you want to say.

Don't try to correct or polish your writing in the drafting stage: Stopping to check spelling or grammar can interrupt your momentum and throw you off balance. Furthermore, it's easier to delete unnecessary or repetitive material when you revise than it is to add new material. If you can't quite articulate an argument or formulate an example, write yourself a note and keep drafting. When you return to your draft, you can fill in these gaps.

**Keeping in touch with your "felt sense."** You attend to many things when you draft. You stop and reread; you reflect about your topic and assignment; you think about your readers. If you're an effective writer, you also look at what you've written not just to see what's on the page but also to consider what *might* be there—that is, you take stock periodically and evaluate how what you've written so far measures up to the meaning you want to get across. Professor Sondra Perl calls this sort of awareness *felt sense*. This felt sense, Perl argues, encourages us to become aware "of what is just on the edge of our thinking but not yet articulated in words."[2]

The ability to develop and maintain felt sense doesn't require magical gifts. Rather, you need to draft for long enough periods so that you can become immersed in your writing. Additionally, as you write words, sentences, and paragraphs, you need to pause periodically to reflect on the extent to which your draft responds to readers' needs and expectations; it's also a good idea to jot down notes on these reflections.

**Allowing time for incubation.** Ideally, you'll come to a natural stopping point, a moment when you feel that you've solved a problem you've been wrestling with or concluded a section you've been working on. At this point, take a few moments to jot down notes about what you've accomplished as well as about what you still need to do. You may also wish to ask yourself a few questions: "What's the best transition here?" "Which examples should I use next?" If you're like many writers, your subconscious mind will present answers when you next sit down to draft.

Sometimes it helps to *stop* thinking consciously about your ideas and just let them develop in your mind while you relax, sleep, or occupy yourself with other projects. After this period of incubation, you'll often spontaneously recognize how to resolve a problem or answer a question. (Don't confuse incubation with procrastination, however. *Procrastination* means avoiding the writing process; *incubation* means recognizing and using the fluctuations of the process to your advantage.)

---

[2]Perl, Sondra. *Writing with the Body*. Boynton Cook Publishers, 2004, p. xii.

---

### for **exploration**

How do you typically draft an essay? How long do your drafting sessions usually last? What do you do when you run into problems? Could one or more of the suggestions presented here enable you to draft more productively? How might you best implement these suggestions? Spend five to ten minutes freewriting in response to these questions.

---

# Developing and Organizing Your Ideas

*thinking rhetorically*

As you draft, you'll become more aware of what you have to say about a subject. Consequently, you'll also become increasingly engaged with issues of organization and structure. "What do I think about this subject?" becomes less important than "How can I best present my ideas to my readers?" This section of the chapter suggests strategies for responding to the second question. Keep in mind that these strategies are only suggestions; your use of them should be based on your understanding of your assignment, purpose, and rhetorical situation.

## USING A THESIS STATEMENT

Academic readers quickly become irritated if writers violate their expectations about how certain kinds of writing should be organized. In general, they expect writing that is straightforward and to the point. For this reason, sharing your working thesis with readers and providing cues about how you will support it are essential.

How to share your working thesis most effectively depends on a number of factors. If you're working on a take-home essay exam for a history class or an analytical essay for a mass media class, for example, you may wish to include in your introduction a *thesis statement*, usually a single sentence that states the main point of your essay.* Your introduction may also preview the main lines of argument you'll use to support your position.

Much academic writing benefits from the inclusion of a thesis statement, but it is not always necessary or even desirable to include an explicit statement of your main point. If you're writing a personal essay for your first-year writing class about what the word *family* means to you, for example, you might decide that you don't want to articulate the main point of your essay in a single sentence. Instead, you might begin with an example that will create interest in your essay and show, rather than tell, what *family* means to you.

*thinking rhetorically*

Whether or not you include a thesis statement, what's important is that you have a clear working thesis and that readers can identify it easily. As you work on your draft, having a working thesis in mind—even if it's not expressed directly—will help you organize your thoughts; it will also help ensure that readers will stay with you.

---

\* For more on thesis statements, see Chapter 6, pp. 145–49.

## DEVELOPING IDEAS

It's a good idea to begin each new drafting session by reviewing the material you've already generated, looking for ideas and details to add or develop more fully. Often in rereading these explorations and early drafts, writers realize that they've relied on words that have meaning for themselves but not necessarily for their readers. Learning to recognize and expand, or "unpack," such words in your own writing can help you develop your ideas so that their significance is clear to readers.

Here is a paragraph from one student's freewriting about what the word *family* means to her. While rereading her writing, she recognized a number of general and abstract words, which she underlined.

> When I think of the good things about my family, Christmas comes most quickly to mind. Our house was filled with such <u>warmth</u> and <u>joy</u>. Mom was busy, but she was <u>happy</u>. Dad seemed less absorbed in his work. In the weeks before Christmas he almost never worked late at the office, and he often arrived with brightly wrapped presents that he would tantalizingly show us — before whisking them off to their hiding place. And at night we did <u>fun</u> things together to prepare for the big day.

Words like *warmth* and *joy* undoubtedly have many strong connotations for the writer; most readers, however, would find these terms vague. This writer realized that in drafting she would have to provide plenty of concrete, specific details to enable readers to visualize what she means.

## FOLLOWING TEXTUAL CONVENTIONS

When you draft, you don't have to come up with an organizational structure from scratch. Instead, you can draw on conventional methods of organization, methods that reflect common ways of analyzing and explaining information. Your subject may naturally lend itself to one or more methods of organization.

Suppose, for example, that you're writing an essay about political and economic changes in Eastern Europe and Asia in recent decades. Perhaps in your reading you were struck by the different responses of Russian and Chinese citizens to economic privatization. You might draw on conventional methods of *comparing and contrasting* to organize such an analysis. Or perhaps you wish to discuss the impact that severe industrial pollution in China could have on the development of a Western-style economy. After *classifying* the most prevalent forms of industrial pollution, you might discuss the consequences of this pollution for China's economy. In some cases, you may be able to use a single method of organization—such as *comparison, definition, cause and effect,* or *problem–solution*—to organize your entire essay. More often, however, you'll draw on several methods to present your ideas.

In considering how best to draw on conventional methods of organizing information, remember that you shouldn't impose them formulaically. Begin thinking about how to organize your writing by reflecting on your goals as a writer and on your rhetorical situation. If your analysis suggests that one or more methods of organizing information represent common-sensical, logical ways of approaching your subject, use them in drafting. But remember that the organization or structure you choose should complement your ideas, not be imposed on them.

## WRITING EFFECTIVE PARAGRAPHS

If you're freewriting or writing a discovery draft, you may not think consciously about when to create a new paragraph or how to structure it: Your goal is to generate ideas. Additionally, by the time you are a college student, you have probably developed a general understanding of how effective paragraphs work, an understanding that grows out of your previous experiences as a reader and writer. Even so, it is helpful to remind yourself about the nature and functions of paragraphs and the expectations that readers bring to them. In this regard, readers expect the following:

- A paragraph will be unified; it will generally focus on one main idea.
- The opening sentence of a paragraph will often, although not always, state what the paragraph is about. (Sometimes the topic sentence may appear at the end of the paragraph or even in the middle, acting as a linchpin between ideas.)
- Paragraphs will often, although again not always, have a clear beginning, middle, and end; that is, they will often state the main idea, support that main idea with evidence, and conclude with a sentence that ties the two together and provides a transition to the next paragraph.✱
- There will be a coherent logic to paragraph development; a paragraph will include transitional words, phrases, and sentences or use other strategies (such as strategic repetition) to make clear how it relates to the paragraphs that precede and follow it.

Paragraphs are remarkably flexible textual units. What is essential is that readers can clearly see and follow the logic of the development of ideas within and between paragraphs.

Transitional devices can play a key role in helping readers stay on track as they move through your text. Some transitional words and phrases—such as *for example, therefore, because, in other words, in conclusion, on the other hand, granted,* and *nevertheless*—indicate how ideas relate to one another logically; others—such as *often, during, now, then, at first, next, in the meantime,* and *eventually*—indicate a sequence or progression; and still others—such as *beside, beyond, above, behind,* and *outside*—indicate spatial relationships. Repetition of key terms or synonyms for those terms can also

---

✱ Chapter 7 (pp. 203–05) explains the structure of a supporting paragraph in a research project.

help readers stay on track. Transitional devices help connect ideas within paragraphs. They can also play an important role in clarifying the development of ideas from paragraph to paragraph.

When drafting, be sure to pay special attention to the paragraphs that introduce and conclude your essay. An effective introductory paragraph announces your topic, but it also engages your readers' interest and attention. Analyzing your rhetorical situation can help you determine appropriate ways to introduce your topic. If you are writing a humorous essay or an essay on a casual subject directed to a general audience, you might begin with an anecdote or an attention-getting question. If you are writing an essay about a serious topic directed to an academic audience, a more straightforward approach would generally be more appropriate. While you might begin with a quotation or question, you would quickly state your topic and explain how you intend to approach it.

Your concluding paragraph is as important as your introductory paragraph. Like the introductory paragraph, your concluding paragraph frames your essay. It reminds your reader that your essay is drawing to a close. Depending on your topic and rhetorical situation, concluding paragraphs may vary in their approach. In some way, however, all bring the issues that you have discussed together in a meaningful and emphatic way. Your concluding paragraph is also your final opportunity to emphasize the importance of your ideas and make a final good impression.

Daniel Stiepleman's essay "Literacy in America: Reading between the Lines" (pp. 173–76) is a good example of effective paragraphing in action. Daniel opens his essay, which analyzes a public service announcement (PSA) from the National Center for Public Literacy, by describing the PSA itself. This description draws the reader's attention and represents Daniel's initial analysis of the PSA. Daniel observes that it is the girl and not the older woman, for instance, "who seems maternal." At this point, this observation seems primarily descriptive, but it will also play a role in Daniel's analysis as his essay progresses. It is important to note that Daniel's essay includes a reproduction of the PSA so that readers can determine whether they think Daniel's description is accurate.

Daniel's second paragraph moves from a description of the PSA to his response. Daniel finds the PSA troubling, but at this point in his essay he is unsure why. He does worry, however, that the PSA's "simple message, though it promotes a position I believe in, I fear does more harm than good." This statement, which is the last sentence of the second paragraph, serves as the thesis statement for his essay.

The initial sentence of the third paragraph establishes a logical connection between the second and third paragraphs: "The problem is with the underlying logic of this PSA." Notice that Daniel does not employ an explicit transitional device. The logic of the relationship between the two paragraphs is already clear. The fourth and fifth paragraphs of the essay explain the difficulties that Daniel sees with the underlying logic of the PSA and provide evidence to support this assertion. The first sentence of the sixth paragraph summarizes Daniel's argument: "The PSA suggests that all the illiterate people in America need to achieve worth is the ability to read and write."

In paragraph seven, his concluding paragraph, Daniel returns to the description of the PSA that opened his essay and extends his description so that it contributes explicitly to his argument. Here are the two final sentences of Daniel's essay as they appear in that paragraph:

> Though the girl is beaming, there is a hesitance I see in the woman's smile and concern in her face. And it is apt; she is shoved into the corner, held there, like so many Americans, beneath the weight of a text that would take the rich and daunting complexity of our multicultural society and give it the illusion of simplicity.

These two sentences evoke the essay's introduction even as they comment in an emotionally charged way on the significance of Daniel's major point. In so doing, they bring Daniel's essay to a powerful conclusion.

Some of Daniel's paragraphs do have topic sentences — the third, fourth, and fifth paragraphs all announce their major point in the first sentence — but others do not. The first paragraph begins with a striking description of the main image in the PSA: "The woman and girl look straight at us." The second paragraph introduces Daniel's troubled response to the PSA: "When I came across this page in the *Atlantic* (see Fig. 1), the image of the girl and the woman was what first caught my eye, but it was the repeated statement 'Because I can read' that captured my imagination." This sentence serves as a transition from the first to the second paragraph, and it also introduces the reservations that Daniel will explore through his analysis. The first sentence of the seventh and final paragraph alludes to the opening paragraph and helps the reader transition to the conclusion.

Daniel's essay is clearly unified and so is each of the paragraphs in the essay. Daniel does not employ many explicit transitional devices, however. Instead, he creates implicit logical connections. His second paragraph, for instance, is structured around this statement: "When I came across this page in the *Atlantic* . . . I grew uncomfortable." In those body paragraphs that have explicit topic sentences — paragraphs three, four, and five — the remaining sentences in the paragraph support the topic sentence.

Daniel's essay is an excellent example of effective paragraphing. Daniel worked hard on his essay, writing multiple drafts and getting responses from peers. To learn more about how Daniel composed his essay, see the case study of Daniel's writing process in Chapter 6 (pp. 160–76). Reading Daniel's case study will help you see how to draw upon and enact the practical strategies described here and in the following chapter in your own writing.

## for **thought, discussion, and writing**

1. Early in this chapter, you used freewriting, looping, brainstorming, clustering, and the journalist's questions to investigate a subject of interest to you. Continue your exploration of this topic by conducting some informal research and drawing on the topical questions (p. 262). Then use the material you have gathered to write a discovery draft on your subject.

2. Choose one of the invention strategies discussed in this chapter that you have not used in the past, and try it as you work on a writing assignment. If you have time, discuss this experiment with some classmates. Then write a brief analysis of why this strategy did or did not work well for you.

3. Choose a writing assignment that you have just begun. After reflecting on your ideas, devise a workable plan. While drafting, keep a record of your activities. How helpful was your plan? Was it realistic? Did you revise your plan as you wrote? What can you learn about your writing process from this experience?

4. Think of a time when you simply couldn't get started writing. What did you do to move beyond this block? How well did your efforts work — and why? After reflecting on your experience, write an essay (humorous or serious) about how you cope with writer's block.

5. Choose an essay that you have already written. It could be an essay for your writing class or for another class. Analyze the essay to determine how effective your paragraphs are, much as this chapter analyzed the paragraphs in Daniel Stiepleman's essay. Here are some questions to consider as you analyze your essay:

   - How effectively does your introduction engage readers? Does your concluding paragraph provide a sense of closure and demonstrate the significance of your topic? How could your introduction and conclusion be improved?
   - Which paragraphs in your essay have explicit topic sentences? Which do not? Can you identify the logic behind this pattern? Could any paragraph be improved by adding or deleting a topic sentence?
   - Can readers easily follow the movement of ideas within and between paragraphs? What transitional strategies might you use to improve the cohesiveness of your paragraphs and to unify your essay?

# 10

# Strategies for Revising, Editing, and Proofreading

**R**evising and editing can be the most rewarding parts of the writing process: Together they give you the satisfaction of bringing your ideas to completion in an appropriate form. Revision challenges you to look at your work from a dual perspective: to read your work with your own intentions in mind and also to consider your readers' or viewers' perspectives. Editing provides you with an opportunity to fine-tune your paragraphs and sentences and, along with proofreading, to provide your readers with a trouble-free reading experience. Although revision and editing occur throughout the writing process, you'll probably revise most intensively after completing a rough draft that serves as a preliminary statement of your ideas and edit once you're happy with the focus, organization, and content of your draft. Proofreading usually occurs at the very end of the process.

Revising and editing are medium-specific activities. Revising a video or podcast is very different from revising an alphabetic text—a text composed primarily of black letters on a white page or screen. As you are probably aware, in most cases, multiple programs can be used to revise and edit digital texts. Someone who wants to edit a video could use Windows Movie Maker, Virtual Dub, Wax, or Wondershare Filmora, to name just a few of the available programs. Programs such as these are constantly being updated, so advice grounded in one version of a program can quickly become out of date. For these reasons, this chapter focuses primarily on the opportunities and challenges of revising and editing alphabetic texts, such as traditional academic analysis and argument.

An important starting point for any discussion of revising and editing involves terminology. In ordinary conversation, the terms *revising* and *editing* are sometimes used interchangeably, but there are significant distinctions between the two. When you revise, you consider big-picture questions about your essay: What are its major strengths and weaknesses? Does it meet the assignment? Are the introduction and conclusion effective given the assignment and your rhetorical situation? Is the essay clearly organized? Given the topic and assignment, does it cover the most important issues? Can the reader move easily from section to section and paragraph to paragraph?

When you revise, you are willing to make major changes to your text—to revise your thesis significantly or to expand on some analytical or argumentative points while limiting or deleting others. Revising requires you to distance yourself from your text—to read it almost as if you had not written it—which is one reason why getting responses to work in progress from readers, such as other students in your writing class, can be so helpful.

Writers move from revising to editing once they have decided that their essay is working well at a global level. Editing generally involves style and clarity. When you edit your writing, you ask yourself questions such as these: Do your sentences flow smoothly, with appropriately varied sentence length and structure? How about diction or word choice? Could you choose more specific, concrete, or emphatic words? These questions all are aimed at improving the impact of your writing. Editing involves more than attention to style, however. It is also the time to ask yourself whether the logic behind your essay is as clear as possible. Would more effective transitions clarify and enrich your argument and add to its impact? Are there ways that your introduction and conclusion could be improved? Proofreading provides an opportunity to make any final changes to grammar, punctuation, and spelling to provide readers with an error-free reading experience.

Revising and editing can help you transform an essay that is so-so at best to one that engages readers and conveys its ideas powerfully and persuasively. But these processes take time, including the time necessary to gain some distance from your writing. You cannot revise and edit your essay effectively if you write it at the last minute, so effective time management skills are essential. As an example of successful revising and editing, see the case study of Daniel Stiepleman's essay analyzing a public service announcement (PSA) that appears in the concluding section of Chapter 6 (pp. 160–76). Be sure to notice that Daniel's essay benefited from multiple drafts and from responses by his writing group.

# Strategies for Revising

You can learn a great deal about revision just by considering the word itself. *Revision* combines the root word *vision* with the prefix *re-*, meaning "again." When you revise, you "see again": You develop a new vision of your essay's logic and organization or of the best way to improve the way it flows.

Revision sometimes requires you to take risks. Often these risks are minor. If you attempt to fine-tune the details in a paragraph, for instance, you need spend only a little time and can easily revert back to the original version. Sometimes when you revise, however, you make large-scale decisions with more significant consequences. You might conclude that a different organization is in order, decide to rework your thesis statement, or consider a new approach to your topic altogether. Trying major changes such as these often requires rewriting or discarding whole sections of a draft, but a willingness to experiment can also lead to choices that make revising less frustrating and more productive. (See the Guidelines for Revising Objectively below.)

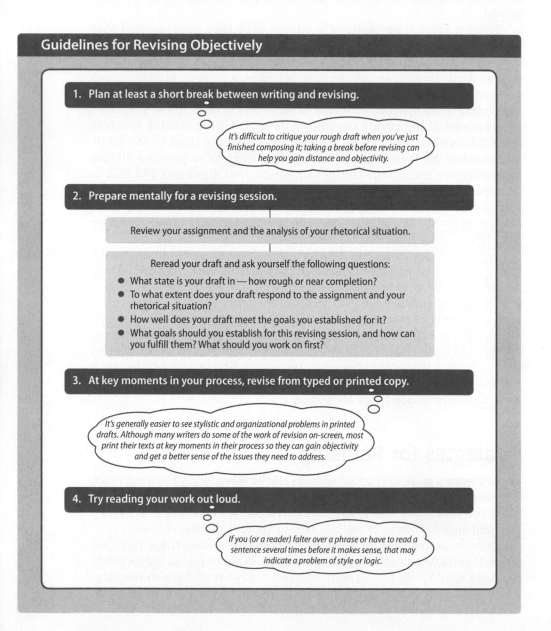

## Guidelines for Revising Objectively

**1. Plan at least a short break between writing and revising.**

*It's difficult to critique your rough draft when you've just finished composing it; taking a break before revising can help you gain distance and objectivity.*

**2. Prepare mentally for a revising session.**

Review your assignment and the analysis of your rhetorical situation.

Reread your draft and ask yourself the following questions:

- What state is your draft in — how rough or near completion?
- To what extent does your draft respond to the assignment and your rhetorical situation?
- How well does your draft meet the goals you established for it?
- What goals should you establish for this revising session, and how can you fulfill them? What should you work on first?

**3. At key moments in your process, revise from typed or printed copy.**

*It's generally easier to see stylistic and organizational problems in printed drafts. Although many writers do some of the work of revision on-screen, most print their texts at key moments in their process so they can gain objectivity and get a better sense of the issues they need to address.*

**4. Try reading your work out loud.**

*If you (or a reader) falter over a phrase or have to read a sentence several times before it makes sense, that may indicate a problem of style or logic.*

---

## for **exploration**

Think back to earlier writing experiences, and freewrite in response to the following questions for five to ten minutes. When, and for what reasons, have you revised your work instead of just editing? Can you see patterns in your decision-making? How would you characterize your experiences with revising? Were they satisfying, frustrating, or a mix of the two? Why?

---

# Asking the Big Questions: Revising for Focus, Content, and Organization

When you revise a draft, begin by asking the big, important questions — questions about how well your essay has responded to your rhetorical situation and how successfully you've achieved your purpose. If you discover — as writers often do — that your essay hasn't achieved its original purpose or that your purpose evolved into a different one as you wrote, you'll want to make major changes in your draft.

## EXAMINING YOUR OWN WRITING

From the moment you begin thinking about a writing project until you make your last revision, you must be an analyst and a decision maker. When you examine your work, you look for strengths to build on and weaknesses to remedy. Consequently, you must think about not just what is in your text but also what is *not* there and what *could be* there. You must read the part (the introduction, say, or several paragraphs) while still keeping in mind the whole.

Asking the Questions for Evaluating Focus, Content, and Organization (p. 280) first is a practical approach to revising. Once you're confident that the overall focus, content, and organization of your essay are satisfactory, you'll be better able to recognize less significant but still important stylistic problems.

---

## for **exploration**

Use the Questions for Evaluating Focus, Content, and Organization to evaluate the draft of an essay you are currently working on. Respond as specifically and as concretely as possible, and then take a few moments to reflect on what you have learned about your draft. Use your responses to make a list of goals for revising.

---

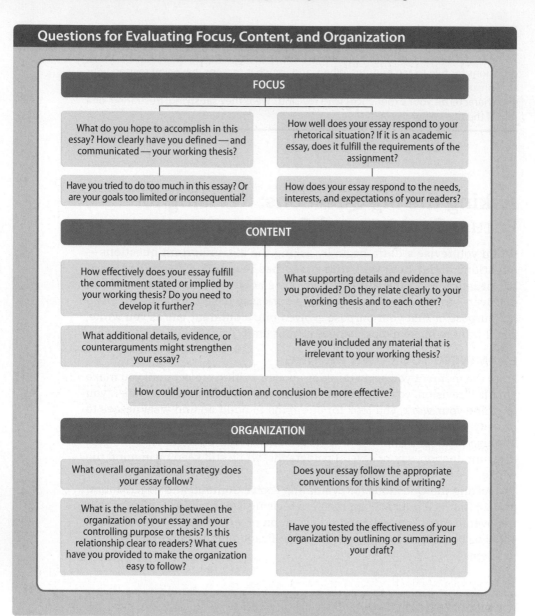

# One Student Writer's Revision for Focus, Content, and Organization

Here is how one writer, Stevon Roberts, used the Questions for Evaluating Focus, Content, and Organization to establish goals for his revision. For an introductory composition class, Stevon was assigned a four- to five-page essay that proposed a solution to a contemporary problem. Stevon decided to write on something he was truly interested in: Internet privacy.

Stevon spent some time discussing the problem with friends and conducted research online, taking notes as he did so. He reread his notes and then did a freewrite (below) to determine his rhetorical situation and figure out what he really wanted to get across. A draft that grew out of his freewrite starts at the bottom of this page.

I am writing an essay for my composition class in which I'm supposed to propose a solution to a contemporary problem. I've decided to tackle the problem of Internet privacy. Since my readers— my instructor and classmates—almost certainly spend at least some time online, I think they'll be familiar with the general context of my discussion. Since the things we do online vary so widely, though, I've decided to narrow my focus to social media—Facebook, Instagram, Pinterest, Twitter, and so on. I do have some practical recommendations to make for ways we can protect our privacy, but I've realized in talking with people and doing some research that making concrete recommendations is not always very helpful: rapid changes in technology mean that my suggestions will quickly become obsolete. For this reason, I've decided primarily to raise awareness of the problem, emphasizing the need for every person who uses technology to understand the dangers of providing personal information online and be alert to new threats.

## STEVON'S EARLY DRAFT

My name is Stevon Roberts. I'm a videographer, a blogger, a student, and a tech enthusiast (at least, that's what it says on my Twitter profile). My last known location was on the corner of NW Beca Avenue and NW 20th Street, at a place called Coffee Culture, in Corvallis, Oregon.

In the past, I would have guarded this kind of information to prevent marketers, hackers, and identity thieves from building a profile to exploit. Identity thieves have gotten very good at compiling seemingly innocuous pieces of information and using them for purposes like credit card fraud. These threats are still very real, and I still take some measures to protect myself. You probably do, too. Most of us know by now how to recognize phishing scams and other threats to our personal security. But with the advent of social media, we've seen huge changes in the way this information is obtained.

Most of us just give information away for free on Facebook, Instagram, Pinterest, Twitter, and other social media services, often compromising security. In the same way that the automobile revolutionized transportation, social media have fundamentally shifted the way we manage our personal information. We learned to mitigate our risks on the road by using safety belts and obeying traffic laws, but most of us probably don't have a good understanding of the appropriate precautions for social media. As these services become more integral to our lifestyles, and more revealing of our identities, protecting our identities will become more critical, both online and in real life.

Other security concerns in the digital realm haven't gone away. Spam, for example, has become so pervasive that world spending for anti-spam software was expected to exceed $1.7 billion in 2008, up from $300 million in 2003 ("Anti-Spam Spending Set to Soar," *Global Secure Systems* 24 Feb. 2005). Apart from reducing the annoyance factor, this can also protect from more serious security threats, such as phishing scams, wherein unsuspecting victims will reply to fraudulent emails with personal information—sometimes even giving away bank account numbers!

Clearly, these security issues are still at the forefront of people's minds, and we're taking steps toward better solutions. But let's put the risks in context and compare our relative response. As of the writing of this essay, Facebook had approximately 1.59 billion users. Many of them are content to settle for the default privacy settings, which aren't all that private. Additionally, many Facebook users will add "applications," including games, quizzes, etc., which have access to many parts of your user profile that you may not want to share. In fact, in a twist of irony, the ACLU has added a quiz that you can take to explain exactly what is exposed when you add these sorts of quizzes (aclunc _privacy_quiz/). The quiz offers some suggestions for changing the privacy settings to protect personal information, but many people simply aren't aware, or don't take the time, to make these adjustments.

But let's not focus on Facebook at the expense of an even larger context. Location services, such as Brightkite, allow you to pinpoint your location on a map. You'd probably be happy to share this information with friends whom you'd like to join you, but you likely wouldn't want to share this information with a stalker, or even an angry ex-boyfriend or -girlfriend. Would you broadcast the location of your home address? Most of us would probably think twice before doing that, but the lines can quickly become blurry. Is it OK to broadcast your location from a friend's house? Your classroom, or your office?

With its instructional tagline "What are you doing?" Twitter gives its users 140 characters to broadcast activities, locations, website URLs, and even pictures (via helper services). An individual post, or "tweet," might cost you a job if, for example, you tell your friends you took a job only for its "fatty paycheck" (Snell). You might risk being overlooked for an interview if you posted a picture from a drinking party.

Similarly, your political views and feelings may be called into question if you endeavor to start a blog, as I have. My blog is not especially personal, but it occurred to me when I started writing that this might be another potential vector for increased risk. It bothered me so much that I wrote to one of my favorite bloggers (Leo Babauta of Zenhabits. net), asking him whether he was concerned about security. He wrote back (via Twitter), "No, I haven't faced security or privacy issues as a blogger (yet). My readers are 100% really cool, nice (and sexy) people." It's worth pointing out that his blog has over a hundred thousand subscribers.

Still . . . social media allow you to compromise your own personal identity and security in ways that are unprecedented. And at the same time, participation in all of these environments is almost obligatory. Very few of my friends have not yet succumbed to the peer pressure to be available on Facebook, Instagram, Twitter, and other social media, despite security concerns. And if you're trying to run a business (or promote your blog), avoiding Twitter is tantamount to professional suicide—these venues are key ingredients for successful marketing. In short, your personal name and profile have almost become like a kind of brand that is expected to be proliferated and maintained in cyberspace. And yet censorship levels must be very high to avoid getting passed over for the next opportunity, because heaven forbid that your future employer doesn't agree with you about the last hot political topic (or whatever).

Stevon shared this essay with the members of his peer response group, who used the Questions for Evaluating Focus, Content, and Organization (p. 280) to analyze his draft. The following analysis reflects both Stevon's own observations about the strengths and limitations of his draft and those of his writing group.

**Focus:** Some of my readers were confused about my main focus. I think I can correct this by revising my introduction and explaining more clearly that we (my instructor, classmates, and I) are all probably too sophisticated now for the "Nigerian royalty" email scams — we've all been there and learned our lessons — but other dangers exist, and we might not all be aware of them: specifically, the dangers presented in giving personal information away while using social media, which many of us are virtually addicted to.

I made one point that readers found really important — the idea that cutting social media off completely is not really an option for most of us, because it's essential for our social and even professional lives — late in the essay; I think I'll move it up closer to the beginning.

Some of my readers wanted more concrete recommendations for what to do to protect themselves. I have to make it clear from the outset that I think awareness and seeking out solutions that work for you are really the only universal solutions anyone can offer — there's too much variety in the kinds of technology people use and it all changes really, really fast. I'm trying to teach them to fish, I guess, instead of giving them fish.

**Content:** Some of my readers were confused about my opening (where I give away private information about myself — what's my point there, exactly?). I think I just need to make the point more clearly in the second paragraph.

A couple of my readers didn't know what "phishing" was — I have to be careful about assuming too much common knowledge in technical terminology.

I realized on rereading one of my sources that a statistic it offered was a bit out-of-date, so I found a more current source.

I need to provide some more examples of some of the risks that people didn't entirely "get," like how having a blog could cost you a job.

Probably most critical is the fact that my readers didn't like my conclusion: They felt like the discussion just dropped off without really "concluding." I think adding a stronger conclusion, reminding readers of my major points, will make the essay much stronger.

**Organization:** I outlined my draft so that its organization was especially clear. In general, it's OK, but I realize that I do ping-pong a bit, especially in the beginning, between old threats like spam and new threats like Facebook quizzes. I need to work on transitions to make what I'm doing there clearer (because that's where some of the confusion about my focus crept in, I think).

I also have to add some clearer transitions between the different kinds of risks I discuss (the usual stuff with marketers and scam artists, and then other, even scarier stuff, like losing a job or being stalked). In the discussion of the latter risks (like stalkers), I lost some readers when I started out talking about Brightkite (it uses GPS technology but my readers didn't immediately know what I was talking about), so I think I'll reorder the presentation of topics here, and start with Twitter and blogs (which people are more familiar with).

Stevon used this analysis to completely rework his essay. The result follows below.

---

Roberts 1

Stevon Roberts
Dr. Mallon
Comp 101
Oct. 17, 2019

Added title to prepare readers for content of essay

### Identity, Rebooted

When you're doing stuff online, you should behave as if you're doing it in public—because increasingly, it is.— Cornell University computer science professor Jon Kleinberg (qtd. in Lohr)

Added new epigraph to provide thought-provoking expert commentary

My name is Stevon Roberts. I'm a videographer, a blogger, a student, and a tech enthusiast (at least, that's what it says on my Twitter profile). My last known location was on the corner of NW Beca Avenue and NW 20th Street, at a place called Coffee Culture, in Corvallis, Oregon.

If someone had told me even five years ago that I would one day regularly broadcast this kind of information about myself to people I didn't know, I wouldn't have believed it. If someone I didn't know

Roberts 2

**Revised pars. 2 and 3 to reflect rhetorical situation — writing to media-savvy readers in age of Facebook — and explained focus to make readers aware of privacy concerns**
**Replaced the term *phishing*, with example that would be more familiar to readers**

had asked me back then for information like this, I would have refused to give it, to prevent unscrupulous people from exploiting it. I was well aware of how expert marketers, hackers, and identity thieves had become at compiling such seemingly innocuous pieces of information and using them for unwanted sales pitches, or even worse, for credit card scams and other kinds of fraud.

These threats are still very real, and I take some measures to protect myself against them. You probably do, too: Most of us are wary of filling out surveys from dubious sources, for example, and most of us know by now how to recognize obvious email scams like the ones purporting to be from "Nigerian royalty." But with the advent of social media, many of us find ourselves in a bind: We want to be connected, so many of us regularly give confidential—and potentially damaging—information away on Facebook, Instagram, Pinterest, and other social-media services.

**Moved up important aspect of argument: Social media matter because we want to be connected**

In the same way that the automobile revolutionized transportation, social media have fundamentally shifted the way we communicate and share personal information. We learned to mitigate our risks on the road by using safety belts and obeying traffic laws, but most of us probably don't yet have a good understanding of appropriate precautions for social media. As these services become more integral to our lifestyles, protecting our identities from those who might use them for nefarious ends will become even more critical. Given the speed with which social media are developing and changing, it's difficult to give specific recommendations. An important first step, however, is becoming aware of the risks you run in broadcasting personal information.

**Clarified and limited primary goal of essay**

**Updated statistics and synthesized these with his own experience to provide concrete examples of problems that remain**

These new concerns about privacy and safety in the digital realm have arrived on the heels of older problems that haven't gone away. Spam, for example, has become so pervasive that, according to a 2009 estimate by Ferris Research, annual spending that year for antispam software, hardware, and personnel would reach $6.5 billion—$2.1 billion in the United States alone (Jennings). As these figures show, though, in the case of spam, most of us can and do fight back: Antispam software eliminates or at least reduces the amount of unwanted email we receive, and it can protect us well from security

Roberts 3

threats like the "Nigerian royalty" scam mentioned above, wherein unsuspecting victims will reply to fraudulent emails with personal information—sometimes even giving away bank account numbers.

Most of us are not yet doing anything about the threats posed by the information we publish via social media, however, and many of us are not even fully aware of them. In order to put the problem in context, let's take a closer look at the kinds of social media we're talking about and the nature and extent of the risks they pose. Participation in social networks like Facebook, Twitter, Pinterest, Instagram, and others has exploded in the last few years: As of the fourth quarter of 2015, Facebook had 1.59 billion users ("Number"). Most of those who participate don't think twice about privacy issues, or they assume that the systems' default privacy settings will protect them. Yet studies done by researchers at M.I.T., Carnegie Mellon, and the University of Texas have demonstrated that it's possible to determine sexual orientation, match identities to "anonymously" stated preferences, and even piece together Social Security numbers from profile information on Facebook and other social networks (Lohr).

As if putting basic profile information out there weren't enough, many Facebook users will add applications like games and quizzes that allow outside parties unmediated access to unrelated information from their profiles. In an attempt to raise awareness of the issue, the ACLU has added a quiz(!) to Facebook that explains exactly what is exposed when you add these sorts of quizzes (Conley). The ACLU's quiz offers some suggestions for changing Facebook privacy settings to protect personal information.

The risks you take in revealing personal information via social media go beyond its possible misuse by marketers, hackers, and identity thieves. For example, with its tagline, "What are you doing?" Twitter gives its users 140 characters to broadcast activities, locations, website URLs, and even pictures (via helper services). A single post, or "tweet," however, might cost you a job, as it did the woman who openly expressed her concerns about taking a job she disliked for a "fatty paycheck" (Snell). You might risk being turned down for an interview if you post a picture from a wild drinking party.

*Marginal annotations:*

Clarified transition, moving from spam (older security concern) to social media

Synthesized experience with information about recent studies to specify "threats to privacy"

Added transition to clarify move from one kind of risk to another; also reorganized section, moving Twitter and blogs to beginning as they were likely to be more familiar to readers

Roberts 4

Similarly, your views and opinions, political and otherwise, may become an issue if you start a blog. I have a blog that's not especially personal, but it occurred to me when I started writing that this might be a potential source of risk: What if my boss saw what I wrote, disagreed, and started treating me differently at work? What if my landlord was bothered enough to refuse to renew my lease? I began to worry so much about it that I wrote to one of my favorite bloggers (Leo Babauta of Zenhabits. net), asking him whether he was concerned about security. He wrote back, "No, I haven't faced security or privacy issues as a blogger (yet). My readers are 100% really cool, nice (and sexy) people." It's worth pointing out that his blog has over a hundred thousand subscribers, so maybe I'm worried over nothing. On the other hand, Mr. Babauta lives on the island of Guam, works for himself, and likely doesn't face many of the same identity expectations that I would as a student and young professional.

One last service that's important to consider is the use of Global Positioning System (GPS) technology in cell phones. Many cell phones now have GPS receivers built in, and as with some Twitter applications, location services such as Brightkite allow you to pinpoint your location on a map with startling accuracy. Broadcasting your location is optional, but many people do so because the technology's there and they don't see how it could hurt. It could hurt: When you broadcast your location, everyone, not just your friends, will know where you are. How about angry ex-boyfriends or -girlfriends or potential stalkers? What if someone were casing your home for a break-in and were able to determine via one of these services that you were away?

Clearly, social media allow you to reveal aspects of your identity and (therefore) compromise your security in ways that are unprecedented. At the same time, for many of us participation is almost obligatory. Most of my friends have succumbed to the peer pressure to be available on Facebook, for example. If you're trying to run a business (or promote your blog), avoiding Twitter is tantamount to professional suicide—these venues are key ingredients for successful marketing. In short, your

---

**Provided some examples to clarify kinds of risks he might be taking in posting blog**

**Responded to question about why readers should be concerned if Babauta wasn't**

**Added discussion about Brightkite and GPS technology in cell phones because readers of draft are unfamiliar with, or unconcerned about, implications**

**Added concluding section to clarify purpose and remind readers of key points**

Roberts 5

personal name and profile have become a brand that you're expected to proliferate and maintain in cyberspace: Without them, you're nothing. Yet, as I have discussed, the risks that accompany this self-promotion are high.

If only because social media are constantly evolving, it is unlikely that a set of specific and concrete best practices for mitigating these risks will emerge. One friend and professional colleague argues that it's simply impossible to manage your identity online because much of it is revealed by others—your friends will post the embarrassing party pictures for you, school or work will post documents detailing your achievements, and Google will determine what appears in the search results when you type your name in. M.I.T. professor Harold Abelson agrees: "Personal privacy is no longer an individual thing . . . . In today's online world, what your mother told you is true, only more so: people really can judge you by your friends" (qtd. in Lohr).

Added quote from expert bolsters claim about ways identities are revealed online

The most positive spin on the current situation is to think of your online identity in terms of a "signal-to-noise" ratio: Assuming you know what you're doing, you are in charge of the "signal" (the information you yourself tweet or allow to appear on Facebook), and this signal will usually be stronger than the "noise" generated by your friends or others who broadcast information you'd rather not share. The key phrase there is "assuming you know what you're doing," and that's where all of us could use some pointers. If you're going to put your faith in your ability to create a strong, positive signal, you need to follow a few key rules. First, realize that there's a potential problem every time you post something private online. Next, make yourself thoroughly acquainted with the privacy settings of any and all social media you interact with. The default settings for any of these programs are almost certainly inadequate because my security concerns aren't the same as Leo Babauta's, and they're not the same as yours. Finally, keep talking (and blogging and Googling) about the issue and sharing any best practices you discover. We need to work together to understand and manage these risks if we want to retain control of the "brand" that is us.

Roberts 6

Works Cited

Babauta, Leo. "Re: Security Concerns?" Received by Stevon Roberts,
11 Oct. 2013.

Conley, Chris. "Quiz: What Do Facebook Quizzes Know about You?"
*Blog of Rights*, ACLU, www.aclu.org/blog/quiz-what-do-facebook
-quizzes-know-about-you.

Jennings, Richi. "Cost of Spam Is Flattening—Our 2009 Predictions."
Ferris Research, email-museum.com/2009/01/28/cost-of-spam-is
-flattening-our-2009-predictions/.

Lohr, Steve. "How Privacy Vanishes Online." *The New York Times*,
www.nytimes.com/2010/03/17/technology/17privacy.html?_r=0.

"Number of Monthly Active Facebook Users Worldwide as of 4th Quarter
2015 (in Millions)." *Statista: The Statistics Portal*, www.statista.com
/statistics/264810/number-of-monthly-active-facebook-users-worldwide
/istic. Accessed 12 Oct. 2016.

Snell, Jason. "Think before You Tweet." *Macworld*, www.macworld.com
/article/1139480/when_not_to_twitter.html.

The Works Cited page includes all sources in correct MLA format. (*Note*: in an actual MLA-style paper, works-cited entries start on a new page.)

# Benefiting from Responses to Work in Progress

You may write alone a good deal of the time, but writing needn't be a lonely process. You can draw on the responses of others to help you re-see your writing and to gain support. When you ask others to respond to your writing, you're asking for feedback so that you can see your writing in fresh and different ways.

Responses can take a number of forms. Sometimes you may find it helpful to ask others simply to describe your writing for you. You might, for example, ask them to summarize in their own words how they understand your main point or what they think you're getting at. Similarly, you might ask them what parts of your draft stood out for them and what they felt was missing.

On other occasions, you may find more analytical responses helpful. You might ask readers to comment on your essay's organization or how well it responds to their needs and interests. If you're writing an argumentative essay, you might ask readers to look for potential weaknesses in its structure or logic.

To determine what kind of feedback will be most helpful, think commonsensically about your writing. Where are you in your composing process? How do you feel about your draft and the kind of writing you're working on? If you've just completed a rough draft, for instance, you might find descriptive feedback most helpful. After you've worked longer on the essay, you might invite more analytical responses.

As a student, you can turn to many people for feedback. The differences in their situations will influence how they respond; these differences should also influence how you use their responses. No matter whom you approach for feedback, though, learn to distinguish between your writing and yourself. Try not to respond defensively to suggestions for improvement, and don't argue with readers' responses. Instead, use them to gain insight into your writing. Ultimately, you are the one who must decide how to interpret and apply other people's comments and criticisms.

## strategies for success

The process of revising multiple drafts is new to many writers. Revising is meant to help you rework your writing to make sure it is as effective and clear as possible. If receiving (and giving) comments on drafts is new to you, be assured that the suggestions and questions from peer and other reviewers should lead to constructive collaboration.

## RESPONSES FROM FRIENDS AND FAMILY MEMBERS

You can certainly ask the people close to you to respond to your writing, but you should understand their strengths and weaknesses as readers. One important strength is that you trust them. Even if you spend time filling them in, however, friends and family members may not understand the nature of your assignment or your instructor's standards for evaluation; they're also likely to be less objective than other readers. All the same, friends and family members can provide useful responses to your writing if you choose such respondents carefully and draw on their strengths as outsiders. Rather than asking them to respond in detail, you might ask them to give a general impression or a descriptive response to your work. If their understanding of the main idea or controlling purpose of your essay differs substantially from your own, you've gained very useful information.

## RESPONSES FROM CLASSMATES

Because your classmates know your instructor and the assignment as insiders, they can provide particularly effective responses to work in progress. Classmates don't need to be experts to provide helpful responses. They simply need to be attentive, honest, supportive readers. Classmates can also read your work more objectively than family members and friends can. To ensure that you and your classmates provide a helpful balance of support and criticism, you and they should follow the Guidelines for Responses from Classmates below.

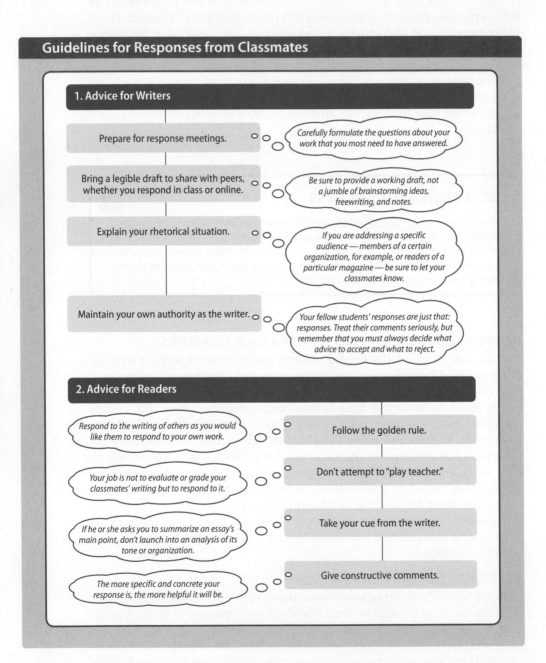

## Guidelines for Responses from Classmates

### 1. Advice for Writers

Prepare for response meetings.
*Carefully formulate the questions about your work that you most need to have answered.*

Bring a legible draft to share with peers, whether you respond in class or online.
*Be sure to provide a working draft, not a jumble of brainstorming ideas, freewriting, and notes.*

Explain your rhetorical situation.
*If you are addressing a specific audience — members of a certain organization, for example, or readers of a particular magazine — be sure to let your classmates know.*

Maintain your own authority as the writer.
*Your fellow students' responses are just that: responses. Treat their comments seriously, but remember that you must always decide what advice to accept and what to reject.*

### 2. Advice for Readers

*Respond to the writing of others as you would like them to respond to your own work.*
Follow the golden rule.

*Your job is not to evaluate or grade your classmates' writing but to respond to it.*
Don't attempt to "play teacher."

*If he or she asks you to summarize an essay's main point, don't launch into an analysis of its tone or organization.*
Take your cue from the writer.

*The more specific and concrete your response is, the more helpful it will be.*
Give constructive comments.

## for **exploration**

Freewrite for ten minutes about responses to your work from classmates, and then draw up a list of statements describing the kinds of responses that have been most helpful.

## for **collaboration**

Meet with a group of your classmates and have each group member read his or her list from the previous For Exploration. Then, working together, list all the suggestions for responses from classmates. Keep a copy of all the suggestions for future use.

## RESPONSES FROM WRITING CENTER TUTORS

Many colleges and universities have writing centers staffed by undergraduate and graduate writing assistants or tutors. If your college or university has one, be sure to take advantage of its services. (The guidelines below can help you get the most from your meeting with a tutor.) Tutors are not professional

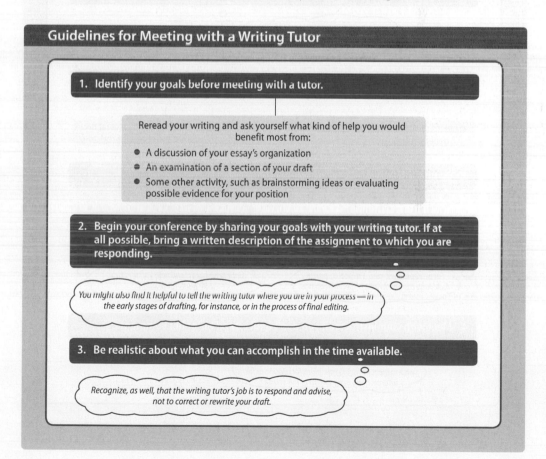

**Guidelines for Meeting with a Writing Tutor**

1. **Identify your goals before meeting with a tutor.**

Reread your writing and ask yourself what kind of help you would benefit most from:
- A discussion of your essay's organization
- An examination of a section of your draft
- Some other activity, such as brainstorming ideas or evaluating possible evidence for your position

2. **Begin your conference by sharing your goals with your writing tutor. If at all possible, bring a written description of the assignment to which you are responding.**

You might also find it helpful to tell the writing tutor where you are in your process — in the early stages of drafting, for instance, or in the process of final editing.

3. **Be realistic about what you can accomplish in the time available.**

Recognize, as well, that the writing tutor's job is to respond and advise, not to correct or rewrite your draft.

editors, nor are they faculty aides standing in for instructors who are unavailable or too busy to meet with students. They are good writers who have been formally trained to respond to peers' work and to make suggestions for improvement. Tutors can provide excellent responses to work in progress.

## RESPONSES FROM YOUR INSTRUCTOR AND OTHERS

Because your instructor is such an important reader for your written assignments, you want to make good use of any written comments they provide. For advice on making the most of them, see the guidelines below.

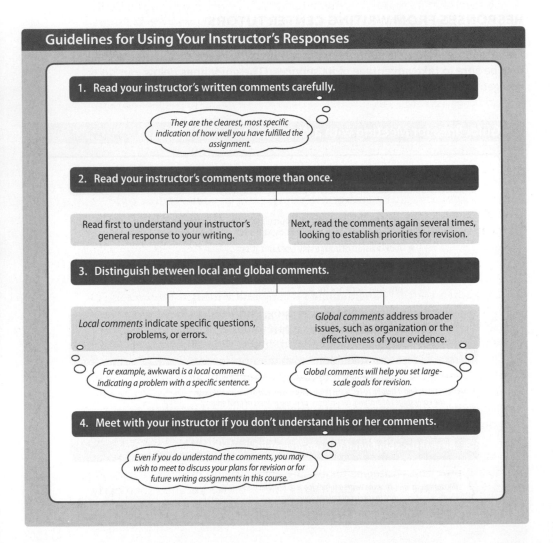

### Guidelines for Using Your Instructor's Responses

**1. Read your instructor's written comments carefully.**

*They are the clearest, most specific indication of how well you have fulfilled the assignment.*

**2. Read your instructor's comments more than once.**

Read first to understand your instructor's general response to your writing.

Next, read the comments again several times, looking to establish priorities for revision.

**3. Distinguish between local and global comments.**

*Local comments* indicate specific questions, problems, or errors.

*Global comments* address broader issues, such as organization or the effectiveness of your evidence.

*For example, awkward is a local comment indicating a problem with a specific sentence.*

*Global comments will help you set large-scale goals for revision.*

**4. Meet with your instructor if you don't understand his or her comments.**

*Even if you do understand the comments, you may wish to meet to discuss your plans for revision or for future writing assignments in this course.*

Friends, family members, classmates, writing tutors, instructors—all can provide helpful responses to your writing. None of these responses, whether criticism or praise, should take the place of your own judgment, however. Your job is to *interpret* and *evaluate* these responses, using them along with your own assessment of your rough draft to establish goals for revising.

# Practical Strategies for Editing

While most writers find it helpful to distinguish between revising and editing, they are not completely discrete processes. While you are writing a first draft of your essay, you may decide that one word is just not right and revise it. In so doing, you are editing—or making a local rather than a global change. Similarly, when you are editing your essay, you may discover that the difficulty you are having with writing an effective transition from one section to another is a larger problem than you previously realized. You now see that the two sections function better logically if they are reversed and the relationship between them is clarified. In this instance, when you make those changes—even though you are primarily focused on editing your writing—you are revising.

As these examples suggest, although it is useful to distinguish between revising and editing, the composing process is not rigid or formulaic. Moreover, individuals vary in how they approach this process. Chapter 4, "Academic Writing: Committing to the Process," discusses four general composing styles. (See pp. 90–94.) Heavy drafters, for instance, typically engage in extensive revising and editing. They tend to write long, loosely focused first drafts that are more like freewrites than essays, hence the necessity of considerable revising and editing. Heavy planners do much of the work of invention, planning, and drafting mentally before they sit down at their computer or put pen to paper. Their first drafts are more like heavy revisers' second or third drafts; their second drafts may require more editing than revision. Those who prefer the third composing style, sequential composers, devote roughly equivalent amounts of time to invention, planning, drafting, and revising/editing; they tend to have distinct stages of revising and editing. The fourth composing style, procrastinators, put off their writing so long that all they can do is to frantically pour out an essay at the last minute; many procrastinators are lucky if they can spell-check their essays before printing them. The following discussion of practical strategies for editing will help you meet the demands of editing, whether you are substituting one word for another in an early draft of your essay or analyzing a later draft to determine how you might improve its style.

## KEEPING YOUR READERS ON TRACK: EDITING FOR STYLE

"Proper words in proper places"—that's how the eighteenth-century writer Jonathan Swift defined style. As Swift suggests, writing style reflects all the choices a writer makes, from global questions of approach and organization to the smallest details about punctuation and grammar. When, in writing, you put the proper words in their proper places, readers will be able to follow your ideas with understanding and interest. In addition, they will probably gain some sense of the person behind the words—that is, of the writer's presence.

While writers address issues of style throughout the composing process, they do so most efficiently and effectively once they have determined that the basic structure, organization, and argument of their text are working. (Why spend a half an hour determining whether a paragraph is coherent and stylistically effective when that paragraph may be gone in an instant?) At this point, the writer can make changes that enable readers to move through the writing easily and enjoyably.

## ACHIEVING COHERENCE

Most writers are aware that paragraphs and essays need to be *unified*—that is, that they should focus on a single topic.✱ Writing is *coherent* when readers can move easily from word to word, sentence to sentence, and paragraph to paragraph. There are various means of achieving coherence. Some methods, such as *repeating key words and sentence structures* and *using pronouns*, reinforce or emphasize the logical development of ideas. Another method involves *using transitional words* such as *but*, *although*, and *because* to provide directional cues for readers.

The following introduction to "Home Town," an essay by the writer Ian Frazier, uses all these methods to keep readers on track. The most important means of achieving coherence are italicized.

> *When glaciers* covered much of northern Ohio, the land around Hudson, the town where I grew up, lay under one. *Glaciers* came and went several times, the most recent departing about 14,000 years ago. *When* we studied *glaciers* in an Ohio-history class in grade school, I imagined our *glacier* receding smoothly, like a sheet pulled off a new car. *Actually, glaciers* can move forward *but* they don't back up—*they* melt in place. *Most likely* the *glacier* above Hudson softened, *and* began to trickle underneath; rocks on its surface absorbed sunlight and melted tunnels into *it*; *it* rotted, *it* dwindled, *it* dripped, *it* ticked; *then it* dropped a pile of the sand and rocks it had been carrying around for centuries onto the ground in a heap. Hudson's landscape was hundreds of these little heaps—hills rarely big enough to sled down, a random arrangement made by gravity and smoothed by weather and time.
>
> —Ian Frazier, "Home Town"

---

✱ See Chapter 9 (pp. 272–74) for coverage of drafting unified paragraphs.

When you read your own writing to determine how to strengthen its coherence, use common sense. Your writing is coherent if readers know where they have been and where they are going as they read. Don't assume that your writing will be more coherent if you simply sprinkle key words, pronouns, and transitions throughout your prose. If the logic of your discussion is clear without such devices, don't add them.

Editing for coherence proceeds most effectively if you look first at large-scale issues, such as the relationship among your essay's introduction, body, and conclusion, before considering smaller concerns. The guidelines below offer advice on editing for coherence.

## FINDING AN APPROPRIATE VOICE

A writer's style reflects his or her individual taste and sensibility. But just as people dress differently for different occasions, so too do effective writers vary their style, depending on their rhetorical situation. As they do so, they are particularly attentive to the *persona*, or voice, they want to convey through their writing.

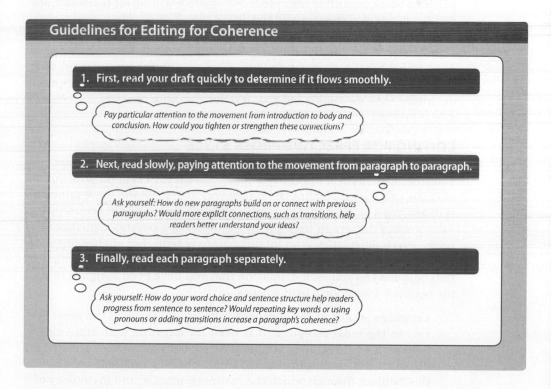

**Guidelines for Editing for Coherence**

1. First, read your draft quickly to determine if it flows smoothly.

   Pay particular attention to the movement from introduction to body and conclusion. How could you tighten or strengthen these connections?

2. Next, read slowly, paying attention to the movement from paragraph to paragraph.

   Ask yourself: How do new paragraphs build on or connect with previous paragraphs? Would more explicit connections, such as transitions, help readers better understand your ideas?

3. Finally, read each paragraph separately.

   Ask yourself: How do your word choice and sentence structure help readers progress from sentence to sentence? Would repeating key words or using pronouns or adding transitions increase a paragraph's coherence?

Sometimes writers present strong and distinctive voices. Here, for instance, is the beginning of an essay by the novelist Ken Kesey on the Pendleton Round-Up, a well-known rodeo held every September in eastern Oregon.

> My father took me up the Gorge and over the hills to my first one thirty-five years ago. It was on my fourteenth birthday. I had to miss a couple of days' school plus the possibility of suiting up for the varsity game that Friday night. Gives you some idea of the importance Daddy placed on this event.
>
> For this is more than just a world-class rodeo. It is a week-long shindig, a yearly rendezvous dating back beyond the first white trappers, a traditional powwow ground for the Indian nations of the Northwest for nobody knows how many centuries.
>
> —Ken Kesey, "The Blue-Ribbon American Beauty Rose of Rodeo"

Kesey's word choice and sentence structure help create an image of the writer as folksy, relaxed, and yet also forceful—just the right insider to write about a famous rodeo. In other situations, writers may prefer a less personal voice, as is often the case in informative writing for textbooks, academic articles, newspapers, and the like.

thinking rhetorically

If you think rhetorically, always asking questions about your rhetorical situation, you'll naturally consider such major stylistic issues as voice. By considering how much you wish to draw on appeals to reason (logos), emotion (pathos), and your own credibility as writer (ethos), you will more easily determine your own voice and your relationship with readers.

## EDITING FOR EFFECTIVE PROSE STYLE

The stylistic choices that you make as you draft and revise reflect not only your rhetorical awareness but also your awareness of general principles of effective prose style. Perhaps the easiest way to understand these principles is to analyze a passage that illustrates effective prose style in action.

Here is a paragraph from the first chapter of a psycholinguistics textbook. (Psycholinguistics is an interdisciplinary field that studies linguistic behavior and the psychological mechanisms that make verbal communication possible.) As you read it, imagine that you have been assigned to read the textbook for a course in linguistics.

> Language stands at the center of human affairs, from the most prosaic to the most profound. It is used for haggling with store clerks, telling off umpires, and gossiping with friends as well as for negotiating contracts, discussing ethics, and explaining religious beliefs. It is the medium through which the manners, morals, and mythology of a

society are passed on to the next generation. Indeed, it is a basic ingre-
dient in virtually every social situation. The thread that runs through all
these activities is communication, people trying to put their ideas over
to others. As the main vehicle of human communication, language is
indispensable.

—Herbert H. Clark and Eve V. Clark, *Psychology and Language*

This paragraph, you would probably agree, embodies effective prose style.
It's clearly organized and begins with a topic sentence, which the rest of
the paragraph explains. The paragraph is also coherent, with pronouns, key
words, and sentence patterns helping readers proceed. But what most distinguishes this paragraph, what makes it so effective, is the authors' use of
concrete, precise, economical language and carefully crafted sentences.

Suppose that the paragraph were revised as follows. What would be
lost?

Language stands at the center of human affairs, from the most prosaic
to the most profound. It is a means of human communication. It is a
means of cultural change and regeneration. It is found in every social
situation. The element that characterizes all these activities is communication. As the main vehicle of human communication, language is
indispensable.

This revision communicates roughly the same ideas as the original
paragraph, but it lacks that paragraph's liveliness and interest. Instead of
presenting vivid examples—"haggling with store clerks, telling off umpires,
and gossiping with friends"—these sentences state only vague generalities.
Moreover, they're short and monotonous. Also lost in the revision is any
sense of the authors' personalities, as revealed in their writing.

As this example demonstrates, effective prose style doesn't have to be
flashy or call attention to itself. The focus in the original passage is on the
*ideas* being discussed. The authors don't want readers to stop and think,
"My, what a lovely sentence." But they do want their readers to become
interested in and engaged with their ideas. So they use strong verbs and
vivid, concrete examples whenever possible. They pay careful attention to
sentence structure, alternating sequences of sentences with parallel structures with other, more varied sentences. They make sure that the relationships among ideas are clear. As a result of these and other choices, this
paragraph succeeds in being both economical and emphatic.

Exploring your stylistic options—developing a style that reflects your
understanding of yourself and the world and your feel for language—is one
of the pleasures of writing. The Guidelines for Effective Prose Style on p. 300
describe just a few of the ways you can revise your own writing to improve
its style.

## Guidelines for Effective Prose Style

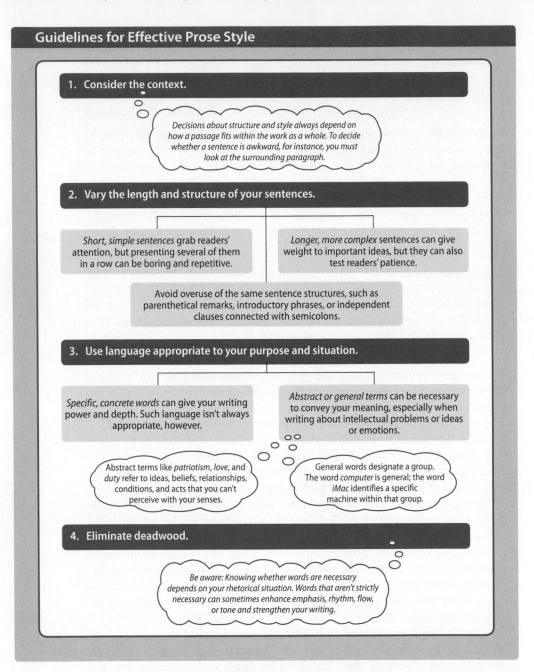

**1. Consider the context.**

*Decisions about structure and style always depend on how a passage fits within the work as a whole. To decide whether a sentence is awkward, for instance, you must look at the surrounding paragraph.*

**2. Vary the length and structure of your sentences.**

*Short, simple sentences* grab readers' attention, but presenting several of them in a row can be boring and repetitive.

*Longer, more complex* sentences can give weight to important ideas, but they can also test readers' patience.

Avoid overuse of the same sentence structures, such as parenthetical remarks, introductory phrases, or independent clauses connected with semicolons.

**3. Use language appropriate to your purpose and situation.**

*Specific, concrete words* can give your writing power and depth. Such language isn't always appropriate, however.

*Abstract or general terms* can be necessary to convey your meaning, especially when writing about intellectual problems or ideas or emotions.

Abstract terms like *patriotism*, *love*, and *duty* refer to ideas, beliefs, relationships, conditions, and acts that you can't perceive with your senses.

General words designate a group. The word *computer* is general; the word *iMac* identifies a specific machine within that group.

**4. Eliminate deadwood.**

*Be aware: Knowing whether words are necessary depends on your rhetorical situation. Words that aren't strictly necessary can sometimes enhance emphasis, rhythm, flow, or tone and strengthen your writing.*

# Proofreading: A Rhetorical Approach to Correctness

Proofreading is the final stage of the writing process. When you proofread, you examine your text carefully to identify and correct errors in grammar, spelling, and punctuation. The goal? To ensure that your writing follows the conventions of standard written English. These conventions represent shared agreements about written texts in English and how they can be best received and understood by readers. You may not be used to thinking about correctness in writing in this way. Your teachers (and perhaps also your parents) may have talked about correctness primarily as a matter of right and wrong. There are reasons they did so: They are aware of the potential negative consequences for those whose writing is viewed as incorrect or error-ridden. When a written text violates readers' expectations, readers may find it difficult to focus on its meaning. They may become irritated at what they view as sloppy or careless writing. They may make judgments about the writer's commitment to the assignment (or to their education). They may even make judgments about the writer's intelligence.

Those who have studied the history of the English language and the conventions of standard written English know that such judgments can be unfair. Textual conventions are shared agreements about what is appropriate in spoken and written communication, and these conventions can and do change over time. Decades ago, for instance, schoolchildren were routinely taught that it was an error to end a sentence with a preposition. This convention led to the construction of some fairly awkward sentences, including the sentence that is often attributed to Winston Churchill: "Ending a sentence with a preposition is something up with which I will not put." Over time this convention changed, and most readers find a sentence like "Who were you talking to?" preferable to the more formal "To whom were you talking?" What was once viewed as a matter of correctness is now viewed as a matter of preference.

Textual conventions are also culturally situated. Where the conventions of writing are concerned, in other words, context and community matter. If a friend texts you and you don't understand something about the message, you might text back a simple "?"—perhaps using an emoji to do so. But if your supervisor emails your work schedule for the week and you think you see an error in the schedule, you would be wise to respond using complete words and sentences and correct punctuation. When you text your friend one way and email your supervisor another way, you are making a rhetorical judgment about what is appropriate in that particular context.

thinking rhetorically

A rhetorical perspective on error can help you understand why observing language conventions is about more than just following rules for rules' sake. The conventions of standard written English play an essential role in the creation and transmission of meaning. Imagine trying to read an extended text with no punctuation. (You may be surprised to learn that the system of punctuation that we use today did not exist before the invention of the printing press around 1440.) You wouldn't know (among other things) where a new sentence began or the previous sentence ended. Punctuation can also be critical to meaning, as the following paired sentences, both of which depend on questionable gender stereotypes, humorously demonstrate:

A woman without her man is nothing.

A woman: without her, man is nothing.

The conventions of standard written English help ensure that the message you intend to convey is the message that the reader receives.

To better understand how deviations from the conventions of standard written English can distract, annoy, or confuse readers, let's look at this issue from the perspective of Aristotle's three appeals, as discussed in Chapter 3 (pp. 64–69). According to Aristotle, when speakers and writers communicate with others, they draw on these three general appeals:

*Logos*, the appeal to reason

*Pathos*, the appeal to emotion, values, and beliefs

*Ethos*, the appeal to the credibility of the speaker or writer

What role might deviations from the conventions of standard written English play in the reception of student writing when read by college instructors? As has been discussed throughout this book, academic writing places a high value on logos, or the appeal to reason. Although successful academic writers employ pathos and ethos in key ways in their texts, logos is particularly important. Anything that interferes with an instructor's ability to focus on content and meaning is a distraction. Numerous errors can cause instructors to turn their focus from the writer's message to the form in which the writer expresses it, so the significance of errors becomes inflated.

What about pathos, or the appeal to emotion, values, and beliefs? In academic writing, students employ appeals to pathos when they demonstrate that they share the commitments, values, and practices of the academic community. Instructors believe that correctness is a sign of respect for readers; they also believe that it represents a commitment to the creation and distribution of knowledge. When students turn in written work that is full of errors, instructors may assume that they do not value—and do not want to be a part of—the academic community.

You have probably already realized that error-ridden writing can cause instructors to question students' ethos as well. Ethos refers to the credibility of the writer. When students do not follow the conventions of standard written English valued by their instructors, they risk losing credibility. At best, instructors may view students as sloppy and careless. At worst, they may make negative inferences about students' commitment to the course—and to their education.

As this discussion indicates, a lot can be at stake when students turn in written work that does not meet the conventions of standard written English. This is why it is important to take the time to proofread your writing carefully. Research suggests that students can recognize most errors in their writing if they learn how and when to focus their attention on correcting their writing, which is what proofreading is all about.

Perhaps the major challenge that proofreading poses for writers is the ability to distance themselves from the texts they have written. For most writers, time away from their text is essential if they are to achieve this distance. Time management thus plays a central role in the proofreading process. If you write an essay for your history or business class at the last minute in a haze of late-night, overcaffeinated exhaustion, you will find it difficult if not impossible to proofread that essay. Thus it is essential to build time for proofreading into your composing process, just as you build in time for research, writing, revising, and editing.

The following guidelines will help you develop the ability to proofread your own writing effectively and efficiently.

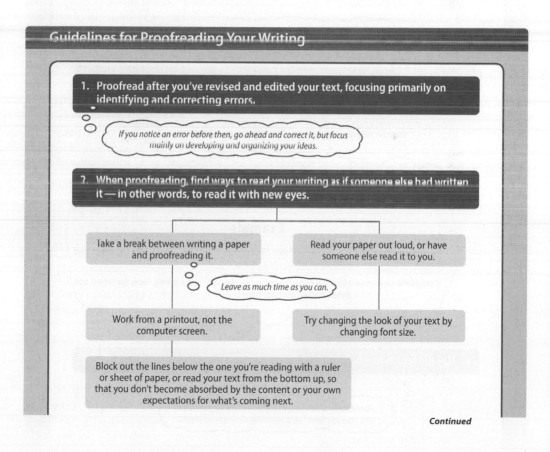

**Guidelines for Proofreading Your Writing**

1. Proofread after you've revised and edited your text, focusing primarily on identifying and correcting errors.

    *If you notice an error before then, go ahead and correct it, but focus mainly on developing and organizing your ideas.*

2. When proofreading, find ways to read your writing as if someone else had written it — in other words, to read it with new eyes.

    Take a break between writing a paper and proofreading it.

    Read your paper out loud, or have someone else read it to you.

    *Leave as much time as you can.*

    Work from a printout, not the computer screen.

    Try changing the look of your text by changing font size.

    Block out the lines below the one you're reading with a ruler or sheet of paper, or read your text from the bottom up, so that you don't become absorbed by the content or your own expectations for what's coming next.

*Continued*

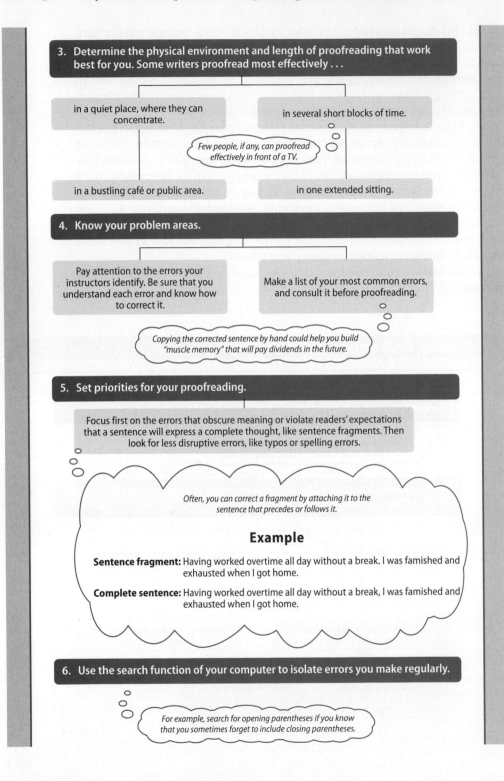

3. Determine the physical environment and length of proofreading that work best for you. Some writers proofread most effectively . . .

in a quiet place, where they can concentrate.

in several short blocks of time.

*Few people, if any, can proofread effectively in front of a TV.*

in a bustling café or public area.

in one extended sitting.

4. Know your problem areas.

Pay attention to the errors your instructors identify. Be sure that you understand each error and know how to correct it.

Make a list of your most common errors, and consult it before proofreading.

*Copying the corrected sentence by hand could help you build "muscle memory" that will pay dividends in the future.*

5. Set priorities for your proofreading.

Focus first on the errors that obscure meaning or violate readers' expectations that a sentence will express a complete thought, like sentence fragments. Then look for less disruptive errors, like typos or spelling errors.

*Often, you can correct a fragment by attaching it to the sentence that precedes or follows it.*

### Example

**Sentence fragment:** Having worked overtime all day without a break. I was famished and exhausted when I got home.

**Complete sentence:** Having worked overtime all day without a break, I was famished and exhausted when I got home.

6. Use the search function of your computer to isolate errors you make regularly.

*For example, search for opening parentheses if you know that you sometimes forget to include closing parentheses.*

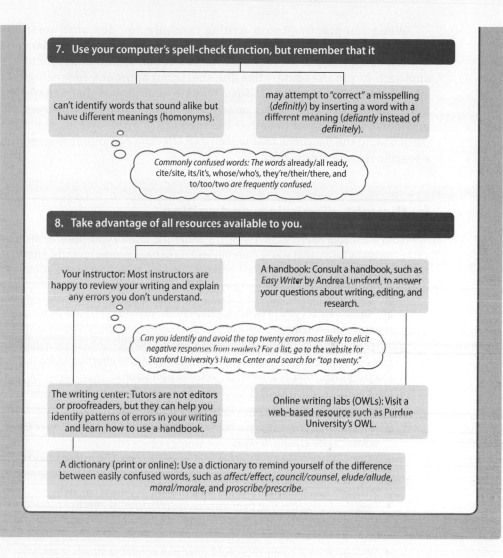

**7. Use your computer's spell-check function, but remember that it**

can't identify words that sound alike but have different meanings (homonyms).

may attempt to "correct" a misspelling (*definitly*) by inserting a word with a different meaning (*defiantly* instead of *definitely*).

*Commonly confused words: The words* already/all ready, cite/site, its/it's, whose/who's, they're/their/there, *and* to/too/two *are frequently confused.*

**8. Take advantage of all resources available to you.**

Your instructor: Most instructors are happy to review your writing and explain any errors you don't understand.

A handbook: Consult a handbook, such as *Easy Writer* by Andrea Lunsford, to answer your questions about writing, editing, and research.

*Can you identify and avoid the top twenty errors most likely to elicit negative responses from readers? For a list, go to the website for Stanford University's Hume Center and search for "top twenty."*

The writing center: Tutors are not editors or proofreaders, but they can help you identify patterns of errors in your writing and learn how to use a handbook.

Online writing labs (OWLs): Visit a web-based resource such as Purdue University's OWL.

A dictionary (print or online): Use a dictionary to remind yourself of the difference between easily confused words, such as *affect/effect, council/counsel, elude/allude, moral/morale,* and *proscribe/prescribe.*

## strategies for success

Proofreading can be especially challenging for many writers. If you find proofreading difficult, try the multiple-reading approach to proofreading. Read your essay first looking for grammatical errors, such as subject-verb agreement, errors involving articles, or pronoun-noun agreement. Then read it again looking for punctuation errors and a third time for spelling errors. It can be especially helpful to keep a list of frequent errors, read your work out loud, and work with a writing center tutor.

When you proofread your writing carefully, you demonstrate in the most specific and concrete way possible that you respect your readers and want to do all you can to facilitate communication with them. A rhetorical approach to proofreading — like the rhetorical approach to writing that informs every aspect of *The Academic Writer* — reminds you that writers who think rhetorically apply their understanding of human communication in general, and of texts (whether the medium is print, oral, or digital) in particular, to the decisions that will enable effective communication within a specific rhetorical situation.

## for **thought, discussion, and writing**

1. To study your own revision process, number and save all your plans, drafts, and revisions for a paper you're currently writing or have written recently. After you have completed the paper, review these materials, paying particular attention to the revisions you made. Can you describe the revision strategies you followed and identify ways to improve the effectiveness of this process? Your instructor may ask you to write an essay discussing what you have learned as a result of this analysis.

2. From an essay you are currently working on, choose two or three paragraphs that you suspect could be more coherent or stylistically effective. Using this chapter's discussion as a guide, revise these paragraphs.

3. Read the essay by Frank Rose on pp. 31–32 (or choose another essay that interests you), and then answer the following questions.

   - How would you describe the general style of this essay? Write three or four sentences describing its style.
   - How would you describe the persona, or voice, conveyed by this essay? List at least three characteristics of the writer's voice, and then indicate several passages that exemplify these characteristics.
   - Find three passages that demonstrate the principles of effective prose style as discussed in this chapter. Indicate why you believe each passage is stylistically effective.
   - What additional comments could you make about the structure and style of this essay? Did anything about the style surprise you? Formulate at least one additional comment about the essay's structure and style.

4. On the next page is a student's in-class midterm essay exam on Nathaniel Hawthorne's short story "Young Goodman Brown." The student didn't have time to proofread the exam response before turning it in. Correct all the errors you can identify. If you are unsure whether something is an error, put a question mark in the margin next to the line where the possible error appears.

Analysis of A Scene in "Young Goodman Brown"

In the short story "Young Goodman Brown," by Nathaniel Hawthorne the longest (it comprises nearly the entire story) and most influential scene is the one where Goodman Brown ventures into the dark woods with the devil. This scene has multiple elements which make it significant to the story, including setting, irony, and suspense.

The setting of this scene really adds to what is going on with the plot. Goodman Brown has just left his sweet young wife back at home in there quiet town and is trekking into the dark, gloomy, mysterious woods with a dark stranger, who later on is revealed as the devil himself. The shadows, darkness, seclusion, and wildness of a forest all contribute to a feeling of unease and suspense. Later on, the burning pine trees create a feeling of hell-on-earth and makes the reader feel as though pour Goodman is slipping deeper and deeper into the devil's clutches.

Irony is another thing apparent in this scene. The fact that the main characters name happen to be Goodman ("good man") is ironic in itself given that he has just left his sweet, good pure wife to converse with the devil, at night, in the middle of a creepy forest. Another example of irony is the number of seemingly "good" townspeople that he encounters as he makes his way deeper and deeper into the forest to attend the devil's communion he sees the minister, a Deacon, a pious Christian woman, and the devil tells him that he has known his father and grandfather, even though Goodman Brown argued earlier that he was from a good Christian family.

Finally, the element of suspense plays a large part in the composition of this scene. One of the most suspenseful moments is when Goodman thinks he hears Faith's voice and then sees her hair ribbon flutter to the ground. Later, he sees her face to face and commands her to, "look up to heaven and resist the wicked one," at which time the scene dramatically ends leaving the reader with a sense of suspense and wonderment at whether or not Faith obeyed the command.

# 11

# Strategies for Multimodal Composing

The term *multimodal composing* may be new to you. When you first encounter the term, you may think something like this: "Oh that must refer to forms of digital communication like wikis, blogs, websites, posts to Twitter and Instagram, and so forth." These are examples of multimodal texts but so is a traditional print essay. "How can this be?" you might wonder. A brief discussion of what modes are should clarify why this is the case.

## Understanding Multimodal Composing

There are five primary modes of communication:

- *Linguistic:* the use of words — written or spoken
- *Visual:* the use of images of all kinds — both static and moving
- *Aural:* the use of sound, from tone of voice to musical compositions
- *Spatial:* the use of design elements, white space, website navigation, and so on
- *Gestural:* movement of all kinds, from a speaker's facial expressions and gestures (whether seen in person or in a photo or film) to a complex dance performance

There are also three primary media of communication: print, oral, and digital. They are not the only possible media, however. Our bodies can serve as a medium of communication, as occurs in the case of oral presentations and dance. Canvas can serve as a medium for painters. The side of a building or railroad car can serve as a medium for graffiti artists. Print, oral, and digital media, however, are especially important and common in college, the professions, and public life. (Texts that emphasize the linguistic mode and that resemble traditional academic essays do not have to employ the medium of print. You might read an essay for your composition or history class on your laptop or e-reader, for instance.

For this reason, some scholars prefer to designate texts that emphasize the linguistic mode as alphabetic texts, a term that acknowledges that these texts are not limited to the medium of print.)

Because print texts draw on a minimum of two modes (the linguistic and the spatial), they are by definition multimodal. It is easy to undervalue the role of the spatial mode when the design elements (margin, spacing, font, and so forth) are standardized (as with traditional academic print essays). Even when students include visuals in print texts, as art history students might do if they insert a reproduction of a painting in their essays, the dominant mode is linguistic, and the dominant medium is print.

In a world of traditional print texts, it was easy for those composing texts to emphasize the role that words (the linguistic mode) play in their development—students and teachers alike would commonsensically say that they *wrote* an essay or report—but in a world where most writers have access to multiple modes and media, design becomes equally important. Students creating a PowerPoint presentation for an oral report or a brochure for a service learning project would probably say that they are *designing, composing,* or *creating* the slide presentation or brochure rather than writing it, even though words would still play an important role in that composition.

Today students live and compose in a world where multiple modes and media abound. While many students continue to compose texts that emphasize the linguistic mode, they are much more likely to include complex visual, gestural, aural, and spatial elements as well. It is quite common for students to create essays with multiple visuals (images, charts, graphs). If they are giving an oral report, they may well create a PowerPoint or Prezi presentation, with sound files and visuals embedded in the slides. They may participate in a class blog, wiki, discussion board, or Facebook page. They may even create films or podcasts to share their ideas.

Students in first year writing classes are also composing texts that take advantage of multiple modes. An increasingly common assignment in these classes, for instance, asks students to revise, or *remix,* a print text to take advantage of other modes and media. A student might remix a research essay in the form of a Prezi or PowerPoint presentation, an audio essay, or a visually rich poster, for example.

Students also create multimodal texts for their own purposes: To share their experiences with family and friends, students studying abroad might create a blog or an Instagram that combines words, images, and design features. Students involved in campus and community organizations on their own or through a service learning program regularly create brochures, posters, websites, podcasts, videos, Facebook pages, and other texts to promote these organizations and their activities. Multimodal composing is a part of most students' daily lives. Even changing the cover photo on your Facebook page is an act of multimodal composition and represents a rhetorical choice about how you want to represent yourself on that site. The rhetorical nature of Facebook cover photos becomes particularly clear when those who are committed to a cause or who want to express their support after a tragedy

thinking
rhetorically

employ a filter (such as the colors of the French flag that many Facebook users adopted after the November 13, 2015, terrorist attacks on Paris) to express their position or their solidarity with the victims of a tragedy. Hashtags can also serve a rhetorical purpose since they help those interested in a topic to find relevant tweets and Instagram posts. A photographer interested in glaciers, for instance, might include this hashtag with all relevant posts: #glaciersartphotographs. That way others who share this interest can easily find these posts, and the photographer can find and follow others as well.

## strategies for success

It may be more difficult to explore multimodal texts if you are returning to school, if you come from an educational background that doesn't use them, or if you have limited access to technology. Don't worry! The world is full of multimodal texts. Take a walk around campus and look for all the ways texts are presented to students. You will see signs, screens, pamphlets, flyers, and many other examples. What are some of your favorites? Which ones would you like to learn how to make yourself?

## for **exploration**

Think about the texts you have created both in school and out of school. (From the perspective of multimodal composition, a text can be an image or a performance as well as a document created with words.) How many of these texts rely mainly on the linguistic mode that characterizes many print texts? How many incorporate other modes (aural, gestural, visual)? Thinking in terms of a range of multimodal projects — such as collages, posters, brochures, blogs, video or audio texts, and slide presentations — are you more comfortable with some than with others? Take five to ten minutes to reflect in writing on these questions.

# The Rhetorical Situation and Multimodal Composing

thinking
rhetorically

As the chapters in Part One of this textbook emphasize, a rhetorical approach to communication encourages you to consider four key elements of your situation:

1. Your role as someone who has (or must discover) something to communicate
2. The audience with whom you would like to communicate

3. The text you create to convey your ideas and attitudes

4. A medium (print, oral, digital)

To make appropriate choices about their writing, effective writers analyze their rhetorical situation. If they are composing a text in a genre with which they are already familiar, they may do so intuitively. But when writers are encountering new genres or undertaking advanced study in their discipline they often find it helpful to do a written analysis.

Chapter 3 provides questions you can use to analyze your rhetorical situation (pp. 56–57) as well as analyses that Alia Sands (pp. 57–59) and Brandon Barrett (pp. 65–67) composed to guide their writing.

Here is an example of a writer's analysis of her rhetorical situation in composing a multimodal digital composition. The writer is Mirlandra Neuneker, whose poster collage about who she is as a writer appears on p. 89. Mirlandra created the collage when she was a student at Oregon State University, using a variety of created and found objects including her favorite pen, sticky notes of all sizes, push pins, a variety of texts, and a hair tie. Since then, Mirlandra has graduated. After working in the financial industry, she decided to embark on a career that would allow more room for creativity while also giving her a flexible schedule. So she created a food blog: *Mirlandra's Kitchen*. Her blog draws on the linguistic, visual, gestural, and spatial modes. As a blog that attracts viewers or visitors from such social media as Google, Pinterest, Instagram, and Twitter, *Mirlandra's Kitchen* is an excellent example of a contemporary composition that draws on multiple modes.

"To be successful," Mirlandra wrote, "my blog must make the fullest possible use of social media, and social media are always evolving. In the early years of *Mirlandra's Kitchen*, Pinterest was the biggest driver of visitors to my blog, but that recently changed so that increasingly large numbers of viewers come to my blog via Google. This makes a difference to me as a writer because as a platform Google encourages long form writing, while Pinterest does not. And there are other consequences as well:

> Because so much of my traffic comes from Google, I must write and create content in a way that Google will consider valuable. I use Google Trends and SEM Rush to do research and determine what content is currently trending and valuable. Everything on my page must be optimized to give me the best chance of ranking with Google. Statistically, if I'm not in the first three search results, a reader will not click on my link. Google also requires things that many people would never think about. For instance, the Alt Text on each image must be filled out. A good Alt Text description makes it clear what is in the image because this description is read aloud to people with visual impairments.

"The shift from desktop to mobile computing is also really important for my blog. [In 2019, 71 percent of the traffic on Mirlandra's blog was mobile, 16 percent desktop, and 11 percent tablet.] There's a lot to think about, and I'm constantly making choices about where to put my energy and what to do next. Analyzing my rhetorical situation reminds me that these are rhetorical as well as practical choices."

The following discussion of Mirlandra's experience with her blog can help you better understand the many challenges and opportunities that those creating multimodal digital texts can face.

**Writer:** I created my blog to share my love of food and cooking. My blog is also a business venture, one to which I'm deeply committed, so I am happy to put in the time and effort to create a blog that will attract readers. It's been a real learning experience, but a fun one.

In my blog, I want to present myself as knowledgeable about food and cooking, but I don't want to come across as a foodie or someone with extensive professional experience. I want every aspect of my blog—from its title to my photo to the font and design to the recipes I create and the photos that illustrate them—to encourage readers to see me as a friend who might be sharing a recipe over tea or across the fence. Some blogs strive for an urban look. I wanted a casual, homey—and yet professional—feel. This is reflected in the cheerful design of my masthead, the bright color scheme,

**A Screenshot from Mirlandra Neuneker's Blog** *Mirlandra's Kitchen* **(mirlandraskitchen.com)**

and the kind of recipes I share (not too difficult, expensive, or fancy). My goal is to create a uniform image or brand for my blog, one that was inviting but also professional and thus trustworthy.

**Reader:** Thanks to Google Analytics I have a lot of information about my readers. In the first ten months of 2019 I've had 695,932 page views. The average reader stays on a page 59 seconds and consumes 1.19 pages on a visit. Of all my traffic, 85.15% is from the US; 6.88% from Canada, 2.73% from Great Britain. The rest comes from every continent in the world. Women comprise 87.4% of my readership. I keep this in mind when I write: My goal is to keep readers on the blog long enough to capture their attention.

I spend a lot of time researching what my readers are interested in. I check the statistics to see what they are searching for online. I watch food trends. This data helps me craft the right recipes at the right times to appeal to readers. I appeal to readers through format, through photos, through recipes that work the first time, through humor, and through the ability to relate.

I do my best to write honestly about my life. While I don't write about deeply personal matters, I share myself in a way that encourages readers to feel that we have a genuine connection. I want every reader to leave my blog feeling encouraged and hopeful about their cooking life and more willing to try new things and take risks.

Perhaps the biggest surprise for me in terms of readers was how important the photos on my blog are. I have always thought of myself as a writer, rather than a photographer. However, my experience tells me that a food blog lives and dies by its photos. When I take a photo I am crafting an argument for readers as to why they should try to make this recipe for their families. As a blogger, if I don't convey that argument and win it, I lose readers. Many readers spend hours every week scrolling through Pinterest. I have less than a second to capture them with a photo that will get them to the blog.

**Text:** I could have the best, most inviting design in the world, but if the recipes I post don't meet the needs of my readers my blog will fail. So of course I spend huge amounts of time researching and developing recipes. I also focus a good deal of time and energy on my writing. I was an English major in college, and I also tutored in our writing center, so I am a confident writer. But I still need to work hard to develop a friendly, engaging style and appropriate content.

Food blogs have well-established conventions. Every food blog has recipes, or it's not a food blog. Most food blogs have an "about" category, and many also have FAQs and information about the blogger. But beyond that there are variations, especially in terms of the number and nature of categories. Some food blogs are more lifestyle-oriented. Others, like mine, keep the focus more on food and recipes.

**Medium:** Blogs are by definition digital texts, so the decision about what medium to use was easy, but beyond that basic decision, there were still many issues I had to address. I had to consider color choices, type and size of font, navigation, overall design, and how the design and layout affected accessibility. I needed a layout that would make sense to someone in their 20s but would also be logical and easy to use for someone in their 70s who might have less computer experience. Photos needed to be a reasonable size for loading, but they also needed to be big enough to be eye catching and engage my readers.

The fact that my readers use different devices to read my blog is critically important. Bloggers must always be looking to the future and thinking about how our work will be read. Will someone be using a smart watch to read my recipe next year?

If you want to have a successful food blog you need to spend a lot of time promoting your posts. I monitor my blog's performance on Google, Facebook, Twitter, Instagram, and Pinterest. Each has advantages and disadvantages. Each is constantly changing in terms of the platform it provides bloggers.

Mirlandra created her blog in 2014. For the first five years or so she focused primarily on getting her blog established, though she also began speaking occasionally on food-related and lifestyle topics. Recently, Mirlandra has expanded her focus to include additional media. Currently, for instance, Mirlandra is offering a "Live at 5PM" digital course on Instagram and Facebook video series, where she tackles a tough kitchen question in five minutes. She also offered a video course "The Confident Kitchen" for the first time in 2019.

When Mirlandra was a student writing primarily traditional print essays, her writing process had a definite conclusion: When the assignment was due, she turned her essay in to her teacher and moved on to the next project. As with many people composing online (bloggers, contributors to wikis and social media sites), Mirlandra's composing process for *Mirlandra's*

*Kitchen* is ongoing, especially as she expands the site to include video and other projects. Nevertheless, she continues to be guided by her understanding of rhetoric and of the rhetorical tradition.

## for **exploration**

Mirlandra Neuneker analyzed the rhetorical situation from the perspective of the writer of her food blog. Now analyze how a digital text, such as the homepage of a website, functions rhetorically from the reader's perspective. Choose a website of interest to you, such as a website you consult regularly or the website for your college or university. Then respond to the Questions for Analyzing Your Rhetorical Situation on pp. 56–57. (Substitute "the writer," "the composer," or "the author" for "you" in each question; for example, the question "Why are you writing?" becomes "Why is the author writing?")

## for **collaboration**

Bring your analysis and a screenshot of your chosen website's homepage to class. In small groups, have each member briefly summarize the results of his or her analysis. After each student has spoken, discuss what the analyses have in common, and identify three important insights into multimodal composing your group gained as a result of this discussion.

# Multimedia Composition and the Importance of Design

As Mirlandra's analysis of her rhetorical situation emphasizes, design plays a key role in the creation and development of her food blog. She writes, "I want every aspect of my blog—from its title to my photo to the font and design . . .— to encourage readers to see me as a friend who might be sharing a recipe over tea or across the fence." The four design principles—*alignment*, *proximity*, *repetition*, and *contrast*—play a key role in all compositions (including images and performances as well as word-based texts). Just as revising and editing are medium specific (revising a film differs greatly from revising an audio essay or a linguistic print or digital text), so too do the opportunities and constraints inherent in design vary depending on medium.

(thinking rhetorically)

## strategies for success

Design preferences vary from culture to culture, nation to nation, and even generation to generation. If the design of texts in your community is different from the designs you see in class, consider sharing your insight with others. Discuss styles, patterns, and other characteristics from your home community with your professor. Multimodal texts offer all of us the perfect opportunity to learn more about each other's rhetorics.

## ALIGNMENT

The principle of alignment relates to the way words, visuals, bodies, or sounds are arranged. In linguistic texts, your goal should be to maintain clear and consistent horizontal and vertical alignment so that readers can follow the text without becoming distracted. (In web design, lack of alignment is a very common design problem, so be sure that you don't mix alignments within a design.) In paintings and other graphic arts, strong diagonals can help guide the viewer's eye.

When creating a presentation, consider the alignment preferences built in to the software: PowerPoint assumes a linear alignment; Prezi allows for a nonlinear alignment with a zoom function and variable transitions and movements. Each offers different advantages and disadvantages, so think carefully about your purpose and rhetorical situation before deciding which to use. If you do not already know how to use Prezi, its steeper learning curve may also play a role in your decision.

thinking rhetorically

More broadly, whatever the medium, alignment involves grouping elements characteristic of various modes of communication in a meaningful way, one that is appropriate to the text's purpose, genre, and situation. Ira Glass, the host and executive producer of the public radio program *This American Life*, for instance, argues that those who listen to public radio have clear expectations about how stories will be organized. In an interview about how his show is designed, Glass refers to this expectation as "the 45-second rule":[1]

> The length of a news spot—if you listen to . . . the news cast at the beginning of *All Things Considered* or *Marketplace*—is 45 or 50 seconds. Usually, there's a couple of sentences from the reporter, then they do a quote from somebody, and . . . two or three more sentences from the reporter, and you're at 50, 45 seconds.
>
> It turns out that we public radio listeners are trained to expect something to change every 45 to 50 seconds. And as a producer you have to keep that pace in mind. For example, in a reporter's story, every 45 or 50 seconds, you'll go to a piece of tape.

As this example indicates, while alignment is often described in visual terms, it functions in powerful ways in other media. Glass's "45-second rule" also calls attention to the interconnections among design principles since it demonstrates the role of contrast in public radio.

---

[1]Glass laid out this and twelve other principles guiding the production of *This American Life* in a lecture called "Mo' Better Radio" given at Macalester College in 1998.

## PROXIMITY

A linguistic text makes effective use of the design principle of proximity when the relationships between text elements (such as headings, subheadings, captions, and items in a list) and visual elements (such as illustrations, charts, and tables) are clear. Your goal should be to position related points, chunks of text, and visual elements together so that your reader's understanding of your meaning is unimpeded. An easy way to evaluate a linguistic text's use of proximity is to squint your eyes and see how the page or screen looks. Do your eyes move logically from one part to another? If not, you'll want to work on the internal relationships.

In a more general sense, and in media other than print, proximity refers to how close various elements of a communication are in space or time and what relationships exist among these elements. When those constructing websites consider how users can best navigate their sites, they are considering issues of proximity. Proximity is especially important to a choreographer who is creating or restaging a dance. Dance is all about physical arrangement, or the relationship of bodies to each other. The word *choreography* actually comes from the Greek words for "dance writing."

## REPETITION

Repetition is important for creating a sense of coherence: A consistent design helps guide readers through the text, whatever the medium. In linguistic texts, repetition can involve elements that are visual, verbal, or both. For example, those writing linguistic texts need to be consistent in the design of typefaces they choose, the placement and use of color, and the positioning of graphic elements such as a navigational banner on a homepage. One example of repetition in a text-based document is the practice of indenting paragraphs: The seemingly subtle indentation actually signals the start of a new topic or subtopic and helps your reader keep track of your argument.

Repetition in music is crucial to holding listener's attention, but too much repetition can become tedious. (Imagine a song with a refrain that goes on too long or lyrics that get repeated too often.) Repetition—good and bad—plays a key role in oral presentations as well. Listeners can only process and retain so much information—they can't go back and reread something they missed or didn't understand—so effective presenters build repetition by including internal summaries and transitions and by providing brief stories, examples, and analogies that reinforce (and thus in a sense repeat) their major ideas. Repetition can be detrimental, however, when speakers engage in what is sometimes called "PowerPoint karaoke" (or "Death by PowerPoint"): When a speaker's presentation consists primarily of reading words on slides, viewers are quickly bored. Effective speakers understand that they must attend to the relationship between their spoken words (and physical gestures) and the information they share with their audience. Too much repetition makes the audience lose interest.

## CONTRAST

A text effectively employs contrast when the design uses difference or surprise to draw the audience in. In linguistic texts, contrast helps organize and orient the reader's interactions with a text, guiding the reader around the elements on a page or screen and making the information accessible. Even the simplest linguistic texts employ contrast in the interplay between white space and text. Margins, double-spacing, and white space around headings or graphics, for instance, frame the text and guide the reader through it. (Take a look at the white space on this page, and try to imagine how difficult the page would be to read if word after word were presented uninterrupted and extending to the borders of the page on all sides.) Visual texts may use contrasting colors or images or fonts to call the viewer's attention.

In both linguistic and visual texts, focal points play an important role in establishing contrast. A focal point—a point that the eye travels to first and that the mind uses to organize the other elements in the composition—may be an image, a logo, or a dominant set of words. When you design a page, flyer, poster, or screen, you should organize the elements so that the focal point makes the relationships among elements clear.

In a medium like film, focal points are constantly changing as camera angles shift from wide angle to close up and so forth. The same is true in dance. At one moment, the focus may be on the lead dancer; the next, it's on the chorus. In aesthetic productions and performances, such as films, opera, plays, or various forms of classical and contemporary dance, the elements of design interact in especially complex and powerful ways.

# Managing the Demands of Multimodal Composition

As Chapter 4, "Academic Writing: Committing to the Process," emphasizes, the demands of writing a traditional academic essay for your history or political science class can be considerable. These demands can become even more significant when you add a digital or oral component, as with websites, presentations, films, audio essays, and podcasts.

This chapter can't provide specific instructions for how best to undertake every possible kind of multimodal project. For one thing, all projects need to be considered in the context of their rhetorical situation. Creating a brief TikTok video to share a special moment with your family is very different from creating an extended video that will play an important role in the defense of your honors thesis, the culminating event of your undergraduate education.

Additionally, the possible technological choices for creating your video are multiple. Someone creating a brief family video would probably use a smartphone; to create a video for a more substantial academic project, he or she might employ a program such as Windows Movie Maker, iMovie, Final Cut Pro, or Adobe Premiere. And, of course, new technologies are being created all the time, even as others fade away.

Some general guidelines nevertheless apply to most multimodal projects, whether it is a relatively simple undertaking (such as an illustrated print essay or a Facebook or Twitter post) or a more complicated project (such as a website or blog, audio essay or podcast, poster, or flyer). See the Guidelines for Multimodal Composing below for details.

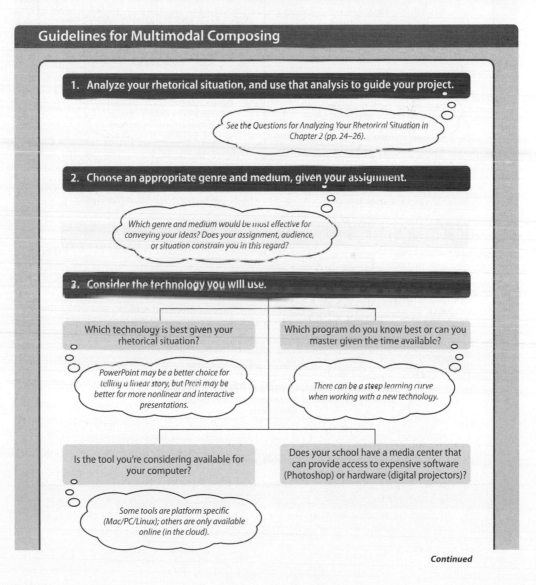

## Guidelines for Multimodal Composing

1. **Analyze your rhetorical situation, and use that analysis to guide your project.**

   See the Questions for Analyzing Your Rhetorical Situation in Chapter 2 (pp. 24–26).

2. **Choose an appropriate genre and medium, given your assignment.**

   Which genre and medium would be most effective for conveying your ideas? Does your assignment, audience, or situation constrain you in this regard?

3. **Consider the technology you will use.**

   Which technology is best given your rhetorical situation?

   PowerPoint may be a better choice for telling a linear story, but Prezi may be better for more nonlinear and interactive presentations.

   Which program do you know best or can you master given the time available?

   There can be a steep learning curve when working with a new technology.

   Is the tool you're considering available for your computer?

   Some tools are platform specific (Mac/PC/Linux); others are only available online (in the cloud).

   Does your school have a media center that can provide access to expensive software (Photoshop) or hardware (digital projectors)?

*Continued*

*Guidelines continued*

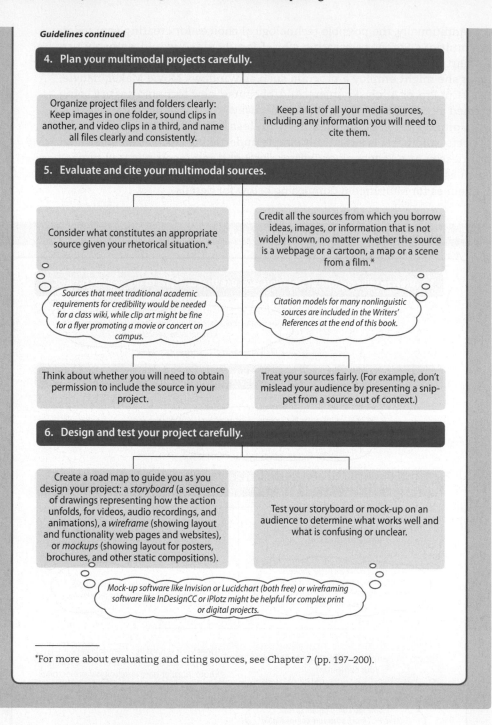

**4. Plan your multimodal projects carefully.**

Organize project files and folders clearly: Keep images in one folder, sound clips in another, and video clips in a third, and name all files clearly and consistently.

Keep a list of all your media sources, including any information you will need to cite them.

**5. Evaluate and cite your multimodal sources.**

Consider what constitutes an appropriate source given your rhetorical situation.*

Credit all the sources from which you borrow ideas, images, or information that is not widely known, no matter whether the source is a webpage or a cartoon, a map or a scene from a film.*

*Sources that meet traditional academic requirements for credibility would be needed for a class wiki, while clip art might be fine for a flyer promoting a movie or concert on campus.*

*Citation models for many nonlinguistic sources are included in the Writers' References at the end of this book.*

Think about whether you will need to obtain permission to include the source in your project.

Treat your sources fairly. (For example, don't mislead your audience by presenting a snippet from a source out of context.)

**6. Design and test your project carefully.**

Create a road map to guide you as you design your project: a *storyboard* (a sequence of drawings representing how the action unfolds, for videos, audio recordings, and animations), a *wireframe* (showing layout and functionality web pages and websites), or *mockups* (showing layout for posters, brochures, and other static compositions).

Test your storyboard or mock-up on an audience to determine what works well and what is confusing or unclear.

*Mock-up software like Invision or Lucidchart (both free) or wireframing software like InDesignCC or iPlotz might be helpful for complex print or digital projects.*

---

*For more about evaluating and citing sources, see Chapter 7 (pp. 197–200).

# Multimodal Composing: Three Student Examples

This chapter includes an example of a multimodal text, a screenshot from Mirlandra Neuneker's blog *Mirlandra's Kitchen* (p. 312), as well as her analysis of her rhetorical situation in creating this text (pp. 312–14). Chapter 4 (p. 89) also includes a collage that Mirlandra created as a student at Oregon State University. This section highlights three additional examples of multimodal texts created by students: a Prezi presentation, a website, and a TEDx talk.

Christopher Buttacavoli created the Prezi presentation "Young People and Risky Behavior: Why Prevention Is the Key to Public Health" for a class in public health at Oregon State University. The Prezi employs the linguistic, visual, and spatial modes; when Christopher presented it in class, however, his public performance added aural and gestural modes. Christopher's decision to use Prezi rather than PowerPoint was rhetorically savvy given his text's emphasis on the interconnections among various health-risk behaviors of adolescents. The result is a visually compelling, dynamic, and well-argued presentation. Shown here is the overview of the presentation.

**An Overview of Christopher Buttacavoli's Prezi Presentation (bit.ly/prezi_publichealth)***

---

*Note: The links in this chapter worked when this book was published, but URLs may change over time. If any of the links cease to function, try searching for the site online using the creator's name and the title of the project.

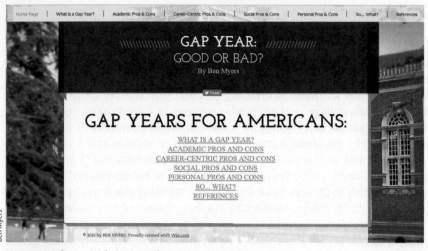

Homepage from a Website (savethetrexes.wix.com/gapyear)

Ben Myers, an undergraduate at Oklahoma State University, created a website on the advantages and disadvantages of gap years for college students as the final project in his first-year writing class and as part of a larger research-based project. The homepage for Ben's site is shown above. After first conducting research on his topic, Ben created his website, which represents a preliminary formulation of his argument. After presenting his website in class and getting feedback, he wrote an eight-page research project on the same topic. The organization of Ben's website reflects the research question that motivated his project: "Gap Year: Good or Bad?" Those navigating his site can move easily from one subtopic to another:

- What Is a Gap Year?
- Academic Pros and Cons
- Career-Centric Pros and Cons
- Social Pros and Cons
- So . . . What?
- References

**thinking rhetorically**

Ben takes full rhetorical advantage of the ability to integrate multiple modes and media into his website. Each page includes at least one video and several visuals, including photos, charts, and maps. On the "So . . . What?" page, Ben takes advantage of the potential for interacting with his readers that digital media affords and provides a survey where they can express their own views on gap years.

The final example is a screenshot from a talk that Ben Myers (the creator of the website, above) gave at a TEDx event at Oklahoma State University, TEDxOStateU 2015, designed to share "ideas worth spreading." Ben

A Video Presentation, Delivered April 10, 2015, at Oklahoma State University–Stillwater and Available on YouTube

competed in an open audition to earn one of the eight spots reserved for students. In his talk "The Disability Conversation," he argues powerfully for the importance of disability advocacy.

His presentation takes advantage of all five modes of communication: linguistic, visual, aural, spatial, and gestural. It is only about eight minutes long, but he uses that time well to share an engaging and thought-provoking mix of personal experience and information with his viewers. At appropriate moments, Ben uses PowerPoint slides to summarize his main points, but they do not dominate his presentation, which is notable for the clarity and persuasiveness of his ideas and his enthusiasm for his topic. Throughout his presentation, his tone is conversational even as he calls attention to the seriousness of his subject. Ben clearly recognizes the rhetorically charged nature of his situation: Many people find discussions of topics like disability uncomfortable. So he begins his talk with a powerful anecdote about his own experience with disability and in so doing puts those attending his talk at ease. Ben then articulates the major point of his talk: "Remaining silent about disability is not helpful." The remainder of his presentation explains why this is the case. Ben concludes his talk with a forceful challenge to his viewers: "Let's start the disability conversation today."

Rhetoric, Aristotle argued centuries ago, is the art of discovering all the available means of persuasion. When Aristotle wrote these words, he imagined a civic space, or *agora*, where the citizens of Athens (who did not include women or the enslaved) would meet face to face to converse and argue. Aristotle could not have imagined the world of print texts that Gutenberg's printing press created, let alone a world enabled by the Internet and World Wide Web. But his emphasis on discovering all of the available means of persuasion applies in all these situations. Thanks to the multiple modes and media of communication available to writers today, new agoras are providing increased opportunities for communication.

## for **thought, discussion, and writing**

1. Develop a flyer, brochure, newsletter, podcast, or web page for a community, church, civic, or other group with which you are involved. If you aren't currently involved in such an organization, develop a text that relates to a project that interests you. Be sure to analyze your rhetorical situation before you begin work on your document. After creating your text, make a list of the five most important decisions that played a role in the development of your text, such as the decision to develop a newsletter rather than a flyer. Then explain the rationale for each decision.

2. Evaluate the effectiveness of the three-minute video "Prezi vs. PowerPoint," developed by the Technology and Learning unit of Pepperdine University. (You can find this video on YouTube by searching with the key terms "Pepperdine" and "Prezi vs. PowerPoint.") Watch this video at least three times; during the second and third times you watch it, take notes on the number of modes it employs and the video's effectiveness as a multimodal composition. Then make a list of the video's top three strengths and indicate two ways you think it could be improved. Finally, based on your own experience with Prezi and PowerPoint, indicate whether you think the video provides a fair assessment of the potential strengths and limitations of each program.

3. Write an essay in which you reflect on your own experiences composing multimodal texts. Are you more familiar and comfortable with employing some modes than others? (For example, are you a confident composer of traditional linguistic research essays but a tentative composer of videos or podcasts?) What are your strengths as a multimodal composer? What areas of improvement can you identify? If you prefer, respond to this assignment using a medium other than print, such as a collage, slide presentation, audio essay, podcast, or video.

4. Choose a linguistic text that you have written for your composition class or another class, and remix it using another medium. Possibilities include creating a collage, brochure, slide presentation, audio essay, podcast, or video.

# Writers' References

# MLA Documentation Guidelines

The *MLA Handbook*, Eighth Edition, published by the Modern Language Association of America, or MLA, offers general principles for citing sources focused on the basic contents of every citation, including the following:

- *Author or authors (followed by a period).*
- *Title of source (followed by a period).* Titles of self-contained works, such as book titles, television series, and website names, are italicized; titles of works contained within other works, such as an article in a magazine or a story in an anthology, are set in quotation marks.
- *Title of the container, or larger work, in which the source appears, if any (followed by a comma).* For example, a newspaper or magazine "contains" the articles that appear within it; a television series "contains" individual episodes. Follow the title of the container with a comma, since the items that follow (other contributors, version, number, publisher, publication date, and location) all relate to the container. If a source has multiple containers—for example, you access an article that appears in a journal (container 1) via a database (container 2)—include information for the second container after the first. Titles of containers are typically italicized.
  - *Other contributors (followed by a comma).* Other contributors may include the editor, translator, producer, narrator, illustrator, and so on.
  - *Version (followed by a comma).* The version may be the edition name or number (revised edition, sixth edition, late edition), director's cut, abridged edition, and so on.
  - *Number (followed by a comma).* The number may include the volume number (for a multivolume work), the volume and issue number (for a journal), the disk number (for a set of DVDs), and so on.
  - *Publication information (followed by a comma).* Publication information may include the name of the publisher, site sponsor, government and agency, and so on.
  - *Publication date (followed by a comma).* The publication date may be a year for books or movies; a month and year or day, month, and year for magazines; day, month, and year for newspapers and episodes of daily television or radio shows; and so on.

- *Source location (followed by a period).* For example, page numbers indicate location for a printed text; the URL or DOI (digital object identifier, a permanent code) indicates location for an online text; a time stamp indicates location for a video or audio file.

- *Additional information (followed by a period).* Additional information may include original publication information for a reprinted book, an access date for an undated online source, or a label for an unusual source type or a source type that readers might not recognize from the citation (as for an editorial or letter to the editor, a typescript, or a lecture).

This appendix helps students make sensible decisions about how to cite sources by providing citation models based on the principles spelled out in the *MLA Handbook.* A number of the models included in the appendix are covered in the *MLA Handbook;* some, however, are not. For example, the *MLA Handbook* provides no model for an editorial or letter to the editor, but one is included in this appendix (p. 348). The model for an editorial is based on that for an article in a newspaper, with an identifying label added at the end of the citation. The appendix provides models for many sources that students consult while conducting research; however, it is not exhaustive. When no model is provided for the type of source you need to cite, base your citation on that for a similar source and add information as needed. Finally, if you are unsure about how to cite a source not included in this appendix, check with your instructor.

# Formatting a Research Project

The Eighth Edition of the *MLA Handbook* provides very little guidance for formatting a research-based writing project, but check the MLA's website (mla.org) for more information. The following guidelines are commonly observed in the humanities, but double-check with your instructor *before* preparing your final draft to make sure the formatting advice provided here is appropriate given your rhetorical situation.

- *First page and title page.* A title page is not often required. Instead, type each of the following pieces of information on a new line, flush left, in the upper left corner of the first page: your name, the instructor's name, the course name and number, and the date. On the next line, include your title, centered, without italics, boldface, quotation marks, or any other treatment.

- *Margins and spacing.* Leave one-inch margins at the top and bottom on both sides of each page. Double-space the entire text, including the identifying information at the top of the first page, title, indented (block) quotations, captions, any footnotes or endnotes, and the list of works cited. Indent paragraphs half an inch.

- *Long quotations.* Set off quotations longer than four typed lines by indenting them as a block, half an inch from the left margin. Do not enclose the passage in quotation marks.

- *Page numbers.* Include your last name and the page number in the upper right corner of each page, half an inch below the top margin and flush right.

- *Headings.* Many instructors and students find headings helpful. Make them concise yet informative. They can be single nouns (Literacy), a noun phrase (Literacy in Families), a gerund phrase (Testing for Literacy), or a question or statement (How Can Literacy Be Measured?). Make all headings at the same level consistent throughout your text, for example by using all single nouns or all gerund phrases. Set headings in the same font as the rest of the text, distinguishing levels by typing the first level heading in capitals, second-level headings in boldface, and third-level headings in italics:

  ## FIRST-LEVEL HEADING
  ### Second-level Heading
  *Third-level Heading*

  Position headings consistently throughout your text. Centered headings are common for the first level; for secondary-level headings, you may indent, set flush left, or run them into the text (that is, you can start the section's text on the same line as the heading).

- *Visuals.* Place tables, photographs, drawings, charts, graphs, and other figures as close as possible to the relevant text. Tables should have a label and number (Table 1) and a clear caption. The label and caption should be aligned on the left, on separate lines. Give the source information below the table. All other visuals should be labeled *Figure* (abbreviated *Fig.*), numbered, and captioned. The label and caption should appear on the same line, followed by the source information. Remember to refer to each visual in your text, indicating how it contributes to the point(s) you are making.

# In-Text Citations

MLA style requires a citation in the text of an essay for every quotation, paraphrase, summary, or other material requiring documentation. In-text citations document material from other sources with both signal phrases and parenthetical references. Parenthetical references should include the information your readers need to locate the full reference in the list of works cited at the end of the text (see pp. 335–63). An in-text citation in MLA style aims to give the reader two kinds of information: (1) It indicates *which source* on the works-cited page the writer is referring to, and (2) it explains *where in the source* the material quoted, paraphrased, or summarized can be found, if the source has page numbers or other numbered sections.

## Directory to MLA style for in-text citations

The basic MLA in-text citation includes the author's last name either in a signal phrase introducing the source material or in parentheses at the end of the sentence. Whenever possible, it also includes the page or paragraph number in parentheses at the end of the sentence.

### SAMPLE CITATION USING A SIGNAL PHRASE

In his discussion of *Monty Python* routines, Crystal notes that the group relished "breaking the normal rules" of language (107).

### SAMPLE PARENTHETICAL CITATION

A noted linguist explains that *Monty Python* humor often relied on "bizarre linguistic interactions" (Crystal 108).

Note in the following examples where punctuation is placed in relation to the parentheses.

**1. AUTHOR NAMED IN A SIGNAL PHRASE** The MLA recommends using the author's name in a signal phrase to introduce the material and citing the page number(s), if any, in parentheses.

Lee claims that his comic-book creation, Thor, was "the first regularly published superhero to speak in a consistently archaic manner" (199).

**2. AUTHOR NAMED IN A PARENTHETICAL REFERENCE** When you do not mention the author in a signal phrase, include the author's last name before the page number(s) in the parentheses. Use no punctuation between the author's name and the page number(s).

The word *Bollywood* is sometimes considered an insult because it implies that Indian movies are merely "a derivative of the American film industry" (Chopra 9).

**3. TWO AUTHORS** Use both the authors' last names in a signal phrase or in parentheses.

For example, Bonacich and Appelbaum report that in Los Angeles, which has the highest concentration of garment manufacturers in the nation, 81% of workers are Asian and Latino immigrants (171–75).

**4. THREE OR MORE AUTHORS** Use the first author's name and *et al.* ("and others").

Similarly, as Belenky et al. assert, examining the lives of women expands our understanding of human development (7).

**5. ORGANIZATION AS AUTHOR** Give the group's full name, abbreviating words that are commonly abbreviated, such as *Association (Assoc.)* or *Department (Dept.)*.

Any study of social welfare involves a close analysis of "the impacts, the benefits, and the costs" of its policies (Social Research Corp. iii).

**6. UNKNOWN AUTHOR** Use a shortened title in place of the author.

One analysis defines *hype* as "an artificially engendered atmosphere of hysteria" ("Today's Marketplace" 51).

To shorten a title, use the first noun in the title plus any adjectives modifying it, leaving out any articles (*a, an, the*), verbs, prepositional phrases, and so on. For example, "The Great Republican Earthquake" becomes "Great Republican Earthquake," and "America's Lurch to the Left" becomes "America's Lurch." If there is no noun in the first part of the title, use the first word (excluding articles) if it will be enough to distinguish the work from other works cited. For example, *Must We Mean What We Say: A Book of Essays* would be abbreviated as *Must.* The word you use in the in-text citation should be the word you use to begin the entry in the list of works cited.

**7. AUTHOR OF TWO OR MORE WORKS CITED IN THE SAME PROJECT** If your list of works cited has more than one work by the same author, include a shortened version of the title of the work✱ you are citing in a signal phrase or in parentheses to prevent reader confusion.

> Gardner shows readers their own silliness in his description of a "pointless,
> ridiculous monster, crouched in the shadows, stinking of dead men,
> murdered children, and martyred cows" (*Grendel* 2).

If two or more works by the same author are referred to, include both titles (abbreviated if necessary) with the word *and* between them: (*Grendel* and *October Light*).

**8. TWO OR MORE AUTHORS WITH THE SAME LAST NAME** Include the author's first *and* last names in a signal phrase or first initial and last name in a parenthetical reference.

> Children will learn to write if they are allowed to choose their own subjects,
> James Britton asserts, citing the Schools Council study of the 1960s
> (J. Britten 37–42).

**9. INDIRECT SOURCE (AUTHOR QUOTING SOMEONE ELSE)** Use the abbreviation *qtd. in* to indicate that you are quoting from someone else's report of a source.

> As Arthur Miller says, "When somebody is destroyed everybody finally
> contributes to it, but in Willy's case, the end product would be virtually
> the same" (qtd. in Martin and Meyer 375).

**10. MULTIVOLUME WORK** In a parenthetical reference, if you cite more than one volume, note the volume number first and then the page number(s), with a colon and one space between them.

> Modernist writers prized experimentation and gradually even sought to blur
> the line between poetry and prose, according to Forster (3: 150).

If you cite only one volume of the work in your list of works cited, include only the author's last name and the page number in parentheses: (Forster 150).

**11. LITERARY WORK** Because literary works are often available in many different editions, cite the page number(s) from the edition you used followed by a semicolon; then give other identifying information that

✱ For more about shortening titles, see model 6, p. 331.

will lead readers to the passage in any edition. For a novel, indicate the part or chapter:

> In utter despair, Dostoyevsky's character Mitya wonders aloud about the "terrible tragedies realism inflicts on people" (376; book 8, ch. 2).

For a poem, cite the part (if there is one) and line number(s) (if included in the source), separated by a period:

> Whitman speculates, "All goes onward and outward, nothing collapses, / And to die is different from what anyone supposed, and luckier" (6.129–30).

If you are citing only line numbers, use the word *line* or *lines* in the first reference (*lines* 33–34). Omit the word *line* or *lines* in subsequent entries. For a verse play, give only the act, scene, and line numbers, separated by periods:

> The witches greet Banquo as "Lesser than Macbeth, and greater" (1.3.65).

**12. WORK IN AN ANTHOLOGY OR COLLECTION** For an essay, short story, or other piece of prose contained within an anthology, use the name of the author of the work, not the editor of the anthology, but use the page number(s) from the anthology.

> Narratives of captivity play a major role in early writing by women in the United States, as demonstrated by Silko (219).

**13. SACRED TEXT** To cite a sacred text such as the Qur'an or the Bible, give the title of the edition you used, the book, the chapter, and the verse (or their equivalent), separated by periods. In parenthetical references, use abbreviations for books with names of five or more letters (*Gen.* for *Genesis*).

> He ignored the admonition "Pride goes before destruction, and a haughty spirit before a fall" (*New Oxford Annotated Bible*, Prov. 16.18).

**14. ENCYCLOPEDIA OR DICTIONARY ENTRY** An entry from a reference work — such as an encyclopedia or a dictionary — without an author will appear on the works-cited list under the entry's title. Enclose the title in quotation marks and place it in parentheses. Omit the page number for reference works that arrange entries alphabetically.

> The term *prion* was coined by Stanley B. Prusiner from the words *proteinaceous* and *infectious* and a suffix meaning *particle* ("Prion").

**15. GOVERNMENT SOURCE WITH NO AUTHOR NAMED** Because entries for sources authored by government agencies will appear on your list of works cited under the name of the country (see model 63, p. 362), your in-text citation for such a source should include the name of the country as well as the name of the agency responsible for the source.

> To reduce the agricultural runoff into the Chesapeake Bay, the United States Environmental Protection Agency has argued that "[h]igh nutrient loading crops, such as corn and soybean, should be replaced with alternatives in environmentally sensitive areas" (26).

If the government agency is also the publisher, begin the citation with the source's title, and include the title (or a shortened form) in the in-text citation.

**16. ELECTRONIC OR NONPRINT SOURCE** Give enough information in a signal phrase or in parentheses for readers to locate the source in your list of works cited. Many works found online or in electronic databases lack stable page numbers; you can omit the page number in such cases. If you are citing a work with stable pagination, such as an article in PDF format, however, include the page number in parentheses.

> As a *Slate* analysis has noted, "Prominent sports psychologists get praised for their successes and don't get grief for their failures" (Engber).

The source, an article on a website, does not have stable pagination.

> According to Whitmarsh, the British military had experimented with using balloons for observation as far back as 1879 (328).

The source, an online PDF of a print article, includes stable page numbers.

If the source includes numbered sections, or paragraphs, include the appropriate abbreviation (*sec.* or *par.*) and the number in parentheses.

> Sherman notes that the "immediate, interactive, and on-the-spot" nature of Internet information can make nondigital media seem outdated (sec. 32).

If using an excerpt from a time-based source (such as an audio or video file), include the time stamp for the section cited.

> Although the Hays Code was written to oust risqué behavior in the movies, its effects were felt in television comedy as well, with shows like *I Love Lucy* and *The Dick Van Dyke Show* depicting their married costars as sleeping in twin beds. But sex did creep in around the edges, if only in the most innocent fashion. For example, much of the humor in the first episode of *Mr. Ed* ("The First Meeting") revolves around Wilbur Post's young wife (Connie Hines) jumping into her costar Alan Young's arms on the slightest pretext (04:22–04:30).

**17. ENTIRE WORK** Include the reference in the text, without any page numbers.

> Jon Krakauer's *Into the Wild* both criticizes and admires the solitary impulses of its young hero, which end up killing him.

**18. TWO OR MORE SOURCES IN ONE CITATION** Separate the information with semicolons.

> Economists recommend that *employment* be redefined to include unpaid domestic labor (Clark 148; Nevins 39).

# Explanatory and Bibliographic Notes

Explanatory notes may be used to provide information or commentary that would not readily fit into your text. Bibliographic notes may be used for citing several sources for one point and for offering thanks to, information about, or evaluation of a source. Use superscript numbers in the text to refer readers to the notes, which may be included as endnotes (typed under the heading *Notes* on a separate page after the text but before the list of works cited) or as footnotes at the bottom of the page (typed four lines below the last text line).

### SUPERSCRIPT NUMBER IN TEXT

Stewart emphasizes the existence of social contacts in Hawthorne's life so that the audience will accept a different Hawthorne, one more attuned to modern times than the figure in Woodberry.[3]

### NOTE

[3] Woodberry does, however, show that Hawthorne *was* often an unsociable individual. He emphasizes the seclusion of Hawthorne's mother, who separated herself from her family after the death of her husband, often even taking meals alone (28). Woodberry seems to imply that Mrs. Hawthorne's isolation rubbed off on her son.

# List of Works Cited

A list of works cited is an alphabetical list of the sources you have referred to in your essay. (If your instructor asks you to list everything you have read as background, call the list *Works Consulted*.) The formatting instructions below are consistent with those offered by the Modern Language Association on their website (mla.org). But check with your instructor if you have any doubts about her or his expectations.

- Start your list on a separate page after the text of your essay and any notes. (For works in media other than print, you may need to include documentation elsewhere, such as on a slide or mentioned in your talk for a presentation.)
- Continue the consecutive numbering of pages.
- Center the heading *Works Cited* (not italicized or in quotation marks) one inch from the top of the page.
- Start each entry flush with the left margin; indent subsequent lines for the entry half an inch. Double-space the entire list.
- List sources alphabetically by the first word. Start with the author's name, if available; if not, use the editor's name, if available. If no author or editor is given, start with the title.
- Italicize titles of self-contained works, such as books and websites, but put the titles of works contained in other works (such as articles that appeared in magazines, newspapers, or scholarly journals; stories that appeared in anthologies or collections; or web pages included on websites) in quotation marks.

## GUIDELINES FOR AUTHOR LISTINGS

The list of works cited is arranged alphabetically. The in-text citations in your writing point readers toward particular sources on the list (see pp. 365–68).

### NAME CITED IN SIGNAL PHRASE IN TEXT

Crystal explains . . . .

### NAME IN PARENTHETICAL CITATION IN TEXT

. . . (Crystal 107).

### BEGINNING OF ENTRY ON LIST OF WORKS CITED

Crystal, David.

# Directory to MLA style for works-cited entries

*Continued*

**1. ONE AUTHOR** Put the last name first, followed by a comma, the first name (and initial, if any), and a period.

> Crystal, David.

**2. MULTIPLE AUTHORS** For works with two authors, list the first author with the last name first, followed by comma. Then include the word *and* followed by the name of the second author, first name first.

> Bonacich, Edna, and Richard Appelbaum.

For three or more authors, list the first author followed by a comma and *et al.* ("and others").

> Lupton, Ellen, et al.

**3. ORGANIZATION OR GROUP AUTHOR** Give the name of the group, government agency, corporation, or other organization listed as the author.

> Getty Trust.

> United States, Government Accountability Office.

If the organization or group is also the publisher, start the entry with the title of the source.

**4. UNKNOWN AUTHOR** When the author is not identified, begin the entry with the title, and alphabetize by the first important word. Italicize titles of self-contained works, such as books and websites. Put the titles of works contained within other works (articles that appear in newspapers, magazines, or journals; web pages that exist within websites; short stories that appear in magazines, anthologies, or collections) in quotation marks

> "California Sues EPA over Emissions."

> *New Concise World Atlas.*

**5. TWO OR MORE WORKS BY THE SAME AUTHOR** Arrange the entries alphabetically by title. Include the author's name in the first entry, but in subsequent entries, use three hyphens followed by a period. (For the basic format for citing a book, see model 6. For the basic format for citing an article from an online newspaper, see model 33.)

> Chopra, Anupama. "Bollywood Princess, Hollywood Hopeful." *The New York Times*, 10 Feb. 2008, www.nytimes.com/2008/02/10/movies/10chop.html.

> ---. *King of Bollywood: Shah Rukh Khan and the Seductive World of Indian Cinema.* Warner Books, 2007.

Note: Use three hyphens only when the work is by *exactly* the same author(s) as the previous entry.

## BOOKS

**6. BASIC FORMAT FOR A BOOK** Begin with the author name(s). (See models 1–5.) Then include the title and the subtitle, the publisher, and the publication date. The source map on pp. 342–43 shows where to find this information in a typical book.

> Bowker, Gordon. *James Joyce: A New Biography*. Farrar, Straus and Giroux, 2012.

**7. AUTHOR AND EDITOR BOTH NAMED**

> Bangs, Lester. *Psychotic Reactions and Carburetor Dung*. Edited by Greil Marcus, Alfred A. Knopf, 1988.

*Note:* To cite the editor's contribution instead, begin the entry with the editor's name.

> Marcus, Greil, editor. *Psychotic Reactions and Carburetor Dung*. By Lester Bangs, Alfred A. Knopf, 1988.

**8. EDITOR, NO AUTHOR NAMED**

> Wall, Cheryl A., editor. *Changing Our Own Words: Essays on Criticism, Theory, and Writing by Black Women*. Rutgers UP, 1989.

**9. ANTHOLOGY** Cite an entire anthology the same way you would cite a book with an editor and no named author (see model 8).

> Marcus, Ben, editor. *New American Stories*. Vintage Books, 2015.

**10. WORK IN AN ANTHOLOGY OR CHAPTER IN A BOOK WITH AN EDITOR** List the author(s) of the selection or chapter; its title, in quotation marks; the title of the book, italicized; *edited by* and the name(s) of the editor(s); the publisher; the publication date; and the selection's page numbers.

> Eisenberg, Deborah. "Some Other, Better Otto." *New American Stories*, edited by Ben Marcus, Vintage Books, 2015, pp. 3–29.

**11. TWO OR MORE ITEMS FROM THE SAME ANTHOLOGY** List the anthology as one entry (see model 9). Also list each selection separately with a cross-reference to the anthology.

> Eisenberg, Deborah. "Some Other, Better Otto." Marcus, pp. 94–136.

> Sayrafiezadeh, Saïd. "Paranoia." Marcus, pp. 3–29.

**12. TRANSLATION**

> Ferrante, Elena. *The Story of the Lost Child.* Translated by Ann Goldstein,
> Europa Editions, 2015.

**13. BOOK WITH BOTH TRANSLATOR AND EDITOR** List the editor's and translator's
names after the title, in the order they appear on the title page.

> Kant, Immanuel. *"Toward Perpetual Peace" and Other Writings on Politics,*
> *Peace, and History.* Edited by Pauline Kleingeld, translated by David L.
> Colclasure, Yale UP, 2006.

**14. BOOK IN A LANGUAGE OTHER THAN ENGLISH** Include a translation of the title
in brackets, if necessary.

> Benedetti, Mario. *La borra del café. [The Coffee Grind].* Editorial Sudamericana,
> 2000.

**15. GRAPHIC NARRATIVE** If the words and images are created by the same person, cite a graphic narrative just as you would a book (model 6)

> Bechdel, Alison. *Fun Home: A Family Tragicomic.* Houghton Mifflin, 2006.

For a collaboration, list the author or illustrator who is most important to
your research before the title, and list other contributors after the title.

> Gaiman, Neil. *The Sandman: Overture.* Illustrated by J. H. William III, DC
> Comics, 2015.

> William III, J, II,, illustrator, *The Sandman: Overture.* By Neil Gaiman, DC
> Comics, 2015.

**16. EDITION OTHER THAN THE FIRST**

> Eagleton, Terry. *Literary Theory: An Introduction.* 3rd ed., U of Minnesota P,
> 2008.

**17. MULTIVOLUME WORK** If you cite only one volume, give the number of the
volume before the publisher. (You may include the total number of volumes
at the end of the citation if that information would help readers find your
source.) Include the publication date for that volume only.

> Stark, Freya. *Letters.* Edited by Lucy Moorehead, vol. 5, Compton Press,
> 1978. 8 vols.

## MLA SOURCE MAP: Books

Take information from the book's title page and copyright page (on the reverse side of the title page), not from the book's cover or a library catalog.

**1** Author. List the last name first. End with a period. For variations, see models 2–5.

**2** Title. Italicize the title and any subtitle; capitalize all major words. End with a period.

**3** Publisher. Use the publisher's full name as it appears on the title page, omitting only terms such as *Inc.* and *Company*. Substitute *UP* for *University Press*. Follow it with a comma.

**4** Year of publication. If more than one copyright date is given, use the most recent one. End with a period.

*A citation for the work on p. 343 would look like this:*

    1          2

Patel, Raj. *The Value of Nothing: How to Reshape Market Society and Redefine*

          3    4

*Democracy.* Picador, 2009.

# THE VALUE OF NOTHING

HOW TO RESHAPE
MARKET SOCIETY AND
REDEFINE DEMOCRACY

— **2** Title and Subtitle

Raj Patel ——————————————— **1** Author

PICADOR ——————————————————— **3** Publisher
New York

**4** Year of Publication————

THE VALUE OF NOTHING: HOW TO RESHAPE MARKET SOCIETY
AND REDEFINE DEMOCRACY. Copyright © 2009 by Raj Patel.
All rights reserved. Printed in the United States of America.
For information, address Picador, 175 Fifth Avenue,
New York, N.Y. 10010.

www.picadorusa.com

Picador® is a U.S. registered trademark and is used by
St. Martin's Press under license from Pan Books Limited.

For information on Picador Reading Group Guides,
please contact Picador.
E-mail: readinggroupguides@picadorusa.com

Library of Congress Cataloging-in-Publication Data

Patel, Raj.
   The value of nothing : how to reshape market society and redefine
democracy / Raj Patel.—1st ed.
      p. cm.
Includes bibliographical references and index.
ISBN 978-0-312-42924-9
   1. Free enterprise.   2. Democracy.   3. Economics.   I. Title.
HB95.P3185 2009
330.12'2—dc22

                                                          2009041546

First Picador Edition: January 2010

Printed on recycled paper

If you cite two or more volumes, give the number of volumes in the complete work and provide inclusive dates of publication.

> Stark, Freya. *Letters.* Edited by Lucy Moorehead, Compton Press,
> 1974–82. 8 vols.

**18. PREFACE, FOREWORD, INTRODUCTION, OR AFTERWORD** After the writer's name, describe the contribution. After the title, indicate the book's author (with *by*), editor (with *edited by*), or translator (with *translated by*).

> Bennett, Hal Zina. Foreword. *Shimmering Images: A Handy Little Guide to*
> *Writing Memoir,* by Lisa Dale Norton, St. Martin's Griffin, 2008, pp. xiii–xvi.

> Dunham, Lena. Foreword. *The Liars' Club,* by Mary Karr, Penguin Classics,
> 2015, pp. xi–xiii.

**19. ENTRY IN A REFERENCE BOOK** If an author is given, begin with the author's name (look for initials and a list of contributors); otherwise, begin with the title. If the entries are alphabetized, you need not include the page number.

> "Ball's in Your Court, The." *The American Heritage Dictionary of Idioms,*
> 2nd ed., Houghton Mifflin Harcourt, 2013.

**20. BOOK THAT IS PART OF A SERIES** At the end of the citation, include the series name (and number, if any) from the title page.

> Denham, A. E., editor. *Plato on Art and Beauty.* Palgrave Macmillan, 2012.
> Philosophers in Depth.

> Snicket, Lemony (Daniel Handler). *The Bad Beginning.* HarperCollins
> Publishers, 1999. A Series of Unfortunate Events 1.

**21. REPUBLICATION (MODERN EDITION OF AN OLDER BOOK)** Indicate the original publication date after the title.

> Austen, Jane. *Sense and Sensibility.* 1813. Dover, 1966.

**22. BOOK WITH A TITLE WITHIN THE TITLE** Do not italicize a book title within a title. For an article title within a title, italicize as usual, and place the article title in quotation marks.

> Lethem, Jonathan. *"Lucky Alan" and Other Stories.* Doubleday, 2015.

> Shanahan, Timothy. *Philosophy and* Blade Runner. Palgrave Macmillan, 2014.

**23. SACRED TEXT** To cite individual published editions of sacred books, begin the entry with the title. If you are not citing a particular edition, do not include sacred texts in the list of works cited.

> *The Oxford Annotated Bible with the Apocrypha.* Edited by Herbert G. May and Bruce M. Metzger, Revised Standard Version, Oxford UP, 1965.

> *The Qur'an: Translation.* Translated by Abdullah Yusuf Ali, Tahrike Tarsile Qur'an, 2001.

## PRINT PERIODICALS

Begin with the author name(s). (See models 1–5.) Then include the article title; the title of the periodical; the volume, issue, and date for journal articles or the date alone for magazine and newspaper articles; and the page numbers. The source map on pp. 346–47 shows where to find this information in a sample periodical.

**24. ARTICLE IN A JOURNAL** Follow the journal title with the volume number, the issue number (if given), the date of publication, and the page numbers.

> Matchie, Thomas. "Law versus Love in *The Round House.*" *Midwest Quarterly*, vol. 56, no. 4, Summer 2015, pp. 353–64.

> Tilman, David. "Food and Health of a Full Earth." *Daedalus,* vol. 144, no. 4, Fall 2015, pp. 5–7.

**25. ARTICLE IN A MAGAZINE** Provide the date from the magazine cover instead of volume or issue numbers.

> Bryan, Christy. "Ivory Worship." *National Geographic*, Oct. 2012, pp. 28–61.

> Grossman, Lev. "A Star Is Born." *Time,* 2 Nov. 2015, pp. 30–39.

**26. ARTICLE IN A NEWSPAPER** Include the edition (*national ed., late ed.*), if listed, and the section number or letter, if given. When an article skips pages, give only the first page number and a plus sign.

> Bray, Hiawatha. "As Toys Get Smarter, Privacy Issues Emerge." *The Boston Globe,* 10 Dec. 2015, p. C1.

> Sherry, Allison. "Volunteers' Personal Touch Turns High-Tech Data into Votes." *The Denver Post,* 30 Oct. 2012, pp. 1A+.

Add the city in brackets if it is not part of the name: *The Globe and Mail* [Toronto].

## MLA SOURCE MAP: Articles in print periodicals

**1** Author. List the last name first. End with a period. For variations, see models 2–5.

**2** Article title. Put the title and any subtitle in quotation marks; capitalize all major words. Place a period inside the closing quotation mark.

**3** Periodical title. Italicize the title; capitalize all major words. Follow the periodical title with a comma.

**4** Volume, issue, and/or date of publication. For journals, give the volume number and issue number (if any), separated by a comma; then list the date and follow it with a comma. For magazines, list the day (if given), month, and year, followed by a comma.

**5** Page numbers. List inclusive page numbers. If the article skips pages, put the first page number and a plus sign. End with a period.

*A citation for a journal article would look like this:*

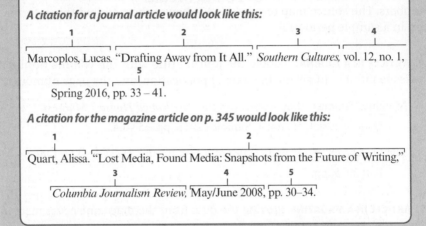

Marcoplos, Lucas. "Drafting Away from It All." *Southern Cultures,* vol. 12, no. 1, Spring 2016, pp. 33 – 41.

*A citation for the magazine article on p. 345 would look like this:*

Quart, Alissa. "Lost Media, Found Media: Snapshots from the Future of Writing," *Columbia Journalism Review,* May/June 2008, pp. 30–34.

**4 Date of Publication**

**3 Periodical Title**

COLUMBIA
**JOURNALISM
REVIEW**

May / June 2008 · cjr.org

*The Future*
**Writin**

Nonfiction's disqui
**ALISSA QUART**

Kindle isn't it, but
**EZRA KLEIN**

**UNDER THE SHI**
A reporter recalls
that got him throu
**CAMERON MCWHIRT**

**LOVE THY NEIGH**
The religion beat i
**TIM TOWNSEND**

**2 Article Title**

# Lost Media,
# Found Media

*Snapshots from the future of writing*

BY ALISSA QUART

**1 Author**

If there were an ashram for people who worship contemplative long-form journalism, it would be the Nieman Conference on Narrative Journalism. This March, at the Sheraton Boston Hotel, hundreds of journalists, authors, students, and aspirants came for the weekend event. Seated on metal chairs in large conference rooms, we learned about muscular storytelling (the Q-shaped narrative structure—who knew?). We sipped cups of coffee and

ate bagels and heard about reporting history through letters and public documents and how to evoke empathy for our subjects, particularly our most marginal ones. As we listened to reporters discussing great feats—exposing Walter Reed's fetid living quarters for wounded soldiers, for instance—we also renewed our pride in our profession. In short, the conference exemplified the best of the older media models, the ones that have so recently fallen into economic turmoil.

Yet even at the weekend's strongest lectures on interview techniques or the long-form profile, we couldn't ignore the digital elephant in the room. We all knew as writers that the kinds of pieces we were discussing require months ... d, and that we were all ... money to do that. It was

**5 Page Numbers**

... but something seems to have changed. For those of us who believed in the value of the journalism and literary nonfiction of the past, we had

become like the people at the ashram after the guru has died.

Right now, journalism is more or less divided into two camps, which I will call Lost Media and Found Media. I went to the Nieman conference par... ... how the ... ision are affecting and afflicting the Lost Media world that I love best, not on the institutional level, but for reporters and writers themselves. This world includes people who write for all the newspapers and magazines that are currently struggling with layoffs, speedups, hiring freezes, buyouts, the death or shrinkage of film- and book-review sections, lim-its on exus... ...work, the erasure of... the general narrowing of institutional ambition. It includes freelance writers competing with hordes of ever-younger competitors willing to write and publish online for free, the fade-out of established journalistic career paths, and, perhaps most crucially, a muddled sense of the meritorious, as blogs level and scramble the value and status of print publications, and of professional writers. The glamour and influence once associated with a magazine elite seem to have faded, becoming a sort of pastiche of winsome articles about yearning and boxers and dinners at Elaine's.

Found Media-ites, meanwhile, are the bloggers, the contributors to Huffington Post-type sites that aggregate blogs, as well as other work that somebody else paid for, and the new non-profits and pay-per-article schemes that aim to save journalism from 20 percent profit-margin demands. Although these elements are often disparate, together they compose the new media landscape. In economic terms, I mean all the outlets for nonfiction writing that seem to be thriving in the new era or striving to fill niches that Lost Media is giving up in a new order. Stylistically, Found Media tends to feel spontaneous, almost accidental. It's a domain dominated by the young, where writers get points not for following traditions or burnishing them but for amateur and hybrid vigor, for creating their own venues and their own genres. It is about public expression and community—not quite John Dewey's Great Community, which the critic Eric Alterman alluded to in a recent *New Yorker* article on newspapers, but rather a fractured form of Dewey's ideal: call it Great Communities.

To be a Found Media journalist or pundit, one need not be elite, expert, or trained; one must simply produce punchy intellectual property that is in conversation with groups of

30   MAY/JUNE 2008

*Illustration by Tomer Hanuka*

**27. EDITORIAL OR LETTER TO THE EDITOR** Include the writer's name (if given) and the title (if any). Include a label indicating the source type at the end of the citation.

> "California Dreaming." *The Nation,* 25 Feb. 2008, p. 4. Editorial.

> Galbraith, James K. "JFK's Plans to Withdraw." *New York Review of Books,* 6 Dec. 2007, pp. 77–78. Letter.

**28. REVIEW**

After the title of the review—if the review is untitled, include the label *Review* in its place—include *Review of* plus the title of the work being reviewed (followed by a comma). Then add *by* plus the names of the author(s), director(s), or producer(s) of the original work (followed by a comma). Finally, add the balance of the information you would need for any article within a larger work.

> Walton, James. "Noble, Embattled Souls." Review of *The Bone Clocks* and *Slade House*, by David Mitchell. *The New York Review of Books*, 3 Dec. 2015, pp. 55–58.

> Lane, Anthony. "Human Bondage." Review of *Spectre*, directed by Sam Mendes. *The New Yorker*, 16 Nov. 2015, pp. 96–97.

**29. UNSIGNED ARTICLE**

> "Performance of the Week." *Time,* 6 Oct. 2003, p. 18.

## ELECTRONIC SOURCES

When citing a website or a web page, include all the information you would need to cite any other source (author, title, and "container" information), and add a permalink or digital object identifier (DOI) in the "location" position. If neither a permalink nor a DOI is available, include the URL (omitting *http://*). If accessing a source through a database, add the information about the database as a separate "container": End the information about the journal with a period, and then add the title of the database (in italics, followed by a comma) and the DOI or permalink URL. If you are accessing the source through a database your library subscribes to, include just the basic URL for the database (*go.galegroup.com*), not the URL for the specific article.

**30. WORK FROM A DATABASE** The basic format for citing a work from a database appears in the source map on pp. 349–50.

> Coles, Kimberly Anne. "The Matter of Belief in John Donne's Holy Sonnets." *Renaissance Quarterly*, vol. 68, no. 3, Fall 2015, pp. 899–931. *JSTOR*, doi:10.1086/683855.

## MLA SOURCE MAP: Articles from databases

Library subscriptions — such as EBSCOhost and Academic Search Premier — provide access to huge databases of articles.

**1** Author. List the last name first. End with a period. For variations, see models 2–5.

**2** Article title. Enclose the title and any subtitle in quotation marks.

**3** Periodical title. Italicize it.

**4** Print publication information. List the volume and issue number, if any; the date of publication, including the day (if given), month, and year, in that order; and the inclusive page numbers.

**5** Database name. Italicize the name of the database.

**6** DOI or URL. Include the DOI (digital object identifier) or URL, preferably a permalink URL (minus *http://*). If accessing the source from a subscription database, include only the URL for the database.

*A citation for the work on p. 350 would look like this:*

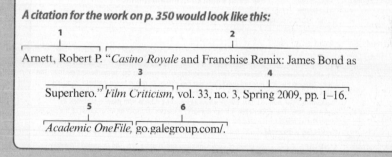

**3 Periodical Title**

**2 Article Title**

| | |
|---|---|
| **Title:** | **Casino Royale and Franchise Remix: James Bond as Superhero.** |
| **Authors:** | Arnett, Robert P.1 ◄─────── **1 Author** |
| **Source:** | Film Criticism; Spring2009, Vol. 33 Issue 3, p1-16, 16p |
| **Document Type:** | Article |
| **Subject Terms:** | *JAMES Bond films   **4 Print Publication Information** |
| | *FILM genres |
| | *BOND, James (Fictitious character) |
| | *SUPERHERO films |
| **Reviews & Products:** | CASINO Royale (Film) |
| **People:** | CRAIG, Daniel |
| **Abstract:** | The article discusses the role of the film "Casino Royale" in remixing the James Bond franchise. The author believes that the remixed Bond franchise has shifted its genre to a superhero franchise. When Sony acquired MGM in 2004, part of its plans is to transform the 007 franchise at par with "Spiderman." The remixed franchise re-aligns its franchise criteria with those established by superhero films. The author cites "Casino Royale's" narrative structure as an example of the success of the film as franchise remixed for the future. The portrayal of Bond as a superhero by actor Daniel Craig is discussed. |
| **Author Affiliations:** | 1Associate professor, Department of Communication and Theatre Arts, Old Dominion University |
| **ISSN:** | 01635069 |
| **Accession Number:** | 47966995 |
| **Database:** | Academic Search Premier |

**5 Database Name**

Macari, Anne Marie. "Lyric Impulse in a Time of Extinction." *American Poetry Review*, vol. 44, no. 4, July/Aug. 2015, pp. 11–14. *General OneFile*, go.galegroup.com/.

**31. ARTICLE IN AN ONLINE JOURNAL** Cite an online journal article as you would a print journal article (see model 24). After the page numbers (if available), include the URL or DOI. If you access the article through a database, include the database name (in italics), followed by a comma, before the DOI or URL.

Bryson, Devin. "The Rise of a New Senegalese Cultural Philosophy?" *African Studies Quarterly*, vol. 14, no. 3, Mar. 2014, pp. 33–56, asq.africa.ufl.edu /files/Volume-14-Issue-3-Bryson.pdf.

Rich, Ruby B. "Evidence of Visibility." *Film Quarterly*, vol. 69, no. 2, Winter 2015, pp. 5–7. *Academic Search Premier*, doi:10.1525/FQ.2015.69.2.5.

**32. ARTICLE IN AN ONLINE MAGAZINE** Provide the usual print publication information for a magazine, but replace the page numbers with the URL.

Leonard, Andrew. "The Surveillance State High School." *Salon*, 27 Nov. 2012, www.salon.com/2012/11/27/the_surveillance_state_high_school/.

**33. ARTICLE IN AN ONLINE NEWSPAPER** Provide the usual print publication information for a newspaper, but replace the page numbers with the URL.

Crowell, Maddy. "How Computers Are Getting Better at Detecting Liars." *The Christian Science Monitor*, 12 Dec. 2015, www.csmonitor.com /Science/Science-Notebook/2015/1212/How-computers-are-getting-better -at-detecting-liars.

**34. COMMENT ON AN ONLINE ARTICLE** If the commenter uses a pseudonym (a pen name or screen name), include it; if you know the author's actual name, include that after the pseudonym in parentheses.

pablosharkman. Comment on "'We Are All Implicated': Wendell Berry Laments a Disconnection from Community and the Land," by Scott Carlson. *The Chronicle of Higher Education*, 23 Apr. 2012, chronicle .com/article/In-Jefferson-Lecture-Wendell/131648.

**35. DIGITAL BOOK** Provide information as for a print book (see models 6–23); then give the electronic publication information, such as the database name (in italics) and the URL, or the digital format (Kindle, Nook). If the book is a reissue of an earlier publication, you may add the original publication information (such as the year of original publication) after the title if it is relevant, given your rhetorical situation.

> Doerr, Anthony. *All the Light We Cannot See*. Scribner, 2014. Nook.

> Goldsmith, Oliver. *The Vicar of Wakefield: A Tale*. 1801. *America's Historical Imprints*, infoweb.newsbank.com.ezproxy.bpl.org/.

> Piketty, Thomas. *Capital in the Twenty-First Century*. Translated by Arthur Goldhammer, Harvard UP, 2014. Google Books, books.google.com /books?isbn=0674369556.

**36. ONLINE EDITORIAL OR LETTER** For clarity, include the label *Editorial* or *Letter* at the end of the citation.

> "City's Blight Fight Making Difference." *The Columbus Dispatch,* 17 Nov. 2015, www.dispatch.com/content/stories/editorials/2015/11/17/1-citys -blight-fight-making-difference.html. Editorial.

**37. ONLINE REVIEW** Cite an online review as you would a print review (see model 28), adding or changing information as needed to reflect the digital container, such as by replacing the page numbers with the URL.

> Della Subin, Anna. "It Has Burned My Heart." Review of *The Lives of Muhammad*, by Kecia Ali. *London Review of Books*, 22 Oct. 2015, www.lrb.co.uk/v37/n20/anna-della-subin/it-has-burned-my-heart.

> Spychalski, John C. Review of *American Railroads—Decline and Renaissance in the Twentieth Century*, by Robert E. Gallamore and John R. Meyer. *Transportation Journal*, vol. 54, no. 4, Fall 2015, pp. 535–38. *JSTOR*, doi:10.5325/transportationj.54.4.0535.

**38. ENTRY IN AN ONLINE REFERENCE WORK** Cite the entry as you would an entry from a print reference work (see model 19), including or changing any information you may need to identify the digital container, such as the URL.

> Durante, Amy M. "Finn Mac Cumhail." *Encyclopedia Mythica*, 17 Apr. 2011, www.pantheon.org/articles/f/finn_mac_cumhail.html.

Hall, Mark. "Facebook (American Company)." *The Encyclopaedia Britannica*, 2 July 2014, www.britannica.com/topic/Facebook.

"House Music." *Wikipedia*, 16 Nov. 2015, en.wikipedia.org/wiki/House_music.

**39. WORK FROM A WEBSITE** For basic information on citing a work from a website, see the source map on pp. 354–55. Include the name of the author; the title of the document, in quotation marks; the name of the website, italicized; the date of publication; the name of the publisher or sponsor if different from the title of the site; and the URL. Include an access date following the URL only if no publication date is available.

Enzinna, Wes. "Syria's Unknown Revolution." *Pulitzer Center on Crisis Reporting*, 24 Nov. 2015, pulitzercenter.org/projects/middle-east-syria -enzinna-war-rojava.

"Social and Historical Context: Vitality." *Arapesh Grammar and Digital Language Archive Project*, Institute for Advanced Technology in the Humanities, www.arapesh.org/socio_historical_context_vitality.php. Accessed 22 Mar. 2016.

**40. ENTIRE WEBSITE** Follow the guidelines for a specific work from the web, beginning with the name of the author, editor, compiler, or director (if any), followed by the title of the website, italicized; the name of the sponsor or publisher, only if different from the author; the date of publication or last update; and the URL. Include an access date following the URL only if no publication date is available.

Halsall, Paul, editor. *Internet Modern History Sourcebook* Fordham U, 4 Nov. 2011, legacy.fordham.edu/halsall/index.asp.

Railton, Stephen. *Mark Twain in His Times*. U of Virginia Library, 2012, twain.lib.virginia.edu/.

*The Newton Project*. U of Sussex, 2016, www.newtonproject.sussex.ac.uk /prism.php?id=1.

*Transparency International: The Global Coalition against Corruption*. 2015, www.transparency.org/.

## MLA SOURCE MAP: Works from websites

You may need to browse other parts of a site to find some of the following elements, and some sites may omit elements. Uncover as much information as you can.

1  Author. List the last name first. End with a period. For variations, see models 2–5. If no author is given or if the author and website title or publisher are substantially the same, begin with the title.

2  Title of work. Enclose the title and any subtitle of the work in quotation marks.

3  Title of website. Give the title of the entire website, italicized.

4  Publisher or sponsor. Include the publisher or sponsor only if that name is significantly different from the title of the website. In the example here, the sponsoring organization is the Nobel Foundation, which is not significantly different from the website title (*Nobelprize.org*), so no sponsor is included.

5  Date of publication or latest update. Give the most recent date, followed by a comma.

6  URL. Use a permalink if available.

7  Date of access. Include an access date only if no publication date is available; insert it following the URL. (See model 39 for an example.)

*A citation for the work on p. 355 would look like this:*

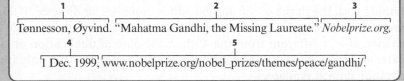

Tønnesson, Øyvind. "Mahatma Gandhi, the Missing Laureate." *Nobelprize.org,*

1 Dec. 1999, www.nobelprize.org/nobel_prizes/themes/peace/gandhi/.

**1** Author

**3** Title of Website

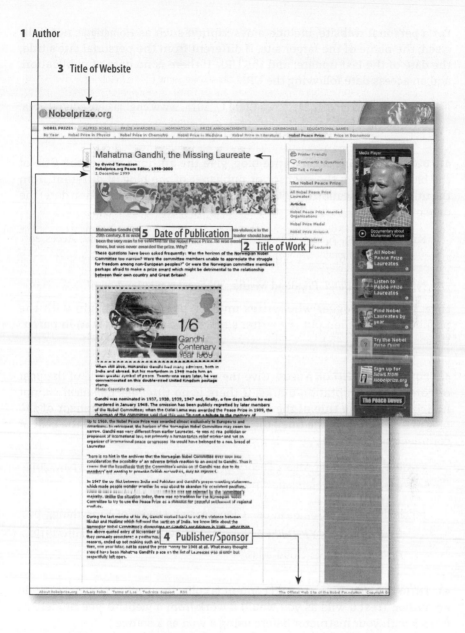

Nobelprize.org

NOBEL PRIZES    ALFRED NOBEL    PRIZE AWARDERS    NOMINATION    PRIZE ANNOUNCEMENTS    AWARD CEREMONIES    EDUCATIONAL GAMES
By Year    Nobel Prize in Physics    Nobel Prize in Chemistry    Nobel Prize in Medicine    Nobel Prize in Literature    Nobel Peace Prize    Prize in Economics

## Mahatma Gandhi, the Missing Laureate

by Øyvind Tønnesson
Nobelprize.org Peace Editor, 1998-2000
1 December 1999

Printer Friendly
Comments & Questions
Tell a Friend

The Nobel Peace Prize
All Nobel Peace Prize Laureates

Articles
Nobel Peace Prize Awarded Organizations
Nobel Prize Medal
Nobel Prize Amount

Media Player

Documentary about Muhammad Yunus

**5** Date of Publication

Mohandas Gandhi (186...) ...non-violence in the 20th century. It is wid... ...leader should have been the very man to be selected for the Nobel Peace Prize. He was nomi... times, but was never awarded the prize. Why?

**2** Title of Work

These questions have been asked frequently: Was the horizon of the Norwegian Nobel Committee too narrow? Were the committee members unable to appreciate the struggle for freedom among non-European peoples?" Or were the Norwegian committee members perhaps afraid to make a prize award which might be detrimental to the relationship between their own country and Great Britain?

1/6
Gandhi
Centenary
Year 1969

When still alive, Mohandas Gandhi had many admirers, both in India and abroad. But his martyrdom in 1948 made him an even greater symbol of peace. Twenty-one years later, he was commemorated on this double-sided United Kingdom postage stamp.
Photo: Copyright © Scanpix

Gandhi was nominated in 1937, 1938, 1939, 1947 and, finally, a few days before he was murdered in January 1948. The omission has been publicly regretted by later members of the Nobel Committee; when the Dalai Lama was awarded the Peace Prize in 1989, the chairman of the Committee said that this was "in part a tribute to the memory of...

Up to 1960, the Nobel Peace Prize was awarded almost exclusively to Europeans and Americans. In retrospect, the horizon of the Norwegian Nobel Committee may seem too narrow. Gandhi was very different from earlier Laureates. He was no real politician or proponent of international law, not primarily a humanitarian relief worker and not an organizer of international peace congresses. He would have belonged to a new breed of Laureates.

There is no hint in the archives that the Norwegian Nobel Committee ever took into consideration the possibility of an adverse British reaction to an award to Gandhi. Thus it seems that the hypothesis that the Committee's omission of Gandhi was due to its members' not wanting to provoke British authorities, may be rejected.

In 1947 the war that between India and Pakistan and Gandhi's prayer-meeting statement, which made people wonder whether he was about to abandon his consistent pacifism, ...made people wonder ...that he was also referred by the committee's majority. Unlike the situation today, there was no tradition for the Norwegian Nobel Committee to try to use the Peace Prize as a stimulus for peaceful settlement of regional conflicts.

During the last months of his life, Gandhi worked hard to end the violence between Hindus and Muslims which followed the partition of India. We know little about the Norwegian Nobel Committee's discussions of Gandhi's candidature in 1948, other than the above quoted entry of November 1... they seriously considered a posthumous... reasons, ended up not making such an... then, one year later, not to award the prize money for 1948 at all. What many thought should have been Mahatma Gandhi's place on the list of Laureates was silently but respectfully left open.

**4** Publisher/Sponsor

About Nobelprize.org    Privacy Policy    Terms of Use    Technical Support    RSS    The Official Web Site of the Nobel Foundation. Copyright ©

For a personal website, include a description such as *Homepage*, not italicized; the name of the larger site, if different from the personal site's title; the date of the last update; and the URL. If there is no date of publication, add an access date following the URL.

> Bae, Rebecca. Homepage. Iowa State U, 2015, www.engl.iastate.edu/rebecca
> -baedirectory-page/.

**41. BLOG (WEB LOG)** For an entire blog, give the author's name; the title of the blog, italicized; the sponsor or publisher of the blog (if different from the title); the publication date; the URL; and (if there is no publication date) the date of access.

> Kiuchi, Tatsuro. *Tatsuro Kiuchi: News & Blog,* tatsurokiuchi.com/. Accessed
> 3 Mar. 2016.

> Ng, Amy. *Pikaland.* Pikaland Media, 2015, www.pikaland.com/.

*Note:* To cite a blogger who writes under a pseudonym, begin with the pseudonym and then put the writer's real name (if you know it) in parentheses. (See model 45.)

**42. POST OR COMMENT ON A BLOG** Give the author's name; the title of the post or comment in quotation marks; if there is no title, use *Comment on*, not italicized, plus the title of the original post, italicized; the sponsor of the blog (if different from the title); the date and time (if available) of the post or comment; and the URL.

> Eakin, Emily. "Cloud Atlas's Theory of Everything." *NYR Daily,* 2 Nov. 2012,
> www.nybooks.com/daily/2012/11/02/ken-wilber-cloud-atlas/.

> mitchellfreedman. Comment on "Cloud Atlas's Theory of Everything," by
> Emily Eakin. *NYR Daily,* 3 Nov. 2012, www.nybooks.com/daily/2012
> /11/02/ken-wilber-cloud-atlas/.

**43. ENTRY IN A WIKI** Because wiki content is collectively edited, do not include an author. Treat a wiki as you would a work from a website (see model 39). (Check with your instructor before using a wiki as a source.)

> "Zion National Park." *Wikipedia,* 18 Mar. 2016, en.wikipedia.org/wiki/Zion
> _National_Park.

**44. POSTING TO A DISCUSSION GROUP OR NEWSGROUP** Begin with the author's name and the title of the posting in quotation marks (or the words *Online posting* if untitled). Follow with the name of the website, the sponsor of the site (if significantly different from the name of the website), the date of publication, and the URL.

> Yen, Jessica. "Quotations within Parentheses (Study Measures)." *Copyediting-L*, 18 Mar. 2016, list.indiana.edu/sympa/arc/copyediting-l/2016-03/msg00492 .html.

**45. POSTING OR MESSAGE ON A SOCIAL-NETWORKING SITE** To cite a message or posting on Facebook, Twitter, or another social-networking site, include the writer's name (or Twitter handle — after the handle, include the author's real name, in parentheses if you know it), the title of the post (in quotation marks), the social-networking site (in italics), the date and time (if available), and the URL.

> Bedford English. "Stacey Cochran explores Reflective Writing in the classroom and as a writer: http://ow.ly/YkjVB." *Facebook*, 15 Feb. 2016, www.facebook.com/BedfordEnglish/posts/10153415001259607.

> Curiosity Rover. "Can you see me waving? How to spot #Mars in the night sky: https://youtu.be/hv8hVvJlcJQ." *Twitter*, 5 Nov. 2015, 11:00 a.m., twitter .com/marscuriosity/status/672859022911889408.

> @grammarphobia (Patricia T. O'Connor and Steward Kellerman). "Is 'if you will' a verbal tic? http://goo.gl/oYrTYP #English #language #grammar #etymology #usage #linguistics #WOTD." *Twitter*, 14 Mar. 2016, 9:12 a.m., twitter.com/grammarphobia.

**46. EMAIL** Include the writer's name; the subject line, in quotation marks; *Received by* (not italicized or in quotation marks) followed by the recipient's name; and the date of the message.

> Thornbrugh, Caitlin. "Coates Lecture." Received by Rita Anderson, 20 Oct. 2015.

**47. COMPUTER SOFTWARE OR ONLINE GAME** Include the author name (if given and different from the title and sponsor); the title, italicized; the version number (if given); the publisher or sponsor; and the publication date.

> *Words with Friends.* Version 5.84, Zynga, 2013.

## VIDEO AND AUDIO SOURCES (INCLUDING ONLINE VERSIONS)

**48. FILM OR DVD** If you cite a particular person's work, start with that name. If not, start with the title; then name the director, distributor, and year of release. Other contributors, such as writers or performers, may follow the director.

> *Birdman or (The Unexpected Virtue of Ignorance)*. Directed by Alejandro González Iñárritu, performances by Michael Keaton, Emma Stone, Zach Galifianakis, Edward Norton, and Naomi Watts, Fox Searchlight, 2014.

> Scott, Ridley, director. *The Martian*. Performances by Matt Damon, Jessica Chastain, Kristen Wiig, and Kate Mara, Twentieth Century Fox, 2015.

**49. VIDEO OR AUDIO FROM THE WEB** If you cite an online video or audio file, add the URL following the date.

> Fletcher, Antoine. "The Ancient Art of the Atlatl." *Russell Cave National Monument*, narrated by Brenton Bellomy, National Park Service, 12 Feb. 2014, www.nps.gov/media/video/view.htm?id=C92C0D0A-1DD8-B71C -07CBC6E8970CD73F.

> Lewis, Paul. "Citizen Journalism." *YouTube*, 14 May 2011, www.youtube.com /watch?v=9APO9_yNbcg.

**50. TELEVISION OR RADIO EPISODE OR PROGRAM** In general, when citing a program, begin with the title, italicized. Then list important contributors (narrator, writer, director, actors), the network, and the broadcast date. Include the URL if citing an episode or program you downloaded or streamed. To cite a particular episode from a series, begin with the episode title, in quotation marks, and add the episode number (if available) before the network.

> "Free Speech on College Campuses." *Washington Journal*, narrated by Peter Slen, C-SPAN, 27 Nov. 2015.

> "The Cathedral." *Reply All,* narrated by Sruthi Pinnamaneni, episode 50, Gimlet Media, 7 Jan. 2016, gimletmedia.com/episode/50-the-cathedral/.

**51. BROADCAST INTERVIEW** Base your citation of a broadcast interview on the citation for a television or radio episode or program (model 50), but add the name of the person interviewed in the author position, and add the interviewer's name (with *Interview by*, not italicized) following the episode title.

> Jaffrey, Madhur. "Madhur Jaffrey on How Indian Cuisine Won Western Taste Buds." Interview by Shadrach Kabango, *Q*, CBC Radio, 29 Oct. 2015, www.cbc.ca/1.3292918.

Tempkin, Ann, and Anne Umland. Interview by Charlie Rose. *Charlie Rose: The Week*, PBS, 9 Oct. 2015.

**52. UNPUBLISHED OR PERSONAL INTERVIEW** List the person interviewed; the label *Telephone interview, Personal interview,* or *E-mail interview*; and the date the interview took place.

Akufo, Dautey. Personal interview, 11 Apr. 2016.

**53. SOUND RECORDING** List the name of the person or group you wish to emphasize (such as the composer, conductor, or band); the title of the recording or composition; the artist(s), if appropriate; the longer work in which the recording is contained (if any); the manufacturer; and the year of issue.

Adele. "Hello." *25*. XL, 2015.

Bizet, Georges. *Carmen*. Performances by Jennifer Larmore, Thomas Moser, Angela Gheorghiu, and Samuel Ramey, Bavarian State Orchestra and Chorus, conducted by Giuseppe Sinopoli, Warner, 1996.

*Note:* If you are citing instrumental music that is identified only by form, number, and key, do not underline, italicize, or enclose it in quotation marks.

Grieg, Edvard. Concerto in A minor, op. 16. Conducted by Eugene Ormandy, Philadelphia Orchestra, RCA, 1989.

**54. MUSICAL COMPOSITION** When you are not citing a specific published version, first give the composer's name, followed by the title (in italics). Do not italicize a work you refer to by form, number, and key.

Mozart, Wolfgang Amadeus. *Don Giovanni*, K527. William and Gayle Cook Music Library, Indiana U School of Music, www.dlib.indiana.edu /variations/scores/bhq9391/.

Beethoven, Ludwig van. Symphony no. 5 in C minor, op. 67. 1807. Center for Computer Assisted Research in the Humanities, Stanford U, 2000, scores.ccarh.org/beethoven/sym/beethoven-sym5-1.pdf.

**55. LECTURE OR SPEECH** List the speaker; the title, in quotation marks; the sponsoring institution or group; the place; and the date. Add the label *Address* (not in italics) at the end of the citation.

Smith, Anna Deavere. "On the Road: A Search for American Character." National Endowment for the Humanities, John F. Kennedy Center for the Performing Arts, Washington, DC, 6 Apr. 2015. Address.

If you streamed or downloaded the lecture or speech, include the URL.

> Khosla, Raj. "Precision Agriculture and Global Food Security." *US Department of State: Diplomacy in Action*, 26 Mar. 2013, www.state.gov/e/stas/series /212172.htm. Address.

**56. LIVE PERFORMANCE** List the title, appropriate names (such as the writer or performer), the place, and the date. To cite a particular person's work, begin the entry with that name.

> *Anything Goes.* By Cole Porter, performed by Klea Blackhurst, Shubert Theater, New Haven, 7 Oct. 2003.

> Snoad, Peter. *The Draft.* Directed by Diego Arciniegas, Hibernian Hall, Boston, 10 Sept. 2015.

**57. PODCAST** For a podcast, include all the following that are available: the speaker, the title of the podcast, the title of the program, the host or performers (if different from the speaker), the title of the site, the site's sponsor (if different from the site's title), the date of posting, and the URL. You may want to include an access date at the end of the citation, if the date the podcast was posted is not provided.

> McDougall, Christopher. "How Did Endurance Help Early Humans Survive?" *TED Radio Hour*, National Public Radio, 20 Nov. 2015, www.npr.org /2015/11/20/455904655/how-did-endurance-help-early-humans-survive.

> Tanner, Laura. "Virtual Reality in 9/11 Fiction." *Literature Lab*, Department of English, Brandeis U, www.brandeis.edu/departments/english /literaturelab/tanner.html. Accessed 14 Feb. 2016.

**58. WORK OF ART OR PHOTOGRAPH** List the artist or photographer; the work's title, italicized; the date of composition; and the name of the museum or other location; and the city. To cite a reproduction in a book, add the publication information. To cite artwork found online, add the URL.

> Bradford, Mark. *Let's Walk to the Middle of the Ocean.* 2015, Museum of Modern Art, New York.

> Clough, Charles. *January Twenty-First.* 1988–89, Joslyn Art Museum, Omaha, www.joslyn.org/collections-and-exhibitions/permanent-collections /modern-and-contemporary/charles-clough-january-twenty-first/.

O'Keeffe, Georgia. *Black and Purple Petunias*. 1925, private collection. *Two
Lives: A Conversation in Paintings and Photographs*, edited by Alexandra
Arrowsmith and Thomas West, HarperCollins, 1992, p. 67.

**59. MAP** Cite a map as you would a book or a short work within a longer
work. For an online source, include the URL. Add the label *Map* (not italicized) at the end of the citation, if the type of work you are citing won't be
clear from the context.

*California*. Rand McNally, 2002.

"Vote on Secession, 1861." *Perry-Castañeda Library Map Collection*,
U of Texas, 1976, www.lib.utexas.edu/maps/atlas_texas/texas_vote
_secession_1861.jpg.

**60. CARTOON OR COMIC STRIP** List the artist's name; the title (if any) of the cartoon or comic strip, in quotation marks; and the usual publication information for a print periodical (see models 24–27). If it won't be clear that you're
citing a cartoon or comic strip, add an appropriate label at the end of the
citation

Lewis, Eric. "The Unpublished Freud." *The New Yorker*, 11 Mar. 2002, p. 80.
Cartoon.

Zyglis, Adam. "City of Light." *Buffalo News*, 8 Nov. 2015, adamzyglis
.buffalonews.com/2015/11/08/city-of-light/. Cartoon.

**61. ADVERTISEMENT** Include the label *Advertisement* at the end of the citation
if your readers won't know the type of work that you're citing.

AT&T. *National Geographic*, Dec. 2015, p. 14. Advertisement.

Toyota. *The Root*. Slate Group, 28 Nov. 2015, www.theroot.com. Advertisement.

## OTHER SOURCES (INCLUDING ONLINE VERSIONS)

If an online version is not shown here, use the appropriate model for the
source, and then end with the URL or DOI.

**62. REPORT OR PAMPHLET** Follow the guidelines for a book (models 6–23
and 35).

*Dead in the Water*. Environmental Working Group, 2006. www.ewg.org
/research/deadwater.

**63. GOVERNMENT PUBLICATION** Begin with the author, if identified. Otherwise, start with the name of the government, followed by the agency. If the author and site sponsor are the same, begin the citation with the title of the source. For congressional documents, cite the number, the session, the house of Congress, the report number, and any other information that will clarify the citation for your readers.

> Canada, Minister of Aboriginal Affairs and Northern Development. *2015–16 Report on Plans and Priorities*. Minister of Public Works and Government Services Canada, 2015.

> Gregg, Judd. *Report to Accompany the Genetic Information Act of 2003*. Government Printing Office, 2003. 108th Congress, 1st session, Senate Report 108–22.

> Russel, Daniel R. "Burma's Challenge: Democracy, Human Rights, Peace, and the Plight of the Rohingya." Testimony before the US House Foreign Affairs Committee, Subcommittee on East Asian and Pacific Affairs, *US Department of State: Diplomacy in Action*, 21 Oct. 2015, 2009-2017.state.gov/p/eap/rls/rm/2015/10/248420.htm.

**64. PUBLISHED PROCEEDINGS OF A CONFERENCE** Include the editor(s), and information about the conference (including its title, dates, and location). If the conference was sponsored by an organization the name of which is not already included in the title of the conference, include that information at the end of the citation as a separate "container."

> Meisner, Marx S., et al., editors. *Communication for the Commons: Revisiting Participation and Environment*. Proceedings of Twelfth Biennial Conference on Communication and the Environment, 6–11 June 2015, Swedish U of Agricultural Sciences. International Environmental Communication Association, 2015.

**65. DISSERTATION** For an unpublished dissertation, enclose the title in quotation marks; for a published dissertation, set the title in italics. Add the label *Dissertation* (not in italics), the school, and the year the work was accepted.

> Abbas, Megan Brankley. "Knowing Islam: The Entangled History of Western Academia and Modern Islamic Thought." Dissertation, Princeton U, 2015.

> Kidd, Celeste. *Rational Approaches to Learning and Development*. Dissertation, U of Rochester, 2013.

**66. DISSERTATION ABSTRACT** Cite a dissertation abstract as you would a dissertation, but add the label *Abstract* (not in italics), followed by information about the "container" in which the abstract appeared.

> Moore, Courtney L. "Stress and Oppression: Identifying Possible Protective Factors for African American Men." Dissertation, Chicago School of Professional Psychology, 2016. Abstract. *ProQuest Dissertations and Theses*, search.proquest.com/docview/1707351557.

**67. PUBLISHED INTERVIEW** Treat a published interview as you would a broadcast interview, with information about the "container" in which the interview appeared at the end of the citation.

> Weddington, Sarah. "Sarah Weddington: Still Arguing for *Roe*." Interview by Michele Kort. *Ms.*, Winter 2013, pp. 32–35.

**68. UNPUBLISHED LETTER** Cite an unpublished letter as you would an email message (see model 46), replacing the subject line with the label *Letter to* followed by *the author* or the name of the recipient.

> Primak, Shoshana. Letter to the author, 6 May 2016.

**69. MANUSCRIPT OR OTHER UNPUBLISHED WORK** Treat a manuscript or other unpublished work as you would its published counterpart, adding information after the title that readers will need to understand the nature of the source.

> Arendt, Hannah. *Between Past and Future*. 1st draft, Hannah Arendt Papers, Manuscript Division, Library of Congress, pp. 108–50, memory.loc.gov /cgi-bin/ampage?collId=mharendt&fileName=05/050030/050030page .db&recNum=0.

**70. LEGAL SOURCE** To cite an act, give the name of the act followed by its Public Law (*Pub. L.*) number, its Statutes at Large (*Stat.*) cataloging number, and the date the act was enacted. To cite a court case, give the names of the first plaintiff and defendant, the case number, the name of the court, the date of the decision, and any other information readers will need to access the source.

> Electronic Freedom of Information Act Amendments of 1996. Pub. L. 104–231. Stat. 110.2048. 2 Oct. 1996.

> Utah v. Evans. 536 US 452. Supreme Court of the US. 2002. *Legal Information Institute*, Cornell U Law School, www.law.cornell.edu/supremecourt /text/536/452.

# APA Documentation Guidelines

The following formatting guidelines are adapted from the American Psychological Association (APA) recommendations for preparing manuscripts for publication in journals. Check with your instructor before preparing your final draft, however.

For detailed guidelines on formatting a list of references, see pp. 370–88. For a sample student essay in APA style, see pp. 240–48.

- *Title page.* Center the title in boldface type, three or four double-line spaces from the top margin. After one double-line space (also centered), include your name, the department and school one line below your name, the course number and course title one line below the department and school, the instructor's name one line below that, and then the due date following one line below the instructor's name. In the top right corner, type the number "1."

- *Margins and spacing.* Leave margins of one inch at the top and bottom and on both sides of the page. Do not justify the right margin. Double-space the entire text, including headings, set-off quotations, content notes, and the list of references. Indent the first line of each paragraph one-half inch (or five to seven spaces) from the left margin.

- *Page numbering.* Type the page number flush right at the top of each page, in the same position as on the title page. Do not include the short title or your name at the top of the page unless your instructor requires it.

- *Long quotations.* For a long, set-off quotation (one having more than forty words), indent it one-half inch (or five to seven spaces) from the left margin and do not use quotation marks. Place the page reference in parentheses one space after the final punctuation.

- *Abstract.* If your instructor asks for an abstract with your paper—a one-paragraph summary of your major thesis and supporting points—it should go on a separate page immediately after the title page. Center the word "Abstract" (in boldface type) about an inch from the top of the page. Double-space the text of the abstract, and begin the first line flush with the left margin. The length of abstracts typically ranges from 150 to 250 words, depending on the length of the source it summarizes.

- *Headings.* Headings (set in boldface) are used within the text of many APA-style papers. In papers with only one or two levels of headings, center the main headings; position the subheadings flush with the left margin. Capitalize words of four or more letters, but do not capitalize articles, short prepositions, or coordinating conjunctions unless they are the first word or follow a colon.

- *Visuals.* Tables should be labeled "Table," numbered, and titled. All other visuals (charts, graphs, photographs, and drawings) should be labeled "Figure," numbered, and titled. Include a *"Note."* below the table or figure to provide any additional information or the source information. Remember to refer to each visual in your text, stating how it contributes to the point(s) you are making. Tables and figures should generally appear near the relevant text; check with your instructor for guidelines on placement of visuals.

## Directory to APA style for in-text citations

# In-Text Citations

APA style requires parenthetical references in the text to document quotations, paraphrases, summaries, and other material from a source. These citations correspond to full bibliographic entries in a list of references at the end of the text.

Note that APA style generally calls for using the past tense or present perfect tense for signal verbs: *Smith (2020) showed; Smith (2020) has shown.*

Use the present tense only to discuss results (*the experiment demonstrates*) or widely accepted information (*researchers agree*).

An in-text citation in APA style always indicates *which source* on the references page the writer is referring to, and it explains *in what year* the material was published; for quoted material, the in-text citation also indicates *where* in the source the quotation can be found.

**1. BASIC FORMAT FOR A QUOTATION**  Generally, use the author's last name in a signal phrase to introduce the cited material, and place the date, in parentheses, immediately after the author's name. The page number, preceded by "p." appears in parentheses after the quotation.

> Zhang (2019) showed that "when academics are strongly motivated to teach and are satisfied with and take pride in their teaching . . . , they tend to develop positive feelings toward their . . . jobs and their . . . universities in general" (p. 1325).

If the author is not named in a signal phrase, place the author's surname, the year, and the page number in parentheses after the quotation: (Zhang, 2019, p. 1325). For a long, set-off quotation (more than forty words), place the page reference in parentheses one space after the final quotation.

For all direct quotations from electronic texts or other works without page numbers, use a locator, such as a heading, a paragraph number, a figure or table number, a slide number, or a time-stamp to indicate where the passage appears. If you use a paragraph number, include the number preceded by the abbreviation "para."

> Driver (2007) has noticed "an increasing focus on the role of land" in policy debates over the past decade (para. 1).

**2. BASIC FORMAT FOR A PARAPHRASE OR SUMMARY**  Include the author's last name and the year as in model 1. Locations (page or paragraph number) for paraphrases or summaries are optional but encouraged for longer or more complex works.

> Instructors' positive feelings about teaching carry over into their feelings about the schools at which they teach (Zhang, 2019).

**3. TWO AUTHORS**  Use both names in all citations. Use "and" in a signal phrase, but use an ampersand (&) in parentheses.

> Bloomberg and Pope (2017) have argued that with global warming we are facing a "*kairos*: a supreme moment at which one simply must act, however implausible or inconvenient" (p. 12).

> Some have argued that we are facing a watershed moment, or "*kairos*," in the fight against global warming (Bloomberg & Pope, 2017, p. 12).

**4. THREE TO FIVE AUTHORS** For works with three or more authors, list just the first author plus "et al." in the first in-text citation.

> Similarly, as Belenky et al. (1986) showed, examining the lives of women expands our understanding of human development.

In subsequent references, also use just the first author's name plus "et al."

> Examining the lives of women expands our understanding of human development (Belenky et al., 1986).

**5. SIX OR MORE AUTHORS** Use only the first author's name and "et al." in every citation.

> As Soleim et al. (2002) demonstrated, advertising holds the potential for manipulating "free-willed" consumers.

**6. CORPORATE OR GROUP AUTHOR** If the name of the organization or corporation is long, spell it out the first time you use it, followed by an abbreviation in brackets. In later references, use the abbreviation only.

FIRST CITATION      (Centers for Disease Control and Prevention [CDC], 2019)
LATER CITATIONS    (CDC, 2019)

**7. UNKNOWN AUTHOR** If the author is unknown, include the work's title (shortened if lengthy) in the in-text citation.

> As a result of changes in the city's eviction laws, New York's eviction rate dropped by over a third from 2013 to 2018 ("Pushed Out," 2019).

**8. TWO OR MORE AUTHORS WITH THE SAME LAST NAME** If your list of references includes works by different authors with the same last name, include the authors' initials in each citation.

> K. Yi (2019) has demonstrated . . .

> D. Yi (2017) has shown that . . .

**9. TWO OR MORE WORKS BY AN AUTHOR IN A SINGLE YEAR** Assign lowercase letters ("a," "b," and so on) alphabetically by title, and include the letters after the year.

> Soot-free flames can be produced by stripping the air of nitrogen and then adding that nitrogen to the fuel (Conover, 2019b).

**10. TWO OR MORE SOURCES IN ONE PARENTHETICAL REFERENCE** List sources by different authors in alphabetical order by authors' last names, separated by semicolons: (Cardone, 1998; Lai, 2002). List works by the same author in chronological order, separated by commas: (Lai, 2000, 2002).

**11. INDIRECT SOURCE** Use the phrase "as cited in" to indicate that you are reporting information from a secondary source. Name the original source in a signal phrase, but list the secondary source in your list of references.

> Amartya Sen developed the influential concept that land reform was necessary for "promoting opportunity" among the poor (as cited in Driver, 2007, para. 2).

**12. PERSONAL COMMUNICATION** Cite any personal letters, email messages, electronic postings, telephone conversations, or interviews as shown. Do not include personal communications in the reference list.

> A researcher studying the effects of the media on children's eating habits has argued that advertisers for snack foods should be required to design ads responsibly for their younger viewers (F. Johnson, personal communication, October 20, 2019).

**13. ELECTRONIC DOCUMENT** Cite a web or electronic document as you would a print source, using the author's name and date.

> Link and Phelan (2005) argued for broader interventions in public health that would be accessible to anyone, regardless of individual wealth.

The APA recommends the following for electronic sources without names, dates, or page numbers:

AUTHOR UNKNOWN. Use a shortened form of the title in a signal phrase or in parentheses (see model 7). If an organization is the author, see model 6.

DATE UNKNOWN. Use the abbreviation "n.d." (for "no date") in place of the year: (Hopkins, n.d.).

NO PAGE NUMBERS. Many works found online or in electronic databases lack stable page numbers. (Use the page numbers for an electronic work in a format, such as PDF, that has stable pagination.) If paragraph numbers are included in such a source, use the abbreviation "para.": (Giambetti, 2006, para. 7). If no paragraph numbers are included but the source includes headings, give the heading, and identify the paragraph in the section:

> Jacobs and Johnson (2007) have argued that "the South African media is still highly concentrated and not very diverse in terms of race and class" (South African Media after Apartheid, para. 3).

# Content Notes

APA style allows you to use content notes, either at the bottom of the page (footnotes) or on a separate page at the end of the text (endnotes), to expand or supplement your text. Indicate such notes in the text by superscript numerals ($^1$). Set footnotes single-spaced in a 10-point font using the footnotes function in your word processor.

SUPERSCRIPT NUMBER IN TEXT

The age of the children involved in the study was an important factor in the selection of items for the questionnaire.[1]

FOOTNOTE

[1]Marjorie Youngston Forman and William Cole of the Child Study Team provided great assistance in identifying appropriate items for the questionnaire.

## Directory to APA style for references

### Guidelines for Author Listings

### Books

### Print Periodicals

*Continued*

# List of References

The alphabetical list of the sources cited in your document is called "References." If your instructor asks that you list everything you have read—not just the sources you cite—call the list "Bibliography." Here are guidelines for preparing a list of references:

- Start your list on a new page after the text of your document but before appendices or notes. Continue consecutive page numbers.
- Center the heading "References" (in boldface type) one inch from the top of the page.

- Begin each entry flush with the left margin, but indent subsequent lines one-half inch (or five to seven spaces). Double-space the entire list.
- List sources alphabetically by authors' (or editors') last names. If no author is given, alphabetize the source by the first word of the title other than "A," "An," or "The." If the list includes two or more works by the same author, list them in chronological order. (For two or more works by the same author published in the same year, see model 5.)
- Italicize titles and subtitles of books and periodicals. Do not italicize titles of articles, and do not enclose them in quotation marks.
- For titles of books and articles, capitalize only the first word of the title and the subtitle and any proper nouns.
- For titles of periodicals, capitalize all major words.

## GUIDELINES FOR AUTHOR LISTINGS

List authors' last names first, and use only initials for first and middle names. The in-text citations in your text point readers toward particular sources in your list of references (see pp. 365–68).

### NAME CITED IN SIGNAL PHRASE IN TEXT

Driver (2007) has noted . . .

### NAME IN PARENTHETICAL CITATION IN TEXT

. . . (Driver, 2007).

### BEGINNING OF ENTRY IN LIST OF REFERENCES

Driver, T. (2007).

**1. ONE AUTHOR** Give the last name, a comma, the initial(s), and the date in parentheses.

Zimbardo, P. G. (2009).

**2. MULTIPLE AUTHORS** List up to twenty authors, last name first, with commas separating authors' names and an ampersand (&) before the last author's name.

Walsh, M. E., & Murphy, J. A. (2003).

Note: For a work with more than twenty authors, list the first nineteen, then an ellipsis (. . .), and then the final author's name with no ampersand before the last author.

### 3. CORPORATE OR GROUP AUTHOR

Resources for Rehabilitation. (2003).

### 4. UNKNOWN AUTHOR
Begin with the work's title. Italicize book titles, but do not italicize article titles or enclose them in quotation marks. Capitalize only the first word of the title and the subtitle (if any) and proper nouns.

*Atlas of the world.* (2019). Oxford University Press.

### 5. TWO OR MORE WORKS BY THE SAME AUTHOR
List two or more works by the same author in chronological order. Repeat the author's name in each entry.

Goodall, J. (1999).

Goodall, J. (2002).

If the works appeared in the same year, list them alphabetically by title, and assign lowercase letters ("a," "b," and so on) after the dates. Works that include only the year (such as books and articles in scholarly journals) precede works that include a year, month, and day (such as articles in newspapers and magazines).

Gladwell, M. (2019a). *Talking to strangers: What we should know about the people we don't know.* Little, Brown and Company.

Gladwell, M. (2019b, January 14). Is marijuana as safe as we think? *The New Yorker.* https://www.newyorker.com/magazine/2019/01/14 /is-marijuana-as-safe-as-we-think

## BOOKS

### 6. BASIC FORMAT FOR A BOOK
Begin with the author name(s). (See models 1–5.) Then include the publication year, the title and the subtitle, the name of the publisher (no location needed), and, if accessed online, the book's DOI or direct-link URL. The source map on pp. 373–74 shows where to find this information in a typical book.

Treuer, D. (2019). *The heartbeat of Wounded Knee: Native America from 1890 to the present.* Riverhead Books.

Kilby, P. (2019). *The green revolution: Narratives of politics, technology and gender.* Routledge. https://doi.org/10.4324/9780429200823

Natterson-Horowitz, B., & Bowers, K. (2019). *Wildhood: The epic journey from adolescence to adulthood in humans and other animals.* Scribner.

**7. EDITOR** For a book with an editor but no author, list the source under the editor's name.

> Yeh, K.-H. (Ed.). (2019). *Asian indigenous psychologies in the global context.*
> Palgrave Macmillan.

To cite a book with an author and an editor, place the editor's name, with a comma and the abbreviation "Ed.", in parentheses after the title.

> Sontag, S. (2018). *Debriefing: Collected stories* (B. Taylor, Ed.). Picador.

---

## APA SOURCE MAP: Books

Take information from the book's title page and copyright page (on the reverse side of the title page), not from the book's cover or a library catalog.

1. **Author.** List all authors' last names first, and use only initials for first and middle names. For more about citing authors, see models 1–5.
2. **Publication year.** Enclose the year of publication in parentheses.
3. **Title.** Italicize the title and any subtitle. Capitalize only the first word of the title and the subtitle and any proper nouns.
4. **Publisher.** Give the publisher's name, dropping any *Inc., Co.,* or *Publishers.*

*A citation for the book on p. 374 would look like this:*

```
     1      2                              3
```
Tsutsui, W. (2004). *Godzilla on my mind: Fifty years of the king of monsters.*
```
          4
```
Palgrave Macmillan.

**2** Publication Year

**3** Title

# GODZILLA®
# ON MY MIND

\*

*Fifty Years of the
King of Monsters*

**3** Subtitle

**1** Author ⟶ WILLIAM TSUTSUI

palgrave
macmillan

**4** Publisher

#### 8. SELECTION IN A BOOK WITH AN EDITOR

Burke, W. W., & Nourmair, D. A. (2001). The role of personality assessment in organization development. In J. Waclawski & A. H. Church (Eds.), *Organization development: A data-driven approach to organizational change* (pp. 55–77). Jossey-Bass.

#### 9. TRANSLATION

Calasso, R. (2019). *The unnamable present* (R. Dixon, Trans.). Farrar, Straus and Giroux. (Original work published 2017)

#### 10. EDITION OTHER THAN THE FIRST

Dessler, A. E., & Parson, E. A. (2019). *The science and politics of global climate change: A guide to the debate* (3rd ed.). Cambridge University Press.

#### 11. MULTIVOLUME WORK

Zeigler-Hill, V., & Shackelford, T. K. (Eds.). (2018). *The SAGE handbook of personality and individual differences* (Vols. I–III). SAGE Publications.

Note: If you cite just one volume of a multivolume work, list that volume, not the complete span of volumes.

#### 12. ARTICLE IN A REFERENCE WORK

Dean, C. (1994). Jaws and teeth. In *The Cambridge encyclopedia of human evolution* (pp. 56–59). Cambridge University Press.

If no author is listed, begin with the title of the article.

#### 13. REPUBLISHED BOOK

Fremlin, C. (2017). *The hours before dawn*. Dover Publications. (Original work published 1958)

#### 14. INTRODUCTION, PREFACE, FOREWORD, OR AFTERWORD

Klosterman, C. (2007). Introduction. In P. Shirley, *Can I keep my jersey? 11 teams, 5 countries, and 4 years in my life as a basketball vagabond* (pp. v–vii). Villard-Random House.

**15. BOOK WITH A TITLE WITHIN THE TITLE** Do not italicize or enclose in quotation marks a title within a book title.

> Miller, K. (2018). *I'll be there for you: The one about* Friends. Hanover Square Press.

## PRINT PERIODICALS

Begin with the author name(s). (See models 1–5.) Then include the publication date (year only for journals, and year, month, and day for other periodicals); the article title; the periodical title; the volume and issue numbers, if available; and the page numbers. The source map on pp. 377–78 shows where to find this information in a sample periodical.

**16. ARTICLE IN A JOURNAL PUBLISHED IN VOLUMES**

> O'Connell, D. C., & Kowal, S. (2003). Psycholinguistics: A half century of monologism. *The American Journal of Psychology, 116*, 191–212.

**17. ARTICLE IN A JOURNAL PUBLISHED IN ISSUES** Include issue numbers for all periodicals that offer them.

> Hall, R. E. (2000). Marriage as vehicle of racism among women of color. *Psychology: A Journal of Human Behavior, 37*(2), 29–40.

**18. ARTICLE IN A MAGAZINE**

> Koch, C. (2019, October). Is death reversible? *Scientific American, 321*(4), 34–37.

**19. ARTICLE IN A NEWSPAPER**

> Finucane, M. (2019, September 25). Americans still eating too many low-quality carbs. *The Boston Globe*, B2.

**20. EDITORIAL OR LETTER TO THE EDITOR**

> Zelneck, B. (2003, July 18). Serving the public at public universities [Letter to the editor]. *The Chronicle Review*, B18.

**21. UNSIGNED ARTICLE**

> Annual meeting announcement. (2003, March). *Cognitive Psychology, 46*, 227.

**22. REVIEW**

Douthat, R. (2019, October 14). A hustle gone wrong [Review of the film
*Hustlers*, by L. Scafaria, Dir.]. *National Review, 71*(18), 47.

**23. PUBLISHED INTERVIEW**

Smith, H. (2002, October). [Interview with A. Thompson]. *The Sun*, 4–7.

---

## APA SOURCE MAP: Articles from periodicals

1 **Author.** List all authors' last names first, and use only initials for first and middle names. For more about citing authors, see models 1–5.

2 **Publication date.** Enclose the date in parentheses. For journals, use only the year. For magazines and newspapers, use the year, a comma, the month (spelled out), and the day, if given.

3 **Article title.** Do not italicize or enclose article titles in quotation marks. Capitalize only the first words of the article title and the subtitle and any proper nouns.

4 **Periodical title.** Italicize the periodical title (and the subtitle, if any), and capitalize all major words.

5 **Volume and issue numbers.** Follow the periodical title with a comma, and then give the volume number (italicized) and, without a space in between, the issue number (if given) in parentheses.

6 **Page numbers.** Give the inclusive page numbers of the article. End the citation with a period.

*A citation for the periodical article on p. 378 would look like this:*

   1       2                              3
Etzioni, A. (2006). Leaving race behind: Our growing Hispanic population
                                          4              5      6
   creates a golden opportunity. *The American Scholar, 75*(2), 20–30.

**2 Publication Date**

**4 Periodical Title**

**5 Volume and Issue Numbers**

**3 Article Title**

RICHA

# Leaving Race Behind

*Our growing Hispanic population creates a golden opportunity*

AMITAI ETZIONI

**1 Author**

ANN BEA
EDWARD H
PHYLLIS RC

ALI
JOSEPH W. GC
D

Jc

For a subscription to THE AMERICAN S
$48 two years, $69 three years; for in
international subscriptions, add $15.
Newstand Services. For more inform
advertising please contact: Linda Mil
THE AMERICAN SCHOLAR, a quarterly jc
Phi Beta Kappa Society, 1606 New
scholar@pbk.org. Manuscripts may be
AMERICAN SCHOLAR assumes no respons
Periodical postage paid at Washingto
P.O. Box 354, Mt. Morris, IL 61054-0
additional revenues, the Phi Beta Ka
deleted should send their name and

Some years ago the United States government asked me what my race was. I was reluctant to respond because my 50 years of practicing sociology—an rerful personal experiences—have underscored for me what we all know to one degree or another, that racial divisions bedevil America, just as they do many other societies across the world. Not wanting to encourage these divisions, I refused to check off one of the specific racial options on the U.S. Census form and instead marked a box labeled "Other." I later found out that the federal government did not accept such an attempt to de-emphasize race, by me or by some 6.75 million other Americans who tried it. Instead the government assigned me to a racial category, one it chose for me. Learning this made me conjure up what I admit is a far-fetched association. I was in this place once before. When I was a Jewish child in Nazi Germany in the early 1930s, many Jews who saw themselves as good Germans wanted to "pass" as Aryans. But the Nazi regime would have none of it. Never mind, they told these Jews, *we determine* who is Jewish and

**6 Page Numbers** practice prevailed in the Old South, where if you had one drop of African blood you were a Negro, disregarding all other facts and considerations, including how you saw yourself.

You might suppose that in the years since my little Census-form protest

Amitai Etzioni is University Professor at George Washington University and the author of *The Monochrome Society.*

20

# ELECTRONIC SOURCES

When citing sources accessed online or from an electronic database, include as many of the following elements as you can find:

- *Author.* Give the author's name, if available.
- *Publication date.* Include the date of electronic publication or of the latest update, if available. When no publication date is available, use "n.d." ("no date").
- *Title.* List the document title, neither italicized nor in quotation marks.
- *Print publication information.* For articles from online journals, magazines, or reference databases, give the publication title and other publishing information as you would for a print periodical (see models 16–23).
- *DOIs, URLs, and Retrieval dates.* For an electronic source, do the following: If a DOI (digital object identifier) is available, include it at the end of the citation with no period at the end. If there is no DOI but you can supply a direct-link URL, do so; if not, omit the URL. Include DOIs as links, using the format "https://doi.org/" and adding the DOI number for the specific work. Include a retrieval statement ("retrieved [month, day, year] from") before URLs only when the online source is designed to be regularly updated. If a DOI or URL is lengthy, you can include a shortened form by using a site like shortdoi.org or bitly.com. If your word processor inserts line breaks automatically or moves a DOI or URL to its own line, you can accept that formatting.

Updated guidelines for citing electronic resources are maintained at the APA's website (www.apa.org).

**24. ARTICLE FROM AN ONLINE PERIODICAL** Give the author, date, title, and publication information as you would for a print document. If the article has a digital object identifier (DOI), include it. If there is no DOI, include a direct-link URL.

> Greengard, S. (2019, August). The algorithm that changed quantum machine learning. *Communications of the ACM, 62*(8), 15–17. https://doi.org/10.1145/3339458

> Daly, J. (2019, August 2). Duquesne's med school plan part of national trend to train more doctors. *Pittsburgh Post-Gazette.* https://www .post-gazette.com/news/health/2019/08/02/Duquesne-med-school -national-trend-doctors-osteopathic-medicine-pittsburgh/stories /201908010181[AJ1]

If the direct-link URL is lengthy, you can include a shortened form.

> Daly, J. (2019, August 2). Duquesne's med school plan part of national trend to train more doctors. *Pittsburgh Post-Gazette*. https://bit.ly/2Vzrm2l

> Vlahos, J. (2019, March). Alexa, I want answers. *Wired*, 58–65. https://www.wired.com/story/amazon-alexa-search-for-the-one-perfect-answer/

**25. ARTICLE FROM A DATABASE** Give the author, the date, the title, and the publication information as you would for a print document. Include both the volume and issue numbers for all journal articles. If the article has a DOI, include it. If there is no DOI, provide a direct-link URL, but only if readers can access the work using that database URL; if not, omit it. The source map on pp. 380–81 shows where to find this information for a typical article from a database.

---

## APA SOURCE MAP: Articles from databases

1. **Author.** Include the author's name as you would for a print source. List all authors' last names first, and use initials for first and middle names. For more about citing authors, see models 1–5.

2. **Publication date.** Enclose the date in parentheses. For journals, use only the year. For magazines and newspapers, use the year, a comma, the month, and the day, if given.

3. **Article title.** Capitalize only the first word of the article title and the subtitle and any proper nouns.

4. **Periodical title.** Italicize the periodical title. Capitalize all major words.

5. **Print publication information.** For journals and magazines, give the volume number (italicized) and the issue number (in parentheses). For journals only, give the inclusive page numbers.

*A citation for the article on p. 381 would look like this:*

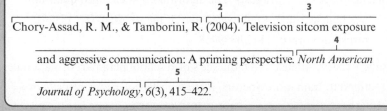

Chory-Assad, R. M., & Tamborini, R. (2004). Television sitcom exposure and aggressive communication: A priming perspective. *North American Journal of Psychology*, *6*(3), 415–422.

**3** Article Title

**1** Author

| | |
|---|---|
| **Title:** | **Television Sitcom Exposure and Aggressive Communication: A Priming Perspective.** |
| **Authors:** | Chory-Assad, Rebecca M.1 |
| | Tamborini, Ron2 |
| **Source:** | North American Journal of Psychology; 2004, Vol. 6 Issue 3, p415-422, 8p |
| **Document Type:** | Article |
| **Subject Terms:** | *TELEVISION comedies |
| | *AGGRESSIVENESS |
| | *ATTITUDE (Psychology) |
| | *TELEVISION programs |
| **Abstract:** | This study examined the relationship between exposure to verbally aggressive television sitcoms and aggressive communication, from a priming and cognitive neo-associationistic perspective. Participants reported their trait verbal aggressiveness and exposure to sitcoms approximately one month prior to their participation in the lab portion of the study. Once in the lab, participants evaluated four sitcoms and engaged in a question-response session that was observed and coded for aggression. Results indicated that increased exposure to television sitcoms was associated with lower levels of aggressive communication. Implications of these results for theory and research concerning the effects of exposure to aggression in a humorous context are discussed. [ABSTRACT FROM AUTHOR] |
| | *Copyright of North American Journal of Psychology is the property of North American Journal of Psychology and its content may not be copied or emailed to multiple sites or posted to a listserv without the copyright holder's express written permission. However, users may print, download, or email articles for individual use. This abstract may be abridged. No warranty is given about the accuracy of the copy. Users should refer to the original published version of the material for the full abstract. (Copyright applies to all Abstracts.)* |
| **Author Affiliations:** | 1West Virginia University |
| | 2Michigan State University |
| **Full Text Word Count:** | 2880 |
| **ISSN:** | 15277143 |
| **Accession Number:** | 15630823 |
| **Database:** | Academic Search Premier |

**5** Print Publication Information

**2** Publication Date

**4** Periodical Title

Ganegoda, D. B., & Bordia, P. (2019). I can be happy for you, but not all the time: A contingency model of envy and positive empathy in the workplace. *Journal of Applied Psychology, 104*(6), 776–795. https://doi.org/10.1037/apl0000377[CJ1]

Le Texier, T. (2019). Debunking the Stanford Prison Experiment. *American Psychologist, 74*(7), 823–839. https://doi.org/10.1037/amp0000401

*Note:* "Stanford Prison Experiment" is capitalized in the example above because it is a proper noun.

## 26. ABSTRACT FOR AN ONLINE ARTICLE

Brey, E., & Pauker, K. (2019, December). Teachers' nonverbal behaviors influence children's stereotypic beliefs [Abstract]. *Journal of Experimental Child Psychology, 188.* https://doi.org/10.1016/j.jecp.2019.104671

**27. DOCUMENT FROM A WEBSITE** The APA refers to works that are not peer reviewed, such as reports, press releases, and presentation slides, as "gray literature." Include all the following information you can find: the author's name; the publication date (or "n.d." if no date is available); the title of the document; the title of the site or larger work, if any; any publication information available in addition to the date; and the URL. Provide your date of access only if a regular update seems likely. The source map on pp. 384–85 shows where to find this information for an article from a website.

Albright, A. (2019, July 25). *The global education challenge: Scaling up to tackle the learning crisis.* The Brookings Institution. https://www.brookings.edu/wp-content/uploads/2019/07/Brookings_Blum_2019_education.pdf

National Institute of Mental Health. (2016, March). *Seasonal affective disorder.* National Institutes of Health. https://www.nimh.nih.gov/health/topics/seasonal-affective-disorder/index.shtml

BBC News. (2019, October 31). *Goats help save Ronald Reagan Presidential Library.* https://bbc.com/news/world-us-canada-50248549

**28. CHAPTER OR SECTION OF A WEB DOCUMENT** After the chapter or section title, type "In" and give the document title, with identifying information, if any, in parentheses. If a source is intended to be updated regularly, include a retrieval date.

Brue, A. W., & Wilmshurst, L. (2018). Adaptive behavior assessments. In B. B. Frey (Ed.), *The SAGE encyclopedia of educational research, measurement, and evaluation* (pp. 40–44). SAGE Publications. https://doi.org/10.4135/9781506326139.n21

Merriam-Webster. (n.d.). Adscititious. In *Merriam-Webster.com dictionary*. Retrieved September 5, 2019, from https://www.merriam-webster.com /dictionary/adscititious

**29. EMAIL MESSAGE OR REAL-TIME COMMUNICATION** Because the APA stresses that any sources cited in your list of references be retrievable by your readers, you should not include entries for email messages, real-time communications (such as instant messages or texts), or any other postings that are not archived. Instead, cite these sources in your text as forms of personal communication (see p. 368).

**30. ONLINE POSTING** List an online posting in the references list only if you are able to retrieve the message from an archive. Provide the author's name, the date of posting, and the subject line. Include other identifying information in square brackets. End with the URL of the archived message.

Murphy, B., Jr. (2018, November 15). The California wildfires, morale at Facebook, and that time Elon Musk gave out credit cards to anyone who asked. *Inc. This Morning* [Newsletter]. https://www.inc.com /bill-murphy-jr/inc-this-morning-california-wildfires-morale-at -facebook-that-time-elon-musk-gave-out-credit-cards.html

lolly12. (2019, September 25). My husband works in IT in a major city down South. He is a permanent employee now, but for years [Comment on the article "The Google workers who voted to unionize in Pittsburgh are part of tech's huge contractor workforce"]. *Slate*. https://fyre .it/0RT8HmeL.4

**31. BLOG (WEB LOG) POST**

Fister, B. (2019, February 14). Information literacy's third wave. *Library Babel Fish*. https://www.insidehighered.com/blogs/library-babel-fish /information-literacy%E2%80%99s-third-wave

**32. WIKIPEDIA ENTRY** Since Wikipedia makes archived versions available, you need not include a retrieval date. Instead, include the URL for the version you used, which you can find by clicking on the "View history" tab on the site.

> Behaviorism. (2019, October 11). In *Wikipedia*. https://en.wikipedia.org/w
> /index.php?title=Behaviorism&oldid=915544724

**33. ONLINE AUDIO OR VIDEO FILE**

> Wray, B. (2019, May). *How climate change affects your mental health* [Video].
> TED Conferences. https://www.ted.com/talks/britt_wray_how_climate
> _change_affects_your_mental_health

> BBC. (2018, November 19). Why do bad managers flourish? [Audio].
> In *Business Matters*. https://www.bbc.co.uk/programmes/p06s8752

**34. DATA SET**

> Reid, L. (2019). *Smarter homes: Experiences of living in low carbon
> homes 2013–2018* [Data set]. UK Data Service. http://doi.org/10.5255
> /UKDA-SN-853485

---

### APA SOURCE MAP: Works from websites

1   Author. If one is given, include the author's name (see models 1–5). List last names first, and use only initials for first names. The site's sponsor may be the author. If no author is identified, begin the citation with the title of the document.

2   Publication date. Enclose the date of publication or latest update in parentheses. Use "n.d." ("no date") when no publication date is available.

3   Title of work. Italicize the title. Capitalize only the first word of the title and the subtitle and any proper nouns.

4   Title of website. Capitalize all major words.

5   Retrieval information. Include the URL. If the work seems likely to be regularly updated, include the retrieval date.

*A citation for the web document on p. 385 would look like this:*

1                    2                                3
Alexander, M. (2001, August 22). *Thirty years later, Stanford Prison*
                                        4                        5
*Experiment lives on.* Stanford Report. http://news-service.stanford.edu

/news/2001/august22/prison2-822.html

**4** Title of Website

**5** Retrieval Information

**2** Publication Date

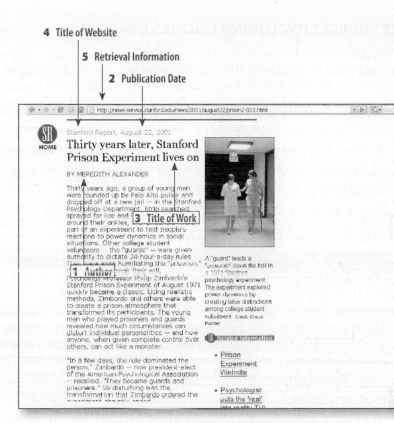

http://news-service.stanford.edu/news/2001/august22/prison2-822.html

Google

**HOME**

Stanford Report, August 22, 2001

# Thirty years later, Stanford Prison Experiment lives on

BY MEREDITH ALEXANDER

Thirty years ago, a group of young men were rounded up by Palo Alto police and dropped off at a new jail -- in the Stanford Psychology Department. Strip searched, sprayed for lice and **3 Title of Work** around their ankles, part of an experiment to test people's reactions to power dynamics in social situations. Other college student volunteers -- tho "guards" -- were given authority to dictate 24-hour-a-day rules.

**1 Author** humiliating the "prisoners" break their will.

Psychology Professor Philip Zimbardo's Stanford Prison Experiment of August 1971 quickly became a classic. Using realistic methods, Zimbardo and others were able to create a prison atmosphere that transformed its participants. The young men who played prisoners and guards revealed how much circumstances can distort individual personalities -- and how anyone, when given complete control over others, can act like a monster.

"In a few days, the role dominated the person," Zimbardo -- now president-elect of the American Psychological Association -- recalled. "They became guards and prisoners." So disturbing was the transformation that Zimbardo ordered the experiment abruptly ended.

A "guard" leads a "prisoner" down the hall in a 1971 Stanford psychology experiment. The experiment explored power dynamics by creating false distinctions among college student volunteers. Credit: Chuck Painter

**Related information**

• Prison Experiment Website

• Psychologist puts the 'real' into reality TV:

**35. MOBILE APPLICATION SOFTWARE (APP)**

> Google LLC. (2019). *Google earth* (Version 9.3.3) [Mobile app]. App Store.
> https://apps.apple.com/us/app/google-earth/id293622097

## OTHER SOURCES (INCLUDING ONLINE VERSIONS)

**36. GOVERNMENT PUBLICATION** If no author is listed, include the department that produced the document in the "author" position. Any broader organization listed can be included as the publisher of the document. If a specific report number is provided, include it after the title.

> National Park Service. (2019, April 11). *Travel where women made history: Ordinary and extraordinary places of American women.* U.S. Department of the Interior. https://www.nps.gov/subjects/travelwomenshistory /index.htm

> Berchick, E. R., Barnett, J. C., & Upton, R. D. (2019, September 10). *Health insurance coverage in the United States: 2018* (Report No. P60-267). U.S. Census Bureau. https://www.census.gov/library/publications/2019 /demo/p60-267.html

**37. DISSERTATION** If the dissertation was informally published by a dissertation indexing service, include the indexing service in the source position. Include a DOI if one has been assigned. If the dissertation was posted online by the granting university, include the university archive, department, or library in the source position and a direct-link URL.

> Bacaksizlar, N. G. (2019). *Understanding social movements through simulations of anger contagion in social media* [Doctoral dissertation, University of North Carolina at Charlotte]. ProQuest Dissertations & Theses.

> Degli-Esposti, M. (2019). *Child maltreatment and antisocial behaviour in the United Kingdom: Changing risks over time* [Doctoral dissertation, University of Oxford]. Oxford University Research Archive. https://ora .ox.ac.uk/objects/uuid:6d5a8e55-bd19-41a1-8ef5-ef485642af89

**38. REPORT FROM A PRIVATE ORGANIZATION**

Ford Foundation International Fellowships Program. (2019). *Leveraging higher education to promote social justice: Evidence from the IFP alumni tracking study*. https://p.widencdn.net/kei61u/IFP-Alumni-Tracking-Study-Report-5

Tahseen, M., Ahmed, S., & Ahmed, S. (2018). *Bullying of Muslim youth: A review of research and recommendations*. The Family and Youth Institute.

**39. CONFERENCE PROCEEDINGS**

Srujan Raju, K., Govardhan, A., Padmaja Rani, B., Sridevi, R., & Ramakrishna Murty, M. (Eds.) (2018). *Proceedings of the third international conference on computational intelligence and informatics*. Springer.

**40. PAPER PRESENTED AT A MEETING OR SYMPOSIUM** Cite the date(s) of the meeting, if available.

Vasylets, O. (2019, April 10–13). *Memory accuracy in bilinguals depends on the valence of the emotional event* [Paper presentation]. XIV International Symposium of Psycholinguistics, Tarragona, Spain. https://psico.fcep.urv.cat/projectes/gip/files/isp2019.pdf

**41. POSTER SESSION**

Wood, M. (2019, January 3–6). *The effects of an adult development course on students' perceptions of aging* [Poster session]. Forty-First Annual National Institute on the Teaching of Psychology, St. Pete Beach, FL, United States. https://nitop.org/resources/Documents/2019%20Poster%20Session%20II.pdf

**42. FILM, VIDEO, OR DVD**

Peele, J. (Director). (2017). *Get out* [Film]. Universal Pictures.

Hitchcock, A. (Director). (1959). *The essentials collection: North by northwest* [Film; five-disc special ed. on DVD]. Metro-Goldwyn-Mayer; Universal Pictures Home Entertainment.

### 43. TELEVISION PROGRAM, SINGLE EPISODE

Waller-Bridge, P. (Writer), & Bradbeer, H. (Director). (2019, March 18). The provocative request (Season 2, Episode 3) [TV series episode]. In P. Waller-Bridge, H. Williams, & J. Williams (Executive Producers), *Fleabag*. Two Brothers Pictures; BBC.

### 44. TELEVISION SERIES

Waller-Bridge, P., Williams, H., & Williams, J. (Executive Producers). (2016–2019). *Fleabag*. Two Brothers Pictures; BBC.

### 45. AUDIO PODCAST

Abumrad, J., & Krulwich, R. (Hosts). (2002–present). *Radiolab* [Audio podcast]. WNYC Studios. https://www.wnycstudios.org/podcasts /radiolab/podcasts

### 46. RECORDING

Nielsen, C. (2014). *Carl Nielsen: Symphonies 1 & 4* [Album recorded by the New York Philharmonic Orchestra]. Dacapo Records. (Original work published 1892–1916)

# Acknowledgments

Pages 26–27, Council of Writing Program Administrators (CWPA), the National Council of Teachers of English (NCTE), and the National Writing Project (NWP), Excerpt from *Framework for Success in Postsecondary Writing*, 2011. Courtesy Council of Writing Program Administrators.

Pages 31–32, Frank Rose, "The Selfish Meme," originally appeared in *The Atlantic*, October 2012. Reproduced with permission of the author.

Pages 74–77, Jean Twenge, Excerpts from *iGen: Why Today's Super-Connected Kids Are Growing Up Less Rebellious, More Tolerant, Less Happy—and Completely Unprepared for Adulthood—and What that Means for the Rest of Us.* Copyright © 2017 by Jean M. Twenge, Ph.D. Reprinted with the permission of Atria Books, a division of Simon & Schuster, Inc. All rights reserved.

Pages 78–79, Jean Twenge, et al., "Increases in Depressive Symptoms, Suicide-Related Outcomes, and Suicide Rates among U.S. Adolescents after 2010 and Links to Increased New Media Screen Time," *Clinical Psychological Science*, Vol. 6(1), 2018. Copyright © 2018 by Sage Publications. Republished with permission of Sage Publications, permission conveyed through Copyright Clearance Center, Inc.

Pages 115–17, Charles Caratti, "Reinstate the Fairness Doctrine!" *Times Advocate* (Escondido, California), December 28, 2018. Reprinted by permission of the author.

Pages 311–14, Mirlandra Neuneker, Rhetorical analysis of her blog, *Mirlandra's Kitchen*. Used with permission.

# Index

## Questions for Analyzing Your Rhetorical Situation

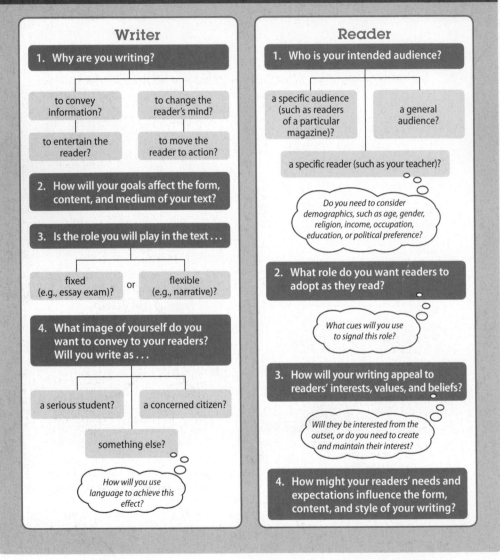

**Writer**

1. Why are you writing?

- to convey information?
- to change the reader's mind?
- to entertain the reader?
- to move the reader to action?

2. How will your goals affect the form, content, and medium of your text?

3. Is the role you will play in the text . . .

- fixed (e.g., essay exam)?
- or
- flexible (e.g., narrative)?

4. What image of yourself do you want to convey to your readers? Will you write as . . .

- a serious student?
- a concerned citizen?
- something else?

*How will you use language to achieve this effect?*

**Reader**

1. Who is your intended audience?

- a specific audience (such as readers of a particular magazine)?
- a general audience?
- a specific reader (such as your teacher)?

*Do you need to consider demographics, such as age, gender, religion, income, occupation, education, or political preference?*

2. What role do you want readers to adopt as they read?

*What cues will you use to signal this role?*

3. How will your writing appeal to readers' interests, values, and beliefs?

*Will they be interested from the outset, or do you need to create and maintain their interest?*

4. How might your readers' needs and expectations influence the form, content, and style of your writing?